D0858356

Human Nature
and Predictability

Human Nature and Predictability

Myles I. Friedman
University of South Carolina
Martha R. Willis
Converse College

LexingtonBooks
D.C. Heath and Company
Lexington, Massachusetts
Toronto

Library of Congress Cataloging in Publication Data

Friedman, Myles I., 1924-
  Human nature and predictability.

  Bibliography: p. 307
  Includes index.
    1. Motivation (Psychology) 2. Human behavior. 3. Social groups.
I. Willis, Martha R. II. Title.
BF503.F74   153.8   81-47582
ISBN 0-669-04684-1   AACR2

Published simultaneously in Canada

Printed in the United States of America

International Standard Book Number: 0-669-04684-1

Library of Congress Catalog Card Number: 81-47582

088916

To Myles, Jr.

Contents

Contents ix

List of Figures

Acknowledgments

We wish to express our appreciation to Dr. George Lackey, Dr. David Garron, and Dr. Sandra Frick for critiquing the manuscript. Their suggestions were responsible for important substantive improvements and clarifications in the text. We also are grateful to Gloria Hicks for her accurate typing and painstaking proofreading of the manuscript.

Introduction

This book presents a promising approach to the understanding of human affairs. *Human Nature and Predictability* is an attempt to integrate theory and research from various disciplines of the behavioral sciences in order to describe and explain human behavior. The behavioral sciences have evolved into discrete, highly specialized fields, including clinical psychology, experimental psychology, industrial psychology, anthropology, social psychology, educational psychology, political science, and sociology. Scientists in each of these fields have pursued specialized research interests and theories that have focused on the particular concerns of their field.

The natural sciences have also evolved into distinct, specialized disciplines such as biology, physics, and chemistry. However, recent progress in the natural sciences is characterized by integration among fields. Generally speaking, the natural sciences are more advanced than the behavioral sciences, and one manifestation of their advancement is the cogent relationships established between one field of science and another. For instance, a chemist and physicist now use the relationships between chemistry, physics, biology, and other branches of science.

The behavioral sciences are ready to profit from the integration of theory and data from the various individual disciplines. It is for this reason that this book has been written. Thus an integrated view of important aspects of human conduct is presented.

Integration is achieved in two ways. First, theory and research findings from the various behavioral science disciplines are applied to certain human attributes, yielding a better understanding of those attributes. Such attributes as human motivation, adaptation, cooperation, and competition have been examined from the various perspectives of the behavioral sciences. Using this approach, for example, a clinical psychologist interested in a particular human attribute might see how theory and research in social psychology, political science, and educational psychology pertain to that attribute. In addition, the individual can see how one particular area of concentration fits into the broader context of the behavioral sciences.

The second way that integration is achieved is by showing how the myriad of activities in which humans engage are attempts to satisfy the same persistent, common motives. Thus, from whatever discipline of the behavioral sciences we view behavior, we see people striving for the same generic kinds of satisfaction. The motivational threads that permeate and integrate human behavior were presented and analyzed in Friedman's book, *Rational Behavior*.

There is still another reason for integrating theory and research across the behavioral sciences. It is a mission of science to search for general principles, because scientific theories and laws must be generalizable. An indicator of scientific progress is the increased ability to generalize scientific principles. One way to increase this ability in the behavioral sciences is to attempt to apply scientific theories and laws across them, an effort that is made in this book.

Human Nature and Predictability is divided into three parts. Part I deals with the behavior of individuals, focusing on motivation, adaptation, mental structure, mental development, and mental process including the higher mental functions. In short, part I is an attempt to determine the motives of individuals, their mental equipment for coping with the environment to satisfy their motives, and the way in which their mental capabilities develop and function.

Part II deals with the social dimension of human behavior, that is, the effect of group membership on behavior. The distinction is made between human groups and the affiliations of lower animals, and the basic elements of the human group are identified. Then, the relationships between the group and its members, between one member and another, and between one group and another are explained. The explanation of group behavior in part II is derived from the explanation of individual behavior in part I. Many explanations of group behavior fail because group behavior is discussed independently of the nature of the individuals. In part I, the motivation of individuals and the way in which each individual seeks to satisfy motives are described; in part II, it is shown that groups form, function, and survive because they help their members satisfy their motives.

Part III deals with how the individual relates to the group by showing how individuals operate in their group milieus to satisfy their motives. In this way psychological and social behavior are meshed, as they should be in any cogent behavioral science theory. Also in part III we see how groups can thwart and frustrate their members.

There is an increased awareness that behavioral science disciplines overlap and that to understand human behavior one must inspect its various facets and integrate the knowledge that is derived from all sources. Humans are both individuals and group members. To understand them we must view them from both perspectives in order to determine how various forces cause humans to behave the way they do.

We chose the title *Human Nature and Predictability* because a unique formulation of motivation is developed in the book. And motivation is certainly a central facet of human nature. The ramifications of viewing human nature from this vantage point are investigated. If humans are motivated as we suggest, how does this affect their thinking; their conduct as individuals; and the formation, maintenance, and interaction of their groups? In seeking the answers to these questions, we are prompted to reconsider the nature of human existence.

As the theory is applied to a particular area of human behavior, a synopsis of salient issues in the area is presented. This enables the reader to become acquainted with the focus and lore of areas that are unfamiliar.

To attempt integration of different facets of human behavior, the approach must necessarily be comprehensive. Covering a wide range of human activities prevents us from dealing with any one activity in great depth or detail. We hope that experts in the various behavioral science disciplines will realize the limitations of our work and will become interested in pursuing implications and applications of the theory in their areas of specialization. Hypotheses derived from the theory are presented at the end of the book to encourage further research.

We have profited a great deal from the work of outstanding social theorists such as Freud. Yet many human problems remain. If we are to improve the human condition, we must explore new theories. In this pursuit we must be willing to suspend our biases and personal commitments to existing theories. Only then can we be free to consider the potential benefits of viewing humans from a different theoretical perspective. We invite you to consider in the pages that follow the contributions of prediction theory to the understanding of human affairs.

Part I
The Individual

1

Motivation

Primary Motivation: Prediction

Since scientific theories are dynamic, the basic assumption of a theory must posit a dynamic underlying force that impels behavior one way rather than another. The other constructs of the theory, then, are organized to show how the impelling force is expressed.

The explanation of *behavior* in this book is based on the assumption that individuals are inherently motivated to predict their relationship with their environment. They are impelled to make, test, and attempt to confirm predictions and are continuously trying to improve their ability to predict.

Individuals must maintain a predictable relationship with their environment to get what they want, whatever that may be. If they are unable to maintain predictability, they are confused and unable to deal with the environment effectively. Consequently, they cannot achieve satisfaction of any kind.

All of us make predictions and attempt to confirm them as a part of our daily routine. Whenever our predictions are not confirmed, we become confused and question our mental faculties. The way in which unpredictability creates confusion and mental instability can be clarified with a few examples.

Suppose you were to make an appointment to meet a friend on a street corner at a specific time. You arrive at the designated time, but your friend is not there. At first you may think that he is late and decide to wait a few minutes for him. However, if he does not arrive within fifteen or twenty minutes, you begin to wonder whether you or he misunderstood the arrangements. You are inclined to become a little confused and question your understanding.

When you make an appointment with a friend, you predict that he will appear at the specified time and place. If your prediction is not confirmed, you begin to question yourself and are compelled to clear up the matter. If you find that you are at fault because you misunderstood the arrangements, the experience would be at least mildly upsetting; but if such misunderstandings continue to occur, you would tend to become seriously disturbed. If you cannot make arrangements with other people and predict their behavior to some degree, you begin to feel incapable of relating to them. You would be unable to work with them effectively or even to live with them successfully.

Consider another example of the impact of unpredictability on mental stability. Suppose you were going to attend a class at school in the middle of a semester. You would predict that a certain route would lead you to the school and that when you arrived at the classroom, you would find your instructor and your classmates there because this is what has occured each time you came to class in the past. If you arrived at the classroom and your instructor and classmates were not there, you would question your understanding. You might check your watch to see if it had stopped, and you might find out whether the class was cancelled. You would continue to probe alternative reasons for the misunderstanding until you were able to find out what had happened and reestablish predictability. If you could not understand the reason for the mistake, you might become quite distressed.

But let us look at a more bizarre set of circumstances. Suppose you arrived at the school site and the school was not there. You would most probably be shaken by the experience—it would seem incredible. In order to reestablish predictability you would have to determine what had happened. If the grounds were covered with rubble, you might reason that the school building was destroyed overnight by some force such as an implosion. However, if grass and tall trees were growing where the school building previously stood, it would seem impossible to find a plausible explanation, and you might be inclined to think you were dreaming or you might question your sanity.

It may be that the way we determine that we are awake, rather than dreaming, is through our ability to predict. When we go to sleep at night, we are aware of our surroundings. We may set the alarm clock to wake us at a certain time, say seven o'clock the next morning, and we fall asleep expecting that when we awaken we will hear the alarm ringing, that the surroundings will be the same as they were the night before, and that the alarm clock will read seven o'clock.

Should we wake in a strange environment that was in no way familiar to us, it would be traumatic because it would be difficult for us to determine whether we were awake or dreaming. When a child falls asleep in familiar surroundings and while sleeping is moved to a strange place, upon awakening the child will tend to be startled, confused, upset, and will ask the parents to explain where they are and how they got there.

We not only are motivated to maintain predictability, we find predicting satisfying and choose to test and polish our predictive powers in our leisure. We play games like chess, Monopoly® , and cards in which we try to outpredict our opponents. Television is replete with very popular quiz shows in which contestants try to predict the answers to questions more accurately than their opponents.

We also enjoy games that challenge our ability to predict even if we are not pitting our wits against others. In solving a crossword puzzle, we predict that filling in the blanks in a certain way will achieve the correct solution. Later we can check our solutions to see if we predicted accurately. Solitary card games provide much the same kind of challenge.

People like to gamble so that they can bet on their predictions; therefore, contests, sweepstakes, and the like pervade our culture. Towns like Las Vegas and Monte Carlo thrive on the desire of people to bet money on their predictions.

We read mysteries and watch mystery stories on television because we like to predict "who done it." We pride ourselves on making accurate and quick predictions with little available information. Often we judge mystery stories to be poor if they give away the solution too early, not allowing us to make our own predictions.

George Kelly (1955) viewed man as an "incipient scientist," seeking "to predict, and thus control, the course of events." Kelly states, "Like the prototype of the scientist that he is, man seeks prediction. His structured network of pathways leads towards the future so that he may anticipate it. Man ultimately seeks to anticipate real events" (pp. 46, 49).

There is a second aspect of the prediction motive implicit in the previous discussion that now shall be made explicit. Not only are individuals motivated to make predictions; once they make a prediction, they are motivated to confirm it. It is through the confirmation of predictions that individuals learn that perceptions of reality are correct.

The tendency to confirm one's predictions was evidenced in a series of studies concerning the performance of machine operators conducted at the Foxboro Company under the direction of Dr. Harry Helson (1949). Helson found that operators establish a performance standard that they expect to meet; when their performance falls below this standard, they expend greater effort to reduce the error. He labeled this the *anticipation dimension of performance*. It suggests that people tend to make predictions about their performance and work in order to confirm the predictions they make.

The notion that individuals make predictions and expect their predictions to come true has been held and contemplated for many years. In the literature of learning theory, much of the work related to prediction has been conducted under the heading of expectancy. Tolman (1949, 1951) was responsible for gaining theoretical legitimacy for expectancy. He contends that if two stimuli are paired, expectancy is the situation in which the individual behaves in the presence of stimulus one as if stimulus two will be present. MacCorquodale and Meehl (1954) formalized expectancy theory. They contend that there are three components to an expectancy: S1, the elicitor of the expectancy; R1, a response following the expectation; and S2, the fulfillment of the expectation. The expectancy process can be diagrammed as S1-R1-S2. For instance, S1 might represent the knob of a television set, which elicits the expectancy that when the knob is turned (R1) the television picture will appear (S2). If watching television is the goal, then the expectancy process is activated.

Bolles (1972), in a similar formulation of expectancy, has proposed the following primary law of learning: "What is learned is that certain events, cues (S), predict certain other, biologically important events, consequences (S*). An animal may incidentally show new responses, but what it learns is an expectancy that represents and corresponds to the S-S* contingency" (p. 402). In short, according to Bolles, their behavior is mainly a function of their expectations.

William K. Estes (1972) uses the word *anticipation* to explain behavior that does not fit neatly into the animal-laboratory-oriented-reward-punishment model. Estes maintains that in the "case of a normal human learner a reward does not necessarily strengthen, nor a punishment weaken, the response which produces it . . . . In any choice situation the individual is assumed actively to scan the available alternatives and to be guided to a choice by feedback from anticipated rewards" (p. 729).

There have also been a number of studies of animal behavior that have given credence to Tolman's statement about expectancy. Hilgard and Bower (1975) reported the following research.

> One of the earliest and most striking observations on reward expectancy was that of Tinklepaugh (1928). In his experiment, food was placed under one of two containers while a monkey was watching but was prevented from immediate access to the containers and food. A few seconds later, the monkey was permitted to choose between the containers and he invariably demonstrated his memory by choosing correctly. This is the standard "delayed response" situation. The behavior which is pertinent here occurred when, after a banana had been hidden under one of the cups, the experimenter, out of the monkey's view, substituted for it a lettuce leaf (a less preferred food). Upon turning over the correct container and finding the lettuce leaf instead of the preferred banana, the monkeys would show "surprise" and frustration, would reject the lettuce leaf, and would engage in definite searching behavior, as though looking for the expected banana. Somewhat the same sort of behavior was found by Elliott (1928) when the food in the goal-box of a rat maze experiment was changed from bran mash to sunflower seed. More systematic experiments were carried out later with chimpanzees (Cowles and Nissen, 1937). There is little doubt that animals have some sort of expectancy for specific goal-objects (p. 130). Reprinted with permission.

Neurological research on brain function is giving increasing credibility to the notion of expectancy. It has been shown that the components of responses evoked by visual stimuli vary with the expectation of the organism (Sutton, Tueting, and John, 1967). The work of Sokolov (1960) suggests that environmental input is matched against a neuronal model that represents an expectancy of the organism.

The fields of psychotherapy and clinical psychology provide additional support for prediction as a motive. Kelly (1955) states that man has a "structured network of pathways" which "leads toward the future so that he might anticipate it. Man ultimately seeks to anticipate real events" (p. 49). Ellis (1976) in a review of *Rational Behavior* (Friedman, 1975) endorsed the basic tenets of prediction theory. He stated that the book deals with a theory of rational prediction that supports Rational Emotive Therapy (RET), although Friedman does not specifically deal with RET. When Alfred Adler first conceived his theory of psychotherapy, he posited the lust for power as the primary motive of individuals. Modern Adlerian theory has shifted the emphasis on motivation to include the individual's desire to predict events and to confirm those predictions.

Franck (1961) states that individuals who have problems in confirming their assumptions tend to respond in a manner that indicates that they are in some emotional distress. When this occurs, people will tend to seek ways to improve the reality of their expectations.

Behavioral research has also pointed to the importance of expectancy. In a study conducted with snake-phobic individuals, Bandura and Adams (1977) found that the systematic desensitization brings about changes in avoidance behavior by creating and strengthening personal expectations of efficacy. They also found that subjects who were able to predict efficacy experienced mediated anxiety arousal. Donahue (1978), in his examinations of negotiation processes and outcomes, found that prenegotiation expectations of subjects were among the most significant indicators of the outcome of negotiations.

Lasswell and Lobenz (1976) are marriage counselors who have found that each partner's satisfaction in a marriage depends on three basic factors: how many needs are being met, how many wants are being received, and how many expectations actually come to pass. Each partner has expectations for his or her own behavior, for the spouse's behavior, and for the marriage itself.

Bettelheim's (1960) account of his experiences in a concentration camp illustrates a struggle to maintain predictability. He writes: "By destroying man's ability to act on his own or to predict the outcome of his own actions, they [the Gestapo] destroyed the feeling that his actions had any purpose" (p. 131). With regard to his own frame of mind, Bettelheim states: "What had most value for me was that things happened according to expectations; that therefore my future in the camp was at least partly predictable from what I was already experiencing and from what I had read" (p. 148).

In social psychology, cognitive-dissonance theory reflects the concept that emotional distress occurs when predictions are not confirmed. Aronson and Carlsmith (1962) state that an individual who has a clear expectation of how he will perform a given task will experience dissonance or psychological discomfort if his performance is radically different from his expectation. Pallak and Pittman (1972) and Kiesler and Munson (1975) supply more recent data on the subject.

The research of Carlsmith and Aronson (1963) provides supportive evidence for prediction theory's assertion that individuals are further motivated to confirm their predictions. They had subjects predict whether or not liquids to be tasted would be sweet or bitter. Even though the same liquids were used throughout the experiment, subjects perceived bitter liquids as less sweet when bitter liquids were predicted.

Research in the field of industrial psychology, too, lends credibility to the individual's inclination and need to predict. In a field study, Cohen (1959) found that telephone workers were more highly motivated, felt more secure, and worked more efficiently when the path to the goal was relatively clear and predictable than when it was ambiguous and unpredictable. A laboratory study by Raven and Rietsema (1957) generally agreed with these findings.

Studies relating to group organization can be viewed as functioning to satisfy the prediction motive. Bales (1950) contends that social structure stabilizes the interaction of group members to reduce uncertainty and unpredictability in the action of others. The research of Sherif (1937), Sherif and Sherif (1956), and Asch (1951, 1956) indicates that group membership is valuable to individuals because they rely upon their groups to help them maintain predictability. The studies show that greater conformity to group opinion occurs when individuals are presented with unpredictable or ambiguous stimulation. (We will delve more deeply into the relationship between the prediction motive and group process in part II of this book.)

Finally, further animal studies provide support for the prediction motive. If predictability is accepted as a primary motivation, it would seem that lack of predictability might be unpleasant and have detrimental effects. Support for this supposition is gained from controlled experiments. Lazarus and Averill (1972) reported research in which rats receiving unsignalled (unpredictable) electric shocks demonstrated more fear responses than did rats who received signalled (predictable) electric shocks. In a similar study, Seligmann (1968) found that rats receiving unsignalled shocks and/or delayed shocks developed more stomach ulcers than rats receiving signalled and/or immediate shocks. Elliot (1975) measured heart rate in relation to application of electric shocks and found no variation relating to probability of occurrence. He did find that heart rate increases as uncertainty relating to when shock will arrive increases.

The preceding data on prediction shows that prediction has a prominent effect on many important aspects of behavior. Bolles (1972) and Estes (1972) show its effect on learning. Bandura and Adams (1977) show its effect on anxiety. Carlsmith and Aronson (1963) show its effect on taste sensation, and Lasswell and Lobenz (1976) on marriage satisfaction. Franck (1961), Aronson and Carlsmith (1962), Pallak and Pittman (1972), and Kiesler and Munson (1975) show its effect on emotional distress. Cohen

(1959) and Raven and Rietsema (1957) demonstrated its effect on work satisfaction and efficiency. In addition, Bales (1950), Sherif (1937, 1956), and Asch (1951, 1956) show its effect on group process; Lazarus and Averill (1972), Seligmann (1968), and Elliot (1975) show its effect on lower animals. There is a preponderance of evidence indicating that prediction affects a wide variety of human behaviors as well as the behavior of infrahumans.

It becomes clear that individuals make predictions and expect their predictions to be confirmed. Although considering prediction to be an important facet of behavior is not new, the proposed theory is distinct in that it posits that the inclination to predict one's relationship with the environment is a basic motive and describes mental process and behavior as organizing to fulfill this motive.

Secondary Motivation: Interests and Preferences

Interests are inclinations to confirm particular predictions. Prediction has been proferred as the primary motive of individuals. Once individuals are assured of maintaining a predictable relationship with the environment, they are inclined to confirm particular predictions that prompt them at the moment. Interests vary as growth and development occur. The infant's interests are primarily instinctual, having the inclination to confirm the predictions that they will eat, drink, and receive tactile comfort. As the child matures and the realm of understanding expands, alternatives are learned. The child is then able to convey interests and to express preferences. *Preferences* are penchants for one alternative over another. A preference is expressed and revealed as a choice among alternatives.

Impulses remain to plague us. We must eat, drink, keep safe from harm, and partake of sex. Nevertheless, we can express preferences if various foods, drinks, refuges, and sex partners are available, and often they are.

Preferences are distinct from impulses in that when a preference is selected consciously the individual does not act impulsively. One deliberates the attainability as well as the desirability of the alternatives, and in choosing a preference the individual will select an alternative that appears attainable as well as desirable. One will probably not choose an alternative that seems unattainable, no matter how desirable it may be.

There is an ever-expanding number of alternatives to be considered in arriving at one's preferences as one's domain of experience expands. However, to achieve those preferences the individual must be able to predict what will happen. Then one can pursue those preferences, whatever they may be.

There is substantial evidence that individuals have preferential interests. Premack's work (1959, 1963, 1966) shows that reinforcements have relative values for individuals and that activities can be arranged in a preferential order for any given individual. He proposed that if a number of activities could be ranked in a preferential order for an individual, then an activity of higher preference should reinforce an activity of lower preference, but not the reverse. He demonstrated the accuracy of his hypothesis in work with monkeys, rats, and children.

In *game theory,* a mathematical theory of the behavior of people in conflict situations, the concept of utility is introduced to account for the motivation of individuals (see Rapoport, 1960, 1962, 1964). The implication is that available commodities have varying utility value for different individuals. One discovers the relative value of commodities to individuals by requiring them to make choices among commodities. Their choices indicate their preferential interests.

There is a respected branch of theory in industrial psychology called *expectancy theory* (and sometimes instrumental theory) that includes the same two motivational components as the present theory, predictability and the attainment of preferences. The early writing on expectancy theory was done by Georgopolous, Mahoney, and Jones (1957). They proposed that if a worker predicts that high productivity will lead to the attainment of personal goals, he will be a high producer. Conversely, if low productivity is predicted to lead to the attainment of personal goals, low productivity will result.

Vroom (1964) formalized many of the postulates that were emerging in expectancy theory. He defines *expectancy* as a probability estimate of a relationship between an action and an outcome. He further contends that a person evaluates a potential outcome on the basis of his perception of the relationship between that outcome and other outcomes for which he has varying preferences.

Porter and Fowler (1968) argue in favor of the expectancy model over the drive model because of the drive model's emphasis on past response-reward connections. They contend that expectancy theories with emphasis on anticipation of future events are more appropriate to a view of humans as creatures capable of delaying gratification and behaving rationally. Research by Mitchell and Biglan (1971) and Heneman and Schwab (1972) provide empirical support for their theory.

Erickson, Post, and Paige (1975) used self-reports and questionnaires to conclude that (1) psychopathology is associated with lower estimates of perceived probability of goal attainment, (2) the lower the perceived probability of goal attainment and the higher the importance of the goal, the more the subjects will experience anxiety, and (3) effective treatment serves to increase the perceived probability of goal attainment.

Stotland (1969) defines *hope* as a shorthand term for an expectation about goal attainment, and distinguishes persons as either "hopeful" or "hopeless." Perceived probability of goal attainment and perceived importance are two factors that direct behavior.

Prediction can be seen as a motive more basic than pleasure when one considers that individuals must maintain a predictable relationship with the environment to obtain their interests, whatever they may be. The maintenance of predictability is superordinate to the pursuit of one's preferences because it is prerequisite to achieving that which is preferred. When the maintenance of predictability is seriously threatened, the individual will forsake an immediate preference in order to maintain a predictable relationship with the environment.

Optimally Predictable Environments

With respect to specific situations, our desire to predict compels us to seek *optimum predictability*. This means that we want any new situation to be somewhat familiar so that we can understand and be able to predict it. If the situation is totally unfamiliar, we have no basis for understanding and predicting it and are bewildered.

Optimum predictability also means that we want a situation with some novelty, so that in predicting it we may improve and extend our ability to predict. It is through the extension of our ability to predict that we gain increasing mastery of the environment. When there is no novelty in a situation, there is no challenge; there is nothing to be learned and we become stagnant.

Both too much and too little predictability for extended periods can disrupt our self-confidence and self-esteem. When there is too little predictability, we question our ability to understand what is going on and lose confidence in our ability to deal with the world in which we live. When there is too much predictability and there are no challenges to pursue, we are unable to improve our ability to predict and may begin to question whether our actions are important and worthwhile.

As time passes, one's circumstances may shift between too much and too little predictability. For example, when we begin a new job, we may feel insecure because the conditions are likely to be too unpredictable. As we learn the job we are no longer overwhelmed by the tasks we have to perform, but there might still be enough novelty to challenge us. After we have mastered all the challenges and the job becomes routine, we may become bored.

When there is either too much or too little predictability for extended periods, our ability to predict is threatened, our mental processes become unstable, and we are unable to negotiate the environment effectively. Under these conditions compensatory reactions are engaged automatically to help us maintain a predictable relationship with the environment and predict events effectively.

Picture a gauge that has too much predictability at one end and too little predictability at the other end, with optimum predictability in the center. When events become confusing the needle on the gauge would move toward too little predictability and compensatory reactions would occur to return the needle to the center. That is, we would seek redundancy and familiarity to make life more predictable. At other times, events become monotonous and boring. Then the needle would move toward too much predictability and compensatory reactions would be engaged to return the needle to the center. Thus we would seek variety and novelty to make life more challenging and adventurous.

There is considerable evidence that too little predictability or confusion will cause individuals to seek familiar and redundant stimuli that are more predictable. Bindra (1959) discusses this phenomenon in his book *Motivation*.

Social psychologists contend that individuals attempt to avoid and remove experiences that are too unpredictable. This notion was introduced in cognitive-dissonance theory by Festinger (1957). However, the earlier explanations of cognitive dissonance tended to be too vague and comprehensive asserting in general that individuals cannot tolerate cognitive inconsistencies. Festinger enumerated four types of inconsistencies. They are logical inconsistency, moral inconsistency, inconsistency of a current behavior with a general trend of behavior, and inconsistency of a current experience with past experience. A good deal of research was conducted on cognitive dissonance—some supported Festinger's formulation and some did not. To accommodate the research findings, Aronson (1968) refined the definition of cognitive dissonance as a conflict between cognition and expectation, a view that is in accord with the present theory. Aronson reviews the relevant research on cognitive dissonance, while Pallak and Pittman (1972) and Kiesler and Munson (1975) supply more recent data on the subject.

Cognitive-dissonance theory has been adopted in industrial psychology where it is generally known as *equity theory*. As suggested in a review of equity theory by Pritchard (1969), Adams (1965) has a version of equity theory that is perhaps the most extensive and explicit. Korman (1971) presents another version of cognitive-dissonance theory.

Evidence that too much predictability or boredom will cause individuals to seek novelty is provided in a study by Brickman and D'Amato (1975). These researchers showed that when stimuli in the form of juke-box records generated boredom, subjects chose other records. May and Hutt (1974) found that four-, six-, and eight-year-old children played more with a push-button light display when there was increased uncertainty as to which bulb would light. Studies in stimulus deprivation also indicate that when there is too much sameness subjects will seek novelty and increased variability. Smith, Myers, and Johnson (1968) state that their data ". . . strongly suggest that one of the profound aspects of sensorially deprived isolation is an effort on the part of the SDSs to seek a return to a homeostatic-like balance of stimulus variability" (p. 626).

In addition, the motivation to escape boredom can be seen in animal experiments using an apparatus called a Butler Box. The animal is placed in the box and learns that by depressing a lever it can see through a window a novel event or a movie of a novel event. The longer the animal is deprived of novel stimulation, the more probable it is that it will press the lever to view a novel experience. Nunnally and Lemond (1973) have reviewed the literature on the subject.

In essence, situations that provide optimum predictability maximize the opportunity to satisfy the prediction motive. This is because optimally predictable situations are sufficiently familiar to allow predictions to be confirmed and sufficiently novel to allow individuals to improve their ability to predict.

Optimum Predictability and Arousal

Prediction theory views too much or too little predictability as conditions that generate arousal. The degree of arousal that is associated with an event is correlated with the intensity of feeling the event provokes. The higher the arousal, the more disturbed and excited the individual will become when the event occurs. In general, prediction theory posits a bipolar continuum. Excessive arousal is generated when situations are either too predictable or too unpredictable. An intermediate optimum level of arousal is generated when situations are optimally predictable.

The notion of arousal and its function was adopted from activation theory. Neuropsychological activation was described by Malmo (1959) in this way: "The continuum extending from deep sleep at the low activation end to 'excited' states at the high activation end is a function of the amount of cortical bombardment by the ARAS (Ascending Reticular Activating System of the brain) such that the greater the cortical bombardment the higher the activation" (p. 384). The term *arousal* is intended to denote the intensity of feeling associated with coritcal bombardment.

Eysenck (1976) offers a definition of arousal in a review article dealing with eighty-five studies and articles. He states that arousal refers to an elevated state of bodily function and a noninformational, nonspecific increment in activity that is physiological. The literature he reviewed tended to offer a unitary concept of arousal, but he speculated that it was possible to separate arousal into autonomic arousal, electrocortical arousal, and behavioral arousal.

When the individual is alert and energetic and there is too much predictability, arousal will increase, signifying a felt state of boredom and a desire to seek novelty and adventure. Boredom is, therefore, an aroused state of mind. Too little predictability will also increase arousal. A prolonged inability to predict events generates excessive arousal and signifies a situation in which the environment is alien and confusing. In this felt state of confusion, the individual will seek out familiar situations in which predictions can be confirmed. Thus, the individual seeks an optimum degree of predictability. The extent to which events are predictable or unpredictable determines the degree of arousal that is generated.

Although most problems concerning predictability are associated with excessively high arousal, some are associated with excessively low arousal. For instance, suppose a person takes an overdose of tranquilizers but must do important work. He may take a stimulant, like coffee, which he predicts will increase his level of arousal and thus allow him to work.

The contention that too little predictability generates arousal is discussed by Bindra (1959). The contention that both too much and too little predictability generate arousal is supported by the research of London, Schubert, and Washburn (1972). They found that boredom increases autonomic arousal as measured by galvanic skin potential, skin conductance, and heart rate. They state that "stimulation which is redundant for the individual . . . produces increased arousal" (p. 33). At the other end of the continuum, rapidly changing (novel) stimulation also causes increased arousal. Thus autonomic arousal seems to reach a minimum at some intermediate level of stimulus change.

Findings of sensory-deprivation studies support the concept that too much sameness generates arousal. Zuckerman, Persky, Miller, and Levin (1969) found that sensory deprivation leads to increased anxiety. Kitamura (1970) showed that sensory deprivation increased arousal and that individuals subjected to sensory deprivation were less able to handle complex tasks.

It seems that as arousal increases, performance increases up to a threshold level. When arousal increases beyond this threshold, it becomes excessive and impairs performance. As arousal continues to increase beyond the threshold, performance becomes so seriously impaired that the individual becomes mentally unstable and is unable to predict and negotiate the environment. Thus excessive arousal, mental instability, and impaired performance are correlated.

The relationship between the degree of arousal and the individual's ability to perform or negotiate the environment has been described by

Malmo (1959). He indicated that the relationship between level of performance and level of arousal forms a curve in the shape of an inverted *U*. Level of performance increases with arousal to an optimal level, then performance declines as arousal continues to increase. It appears, then, that there is a threshold level of arousal for a given individual and that when the threshold level is exceeded the individual's level of performance will begin to fall. As arousal increases beyond this threshold the individual's performance will continue to fall.

According to Eysenck the curvilinear relationship between arousal and performance was propounded by Hebb (1955). Evidence (Gale, 1973) that introverts are characterized by higher cortical arousal than are extroverts allows Eysenck's (1974) further work to stand as additional support.

The way in which boredom and confusion cause excessive arousal and impaired performance can be illustrated as follows. Too little predictability may stem from being confronted with a serious problem and repeated failures to predict a solution. Perhaps we are worried about bills we must pay and cannot think of a way to pay them. Under such duress, arousal may increase beyond the threshold level mentioned, and we may become so worried that we cannot think straight and deal with the problem realistically.

In the case of too much predictability, we may have plenty of energy but be trapped in a routine that bores us immensely. An example is the factory worker who does the same task over and over. The worker tries to control feelings of boredom because he knows that he needs the money, but as his boredom increases and his dilemma persists, this may cause arousal to rise and performance to be impaired—leading to repeated mistakes, even to injury.

There is evidence that it is the unpredictability of arousing stimulation rather than the arousing stimulation itself that impairs performance. Kryter (1970) showed that individuals can adapt to a higher level (over 90 db) of steady noise when they are performing complex tasks. Glass, Singer, and Friedman (1969) demonstrated that subjects exposed to unpredictable noise showed less tolerance for frustration and made more errors on a proofreading test than the subjects exposed to predictable or steady noise. Cohen, Glass, and Singer (1973) generalized these findings beyond the laboratory. They studied children who lived in a high-rise apartment over an erratically noisy expressway. They found that children who lived on the top floors performed better on tests of auditory discrimination and reading ability than children who lived on lower floors.

For an excellent in-depth look at the mechanisms involved in the process of arousal, see the detailed theoretical and empirical works of Pribram (1970) and Berlyne (1960).

2 Boredom and Confusion

There are two possible reasons for the mental stress that occurs when optimum predictability is violated. First, the situation may be too predictable—stimulation is redundant and monotonous. This state is *boredom*. Bored individuals seek relief and restoration of optimum predictability by pursuing variation and novelty. Second, the situation may be too unpredictable—stimulation is too unfamiliar and variable. This state is *confusion*. Confused individuals seek relief and a return to optimum predictability by pursuing familiar and redundant stimulation.

Boredom

One of the least understood and the most subtly perplexing feelings of humans is boredom. The importance of boredom tends to be overlooked because we have not considered it a serious malady. When we glibly say that "no one ever died of boredom," it is merely living that seems to concern us. When humans, like lower creatures, spent the major portion of their time battling the elements of nature for their survival, there was little time to be bored. However, as survival is insured and as more and more leisure time becomes available because of the shorter work week, increased technology, retirement, and increased longevity, boredom becomes an increasingly ticklish and prevalent problem.

Many definitions of boredom imply that it is an unpleasant or aberrant state. Biderman and Zimmer (1961) define boredom as "a general state of restlessness related to inactivity, and often anxiety or fear of extreme proportions" (p. 73). Hartocollis (1972) sees the experience of boredom as involving feelings of impatience, frustration, dissatisfaction, want, and need. Wangh (1975) also speaks of awareness of discomfort and feelings of vague longing.

Bernstein (1975) discusses boredom and its manifestations in relation to trends occurring in our society today. He sees such phenomena as graphic sex and violence in movies as an ever increasing attempt to provide new and varied stimuli to fight off boredom.

Prediction theory contends that when individuals are subjected to repetitive, monotonous, or boring situations they will seek novel stimulation to find relief and return to a state of optimum predictability. There is evidence in the literature that supports this position. Grubb (1975) found a trend toward higher levels of boredom in assembly-line workers as tasks were more repetitious. He also found that workers who experienced greater levels of job boredom tended to engage more frequently in leisure activities perceived by them as offering novelty.

Prediction theory suggests that to avert boredom, attention tends to dwell on novel, complex stimulation because it is challenging. Berlyne and Ditkofsky (1976) exposed subjects to a field consisting of dots of one color. They found that subjects were then more likely to identify stimulus objects of a different color when presented in a display. After repeated trials, they concluded that individuals tend to attend to novel or odd visual stimuli more often than to redundant stimuli. Studies performed by Yarbu (1967), Antes (1974), Welch (1974), and Thomas (1965) further confirm this contention.

Boredom is much more common than is evident at first glance. Even the very young child, for whom almost every experience contains some novelty, exhibits signs of boredom. The child continuously prompts the parents to play and teach new things. The child constantly seeks the novel and asks for explanations of how things work.

Children seem to have less reason for boredom than adults because so many things are unfamiliar. However, with children there seems to be a greater craving for exploration and novelty and a greater aversion to redundance, while adults seem to be more content with routine.

The adolescent, too, craves novelty. Parents suggest that their daughters and sons become "solid citizens," doing the chores assigned at home and school. Adolescents are often criticized for being impulsive when, in fact, they are driven to break away from the boring rituals and routines that parents and schools impose. Adults find it hard to understand why adolescents feel an urgent need to leave home. It could be that adolescents are willing to accept the risks and dangers of striking out on their own in order to escape the boredom inherent in a stable and secure home life.

Security is often equated with a large amount of predictability; parents praise themselves for providing a secure environment for their children. What they do not seem to understand is that their interpretation of a secure environment is to the adolescent an overly predictable ritualistic environment devoid of challenge and excitement. Of course, when adolescents return from precarious adventures, the accounts of which usually anger and frighten parents, they frequently appreciate for a while the security that a structured home environment may provide.

It is sad that the rituals that the adult so conscientiously tries to sell to the adolescent as the "good life" plague and frustrate the adults themselves. The point is that personal security is not derived from the adoption of a ritualistic, redundant code of conduct; security comes from mastering new situations and from improving one's ability to predict. It comes from probing and learning to predict new and challenging happenings and, as a result, developing self-confidence that new situations in the future will be predicted and controlled. Many adults are so obviously bored with conforming to social rituals that the adolescent often regards the adult as hypocritical and ludicrous. It is as if the adolescent were saying to the adult, "If conforming to social rituals is so right, why aren't you happy?" and the adolescent is quick to remind the adults of their complaints and dissatisfactions.

Boredom has one particularly important value that we should emphasize. It is when people are attempting to escape boredom and pursue novelty that they are most likely to discover and invent new things, and it is discovery and inventions that highlight the superior accomplishments of human beings. We have examples of Archimedes relaxing in a bath, Newton in an orchard, and Einstein in a patent office at the time of their discoveries of buoyancy, gravitation, and relativity.

When individuals are in a state of too much predictability, they need only to find novel stimulation to overcome their boredom. Entertainment media, such as television, provide escape from boredom. Most often one needs only to switch channels to find novelty and adventure.

Confusion

Just as too much predictability or boredom produces mental stress, too little predictability causes stress. According to prediction theory, when stimuli are so unfamiliar or change so rapidly that an individual is unable to predict with accuracy, the individual is said to be in a state of confusion. Biderman and Zimmer (1961) define confusion as a temporary anxiety state associated with symptoms of headache, restlessness, poor concentration, ideas of physical disease, poor appetite, and exaggerated startle reaction. Carlsmith and Aronson (1963) demonstrated that events that do not confirm an individual's expectancies are perceived by the individual as unpleasant. Thus confusion may also be viewed as an aberrant and unpleasant state.

If Malmo's (1959) conception of arousal as an inverted U-shaped curve is accepted, confusion would represent a situation in which stimuli are excessive and/or unfamiliar. This situation is in contrast to one in which stimuli are minimal and/or redundant—the state of boredom. Keen (1977) sees healthy individuals as being able to withdraw from situations in which stimuli are excessive and seek out situations with decreased stimuli. Berlyne and Lewis (1963) investigated the effects of heightened stimulus situations on exploratory behavior and found that subjects with high arousal were less prone to seek out challenging or interesting stimuli. McReynolds and Bryan

(1956) found that individuals tend to seek out and assimilate new and novel percepts as long as previous percepts had been assimilated. McReynolds (1956) defines a *percept* as "that which one is, or assumed to be, aware of . . ." (p. 294). McReynolds and Bryan further found that, as the level of unassimilated percepts increased, the tendency to seek out novelty was inhibited. Since the study performed by McReynolds and Bryan utilized neuropsychiatric patients as subjects, Haywood (1962) sought to replicate the results using a group of college students in an introductory psychology course and found similar results. This supports the notion that as individuals become confused they avoid novel stimulation and suggests that they seek optimum predictability.

As was previously mentioned, there is evidence that it is the unpredictability of stimulation rather than the stimulation itself that generates stress and frustration. Glass, Singer, and Friedman (1969) and Glass and Singer (1977) showed that subjects exposed to unpredictable noise showed less tolerance for frustration than subjects exposed to predictable or steady noise. Rogers and Mewborn (1976) demonstrated that heart rate increases when subjects are uncertain when an electric shock will arrive but does not increase if subjects are uncertain that shocks will occur.

Although it is asserted that individuals seek optimum predictability, the optimum level of predictability may vary from one individual or type of individual to the next. Eysenck's (1975) research demonstrated that introverts tend to be more highly aroused than extroverts and that extroverts need more novelty in task performance than introverts. Hill (1975), in a study designed to test Eysenck's hypothesis, found that extroverts built more variety into their performance at monotonous tasks than did introverts. Quay (1965) found that adult and adolescent sociopaths show lower responsiveness to stimuli than do normals or neurotics. He believes that this suggests that hedonistic and thrill-seeking behaviors in sociopaths may represent a pathological mode of stimulation seeking. Whitehill, DeMeyer-Gapin, and Scott (1976) conducted a study with antisocial preadolescent children and found that in an experimental setting designed to be boring, antisocial preadolescents engage in more stimulation-seeking behaviors than do normal or neurotic children. Zentall (1975) observed behaviors of hyperactive children and found that when these children are isolated, they appear to create stimuli. His observations also show that these children tend to be less distractable under conditions in which stimuli (visual, auditory, and tactile) are increased. Zentall seems to feel that these children have higher arousal levels and may require more stimuli to overcome a state that may be defined as boredom. London, Schubert, and Washburn (1972) found that measures of intelligence correlated positively with rated boredom, suggesting that boredom may result from an inadequate information flow.

It also is probable that the effect of environmental stimulation on the same individuals varies from time to time. When individuals are alert and energetic, they are interested in predicting their environment and improving their ability to predict. Under these circumstances, confusing or boring stimulation will arouse and irritate them. On the other hand, when they are fatigued they are interested in resting, not predicting. Then, boring stimulation, such as counting sheep, would be calming and put them to sleep. Confusing stimulation would tend to be irritating and prevent them from resting. However, should fatigued individuals need to do important work, they may take a stimulant or engage in stimulating physical exercise that they predict will increase their level of arousal and allow them to work. Further research is required to identify variations among individuals and for the same individual under different conditions.

Problems involving too little predictability plague us from birth, since life is too complicated for us to understand all the things that affect us. The news media remind us continuously of the complex problems that we can, at best, only partially grasp. So we must learn to live with unpredictability and try to learn to predict those things that affect us directly. We must at least learn to take care of ourselves, relate to others, and work productively. In addition, we must learn to depend on others for the things that we cannot provide for ourselves.

Infants find almost everything unpredictable at first. They learn how to predict from their parents, as well as from their own observations. To feel secure, babies must first learn to predict that their basic requirements will be provided because they are dependent on adults for their survival. They must be able to predict that they will receive food when they are hungry and that certain actions on their part, like crying, will result in the parents' bringing food. Infants are then able to act in their own behalf to fill their needs.

The roles of adults in our society often provide too little predictability. Historically, the American family was a closely knit unit in which the roles of the members were complementary. The husband worked in the field, and the sons helped. The mother cared for the home and the daughters helped, and mothers and daughters also helped in the field. Each contributed to the welfare of the family and there was little basis for open conflict among them.

Now in our technological society things are different. The family is becoming diffuse and disintegrated; adult roles overlap and conflict, and family togetherness has been replaced in many cases by dispersion. The family members find their pleasures and spend their time away from home in the larger community that does not offer the security the traditional family did. It is a complicated maze of alternatives and pressures that is not easily understood. The individual has a hard time finding a satisfactory niche because, although there are many opportunities, for most of them success is unpredictable. Specialized knowledge is needed to be able to understand and take advantage of the opportunities with any expectation of success.

How we feel about objects and individuals is to some extent a function of how well we can predict them. In a previously cited study by Carlsmith and Aronson (1963) an example was provided. These experimenters led subjects to believe that a liquid they were about to taste was either sweet or bitter. When this expectation was not confirmed, the subjects judged the taste of the liquid to be more unpleasant. The researchers also showed that individuals will tend to judge situations to be less pleasant when they cannot predict events.

In general, it is often too little predictability that underlies our problems. We have said that too much predictability is more easily remedied than too little predictability because there are usually many ways that one can find novelty and diversion when bored. The only time that bored individuals are inclined to remain frustrated is when they are unable to escape boredom and feel entrapped by too little predictability.

For example, a man may be bored because his work is monotonous— there is too much predictability. But all that he would need to do to alleviate his boredom is to find another job that is more challenging. Too little predictability entraps him insofar as he cannot find a more challenging, suitable job at which he can predict success. So it is too little predictability, rather than too much predictability, that produces his frustration and erodes his self-confidence. If he could find a suitable substitute, he would take it. His confidence is eroded because he is unable to predict a suitable substitute. Too much predictability initiates the problem of boredom and too little predictability maintains the problem. In this case, the man might have to enroll in night school in order to upgrade his skills to qualify for a more challenging job at the same pay. If he were to complete his preparation, he could predict success at the new job and he would not feel entrapped.

Examples of Boredom and Confusion

A particularly interesting way to study human behavior is to examine the behavior of characters in novels, short stories, plays, and poetry. Usually the author who receives great acclaim in the literary world is one who is adept at delving into and describing the actions, thoughts, and feelings of human beings. A large number of writers have dealt with boredom and confusion, and a few of them are mentioned here to illustrate our discussion, although some examples may be subject to other interpretations.

In Ibsen's play *The Doll's House,* we find that Nora, the central character, was bored by the conventional strictures of a marriage based on economic security and the female role to which she was confined. She realized that she had merely exchanged one confining situation for another—her father had allowed her no life of her own, and now her life with her husband Torvald was equally restricted. In Nora, Ibsen has given us an example of an individual who is finding events and situations to be too predictable and stimulation to be too redundant.

James Thurber gives us a description of an individual whose life is monotonous, humdrum, and too predictable. Walter Mitty (in *The Secret Life of Walter Mitty*) is a man whose existence is plagued by a wife who constantly treats him as if he were a child, nags him, and gives him orders. He is able to get away from the tedium and boredom of such a routine through daydreaming. In his fantasies he places himself in much less predictable situations where he is, for instance, the fearless pilot of a plane, a highly qualified physician, and the defendant in a murder trial.

Shakespeare made use of confusion in his play *The Comedy of Errors*. In this tale Aegeon, a merchant from Ephesus, had been shipwrecked along with his wife, their twin sons, and twin male slaves. Aegeon had managed to rescue only one member of each of the sets of twins. His wife, one son, and one slave were separated from him and never heard of again. Many years later Aegeon and his party are in Syracuse where, unknown to him, his lost wife, son, and slave now reside. Confusion reigns among all the parties when by chance they meet each other individually. None of the characters behave in the manner predicted by the other characters. Shakespeare describes the characters' bewilderment as they find too little predictability in their environments.

Jean Paul Sartre paints a picture of hell in *No Exit* where the three characters, Garcin, Inez, and Estelle, are placed in a drawing room together to spend eternity. Garcin is confused because he had predicted hell to be an extremely hot place with torture chambers and instead he is in a room decorated in an Empire style.

In Camus' *The Guest* we find two characters who are confused because each is not confirming the other's predictions. Daru is a schoolmaster who is given the responsibility of delivering an Arab prisoner to the police headquarters. Daru houses and feeds the Arab, expecting him to escape and, therefore, rid him of the burden of taking away the freedom of a human being. The Arab is bewildered that Daru will sit and eat with him, serving him as he would any guest in his home. Daru gives the Arab every opportunity to escape, and yet he does not do so. None of the characters have their predictions confirmed so confusion reigns.

F. Scott Fitzgerald gives us a look at the boredom among some wealthy individuals during the early part of this century in his book *The Great Gatsby*. Tom and Daisy Buchanan are among the idle rich who find the stimulation in their lives at so low a level that they pursue variation and novelty and look for new diversions. They travel, buy expensive items, and seek out new relationships in their attempts to decrease the predictability (boredom) of their environment.

Joseph Heller's *Catch-22* revolves around contradiction, which causes a great deal of confusion among a group of Air Force personnel during a time of war. A *catch-22* is a contradictory rule or statement of policy, such as (1) to be grounded a pilot must ask for mental discharge, but to request a mental discharge was accepted as proof of sanity, and (2) one could only see the major about military matters when he was in his office, but when he was in his office no one was permitted to enter.

We could continue at great length giving examples of individuals in literature who are bored or confused. There are Dostoevsky's main character writing to fill time and dispel boredom in *Notes from the Underground*, Lermontov's Pechorin of *A Hero of Our Time* whose boredom causes him to seek entertainment, and several of Kafka's central figures who are confused when they find themselves in existential dilemmas.

According to prediction theory, all psychological problems are of two types. A psychological problem is either a problem of boredom or a problem of confusion. *When a preference is pursued because of a psychological problem it is implicit that the satisfaction of the preference results in the relief of boredom or confusion as the case may be.* This does not mean that the satisfaction of all preferences relieves boredom or confusion. The satisfaction of a biological preference, for example, that is not related to a psychological problem would not. If individuals are hungry and prefer to eat, the eating of food would satisfy a biological preference, but it would not necessarily result in the relief of boredom or confusion because no psychological problem may be present. On the other hand, if after repeated deliberate attempts to acquire food individuals are unsuccessful, they become confused and a psychological problem exists. In this case the subsequent acquisition of food not only satisfies the biological preference for food, but relief from confusion would result as well.

3 Adaptation

This chapter focuses on adaptation and the relationship between the prediction motive (discussed in chapters 1 and 2) and adaptation. Too often motivation and adaptation are considered independently without relating the two. In general, it is believed that individuals are motivated to survive and adapt, although particular impulses at times may operate to the contrary. Therefore, any cogent theory of behavior should explain how motivation promotes adaptation. Adaptation refers to survival, subsistence, and successful living. Adaptation for humans may be manifested by such things as the maintenance of physical and mental health, the acquisition of wealth and status, or being victorious in competition.

In prediction theory motivation promotes adaptation as follows. As stated at the beginning of chapter 1, the motivation to predict impels individuals to make, test, and attempt to confirm predictions and continuously try to improve their ability to predict. Such behavior is termed *rational behavior*. It is implicit that rational behavior includes making plans to confirm predictions. Rational behavior leads to adaptation.

Let us look at just a few examples that show the connection between rationality and outstanding achievements. People conceived of landing on the moon long before it was possible to realize the achievement. Initially, plans were conceived that predicted a landing on the moon; then the plans were implemented, tested, and revised. Confirmation of the prediction was obtained when we reached the moon. The construction of a new advanced airplane proceeds in a similar manner—plans are made which predict the construction of an airplane that will fly farther and faster than its predecessors. The pursuit of a cure for cancer is proceeding in much the same fashion.

While people share the ability to predict with other animals, it is in a superior ability to conceive and confirm predictions that they excel over other animals, and it is this rational ability that contributes heavily to the outstanding achievements of human beings. Many explanations of human behavior give short shrift to the rational side of human nature. They tend to focus on what we share with other creatures, rather than to highlight and dignify our excellence.

The practice of rationality by individuals results in the improvement of their ability to predict, and ultimately it is the ability to predict accurately that contributes to adaptation. That is, making, testing, and attempting to confirm predictions improves one's ability to predict accurately. The ability to predict accurately enables one to confirm his or her predictions more often, and it is the confirmation of one's predictions that characterizes success.

The sports coach must be able to predict the game strategies that will win games, or the coach will be replaced. Students must learn to predict that the use of certain study skills will enable them to learn the material assigned, or their learning will be handicapped. Students are constantly engaged in predicting what will be on tests and what the instructor will ask them. The teacher must be able to predict that the methods used in teaching will result in students' learning.

Successful individuals select goals they wish to pursue and make plans that they predict will achieve the goals. They then proceed to implement, test, and revise the plans in pursuit of the goals. The successful football coach conceives of a plan to win the game and revises it, as conditions dictate, to maximize the probability of winning the game. The successful business executive projects an amount of profit as the goal of the enterprise for the year, makes plans to achieve the goal, mobilizes the resources of the organization, implements the plan, and adjusts it to maximize the chances of achieving the goal.

Thus the prediction motive impels individuals to behave rationally. The practice of rationality improves their ability to predict, and accurate prediction results in adaptation.

Let us now consider evidence showing the relationships between the ability to predict and adaptation.

Prediction and Performance

As reflected in successful performance, in general, good predictors appear to be good performers. Franck (1961) sees optimal functioning or performance as the ability to predict accurately.

Industrial psychologists have been well aware of the importance of prediction in adapting to work tasks. Poulton (1957) identified three types of anticipation based on the type of information used. *Effector anticipation* is based on the machine operator's ability to predict the amount of muscle activity necessary to control the machine. For instance, an automobile driver learns to predict precisely the muscle movements and force necessary to steer the car. *Receptor anticipation* pertains to predicting coming events as when the driver predicts the actions that will be required when viewing a curve in the road ahead. This previewing allows the operator to prepare the proper response in advance. Leonard (1953) and Wagner, Fitts, and Noble (1954) showed the value of previewing in improving performance. *Perceptual anticipation* is anticipation based on input cues. The subject learns with practice the predictable aspects of the input. Such is the case when a driver takes the same route to work each day and as a result learns to predict the coming curves in the road.

The findings of research on anticipation indicate that machine operators use advance information to predict future events as a basis for preparing for the coming events. Adams and Xhigriesse (1960) showed that accurate anticipation increased with the predictability of the task and with pretraining, which made the task more predictable to begin with. Thus people try to predict to improve their performance, and the predictability of the task at hand aids them.

Predictive ability has been shown to contribute substantially to effective reading.[1] Goodman (1970) says that reading is a process through which "available language cues are selected from perceptual input on the basis of the reader's expectations" (p. 260). As this partial information is processed, tentative decisions are made to be confirmed, rejected, or refined as reading progresses. Goodman refers to reading as a "psycholinguistic guessing game." Research documents the importance of prediction in reading. Greeno and Noreen (1974) measured reading time when subjects were led to expect content of later sentences as opposed to absence of this condition. Reading time was more rapid when preceding sentences supplying expectations were present. When expectations were disconfirmed or contradicted, reading time was slower. Henderson and Long (1968), in an article in *Psychological Reports*, investigated the relationship between reading ability and the ability to predict story outcomes. They found that superior readers had much greater ability to predict outcomes than did poor or average readers. Benz and Rosemier (1966) found that the ability to use context to predict the meaning of words was the single word analysis skill that best differentiated good, average, and poor comprehenders. Friedman and Rowls (1980) comprehensively cover the relationship between prediction and reading in their book, *Teaching Reading and Thinking Skills*.

Research also supports the contention that optimum predictability and arousal enhance performance. Eysenck (1975, 1976) demonstrates in several studies that high and low levels of arousal are associated with poor recall performance in semantic memory tasks, while an intermediate level of arousal is highly correlated with speed of response.

With regard to boredom, Heron, Bexton, and Hebb (1953) found decreased abilities to problem solve in subjects given monotonous tasks. Davenport (1974) exposed subjects performing a visual vigilance task to random, variable, fixed, and continuous interval schedules of background music. Subjects exposed to the random or variable interval schedules (less predictable) performed at a significantly higher level than did subjects exposed to fixed interval or continuous schedules. Finally, Thackery, Jones, and Touchstone (1974) found that extroverts (who have lower arousal levels than introverts) did not perform as well on monotonous and repetitive tasks as did introverts.

The importance of prediction in interpersonal behavior was pointed out in a study by Hayden, Nasby, and Davids (1977). They evaluated emotionally disturbed boys in residential treatment in terms of their predictive accuracy in sequencing social behavior, their level of social adjustment, and the structural characteristics of their interpersonal conceptual systems. They found that the more accurate a subject was in predicting the sequence of another individual's behavior the more appropriate was his interpersonal behavior.

Prediction and Problem Solving

The importance of *hypothesis testing*—a means for testing predictions—in problem solving has been highlighted by a number of researchers. Bruner, Goodnow, and Austin (1956) suggested that individuals create and test hypotheses. Restle (1962) and Bower and Trabasso (1964) conceived a model of the process of hypothesis testing. A more recent explanation of hypothesis testing comes from Levine (1974). Levine contends that to deal with a current problem, individuals first categorize or type the problem. Once the problem is classified, individuals deliberate and sample ideas from the category and hypothesize solutions. Each hypothesis represents an alternate solution. Hypotheses are then tested against feedback in an attempt to confirm them and solve the problem. When individuals' predictions are tested and confirmed, they are accepted as correct. When feedback indicates predictions are wrong, another hypothesis is chosen and tested. Subjects continue this lose-shift/win-stay strategy until a solution is eventually achieved. This line of reasoning and the research that supports it led to the development of what Levine calls H or hypothesis theory. (Brown [1974] reviews hypothesis theory.)

Prediction and Mental Stress

Prediction not only affects performance and problem solving; there is evidence that the ability to predict is related to mental stress.

The findings reported in the first chapter suggest a bipolar continuum with boredom and confusion at opposite poles and optimum predictability in the center. Prediction theory posits that boredom and confusion impair performance and adaptation, and optimum predictability enhances performance and adaptation. When an individual is under mental stress in the maladaptive state of boredom or confusion, that person can find relief by returning to a state of optimum predictability. The continuum suggested might be portrayed as follows:

Maladaptive Boredom ⟶ Adaptive Optimum Predictability ⟶ Maladaptive Confusion

A counseling study lends credibility to the above formulation. Savitz (1979) developed and validated an interview schedule that diagnoses bored, confused, and adaptive stress of mind. Adult outpatients suffering from psychological problems and diagnosed as bored or confused were studied. An experimental group was counseled one hour a week for four weeks using a method designed specifically to relieve their boredom or confusion. Bored clients were shown how to introduce variety and novelty into their lives, and confused clients were shown how to simplify and regulate their lives and involve themselves with familiar situations. A control group received no counseling. At the end of the four weeks those counseled and those in the control group were given a postdiagnosis. When compared to the control group, a significantly greater number of those in counseling recovered from their boredom or confusion.

An interesting example of the relationship between adaptation, mental stress, and optimum predictability can be seen in professional accounts of the process known as *brainwashing*. In brainwashing, the subjects are placed in a "topsy-turvey" world in which none of predictions they are accustomed to making are validated. However secure they may have been in the past, they soon become very insecure. The subjects become desperate to establish a predictable relationship with the environment once again. The only way that the subjects can reestabish predictability is to formulate predictions that the environment will confirm.

The brainwashers arrange the environment so that only certain predetermined predictions are confirmed. These predictions are based on the values of the social group to which the brainwashers belong and into which they are attempting to indoctrinate the subject. While holding the subjects in the helpless state of unpredictability, they encourage them to try their way of behaving, suggesting that they need only adjust to the inevitability of the demands of the environment in which they find themselves, as anyone must, in order to establish a predictable relationship with the new environment.

The brainwashers claim that they are not punishing them. They challenge the subjects to illustrate one instance in which they actively attempted to harm them. They suggest that they are asking them to conform to the same environmental demands to which the brainwashers themselves must conform and they offer to help the prisoners adjust. Placing them in an unpredictable environment, they offer to teach the prisoners how to predict and control themselves in this new environment, suggesting that "when in Rome do as the Romans do." The claim is that the subjects succumb to the conversion. They enter brainwashing with one set of values and predictions and emerge with another. They relinquish the predictions they learned from their former reference groups and learn the predictions that emanate from the social values of the group into which they are being indoctrinated.

One procedure that allegedly was used in the prisoner-of-war camps by the Communists during the Korean War to begin the brainwashing process was as follows. Upon arriving at the prison camp a small group of American soldiers was taken to an open field, given shovels, and told to dig a line of trenches. Each soldier was to dig one trench approximately seven feet long, four feet wide, and six feet deep. The trenches, of course, were about the size of a grave. When the trenches were finished, each soldier was asked to stand behind the trench that he had dug. When this was accomplished, a line of trenches was formed with a soldier standing behind each trench. Then a platoon of Communist soldiers, led by an officer, marched onto the field and stopped, facing the American soldiers from a distance of about forty feet. The arrangement closely resembled that of a firing squad. When the Communist soldiers were in place, the officer gave the commands in English, "ready, aim, fire," and the Communist soldiers fired into the air over the heads of the American prisoners. Then, the Communist officer walked over to the line of American soldiers, shook their hands, smiled at them, and welcomed them to the prison camp. He explained to them that the ritual represented a welcoming salute honoring their arrival, and the trenches were for garbage. He thanked them for digging the trenches, and they stood there while the trenches were filled with garbage. They were then asked to cover the garbage with dirt and were dismissed.

Thus brainwashing involves the systematic destruction of the person's ability to predict by placing the individual in a world that will not allow for confirmation of predictions. The technique implicitly recognizes that the ability to predict is a necessity of life and that people are strongly motivated to predict.

Bettelheim's (1960) account of his experiences in a concentration camp illustrates a struggle to maintain predictability. He writes:

> Besides traumatization, the Gestapo relied mainly on three other methods of destroying all personal autonomy. The first was that of forcing prisoners to adopt childlike behavior. The second was that of forcing them to give up individuality and merge them into an amorphous mass. The third consisted of destroying all capacity for self-determination, all ability to predict the future and thus to prepare for it. . . . By destroying man's ability to act

on his own or to predict the outcome of his own actions, they destroyed the feeling that his actions had any purpose. (pp. 131, 148)

The Predictive Ability Test

Because there is limited research in fields other than reading and industrial psychology that show the relationship between prediction and successful performance, and because there are many measures of successful living and adaptation but none of predictive ability available, Friedman has constructed a test of predictive ability. His task was to construct a valid and concise test of predictive ability so that scores on the test could be correlated with measurements of successful living and adaptation. It was reasoned that if predictive ability correlates positively with different indexes of successful living, it contributes to adaptation. The scores on the Predictive Ability Test (PAT) were correlated with social adjustment, success in education, and job status as indexes of successful living. The PAT scores correlated with social adjustments significantly and substantially higher than scores on an IQ test. There also was a high positive relationship between the PAT scores and measures of success in education such as successful completion of course work, highest school grade completed, grade-point average, and academic-achievement-test performance. In addition, the PAT scores were significantly and positively related to measures of job status. The PAT proved to be a better indicator of status achievement than an IQ test. Sample items from the PAT are in the appendix along with more details of the research reported above.

The composite evidence indicates that predictive ability as measured by the PAT is substantially correlated with important indexes of successful living. The relationship becomes more impressive when you consider that predictive ability is only one variable, and other variables must also contribute to successful living.

Prediction and Self-Confidence

A major reason the ability to predict contributes to adaptation is because it generates self-confidence. As individuals are able to confirm their predictions, they develop self-confidence in their ability to predict. And as they develop confidence, they anticipate success in predicting and become more persistent in pursuing the confirmation of a prediction. Also, they become more adventurous and less afraid of the unknown. Their confidence compels them to believe that sooner or later they will be able to confirm their predictions.

The self-confident person, then, can tolerate unpredictability and delay in confirming predictions. The confidence one has in one's ability to predict will cause one to pursue novelty more often and not to become frustrated and impatient when predictions are not confirmed immediately.

A person's insecurity or lack of self-confidence stems from a past inability to predict. This in turn causes the person to fear and anticipate unpredictability in the future. Such an individual suffers from a fear of the unknown, regarding the world as alien and dangerous. When the lack of self-confidence becomes pronounced, the individual tends to feel worthless, pessimistic, and despondent.

Much of the research on self-confidence has been conducted in the school setting. Anderson (1975) concludes that the time a student attends to a learning task contributes most heavily to the amount learned. A student who lacks self-confidence is not motivated to persist at a learning task and is likely to be distracted and to withdraw from the challenge of learning. Further, the student may disrupt the teacher and other pupils.

Coopersmith (1968) showed that students with low self-esteem lacked self-confidence and were generally less successful in and out of school. In his original study, Coopersmith discovered a number of differences between students with low self-esteem and those with high self-esteem. High-esteem students had less difficulty making friends, tended to be more academically and socially successful, realistically appraised their own abilities, and were confident that success would result from their efforts. Low-esteem individuals, on the other hand, lacked these characteristics. In addition, they showed a marked tendency to be overly sensitive to criticism, followers rather than leaders, less original and creative, and less active.

Self-confidence is an attitude one has toward one's self and one's ability to be successful. There are other related terms that are used to describe this attitude, such as self-esteem, self-concept, and self-regard. In general, those who have low opinions of themselves, however one may wish to state it, lack self-confidence and exhibit undesirable behavior.

In the school setting, teachers can enhance the self-confidence of students by arranging the teaching and learning environment in such a way that predictions are confirmed, challenge is provided at appropriate times, and punishment is not possible. Students are rewarded when validation of their predictions is achieved; they are punished when a program predicted to lead to a goal is not confirmed and there is no feedback as to how the program might be modified to achieve the goal. Students are challenged when program modifications for achieving the goal are provided (Willis 1974).

With respect to reading, Athey and Holmes (1969) found poor readers to be more socially independent, lower in self-concept, and exhibiting more school-related dislikes than average and good readers. Frerichs (1971) determined that good readers were higher in self-esteem than poor readers. Woolf

(1965) ascertained that poor readers were higher in anxiety and lower in self-concept than good readers.

Kulhavy, Yekovich, and Dyer (1976) showed that self-confidence facilitates learning and the amount of effort expanded to confirm predictions. Their study involved feedback (yes or no), self-related assuredness of answer, and one-week retention. They found that (1) high-confidence responses when reinforced as correct were remembered best, and (2) high-confidence responses when reinforced as incorrect were studied longer and corrected at a high rate. However, low-confidence responses whether (3) correct or (4) incorrect were forgotten, feedback having little effect.

Kifer (1975) conducted research on the personality traits of self-esteem and positive self-concept (self-confidence indicators). He reported that the pattern of success and failure and the accumulation of these experiences is related to positive inclination of these traits in individuals. It appears that this research supports the idea that the ratio of success to failure, which is perceived by a person, is the basis for beliefs about one's ability to make successful predictions with respect to classroom tasks.

In a study conducted by Schneider and Posse (1978) subjects were asked to predict success or failure of each move in a game of skill with nine levels of difficulty. They were also asked to indicate their degree of confidence in each prediction, and they were allowed to play the game at the level of difficulty of their choice. The study showed that individual choice behavior was a reliable and valid measure of degree of confidence subjects had in their predictions.

Autonomy has often been used as an index of personal adjustment. Some psychologists contend that maturation proceeds from total dependence toward autonomy and that when the individual becomes autonomous, that person is well adjusted. If autonomy is regarded as the ability to control the sources of one's satisfaction with a minimum of assistance from others, as it often is, then autonomy leaves something to be desired as an index of adjustment. What we are suggesting is that self-confidence does not require autonomy—it requires the ability to predict. Therefore, individuals may be well adjusted without being autonomous. That is to say, individuals may be self-confident without being able to control the sources of their own satisfaction as long as they can predict that others will provide satisfaction for them. Moreover, there is reason to believe that if self-confidence is not developed in early childhood when autonomy is impossible, the chance of becoming a relatively autonomous adult may be substantially impaired.

Infants have very little control over their own satisfaction and must depend on adults to minister to their needs. To insure their survival, infants must rely on the simple signs and symbols they can express to communicate their needs to the ministering adults. Still, infants would feel secure and gain self-confidence if their requests were granted by adults in spite of their lack of autonomy.

It does not appear to be individuals' ability to control their relationship with the environment that yields self-confidence, as much as their ability to predict accurately. Autonomy seems to be imposed upon individuals rather than sought by them. All societies require an increasing degree of autonomy for individuals as they grow older. Thus the push toward autonomy appears to be more external than internal, especially when one considers the propensity of individuals to surrender autonomy for dependence, as Eric Fromm (1971) made eminently clear in his book *Escape from Freedom.*

Self-confidence depends on the ability to predict new and challenging situations. A momentary feeling of security may be derived from retreating to familiar surroundings in the face of too little predictability, but lasting self-confidence comes from the knowledge that you can meet and learn to predict new situations because you have successfully done so in the past.

We have seen that predictive ability contributes to adaptation and successful living. Researchers in the fields of reading and industrial psychology have been leaders in the behavioral sciences in bringing forth evidence that it is the ability to predict that enhances success. We will probably soon see an increase in the amount of research into predictive ability as it relates to such arenas as clinical psychology, marriage counseling, political campaigning, and classroom teaching. Clinical psychologists are interested in adaptive states of mind and should therefore be helping their clients in learning to predict life situations. Likewise, marriage counselors could endeavor to increase their clients' accuracy in predicting what can and cannot be expected in a marriage relationship. For those seeking political office, the ability to predict what a constituency wants and what can be achieved after election to a particular office could add greatly to the office seekers' adaptation. Teachers are certainly interested in achieving optimum predictability in the classroom both for their own comfort and success and the enhancement of learning by their students.

Obviously the list of persons who will benefit from research into predictive ability could go on and on. All of us want to be successful at living and adapting to the world around us.

Prediction and Identification

Although the improvement of the ability to predict is the ultimate goal in promoting adaptation, it is important to acknowledge that accurate identification is prerequisite to accurate prediction. This is because it is necessary to identify what is happening in order to predict what may happen in the future. In short, predictions are based on the identification of trends.

Sometimes predictions are based on the identification of a present trend. Seeing two cars on a collision course might prompt you to predict an accident. Watching clouds form and hearing a clap of thunder may cause you to predict rain. Seeing a lighted firecracker might prompt you to expect an explosion. In each of these cases the identification of an immediate trend is the basis for making a prediction.

Predictions are sometimes based on the identification of more protracted trends. In such instances, past records are consulted, present information is obtained, and a prediction is projected based on the indicated past-present trend. The population rate forecast is based on the past-present trend of births. Economic conditions are predicted from the trend indicated by past and present economic indicators. The ecologists' prediction that our natural resources are being depleted is based on our increased abuse of the environment.

Whether trends are long or short term, individuals must learn to identify trends as a basis for making predictions. However, formal learning usually begins with simpler forms of identification, such as the identification of single objects or events. Such learning is manifested by the ability to name things. After learning to identify static events, children are taught relationships and how things change over time. Eventually they are taught to identify trends. This occurs when they study such subjects as history and the life cycles of plants and animals. Once they learn to identify a trend they can base a prediction on it.

The remaining chapters in part I are concerned primarily with identification and prediction skills, that is, how they develop and operate to facilitate prediction. Although a great deal remains to be discovered about the operation of the mind, the following explanations of mental process are intended to be consistent with current evidence interpreted from the perspective of prediction theory.

Note

1. It might be mentioned in passing that the field of reading provides some evidence that secondary motivation, the pursuit of preferential interests, enhances performance. Two studies conducted by Asher and Markell (1974) and Estes and Vaughan (1973) demonstrate that the selection of preferred reading materials enhances reading comprehension.

4 Mental Structure

In this chapter the content and structural components of the mind are considered. Mental content and structure provide the basis for making predictions and the identifications that are necessary for predicting. Once mental structure and content are understood, learning can be addressed, as well as the dynamics of identifying and predicting in subsequent chapters.

In prediction theory the basic structural unit of the mind is called a *neuroprint*, which is a mental coding of the relationship among stimuli or events. We know about stimuli through their composition, that is, the relationship of their parts to the whole. For instance, we recognize people by noting the relationships among the features of their faces and bodies; a tricycle is recognized because of the relationship between its three wheels, frame, seat, pedals, and handlebars; a bathroom is recognized because of its related parts, that is, a lavatory, toilet, and bathtub. An event such as a sunrise is understood in terms of the relationship between the sun and the earth; and the life cycle of a plant or animal is known through the relationship of one developmental stage to another. Neuroprint is the term used to refer to any and all codings of the mind. Particular types of mental codings represent particular types of neuroprints. The *theoretical construct neuroprint* is introduced because a term is needed to refer in general to codings or recordings in the mind, as explained further.

There are neuroprints in the mind present at birth that direct the behavior of the infant and its development. These inherited neuroprints represent one type of neuroprint. Inherited neuroprints include instincts and reflexes. Although inherited neuroprints underlie and influence mental development, they will not be analyzed in this book. They are not central to the understanding of prediction theory and its implications for the behavioral sciences, which is the focus of this book. The explanation of inherited neuroprints requires delving deeply into the biological sciences. The only neuroprints that will be considered are ideas, which are neuroprints that are products of learning.

Ideas

Ideas are neuroprints that make us aware of the composition of events and the way we feel about them. They are a product of learning. The ideas we have represent our understanding of the relationship between events as a result of what we have learned about them. Ideas make us aware of the relationships among the parts of our body, the relationships among the things we see in our environment, and the relationship we have with our environment. Ideas permit us to be aware of the composition or content of events and how we feel about the events. Thus ideas give meaning to experience.

For instance, as a woman drives to her office, she is aware of the road before her and the scenery she is passing, as well as the traffic problems confronting her at the moment. She is aware of even more than she sees—she knows there is a back seat behind her and perhaps a package on the seat. Moreover, as she travels her mind may wander to an experience she had playing with her child the previous evening or to the work she must accomplish when she arrives at the office. Thus ideas represent the awareness one has about what is happening, what has happened, or what may happen.

Ideas include also one's feeling about one's experiences. As a woman proceeds to her office, she is aware not only of what is happening but also of the feelings she has about the events. As she views the scenery along the road, she is aware not only of its composition but also of the way it makes her feel—its beauty or its ugliness. If she should be threatened by an oncoming car, she might be frightened by it; or if she should reminisce about her child, a feeling of pleasure may come over her. An individual's feelings about experiences represent the way in which one values the experience.

A little introspection may clarify further the proposition that ideas contain affect as well as content and that the content of ideas indicates what one's feelings are about. Think of both the content and feelings that the ideas which are stimulated by certain words bring to mind. "Ice cream," "circus," and "Christmas" usually portray situations that generate positive feelings. "Cancer," "traffic accident," and "murder" portray situations that generate negative feelings.

When the content of an idea is vivid and detailed, the individual has a keen awareness of the event that the idea represents. However, some ideas represent faint impressions of events because the content is vague. In such cases, one may be aware of the intensity of one's feelings but only vaguely aware of the event associated with the feelings. Thus it is the content of an idea that lends clarity to one's experiences and indicates what one's feelings are about.

Ideas and Prediction

There are two forms of ideas that facilitate prediction; programs and master neuroprints.

Programs

Programs are neuroprints that represent sequences of activities. Programs are the mental equipment for making predictions because predictions are inherent in them. In essence, programs are mental recordings of "if this . . . then that" relationships so that when "this" occurs "that" is predicted to follow. For instance, by knowing that if you take aspirin then your headache may subside, you can predict that taking aspirin can relieve a headache.

A program may define a trend or a procedure. When a program defines a *trend* it provides a basis for predicting events; when a program defines a *procedure* it provides a basis for controlling events as well as predicting events. For instance, the sun rising and lighting the earth is a trend. Knowing this trend one can predict that when the sun rises it will become light outdoors. This program does not, however, provide a basis for controlling events. On the other hand, the procedure of taking aspirin to relieve a headache does provide a basis for controlling headaches. Prediction is implicit in procedures—one predicts that if one takes aspirin one's headache will subside.

A program may contain one "if this-then that" sequence, or it may contain a chain of such sequences. If it contains a chain of sequences, we will refer to each component sequence as a *subroutine* of the program.

A child may learn a program procedure to obtain a glass of water. The first subroutine of the program might be to open the kitchen cabinet, the second to take a glass, the third to fill it with water, and the fourth to drink the water. Each subroutine of the program is performed in sequence in order to execute the program.

Programs not only allow predictions to be made, they are also the basis for testing and confirming predictions. Predictions are tested by following the operations prescribed in the program and are confirmed when events actually turn out as the program prescribes. If they do, the program is reinforced and retained in the mind. If not, the individual's inclination to predict accurately causes the program to be modified to accommodate actual events.

In learning to obtain a glass of water the child first learns the program sequence, then tests the program by executing the subroutines in order. If the child is successful, the program will be reinforced in the child's mind. If not, the program will be modified so that it will work or another program will be substituted for it.

Programs both guide action and process information. However, there are programs that primarily guide action and programs that primarily process information. The above example of the child getting and drinking water is an illustration of a program that primarily directs action.

Information-processing programs represent a set of procedures that are followed to store, retrieve, and analyze information. The program used to obtain information from the library is an example of an information-processing program. To find the information you are seeking you would first check the card catalogue, then note the titles, authors, and numbers of the relevant reading references. Next, the reading material is located in the stacks by means of the numbers assigned to them. Finally, you receive the material and review it to find the information you are seeking. You also follow a program when you use the index or table of contents to locate information in a book. The alphabetical arrangement of dictionaries, encyclopedias, and telephone directories represent programs for finding information in them.

Programs vary in degree of flexibility. An *inflexible program* is one in which the operations controlled by the program are performed in a fixed order. Such programs are executed automatically, and they include habits such as the program that governs the shifting of the gears of a car.

A *flexible program* is a fixed sequence of activities within which certain activities can be performed in more than one order. For example, the program governing driving a car prescribes a fixed sequence in that one must enter the car before driving it. However, certain activities one performs within the sequence in preparation for driving are flexible. Turning on the lights, adjusting the seat, and fastening the seat belt can be performed in any order. Another example is shopping. One leaves home to shop and returns home after shopping. These activities occur in a fixed order. While shopping, the items on the shopping list usually can be purchased in more than one order.

In conclusion, programs are the means of satisfying the prediction motive because they are the basis for making, testing, and confirming predictions. Thus programs are the key to rationality which, as we said, involves making, testing, and attempting to confirm predictions. In addition, it is the learning of new programs that improves one's ability to predict.

Master Neuroprints

Earlier we defined interests as penchants to confirm particular predictions. The master neuroprint is the means of satisfying interests. A *master neuroprint* contains an interest, a goal predicted to satisfy the interest and a program that leads to the goal.[1] When children learn that drinking water will quench their thirst, a master neuroprint is coded in the mind. The interest is confirming the prediction that their thirst will be quenched. The goal is the drinking of water, and the program is the set of actions or operations involved in obtaining and drinking the water. Once the master neuroprint has formed, children know how to confirm the prediction that their thirst will be quenched and they can satisfy this interest in the future. So, master neuroprints are our mental equipment for satisfying interests.

A master neuroprint may be illustrated as follows:

An Interest ──────▶ Program ──────▶ Goal

It is the master neuroprint that indicates whether we have positive or negative feelings toward something. If the content of a master neuroprint indicates that moving away from an object will satisfy an interest, we will have negative feelings toward the object and try to avoid it. When a child is bitten by a dog, the master neuroprint that forms will indicate that avoiding dogs will prevent getting bitten again, and the child will have negative feelings toward dogs and avoid them. On the other hand, if the content of a master neuroprint indicates that obtaining an object will satisfy an interest, we will have positive feelings toward the object and seek it. It is a master neuroprint that indicates that obtaining food will reduce hunger; we therefore have positive feelings toward food and seek it. Master neuroprints are used to satisfy both primary and secondary motivations. They satisfy primary motivation because they contain programs that are the means of enhancing prediction in general. They satisfy secondary motivation in that they can be used to confirm the particular prediction of interest to the individual at the time.

Images and Concepts

We have explained how programs and master neuroprints facilitate prediction. Images and concepts also facilitate prediction in a complementary way. Images permit familiar events to be predicted. Concepts permit novel events to be predicted.

Images

An *image* is an idea (neuroprint) of a sensory experience. An image of an event forms as a result of sensory exposure to the event. The learning process that produces images is sometimes referred to as memorizing. In general, memorizing is facilitated through spaced review of the event and interest in it.

An image represents the composition of the event and the way it makes the individual feel. Once an image of an event is formed, it permits the individual to recognize the event. For instance, when an individual is exposed to an object such as a dog, an image of the dog will form in the mind. Subsequently, when seeing the dog, the individual will recognize it as familiar to past experience. The person will also be aware of its composition and the feelings produced by seeing the dog. Thus images are ideas of sensory events that have been experienced in the past.

In addition to acquiring images of individual events, individuals acquire images of programs. An image of a program forms when individuals are exposed to sequences of activities and memorize them. Such is the case when individuals learn to tell time. Learned inflexible programs that are executed automatically are generally thought of as *habits*. Learning to tell time, count, and recite the alphabet result in the formation of habits. Thus images govern habits.

Images also form representing master neuroprints. Images of master neuroprints form when individuals learn that interests are satisfied through the attainment of goals by means of programs. When the infant observes that when the mother brings milk and feeds it to him his hunger is satisfied, the infant learns a master neuroprint. The image of the master neuroprint depicts the interest as the satisfaction of hunger, the goal as the acquisition of milk, and the program as the mother's activities in providing the milk for him.

It is the contention of prediction theory that the individual is more prone to record images of sequences of events rather than static events because sequences allow predictions to be made. Penfield (1951), a neurosurgeon, stimulated electrically various parts of the human brain and observed what the subjects experienced. He found that when the temporal lobes of the brain are stimulated, the experiences reported by the subject are not single static memories but rather sequences of events as they were experienced initially.

So far we have considered images that represent concrete events that have been observed in the past. We also have images of events that did not happen—dreams and hallucinations are examples of such images. Further, images of concrete events become colored and distorted, as one's recollection of past experiences changes with time. It seems that images of past experiences become associated with neuroprints already stored in the mind and change as a result of the storage and retrieval process.

Concepts

A *concept* is an idea (neuroprint) representing a category of images that have common characteristics. When an image of a sensory event is formed, it is compared with other images and categorized with similar images as a part of the storage process. The categorization of similar images forms concepts. The process of categorization results in the individual's recognizing an event as a special case of a general category of events. A concept is not created directly by a sensory experience but by the categorization of images that have been associated as having something in common. An apple is a sensory event represented by an image. The term *apple* is a concept representing a category of images of items similar to apples.

Thus a concept cannot be experienced directly as a sensory event, although it is inferred from sensory experience. In other words, an image represents a sensory event; a concept does not represent a sensory event, but, rather, a category of images that depicts events with similar characteristics.

The process of conceptualization does not end with the formation of images into categories. Once categories have been formed, they can be compared for similarities and differences and this leads to the formation of more general or higher level concepts. For example, vegetables and meats, which are both concepts, may be classified together within the category of *food* as parts of a higher level concept. Concepts, therefore, permit the individual to have ideas about the similarities and differences among events and objects. When one is able to make distinctions between the similarities and differences among events, one is able to understand alternatives, which is the basis for making choices. For example, if individuals understand that food will satisfy their hunger, they are aware of a variety of food items that can satisfy their hunger and choose among them.

Programs may also be categorized together to form a concept. This may mean that the programs in a category share in common their ability to control some of the same operations. Therefore, one program in the category might be substituted for another. For example, cursive writing, printing, and typewriting might be categorized together to form the concept *writing* programs. The programs in this category represent alternative procedures for writing.

Master neuroprints, too, can be categorized to form a concept. For instance, master neuroprints that define different ways of satisfying hunger might be grouped together to form a concept.

Concepts produce ideas about categories of events that represent an impression of the features that the items in a category share in common. For example, we have an idea of the concept *people* as a general representation of the common characteristics of people.

When an idea of an event is elicited, the event to which the idea corresponds is recognized as familiar. When an idea is produced by an image, the corresponding event is recognized as familiar to a specific event in the individual's past experience. When an idea is produced by a concept, the corresponding event is recognized as containing the features or attributes of a category of events.

The assertion that individuals form concepts by categorizing their experiences is amply supported in the literature on the subject. In their book *A Study of Thinking*, Bruner, Goodnow, and Austin (1956) suggest that people tend to categorize events because categorization simplifies the environment for them; it reduces the need for learning since new events are viewed as belonging to old categories, and it facilitates identification when objects can be recognized as members of categories.

For Piaget, the process of categorizing is an important aspect of mental development. Children are said to have reached the "concrete operations" stage of development when they are able to classify experiences. The operation of classifying is considered the mental equivalent to the motor act of grouping together objects recognized as similar. The ability to classify objects is illustrated in a study reported by Piaget and Szeminska (1941) entitled *The Child's Concept of Numbers*.

The *schema*—Piaget's term for the mental representation of events—is considered to be based on common elements. Inhelder (1958), Piaget's associate, defines a schema as "the structure common to all those acts which—from the subject's point of view—are equivalent" (p. 122). It should also be noted that the Gestalt Law of Similarity (which states, in essence, that in perception individuals tend to group similar events together) reinforces the position that individuals tend to categorize their experiences.

Travers (1973) summarizes the process of categorizing as follows: "The process of generalization and discrimination are seen to operate in categorizing behavior, an important aspect of behavior through which the countless situations and events encountered by the learner are grouped. Both human and subhuman animals demonstrate through their behavior this tendency to categorize the situations they encounter" (p. 143).

The products of the categorization of experiences have been well known since the early days of psychological research. Studies in stimulus and response generalization demonstrate the effects of categorization. For example, stimulus generalization was demonstrated in Pavlov's training of dogs. Dogs conditioned to raise a front paw each time a tone of 440 vibrations per second is sounded will make the same response when a tone of 220 vibrations per second is sounded. Response generalization has also been demonstrated in research when one stimulus is shown to elicit a range of responses in the individual.

Garner (1974) has shed light on the response of the central nervous system to sensory input. He contends that when a sensory input is examined and interpreted it is implicit that the perceived element is classified as a member of a set or category of elements. Ingling (1972) offers some evidence that individuals tend to recognize an object as a member of a category rather than recognize the idiosyncratic features of the object. He suggests that categorical identification is more economical and rapid because an identification can be made without taking into account all of the features of the object.

There is also considerable research that supports the position that people categorize their experiences. To begin we cite the research on chunking. The *chunking hypothesis* was described by G.A. Miller (1956) who stated that immediate reproductive memory is limited in terms of the numbers of chunks of elements rather than the number of individual elements. Bower (1969) demonstrated this. Subjects were exposed either to a list of nouns or three-word statements such as Happy New Year and then asked to recall them. The subjects recalled as many three-word statements as they did individual nouns. The terms are said to be learned chunks or groups. Hilgard and Bower (1975) conclude that "the way a person learns a longer list of words, say of 14 unrelated words, is to organize the lower-order units into seven or fewer higher-order units or chunks. Learning, then, was to be viewed as a matter of segregating, classifying, and grouping the elementary units into a smaller number of richer, more densely packed chunks" (p. 585).

Underwood's (1969) study showed that information is chunked into categories and that when words can be categorized they are learned more rapidly. He presented to his subjects lists of words that did not obviously belong in categories and others that did. The words that did belong in categories, for example, were names of countries, birds, diseases, and elements. The words on the lists were presented in random order, so that categories of words were not evident. The words were read aloud to subjects, and then they were asked to recall the words. The words that could be categorized by the subjects were categorized by them. The subjects categorized all the diseases together, all the countries together, and so on. Further, the lists that included categories of objects were remembered more readily than the lists that did not include categories that were evident.

Shuell (1969), Tulving (1967), and Tulving and Patterson (1968) have summarized the results of studies by Bousefield which bear on the individual's tendency to categorize. The subject is read a list of words and is then asked to recall them. If categories of words are selected by the researcher and presented, the subject is likely to recall them in categories. If the words have been selected by the experimenter at random, the subject will attempt to categorize them. This research suggests that individuals tend to organize objects into categories.

When research on categorizing is conducted using words as stimuli, it is difficult to determine whether the individual's tendency to categorize is due to an inherent tendency to categorize or because the words were taught categorically. A study by Preusser and Handel (1970) demonstrates that individuals tend to categorize the data that are unfamiliar due to the fact that individuals were taught to categorize the particular data previously. Preusser and Handel presented subjects cards with geometric patterns on them. The geometric forms on the cards were familiar (circles, squares, and triangles), but the patterns on the cards were novel. However, there were similarities or common geometrical characteristics among the different cards which could be detected. The order in which the cards were placed before the subjects was randomized, and the subjects were asked to group the cards together in any way that made sense to them by placing them together physically. The subjects grouped cards with similar geometrical characteristics together.

The results of this study indicate that individuals will attempt to categorize unfamiliar information, probably because they are inherently impelled to categorize. However, we cannot discount the possibility that individuals have been taught to categorize unfamiliar information.

The term *concept* was used to denote a category of events because it serves as a bridge between the findings and theory on categorizing that stem from studies of memory and the research of concept learning. In concept learning a concept is regarded as knowledge of a category of events. Learners demonstrate their understanding of a concept when they are able to (1) state the critical attributes of the concept, that is, the criteria for inclusion in the category, and (2) distinguish examples from nonexamples of the concept category.

Hull (Hilgard and Bower 1975) introduced the term concept as we are using it. Bruner, Goodnow, and Austin (1956) added to our understanding of concepts, and Bourne (1966) and Byers (1967) summarized much of the research on concepts up to that time. Since these summaries, much of the work on concepts has centered around the teaching of concepts. Markle and Tiemann (1969) described how concepts are learned and should be taught. A more recent summary of the research on the teaching of concepts is presented by Goodwin and Klausmeier (1975).

Concepts generally refer to public categories. Not only do individuals tend to categorize experiences on their own, society categorizes information and teaches the categories to its members. Social categories are usually presented in the form of word definitions in dictionaries, encyclopedias, and textbooks. The word definitions state the criteria for identifying an object or event as a member of a category the word represents.

It is illuminating to realize that most words represent categories. When you look up most words in the dictionary you are given defining criteria for a category. Should you look up the word *mammal* in the dictionary, you would be given the following criteria for the concept: (1) vertebrate, (2) skin is covered with hair, (3) has mammary glands. Only proper nouns and some uses of personal pronouns represent concrete sensory events. Proper nouns are names for concrete events—your name represents you. Quite often a personal pronoun is used to designate a concrete event, such as when a man is referred to as *he*. However, a personal pronoun such as *he* can be used to designate a concept category. The statement, "The dog is a *he*," indicates that the dog belongs to the category *male*.

In conclusion, the evidence indicates that individuals tend to categorize information, and the ability to categorize facilitates learning. In addition, societies categorize public information and teach these concept categories to their members. A great deal of attention and research has been devoted to the teaching of concepts, which has become a major issue in education. Our concern here is with concepts as mental content; the teaching of concepts is beyond the scope of our inquiry. (See references for more about the teaching of concepts.)

We have posited and defined two types of ideas—images[2] and concepts. The contention that there are two kinds of ideas or memories stored in the mind has been gaining credibility recently, and there are prominent similarities between the distinctions we have made and the distinctions of others.

Tulving (1972) distinguished between episodic and semantic memory. *Episodic memory* refers to a record of the incidents that happen to the individual and is similar to Friedman's definition of image in that both are referring to a record of sensory experience. Tulving's *semantic memory* is similar to Friedman's definition of concepts in that they are both referring to generalities inferred from sensory experience rather than experienced directly through the senses. Friedman defined three different types of generalities or concepts—concepts pertaining to (1) individual events or objects, (2) programs, and (3) master neuroprints. Programs and master neuroprints represent general principles for problem solving. Tulving refers primarily to general principles for problem solving in his discussion of semantic memory.

Kintsch and Keenan's (1973) remarks suggest that episodic memory records specific concrete events such as remembering the characteristics of a chisel after using one, whereas semantic memory categorizes concrete events such as remembering that a chisel belongs to the category tool. This indicates further the similarity between Friedman's definition of an image and the definition of episodic memory, and the similarity between Friedman's definition of a concept and the definition of semantic memory.

Another dichotomy of types of memory is iconic and symbolic memory discussed by Entwistle and Huggins (1973). *Iconic memory* is similar to Tulving's episodic memory and Friedman's definition of image in that iconic memory refers to the recording of sensory experience. *Symbolic memory* is similar to Tulving's semantic memory and Friedman's definition of a concept in that symbolic memory represents an abstract symbolizing of sensory experience.

Before leaving the subject of ideas or memories, we should consider meaning because ideas give meaning to one's experiences. First, images give meaning to experience because they are recordings of the content of sensory experiences together with the feelings one has about the experiences.

Second, concepts give meaning to experience because they are recordings of the common attributes of events; identifying a sensory event as a member of a category imputes to the sensory event the same characteristics as the category. Thus if an unfamiliar sensory event has the same characteristics as a concept, the sensory event has meaning for the individual in that it is known to have the same properties as other members of the concept category.

We indicated earlier that images and concepts enhance prediction in a complementary way. Images are the basis for making predictions about familiar events. Concepts are the basis for predicting novel events. Because images are ideas of past experiences, when an identification is based on an image, the identified event is familiar to the individual's past experience. When a prediction about the event is based on a program or master neuroprint image, the individual will predict a familiar outcome. A person will be inclined to predict that events will turn out in the future as they have in the past.

When a novel event appears, its identification cannot be based on an image because the event has not been experienced before and an image has not formed. However, if the novel event corresponds to a concept, it can be identified as a member of the concept category. Then it will be known to possess the same characteristics as members of the category. Further, once identified it can be predicted to behave as other members of the category do. For instance, if a strange creature standing on the ground is identified as a member of the concept category bird, one can predict that it will probably fly.

This short explanation of the relationship between prediction and images and concepts serves as an introduction. Further explanations and clarifications will be offered in the following chapters.

Emotion

Too much or too little predictability generates emotion. The intensity of emotion is the intensity of affect or feeling associated with arousal. As arousal increases there is an increase in the intensity of feeling, which is regarded as an increase in the intensity of emotion. To be very emotional is to be very aroused. Emotion is given specificity by the content of ideas. Therefore, specific emotion is a product of learning.

When arousal is high and the individual feels intensity without knowing what the intensity of the feelings is about, we sometimes refer to this condition as "free floating arousal or anxiety." This simply means that the feelings are nonspecific because an idea has not formed through learning which designates what the feelings are about. In order to have an idea of what your feelings are about, an idea must form, the content of which indicates why you feel the way you do.

For example, you know what being sunburned is because you have learned about it from experience, and your ideas indicate the characteristics of sunburn. If you cannot characterize a feeling in terms of the conditions that produce it, you cannot identify the source of the emotion or feeling. The identification and description of emotion depend upon the content of ideas.

To elaborate, the minds of newborn infants contain very few ideas because there has not been sufficient time for learning. Therefore, their feelings are relatively undifferentiated and are characterized mainly by variation in intensity rather than content. As infants learn to associate their feelings with an increasing number of specific events, their inventory of ideas becomes more differentiated and so do their feelings. This is a refining and differentiating process that changes the amorphous feelings of early childhood to the more graded and distinct feelings of maturity. Thus at any given stage of maturity the individual's feelings become more modulated and distinct than at an earlier, less differentiated state. This does not mean that adults are incapable of extreme feelings; rather, adults will tend to express a greater variety of feelings and probably extreme feelings less often.

Evidence that adults will express extreme feelings less often than children was provided in a study that required both adults and children to react to pictures of paintings (Friedman 1967). The subjects were asked to indicate on a bipolar four-point scale the extent to which they liked or disliked each painting. The children expressed significantly more extreme reactions to the paintings than the adults.

In summary, the following chart shows the types of ideas described in this chapter. Figure 4-1 shows that two kinds of ideas are coded in the mind—images and concepts—and that images and concepts may represent master neuroprints, programs, or individual objects and events. An image represents a master neuroprint when it records a means of satisfying a personal interest that was observed through the senses, and an image represents a program when it records an activity sequence that was observed through the senses. An image represents an individual object or event when it records an object or event that was observed. A concept represents a category of master neuroprints when it records programs that satisfy the same personal interest. A concept represents a category of programs when it records similar activity sequences, and a concept represents a category of individual objects or events when it records static objects or events with the same characteristics.

	Master Neuroprints	Programs	Individual Objects and Events
Images	Mental codings of observed programs that satisfy personal interests	Mental codings of observed activity sequences	Mental codings of observed objects and events
Concepts	Mental codings of categories of programs that satisfy personal interests	Mental codings of categories of activities	Mental codings of categories of objects and events

Figure 4-1. Types of Ideas

In this chapter we have considered the structure and content of ideas that provide the basis for predicting and identifying. Programs were described as the structural components most essential to satisfying the prediction motive because they represent sequences that indicate predictions that can be made. Programs also permit the identification of sequences. Master neuroprints were described as ideas that facilitate prediction in general and the satisfaction of specific interests. They facilitate prediction because they contain programs. They satisfy interests because they facilitate the confirmation of a particular prediction the individual may have a penchant to confirm at a particular time. In addition, images were described as ideas of past experience, whereas concepts were described as categories of images with common characteristics. We showed how images and concepts represent programs, master neuroprints, and individual events. However, we indicated that ideas of programs and master neuroprints are more likely to be learned than ideas of individual events because programs and master neuroprints provide the means of satisfying the prediction motive.

Finally, we provided an introductory explanation of why images permit familiar events to be predicted and why concepts permit novel events to be predicted.

Notes

1. Although master neuroprints are discussed only with respect to the learning of ideas that contain them, most inherited neuroprints probably

are master neuroprints that are executed automatically. The interest in an inherited master neuroprint would be associated with survival, and when survival is threatened the program portion of the master neuroprint would engage automatically to reduce the threat. The goal is the condition that results in the removal of the threat.

2. In the original version of prediction theory presented in *Rational Behavior*, Friedman used the term *memory* instead of the term *image*. The terms were changed because he found that the term memory is used in many different ways and causes problems of interpretation. The term image is more compatible with the meaning he wishes to convey. Also, the term *abstraction* was used instead of the term concept in the original version. He continues to use the term abstraction but in a more generic sense (see chapter 5). From Friedman's present view, a concept is one kind of abstraction.

5 Learning

Now that we have described the content and structural components of the mind, we can consider how learning occurs. We are concerned primarily with how the ideas that facilitate prediction and identification are learned. First, we will consider some factors that influence learning as they are discussed in the literature and relate them to prediction theory; then we will offer an account of learning based on the factors previously considered.

Factors Affecting Learning

Abstraction

Abstraction is defined as the identification of an event based on a limited set of its attributes. One important factor that underlies the development of ideas is that individuals do not seem to store in their minds the totality of an experience. Rather they abstract and store only a set of attributes of the experience.

Underwood (1969), Murdock (1974), and Tulving and Watkins (1975) in theoretical discussions indicate that what is stored in the mind is a set of attributes of an experience. Research demonstrates that visual symbols are processed as a set of features. Ellis and Daniel (1971), using randomly designed figures, found that individuals stored in memory a record of the distinctive features of the figures, rather than the figures as total units. Studies on the processing of words yielded similar results. Nelson, Brooks, and Fosselman (1972) showed that words were recognized as a set of features of which the first and last letters are most important. Visually presented words are not retained in memory as total units.

Research on the tip-of-the-tongue phenomena also indicates that words are stored and retrieved as a set of characteristics. Brown and McNeill (1966) conducted a study in which the definitions of rare words were read to the subjects, and the subjects were asked to state the words being defined. Of the total group some subjects said that they could not recall a word but that it was on the tip of their tongues, such as how many syllables it had, the first letter of the word, and other words that had similar sounds or meanings.

The subjects in the tip-of-the-tongue group were able to recall features of the words they were attempting to recall, even though they could not

53

recall the target word. They were able to identify with better than chance accuracy the number of syllables, the first letter, and suffixes in the target word. In addition, the subjects could judge which of two words most resembled the target word.

So it appears that the images that are stored in the mind consist of a set of attributes of an event, and we remember an event in terms of the attributes that are recorded.

Attribution theory can be applied to the learning of concepts as well as to the learning of images. Once the attributes of events are recorded as images, the attributes of one image can be compared to the attributes of other images for similarities and differences. When similarities are found among the attributes of different images, a concept category has formed in the mind. Once the concept has formed, any new event that possesses the attributes of the concept category is assumed to behave as other members of the category.

Short-term and Long-term Memory

A second major factor that influences any interpretation of learning is the distinction between long- and short-term-memory systems as subsystems of the total memory system. We will not attempt to define long- and short-term memory because there is some variation in the literature with respect to their precise characteristics. For our purposes a discussion will suffice.

One piece of evidence indicating that there is a long- and a short-term-memory mechanism is reported by Pines (1974). A patient after brain surgery gave evidence that his short-term and long-term memories were intact, but he was unable to transfer current experience from his short-term memory to his long-term memory. The patient was able to read a story and remember the beginning of the story before he reached the end. But soon afterward the memory of the story faded, and he could read it again as if it were new to him.

Another study that indicates that there are two memory systems was conducted by Kleinsmith and Kaplan (1963). They measured the subject's degree of emotional arousal by means of galvanic skin response when presenting him with pairs of words. They found that when a pair of words generated high arousal the retention of the association was reduced for short-term memory but increased for long-term memory. It would seem that the two memory systems are discrete if a condition that improves the long-term memory impairs short-term memory.

Two other factors distinguish short- and long-term memory. First, the capacity of long-term memory is relatively larger than short-term memory. Second, the causes of forgetting appear to be different for the two systems.

Forgetting in short-term memory occurs as a result of fading—to be kept in short-term memory, information must be rehearsed. For instance, after looking up a phone number one repeats it over and over to keep it from fading before dialing the number. On the other hand, information contained in long-term memory does not readily fade with time. Bahrick, Bahrick, and Whittlinger (1974) show that subjects remember their high school classmates long after graduation. Graduates were able to match pictures with names of classmates with 90 percent accuracy fifteen years after graduation and with 60 percent accuracy after forty-eight years. So there is evidence that decay or fading from long-term memory is slow.

It appears that with respect to long-term memory forgetting is caused by interference. Interference occurs in two ways, retroactively and proactively. In retroactive interference new learning interferes with the retention of material already learned; in proactive interference earlier learning may have a depressing effect on later learning. For both types of interference the earlier and later learnings are inconsistent or contradictory. The inconsistency tends to cause forgetting.

Watkins (1974) states three characteristics of short-term memory. First, it is a store from which information is selected to transfer to long-term memory. Second, short-term memory is the conscious aspect of memory— the information we are conscious of is contained in short-term memory. Third, short-term memory involves retrieval. Short-term memory not only includes perceptions of immediate sensory events but also perceptions or images retrieved from long-term memory, such as an image of a past occurrence. In addition to the three characteristics described by Watkins, short-term memory may be the locus where incoming information is organized prior to memorization and transfer to long-term memory.

With respect to prediction theory, short-term memory produces images. That is to say, when we are conscious of an event we have an image of the event, whether the image is of an immediate sensory event or is a result of retrieval from the long-term-memory store. Long-term memory contains both images and concepts. This is consistent with other interpretations of long-term memory (see chapter 4). To elaborate, Tulving (1972) suggests that long-term memory is organized in two distinct ways, episodic and semantic memories, while others refer to the dichotomous content of long-term memory as iconic and symbolic memory. As was mentioned previously, our term *image* and the terms *episodic* and *iconic memory* refer to recordings of sensory experiences. Our term *concept* and the terms *semantic* and *symbolic memory* refer to abstracted generalizations of the images, and our term *concept* refers to an abstraction category.

It is long-term memory that gives meaning to experience. If a current stimulus is totally unfamiliar, it is not stored in memory and can have no meaning. If it is stored in memory and is familiar as an image, it may have meaning because it produces the content and feeling of an experience and may be associated with satisfying the prediction motive, or an interest, or both.

Additional meaning can be imputed to an event as a result of categorizing it in long-term memory. For example, meaning is imputed when a particular animal is identified as a horse. This indicates that it has the attributes of "horseness" and will behave as a horse. Categorizing an animal as a horse enables one to make predictions about it and to determine whether or not it is a source of satisfying a personal interest.

There is some evidence that long-term memory represents meaning whereas short-term memory represents sensory images. Errors in recall experiments indicate that for short-term memory the subject will substitute a similar sounding word for the correct word, such as substituting log for dog. In erroneously recalling information from long-term memory, the subject provides similar meaning such as substituting the word terrier for dog. The fact that different types of recall errors are made in the two systems offers further evidence that long- and short-term memory are distinct subsystems of memory.

Although we have been able to distinguish long-term and short-term memory, describe the properties of each, and relate them to prediction theory, it is much more difficult to describe the interaction between the two systems. Attempts up to this point have given us a recursive sequence of steps often portrayed as a sequential system of boxes (see Atkinson and Shiffrin 1965, 1968).

The sequence usually portrays a perceptual trace of an arousing event entering the short-term memory store where mnemonic activity is engaged, such as rehearsal. As a result of rehearsal in short-term memory, the memory structure is transferred to long-term memory. Since such renditions are based largely on research pertaining to the processing of verbal information, we can use verbal input to illustrate the sequence. A researcher interests subjects in recalling a list of words in serial order. (1) A perceptual trace of the word, say its pronunciation, enters short-term memory. (2) The pronunciation of the word would be rehearsed subvocally along with other words on the list. (3) As a result of rehearsal, the words would transfer to long-term memory and the subjects would be able to recall them at a later time when the researcher asked them.

Although this may be an oversimplified version of the sequential process, it is sufficient to allow us to point to some limitations of our current renditions of the memory process and the limited knowledge we have of how memory actually operates.

To begin, the rendition assumes that rehearsal causes the transfer of information from short-term to long-term memory. However, this notion is gleaned largely from research on the processing of verbal material, when most often rehearsal involves the repeated subvocal pronunciation of linguistic symbols. This type of rehearsal might be more difficult if the stimulus to be transferred to long-term memory were novel, nonverbal material. So it remains for us to consider other possible reasons why rehearsal facilitates transfer. Maybe it is the repeated or prolonged consciousness of a stimulus that causes the transfer, in which case rehearsal would represent one way of prolonging consciousness of a stimulus. Consciousness may also be prolonged if the stimulus repeatedly appeared in the individual's perceptual field. In such a case rehearsal might not be needed to cause transfer to long-term memory. It seems that we are dealing with factors that affect memorizing. These factors have long been familiar to psychologists. They are the factors that facilitate habituation, and the repetition of stimulation is only one of these factors. Further, rehearsal is only one form of repetition. Other factors that affect habituation are the recency, frequency, and intensity of stimulation.

It is important to realize that the laws of habituation apply to rote learning, and that rote learning has not proved to be the most effective way for humans to learn. Many studies show that meaningful information is much more readily retained than meaningless information, such as nonsense syllables.

Another limitation of the sequential version is that there is reason to believe that the short- and long-term-memory systems are parallel rather than sequential. The perceptual trace of an input item might well be entered into long- and short-term memory simultaneously. Long-term memory is used for pattern recognition and coding. Hence, input from long-term memory would be necessary for a code to be entered into short-term memory. Further, comparisons between a perceptual trace and long-term memory would need to be made to determine the novel and known aspects of input information, so that the individual could distinguish between known information and the new information to be memorized. If you are given a list of words you already know and are asked to memorize them in serial order, the only task for you is to memorize the order in which the words appear on the list.

It is only necessary to memorize totally unfamiliar stimuli, that is, stimuli that are not represented either by an image or a concept. If a stimulus elicits an image, it is familiar as a sensory experience. It does not need to be memorized because it is already in long-term memory. If a stimulus has never been observed before, but it matches a concept in long-term memory, the stimulus is known to possess the attributes of the concept category and is familiar in this way.

There is one study that suggests that perceptual input does not need to be processed in the short-term-memory mechanism in order to enter long-term memory. Shephard (1967) showed subjects 540 words in random order one after the other then tested them to determine whether they could remember the words. In the test the subjects were presented with pairs of words, one belonging to the list they had seen and one new, and they were asked which of the pair they had seen previously. After the subjects had seen the words only once they were able to identify them with 88.4 percent accuracy. Shephard employed the same procedures using pictures and sentences rather than individual words, yielding about the same for sentences and 96.7 percent correct for pictures. The test for pictures was given after 7 and again after 120 days had elapsed. Even after 7 days the subjects remembered the pictures they had seen with 87.0 percent accuracy; after 120 days the percentage of recognition dropped to 57.7 percent. The study suggests that a brief exposure to stimuli resulted in their entering long-term memory.

Hierarchical Organization

Another factor that affects learning appears to be the hierarchical organization of mental content. This was alluded to in chapter 4 when we suggested that images are categorized on the basis of common characteristics, then categories are combined because of their common characteristics to form more general categories. Thus early learning proceeds from the specific to the general as images are formed into categories and categories are combined to form more general categories. The result of this process is the development and organization of the content of the mind into *representational class-inclusion hierarchies* in which the lower levels of the hierarchy are represented and included in the higher levels.

Class-inclusion hierarchies are often shown as hierarchical trees. The following is an example of such a hierarchy.

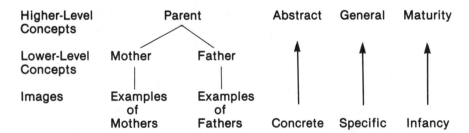

The diagram suggests that the initial learning of infants consists of the memorizing of images of concrete events, such as particular mothers and fathers they observe. Then, common characteristics are noted among the particular mothers and fathers. The child learns that mothers are women with children and that fathers are men with children. As a result the concepts mother and father form in the child's mind. Subsequently the child detects that mothers and fathers have common characteristics—they are both adults with children. Thus the more general concept parent forms in the child's mind.

The contention is that from infancy to maturity natural learning proceeds as described from the specific to the general and from the concrete to the abstract. Here we are describing the natural storage process not the retrieval process. Further, we are not contending that the more general, abstract concept *parent* cannot be taught before the more specific concepts *mother* and *father*. What we are saying is that the child will tend to learn more specific concrete concepts before learning more general abstract concepts. However, once intricate idea hierarchies develop in the mind with maturation, learning can take place and often does from the general to the specific. For instance, once the concept *adult* has been learned, the individual can identify any particular individual as an adult by noting that the person has the characteristics of adulthood. In short, the initial learning of the child proceeds inductively from the specific to the general. Once concepts form, learning can proceed deductively from the general to the specific, as the individual identifies particular objects as members of concept categories that are already in mind. It should be kept in mind, however, that we may well be correct about the hierarchical organization of mental content, even though our description of the storage and retrieval processes are not adequate.

The proposal that the content of the mind is organized hierarchically is not new—many have contended this. Ausubel (1963) states that "The model of cognitive organization proposed for learning and retention of meaningful materials assumes the existence of a cognitive structure that is hierarchically organized in terms of highly inclusive perceptual traces under which are subsumed traces of less inclusive subconcepts as well as traces of specific informational data" (p. 24). Kintsch and Keenan (1973) and Kintsch (1975b) also describe long-term memory as hierarchically organized. They provide evidence to show that retrieval of information proceeds within the framework of such an organization. One first searches for a block or category of information, then one searches within the category for the needed information. Johnson (1970) presents a model and tests of how a hierarchical memory structure could be retrieved.

Bower et al. (1969) demonstrated that the hierarchical presentation of information to subjects greatly facilitated recall in a free-recall task. The following hierarchy was presented to subjects.

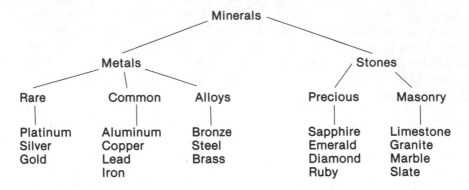

The results of the study show recall was two to three times better when the words were presented in the above hierarchical format than when the words were presented randomly. Bower suggests that the subjects appeared to use the hierarchical tree as a retrieval plan, starting at the top and unpacking successive levels in recursive fashion. Atwood and Shavelson (1976) obtained similar results. So one adaptive feature of the hierarchical organization of information is that it facilitates retrieval.

The Bower and the Atwood and Shavelson studies showed that people benefit from hierarchical organization in retrieving verbal information. Preusser and Handel (1970) demonstrated that people tend to organize information for storage hierarchically. They gave subjects cards containing hierarchically related words and found that subjects tended to organize the words into hierarchies. They obtained similar results working with graphic designs. Organizing unfamiliar graphic patterns into hierarchies shows that the skill of hierarchical organization was previously learned.

Thus there is evidence that individuals not only categorize information; in addition, they organize the categories into representational class-inclusion hierarchies.

Levels of Learning

Images

Images represent the first level of learning and are the first ideas that form. When an event is totally unfamiliar, that is, there is no corresponding image or concept in the mind to produce an idea of the event, it must be memorized in order to be recognized. This involves exposure to the event for a sufficient period of time to enable the perceptual image or traces of the event to be recorded as a permanent image in the mind. Exposure may involve the presence of the event or the rehearsal of the perceptual trace of the event in short-term memory. For an accurate image to form, the features or characteristics of the event must be imprinted accurately in the image.

The need to improve predictability stimulates two mental functions that direct the formation of images: the *content function*, which interprets the specific composition or content of an event; and the *arousal function*, which is a nonspecific, intensity function that generates a degree of feeling associated with the event.[1]

When an event occurs it initiates either no arousal or some degree of arousal in the individual, which represents the intensity of feelings the individual had about the event. As the individual is exposed to the event, an image forms that represents the event, and the intensity of feeling is contained in the image or idea. After the image had been formed and the event appears, the image will be brought to mind and the individual will tend to react to the event with the intensity of feeling contained in image of the event. For example, when a child learns to recognize a dog, the dog may be threatening him. If he is mildly threatened he may be somewhat apprehensive of the dog. However, if the dog is vicious, he may be dreadfully afraid of the dog. The image that forms representing the dog will contain the intensity of fear he had when the image was forming. And, on a subsequent encounter with a dog, the image will be elicited, the dog will be recognized, and the child will tend to feel about the dog the same intensity of fear contained in the image.

The formation of an image is directed by the content function as well as the arousal function. The degree of heat felt by the individual, upon exposure to a heat source, will determine the degree of arousal associated with the source. However, the content function will operate to record the composition of the heat source so that it may be recognized and understood. The content function enables the individual to distinguish the sun as a source of heat from a fire or a radiator because of the differences in their composition. In short, the arousal function interprets the intensity of feeling associated with an event, while the content function defines what the feeling is about. The two functions combine to direct the formation of images.

It is important to realize that you can describe the content of an idea without describing the feelings associated with it. For example, you can describe the features of a dog as represented by your idea of a dog without describing your feelings about dogs. On the other hand, it is difficult, if not impossible, to offer an idea of how you feel without describing the content of the idea to convey what your feelings are about. For instance, you cannot convey that you are afraid of dogs without referring to dogs.

Additionally, a teacher may wish to teach content by describing the features of an object. However, the learner will attach feelings to the content being presented that will be included as a part of the idea being formed.

The point is that although content may be taught by itself, what will be learned is content and the feelings associated with it. For example, a teacher may describe what a German Shepherd looks like, but the learner will attach feeling impressions to the content presentation, and the idea that forms will include both content and feelings.

As the image of an event forms, and the individual is repeatedly exposed to the event, recognition of the event occurs even more automatically and rapidly. In essence, when the process of memorization has been completed, a habit has formed permitting the individual to recognize the event automatically without deliberation.

Of the various "laws of learning" that are offered by psychologists, those that describe the conditions that influence the formaton of habits seem to be closely related to the process of memorizing. Interpreted within the framework of memorization, it might be said that the memorization of an event would be enhanced by frequent, recent, repetitive, intense exposure to the event. The Law of Contiguity, which suggests that memorization would be facilitated if the elements of an event are close together (contiguous) in space and time, would also apply. This suggests that when the characteristics of an event are perceived as being together, they can be viewed as features of the same event and not as different events.

The laws that govern the formation of habits may be sufficient to guide the memorizing of simple stimuli such as a single letter of the alphabet. However, the Gestalt laws of perception gain importance as the stimuli to be memorized become more complex. The Law of Proximity buttresses the Law of Contiguity by indicating that things which are close together in time and space will be more readily perceived and learned. In addition, the Gestalt laws suggest that an event can more readily be perceived if it is presented in distinct contrast to its background. This circumscribes and more clearly defines the event to be memorized. As for the event itself, these laws suggest that perception is facilitated if the relationship between the parts of the event and the whole can be readily perceived. This can be construed to imply that an accurate idea of an event will form more readily when the relationship between the parts of the event and the whole event can be perceived distinctly.[2]

It is also of interest to note that the Gestalt Law of Similarity indicates that individuals tend to group similar things together. This fortifies the statement that images with similar characteristics are grouped together to form concepts.

*The Identification of Programs
and Master Neuroprints*

The individual learns to identify programs as well as individual events. Ideas representing programs form as the individual learns that events are sequentially related in space and time. Because the understanding of relationships is the basis for making predictions, one is more inclined to learn about the relationship between events than to learn about events in isolation.

The relationship between events may form a set, a series, or a sequence. A *set of events* would represent events that are related to each other in space and appear at the same point in time. For example, all of the parts of an automobile are expected to be seen at the same time in a certain proximity to one another in space.

A *series of events* would represent events that are related to each other in space but do not appear at the same time. Further, a series of events appears close to each other in time but not in a fixed order. For example, if you were to meet a number of friends for lunch at noon, you would expect them to arrive about noon, but you would not expect them all to arrive at the same time. Nor would you know in which order they might arrive.

A *sequence of events* would represent events that occur in a fixed order over time. Programs define a sequence, although any given program may include sets and series. When the individual learns that events precede certain events and follow others, a sequence is learned. For example, when a boy learns that in dressing his father puts on his socks before his shoes, he is learning a sequence.

In learning a sequence, one may learn that some events are prerequisite to other events and some events are consequences of other events. Such sequences define *cause-effect relationships*. In addition, an individual may learn that within a sequence certain events need not occur in a fixed order but may occur as a series. In a series there is some flexibility in the order in which operations need to be performed.

Some of the programs the individual learns are trends, while others are procedures. When individuals learn that heavy cloud formations often lead to rain they learn a trend; when they learn how to control a sequence of activities to produce an effect they learn a procedure. Such is the case when children learn to dress themselves.

The individual memorizes master neuroprints as well as programs. When children learn the program that leads to the candy store, they have learned a way of obtaining candy when they want it. The interest of the children is to confirm the prediction that they will obtain candy; the goal is to eat the candy; the program is the procedure for getting the candy.

So far we have described how images are formed as a part of the storage process leading to the recognition of sensory events. Images also are produced as a result of the retrieval process, as happens when the individual reminisces about a past experience. In addition, the retrieval process can conjure images of events that are not direct representations of stimulus input. Such is the case when the individual dreams at night, daydreams, or has images of events that did not happen.

When images form, identifications and predictions can be made from past experiences. Based on the content of images, individuals can identify the composition of objects and events that they have observed before and they can identify the way they feel about the objects and events. Program and master neuroprint images permit individuals to predict outcomes that have occurred in the past and the way they may feel about the outcome. Thus before concepts are learned, infants are restricted to identifying and predicting based on images. They can only identify events that they have observed before and memorized and they will be prompted to predict that events will turn out in the future as their images indicate they turned out in the past.

Concepts

Concepts represent the second level of learning and are formed by comparing memories of events for similarities and differences and grouping events with similar features together to form a category of events. Thus a concept is defined by enumerating the features that the events in a category have in common. In order for a concept to be defined clearly, it is important that the necessary and sufficient criteria (features) for inclusion in the category be stipulated. For example, the term *poison* is a concept. The features that would provide the necessary and sufficient criteria identifying poison would be (1) a substance that when taken into the body (2) makes one ill.

A concept can be learned by memorizing the necessary and sufficient criteria that define the concept. Such learning occurs in school when students are required to memorize the criteria that define such concepts as mammals in the study of zoology and intelligence in the study of psychology.

In addition, individuals can infer for themselves the similar features of a number of images of events to form a concept. A concept may be inferred when the individual realizes that a number of events have common characteristics. For example, a child may infer that certain animals have wings and later learns that such animals are called birds. The individual may also realize that certain lower level concepts have common characteristics and infer a higher level, more general concept. For example, one may infer that vegetables, meat, and beverages all provide nourishment and understand what a nutrient is. When the individual infers a concept, the ability to recognize events increases even though the individual may not have learned the formal social labels for the concept inferred.

Clark (1977), in summarizing, provides evidence that concept learning skill develops with age and that young children attend most readily to the sensory attributes of objects. Thus they tend to think in terms of images rather than concepts.

Moran (1976) trained third graders in transferable and generalizable problem solving successfully, claiming support for the information-processing view that children this age can generalize rather than the Piagetian idea that they cannot. Sugimura and Terao (1975) compared four-year-olds to six-year-olds and found that both groups were significantly better at identification than at abstraction but with a greater difference in abstraction (that is, sixth graders were developing this skill). Doran and Ngoi (1976) have results on sixth graders that would indicate that once the skill of recall is acquired, generalization may be acquired even before application.

Powers, Stavens, and Andreasen (1975) tested first graders, fourth graders, and adults (representing Piaget's preoperational, concrete-operation, and formal-operational stages) and found sorting behavior to increase with age.

Klausmier's summary of his concept research (Levine and Allen, 1976) states that the ability to discriminate among objects is present before the age of two, whereas hypothesizing and evaluating the attributes of certain concepts, for example, noun, is not found in most people until the age of sixteen. If the traits of a concept are readily perceptible, the operations emerge earlier than if they are unobservable and must be inferred. The above studies would indicate that children's ability to abstract and classify increases over the years from age three to eleven and on to adulthood.

We will describe the formation of concepts within the master-neuroprint format because this includes programs and individual events. Further, learning probably proceeds in this format because the individual is more likely to learn in a master-neuroprint format than any other way.

There is, in a sense, a double motivation. First, master neuroprints satisfy one's desire to predict. Second, they lead to the satisfaction of a particular interest of the moment. The learning of a program satisfies the predictive motive because one event in the sequence can be predicted from another. However, a program does not satisfy a particular interest.

Individuals should be least motivated to learn an event in isolation. This is because it would be difficult for them to understand how the learning contributes to their ability to predict or how it can lead to the satisfaction of an interest. Let us trace the way in which guilt is learned as a means of illustrating the process. First, we can define *guilt* as the feeling of wrongdoing associated with a set of events in a concept.

The first image of wrongdoing that is learned by young children is retained in a master-neuroprint memory. Children memorize specific acts on their part that result in a retaliation from parents or in a reprimand that is often accompanied with a threat of retaliation. Children learn to regard an act as a wrongdoing and predict punishment as a consequence and forgiveness afterward. We must realize that young children are totally dependent on adults, usually parents, for survival. Any displeasure expressed by parents (or guardians) about their actions may be regarded by them as a profound threat. They must be assured constantly that the parents care for them and are willing to provide for their needs or they will feel severely threatened.

Toilet training is an example of how a master-neuroprint image may form which provides a foundation for the development of guilt. Children learn that their parents are pleased when they eliminate in the toilet and are displeased when they soil their clothing. The act of soiling is then regarded by the children as a specific wrongdoing for which the parents will scold, and they would become interested in not soiling. They learn, in addition, that after they are scolded and feel displeasure, the parents will forgive their misbehavior. This temporarily removes the threat of parental retaliation.

You should keep in mind that one's ideas contain programs that depict one's own activities, the activities of others, or both.

The master-neuroprint image of the above learning would be represented as follows:

Soiling $\longrightarrow$ Scolding $\longrightarrow$ Forgiven by Parents

As additional acts bring scolding or spanking from parents, master-neuroprint images would form representing them. For instance, children might learn that they will be scolded or spanked for getting dirty, or for hitting a sibling. The formation of such master-neuroprint images provides the basis for generalizing about wrongdoing in the formation of a master-neuroprint concept as in figure 5-1.

Figure 5-1 indicates that five individual master-neuroprint images have been categorized together to form a master-neuroprint concept. The master-neuroprint concept represents experiences that have led the individual to

An Interest	Program	Goal
Wrongdoing (Feeling of guilt)	Expiation	Forgiveness (Relief of guilt)
1	1	1
2	2	2
3	3	3
4	4	4
5	5	5

Figure 5-1. Formation of a Master-Neuroprint Concept

understand that wrongdoing produces guilt feelings and to develop an interest in confirming the prediction that the guilt will be relieved. The individual also understands that wrongdoings can be expiated (program),
which leads to forgiveness and the consequent relief of guilt (goal).

The five individual master-neuroprint images that are categorized
together to form the master-neuroprint concept might be as in figure 5-2.

Prediction theory's version of the development of ideas can be extended
and refined by including Piaget's most recent interpretation of the development of ideas. Piaget and Inhelder (1973) suggest that the first stage of ideation involves the historical recording of images of events the infant
observes.

In the second stage of ideational development, the images that are
recorded enable the infant to recognize objects and events. These images are
the recordings of the infant's interaction with the environment. The images
in the mind enable the child to recognize past interactions with the environment and remember ways environmental objects were previously manipulated. A five-month-old infant may learn to recognize a nursing bottle as
something to be sucked and perform this activity when the bottle is seen.
However, at this stage of development the infant is unable to recall the objects that can be recognized. That is, the infant cannot produce images of
objects without their being present.

At the third stage of ideational development the baby is able to
recognize and recall objects and events with specific reference to the past.
Thus the images in the mind permit the child to recall past experiences.

At a later stage of ideational development, the concrete operations
stage, the child understands concepts. The infant not only has images of
past sensory events but has organized them into concept categories and

An Interest	Program	Goal
Wrongdoing—Guilt	Means of Expiation	Forgiveness and Relief from Guilt
Soiling	Scolding	Hugging from parent
Hitting sibling	Spanking	Verbal forgiveness from parents
Losing coat	Allowance withheld	Allowance restored
Stealing candy	Returning candy	Forgiving self
Destroying sibling's toy	Confessing to parents and begs forgiveness	Verbal parental forgiveness

Figure 5-2. Example of a Master-Neuroprint Concept

can then recognize and recall that a particular sensory event is a member of an understood category.

The recent research reported by Piaget and Inhelder pertains to the latter two stages of ideational development; one study involves the concept of seriation. A child is shown a series of rods arranged in order of size:

The child is asked to remember what has been seen, then a few days later the child is asked to draw what had been seen. The four-year-old does not draw a series of lines of progressing length because the four-year-old had not learned the concept of seriation.

About eight months later they asked some of the children to reproduce what they had seen. The interesting finding was that their reproductions more closely resembled the series of rods that they had seen previously, and some of the children who had not been able to reproduce the series were then able to do so. The improvement in their representations was due to their improved understanding of seriation. This finding shows that although the children could recall the information, they were not able to reproduce it accurately until they had learned to conceptualize seriation.

When concepts are learned, they can be compared for similarities and differences and, as a result, new concepts can be learned. When similarities in concept categories are identified, a new, more general concept can be learned. Such would be the case when individuals learn that mothers and fathers have in common that they are both adults with children, the criteria defining parent. Conversely, when distinctions are detected within a category new, more specific categories may be learned. For example, it might be learned that mothers and fathers are subtypes of parents in that mothers are women with children whereas fathers are men with children. As individuals detect similarities and differences among concrete events and concepts, their conceptual repertoire becomes increasingly more intricate and refined.

As indicated earlier in the chapter, it is quite possible that as learning proceeds images and concepts are organized into class-inclusion hierarchies indicating the relationships among ideas.

The development of idea hierarchies may be summarized as follows. Ideas develop in a hierarchical manner. Lower levels of the hierarchy develop first and are represented in the higher levels and often development at the lower levels is prerequisite to development at the higher levels. Images represent the first ideas that form. The earlier images that form permit recognition, while later images permit the recall of events in their absence. Once a number of images are learned they are categorized to form lower level concepts. Then lower-level concepts are categorized to form higher-level concepts.

The idea hierarchy may be represented as shown in figure 5-3. The figure illustrates that ideas form portraying objects, programs, and master neuroprints. First, images form representing objects, programs, and master neuroprints that have been observed through the senses. Then, low-level concepts form representing categories of objects, programs, and master neuroprints that are included in a category because they have common characteristics. Then, higher-level concepts form when lower-level concepts are combined because of their common characteristics. Higher-level concepts contain more items than lower-level concepts.

Of course, ideas of programs include events and objects, and master-neuroprint ideas include both individual objects and events and programs.

As individuals mature and learn, more ideas form and their idea hierarchies expand and become more elaborate. It is implicit that young children who have learned fewer concepts are less able to make distinctions and, consequently, would tend to overgenerlize. Novack and Richman (1980) lend support to this view in their research. They have shown that young children (five and seven years old) do have a tendency to overgeneralize.

As individuals' learning of concepts increase, so does their ability to identify and predict. They are no longer limited to identifying and predicting events based on images of past experiences. The learning of concepts enables them to identify and predict novel events that have not been previously experienced. They might identify a strange creature as a fish because it has the characteristics of the known concept fish. It has gills, fins, and is found in water. In addition, they might predict that the fish will swim because this also is a characteristic of the concept category.

Concepts also allow greater flexibility of behavior, when compared to images. Behaviors based on images are more ritualistic and habitlike because things tend to be done in the future as they were done in the past. Concepts provide alternative ways of behaving because they contain images with similar characteristics, often representing a choice. For instance, a master-neuroprint concept may include master-neurorprint images that indicate alternative ways of relieving a headache. (More will be said about the functions of images and concepts in these regards in the coming chapters.)

Let us summarize the salient issues in this chapter by relating learning to identification and prediction. The initial learning of infancy is the learning of images. Thus images are the first resources for identifying and predicting. Images of programs and master neuroprints are the initial primitive ideas that facilitate prediction. They are learned through memorizing and

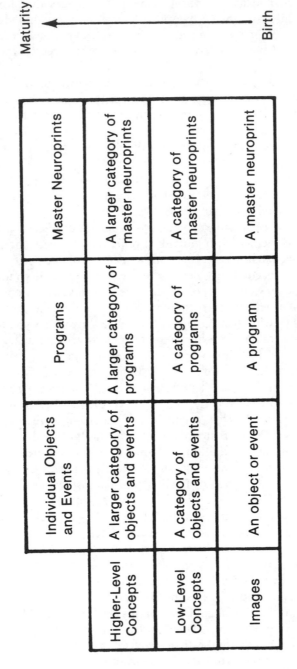

Figure 5-3. The Idea Hierarchy

facilitate the prediction of familiar, previously observed events. Images prompt individuals to predict that events will occur in the future as they have in the past. When concepts are learned, identification and prediction are enhanced. Concepts enable individuals to make identifications and predictions about events that have not been previously experienced. Concept categories also enable the individual to consider alternative ways of identifying and predicting. Concepts of programs indicate alternative ways of controlling similar operations, such as indicating alternative ways of swimming. Concepts of master neuroprints indicate alternative means of satisfying the same interests, such as indicating different ways of confirming the prediction that money will be acquired. As lower-level concepts form into higher-level concepts and vice versa, one's idea hierarchy becomes increasingly more intricate and differentiated and provides a basis for more alternative ways of identifying and predicting. As this happens, individuals develop the potential for more flexible behavior and more effective predicting.

Notes

1. Each interaction between environment and organism involves at least two components: discrete interaction by way of the brain's sensory mode, specific, classical projection systems and its core homestadts; and a "nonspecific," relatively diffuse interaction by way of reticular and related formations. These nonspecific systems act as a bias on the specific reactions; the set point or value toward which a specific interaction tends to stabilize is set by the "nonspecific activity" (Pribram 1967, p. 12).

2. A comprehensive review of the laws of learning is in *Theories of Learning* by E. Hilgard and G. Bower, 1975.

6 Mental Process and Behavior

In the preceding discussion of the formation of idea hierarchies, learning and the storage process were described. This chapter describes how information is retrieved and employed to facilitate identification and prediction.

The key to understanding the relationships among mental process, prediction, and behavior is the matching process. In order to predict, the individual must match events with neuroprints in the mind for correspondence. If there is a match, then predictability is being maintained; if there is a mismatch, then events are unpredictable. Bear in mind that programs enable predictions to be made in the first place and tested in the second place and that the individual is continually matching events with programs for the confirmation of predictions. The work of Sokolov (1960) and Picton and Hillyard (1974) suggest that environmental input is matched against neuronal models in the brain, which represent expectancies of the individual.

The Servoprogram

The servoprogram governs the matching process. A *servoprogram* is a reflexive program that governs the adjustment of events and neuroprints. The notion of a servoprogram is adapted from the term servomechanism. *Servomechanisms* sense information and make performance adjustments according to a criterion. A thermostat is an example of a servomechanism. It senses temperature changes and turns the heat on and off to maintain the criterion level of temperature at which the thermostat is set.

Servoprograms control the matching functions of behavior. Programs are adjusted to match events, and events are adjusted to match programs in order to confirm predictions. For example, an individual building a model airplane might assemble existing materials according to the program designated by the blueprint, or the person might modify the material, the plan, or both to gain a match between them in the construction of the plane. Servoprograms are part of the individual's inherited perceptual equipment. By contributing to the modification of ideas and events to improve prediction they are indispensable to the learning process.

Optimum Predictability

In matching neuroprints and events the individual seeks optimum predictability. Too little predictability, that is, a pronounced mismatch, generates
disorientation and *confusion*. Too much predictability, that is, monotonous
matching, generates *boredom*. In the case of too little predictability, there is
a search for redundance and familiarity to facilitate the immediate confirmation of a prediction, while in the case of too much predictability there is a
need to seek novel stimulation to extend one's ability to predict.

When optimum predictability is violated and boredom (a monotonously
repetitive matching) or confusion (a pronounced mismatch) occurs, the
servoprogram automatically selects neruoprints to restore optimum predictability, as will be explained further.

The Feedback Loop

Because each program includes a series of predictions (which are defined by
the subroutines of the program), each prediction must be tested against sensory feedback to determine whether events are proceeding as prescribed by
the program. The testing of each individual prediction in a program against
sensory feedback defines a *feedback loop*. The feedback loop is the basic
unit for analyzing the testing of predictions. Thus as a program proceeds to
guide behavior, a series of feedback loops are completed to test the predictions in the program—to determine whether the individual is on the "right
track." For example, the route to a person's office is a program that is
followed to get there. The program includes predictions of many milestones
that are expected to be passed on the way. As each milestone is passed en
route, a feedback loop is completed. If there is correspondence between sensory feedback and the program depicting the route, the individual would
continue to follow the dictates of the program until arriving at the office, at
which time new stimulation would occupy attention and a new program
would be selected to deal with it. If there were a mismatch when any feedback loop was completed, it would indicate that the individual had gone
astray, resulting in an adjustment to behavior to produce a match, for example, steer back on the road after straying off it. Or in the case of a gross
mismatch, a new program would be selected in an attempt to restore predictability, for example, a new program would be selected if the individual
were lost. Lackner (1974) presents a study that illustrates the importance of
visual, tactile, and kinesthetic feedback in task performance.

Matching occurs between neuroprints and events and between one
neuroprint and another because there is correspondence between them, that
is, they fit together. There is neurological evidence that environmental

events are matched with mental expectations. Miller, Galanter, and Pribram (1960), in their book *Plans and the Structure of Behavior*, offered the first version of how the matching process operates to confirm predictions. They suggest that the basic unit of behavior is the TOTE, which stands for test, operate, test, exit. The following is a description of the TOTE.

1.   The prediction to be confirmed or the goal is matched with a stimulus for congruity. This is the initial test phase.
2.   If a discrepancy exists, control shifts to the "operate" phase and action is taken to reduce the discrepancy so that the goal may be achieved.
3.   The result of the operation is then tested for congruity to the goal. This is the second test phase.
4.   If the goal is achieved, the process exists or stops completing the TOTE.

They offer the following figure 6-1 as an example of the TOTE process.

The first testing phase involves the goal or prediction to be confirmed—the testing of the nail to see if it is flush with the surface of the board. If it is not flush, the second phase is entered and control shifts to the hammer operations. The hammer is lifted and the nail is struck. Then control shifts to the second test phase, and the nail is inspected to see if it is now flush. If it is, the process terminates and control is passed to a higher unit

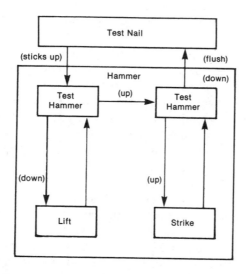

Source: From G.A. Miller, E. Galanter, and K.H. Pribram, *Plans and the Structure of Behavior* (New York: Holt, Rinehart and Winston, 1960) p. 36. Reprinted with permission.

Figure 6-1. Example of the TOTE Process

of the plan which the person is executing. If not, the program can recycle until the prediction is confirmed.

A number of TOTEs may be arranged hierarchically to represent a person's overall plan. The plan may be to build a bench, which would require many subplans or TOTEs such as buying material, sawing, and attaching together pieces of wood. The nailing TOTE illustrated would be a subroutine of attaching pieces of wood. Although the plans and subplans are executed programmatically as a procedure, the total plan is organized and stored hierarchically. That is, each plan or TOTE is represented in a higher order plan or TOTE.

The Miller, Galanter, and Pribram explanation of the most fundamental unit of behavior posits a matching process aimed at the confirmation of predictions. Further, their contention that TOTEs are hierarchically organized in the mind is in keeping with our description of the hierarchical organization of information in the mind in the last chapter.

The development of cybernetics (Winer 1948) brought with it the notion of programs describing feedback and servomechanisms such as the TOTE and the use of computers to stimulate the information-processing process of the mind. Figure 6-2 represents the feedback system that might be involved in maintaining optimum predictability. The interpretation of the figure is written as a computer program might be written.

Although the thought processes we are describing might be diagrammed as flow charts and interpreted as computer programs, we will revert to exposition. We will leave the translation of thought into flow chart diagrams and computer programs to experts in those fields.

Matching for Identification: Of an Initiating Event. Matching for identification takes place between neuroprints in the mind and sensory events. When there is a match between neuroprints and events the individual is identifying the events, but when there is a mismatch between events and neuroprints the individual is unable to identify the events. If current events cannot be identified, then coming events cannot be predicted. Identification is prerequisite to prediction and connects mental activity with concrete events.

According to the evidence presented in chapter 4, neuroprints are coded as a set of attributes. The identification of a sensory event probably involves matching the attributes of the event with the attributes of neuroprints. The notion that perception and identification involve the matching of sense perceptions and mental recordings is not new. An old theory that has currency and credibility today takes this position. The theory is called the "template matching theory" (see Neissen 1967). According to this theory, an object, such as a dog, is perceived. An identification is made by matching the perception of the dog with representations stored in memory. If a match is achieved, the object is indeed identified as a dog.

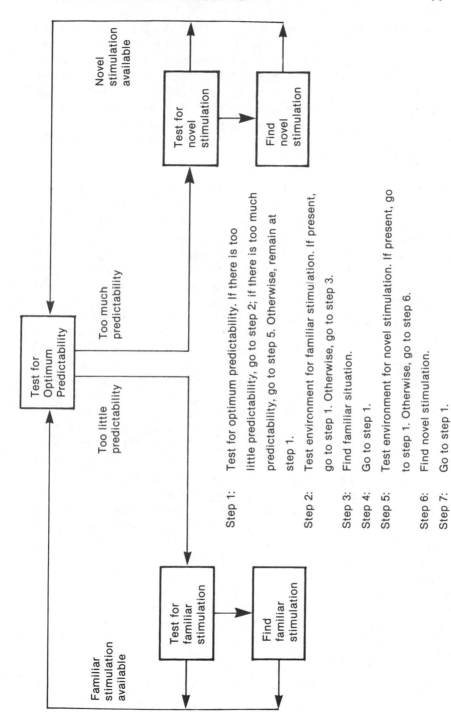

Step 1: Test for optimum predictability. If there is too little predictability, go to step 2; if there is too much predictability, go to step 5. Otherwise, remain at step 1.

Step 2: Test environment for familiar stimulation. If present, go to step 1. Otherwise, go to step 3.

Step 3: Find familiar situation.

Step 4: Go to step 1.

Step 5: Test environment for novel stimulation. If present, go to step 1. Otherwise, go to step 6.

Step 6: Find novel stimulation.

Step 7: Go to step 1.

Figure 6-2. A Plan for Maintaining Optimum Predictability

Matching for Prediction. Once an event is identified, coming events can be predicted by matching in the mind the neuroprint that identifies the event and a program neuroprint already coded in the mind. A match for prediction is made because the initiating event is a component of the program—there is some degree of correspondence. Because programs represent a sequence of events, they indicate that one event will follow another. When a match for prediction is made, the program that is elicited generates the expectation that coming events will occur in sequence as the program prescribes and that prediction is made.

Matching for Identification: To Test the Prediction against Sensory Feedback. After a prediction is made, activity is monitored through the senses to determine whether or not events occur as prescribed by the program. If they do, the prediction is confirmed. The program neuroprint is reinforced because by contributing to the confirmation of a prediction, it satisfied the basic prediction motive. If events do not occur as the program predicts, the program neuroprint often is modified to accommodate the actual events that occurred.

Allport (1955), in a seminal review of the literature on the perception of indistinct stimulation, concludes that the structuring of inputs to the perceptual systems is preceded and accompanied by a state of expectancy. He contends that what is perceived is affected by what the individual predicts he will perceive at a particular place and time. More recent writings such as that of Salley and Murphy (1960) hold the same point of view. Anderson, Kulhaven, and Andre (1970) demonstrated more time is spent on feedback after a wrong answer, while Meyer (1960) showed that feedback facilitates learning in programmed instruction. Geller (1974) found that the reaction time to correctly predicted (previous trial) stimuli was a decreasing function of the (manipulated) rate of reinforcement as correct, while reaction time to incorrectly predicted stimuli was not.

Good (1973) worked with four groups on a free-association task. The groups were led to anticipate that they would (1) be evaluated and do poorly, or (2) be evaluated and do well, or (3) not be evaluated and do poorly, or (4) not be evaluated and do well. He found that the only condition that facilitated free associations was when the subjects thought they would be evaluated and do well. According to prediction theory, this group thought their predictions would be confirmed, while groups that thought they would do poorly would not anticipate confirmation. The groups that expected no evaluation would believe that there would be no way of knowing whether their predictions were right or wrong; they expected no feedback.

Where there is life there is always activity. A motor program may direct the actions of the individual to obtain something from the environment.

When such a motor program is elected, the individual acts in accordance with the program. On the other hand, a program may predict a sequence of activities that will occur in the environment. In this case the individual observes environmental activity and processes the information.

The following is an illustration of the matching process.

Matching for Identification: Of an Initiating Event. An adult hears his child talking and becomes interested in identifying what the child is saying. A match for identification is made between the sounds the child is uttering and an idea in the adult's mind. Suppose the adult hears the child say one, two, three, and this matches an idea in the adult's mind. The adult heard the sounds many times before and memorized them. Consequently there is a memory in his mind corresponding to the sounds so that he identifies the sounds when he hears them.

Matching for Prediction. Once the sounds have been identified a matching for prediction ensues. The memory of the numbers one, two, three are matched with the program in the adult's mind. A match is made with the counting program because the initiating event is a component of the program; therefore, there is correspondence. When the match is made, the adult is aware that his child is counting and is able to predict that he will hear the child say the numbers four, five, six, and so on in the sequence prescribed by the counting program.

Matching for Identification: To Test the Prediction against Sensory Feedback. The adult continues to listen to what his child is saying. He monitors what the child is saying to determine whether the child's next utterances are the numbers four, five, six, and so on as the counting program predicts they will be. Of course this whole matching process takes place in an instant, automatically, without any concentration on the part of the adult.

Thought

Now *thought* can be defined, based on previous discussions, as the process of matching events and neuroprints for purposes of identification and prediction. Thought serves both to prepare for and guide action. The preparation for action occurs when an event occurs and the mind uses information-processing activities to match the event for identification and prediction. Thought guides action when a program has been selected to guide action to obtain something from the environment and a match is sought between environmental events and the program. Moreover, thought occurs at all levels of the idea hierarchy. It can involve images and concepts.

To continue the description of thought, consider two complementary modes, automatic thought and deliberate thought.

Automatic thought is the relatively rapid, involuntary execution of the matching process as the individual attempts to predict familiar events. Automatic thought involves the execution of habits.

Deliberate thought, or deliberation, is the relatively slow execution of the matching process through ideation. Deliberate thought operates through ideation when events are unfamiliar, and the relationship between events and ideas is consciously reviewed.

The prediction of novel events may be achieved through deliberation in one of two ways: memorization or conceptualization. If the event is totally unfamiliar it has to be memorized, because there would be no ideas in the mind to match the event. Once memorized, the idea representing the event could be matched for prediction. On the other hand, if some features of the novel event are familiar, deliberation involves matching the familiar features with concepts in search of a prediction. In this instance, the individual may preview in his or her mind the probability that one idea or another would lead to the confirmation of the prediction sought, and select one of the alternatives of a concept.

Hypothesis-sampling theory, introduced by Bruner, Goodnow, and Austin (1956) and modified, most notably by Levine (1959, 1963), has been a popular theory of concept acquisition. As was mentioned in chapter 3, the theory would argue that the individual generates a set of hypotheses involving many dimensions of the problem and samples and tests them, narrowing down the set until the correct one is found (see Brown 1974; Bourne and Dominowski 1972). The theory will be discussed further at the end of chapter 7.

The individual may deliberate concepts that contain alternative interests, programs, and/or goals. The concept *personal problems* might contain a number of worry-causing interests. Worry-causing interests would be the common characteristics for inclusion in the concept. The individual might deliberate the concept to decide which interests to attend to and in what order.

Goals may also form concepts. The concept *food* includes items that have in common the fact that they may be safely eaten to reduce hunger. When one is hungry, one may deliberate the items in this concept to decide the food item one wishes to pursue as a goal. If the item cannot be obtained, another item may be chosen from the category.

Programs, too, may form concepts. A concept may form that includes various ways of acquiring food—one program might lead to the refrigerator, another might lead to a restaurant. The individual can deliberate these alternative means of obtaining food when that is the goal.

When alternatives in a concept have been deliberated and a choice is made, a preference is expressed.

The Complementary Nature of Automatic
and Deliberate Thought

Automatic and deliberate thought are complementary in the sense that automatic thought is used to predict familiar events while deliberate thought is used to predict unfamiliar or novel events. But there is something uniquely adaptive about the reciprocal relationship between these two thought processes.

Familiar events can be predicted automatically in a routine manner that is adaptive because automatic thought is faster, and innumerable activities can be directed automatically at the same time, such as the many automatic functions of the body. Moreover, the relegation of routine matters to automatic thought permits the deliberative process to be free to deal with the novel, unusual, threatening events that may emerge and demand attention. So when events can be predicted automatically, they will be.

On the other hand, when events are being directed automatically and they become either too predictable (boring) or too unpredictable (confusing), the individual will become aroused and deliberation will be initiated. Then the individual becomes aware of the event, related ideational material is elicited, and the individual attempts to restore optimum predictability. In the case of too much predictability, the matching process is monotonously repetitive. To restore optimum predictability, ideational material is elicited that directs activity toward novelty and variability so that new predictions may be attempted in order to improve the ability to predict. In the case of too little predictability, there is an arousing mismatch or discrepancy because of an unfamiliar event. To restore optimum predictability, ideational material is elicited that directs activity toward redundancy and more familiar events to enhance the confirmation of prediction.

When an unfamiliar event has been deliberated often enough to become familiar, a habit may form, and the event subsequently will be dealt with automatically. It is in this way that automatic and deliberate thought operate reciprocally to improve prediction. Thorngate (1976) believes habit to be a more common determinant of social behavior than cognition.

These examples will clarify the relationship between automatic and deliberate thought. Let us begin by considering habit as automatic thought.[1] (Deliberated thought is dealt with extensively in chapters 7 and 8.)

Images, Habits, and Prediction

Images permit predictions to be made about familiar events. When predictions are based on images of concrete experiences, we are prompted to predict that events will turn out in the future as they have in the past because such images are mental representations of past experiences. Thus when an impinging event elicits such an image, the outcome in the image will have been experienced before. *Habits* are images that contain inflexible programs that tend to be executed automatically with little or no concentration. An example follows. Suppose a mother teaches her infant son how to hold his baby bottle so that he can drink from it without assistance. When the baby learns to execute the program smoothly, a habit has been learned and the baby executes the habit automatically. The subroutines of the program may be executed in this order: (1) reach for the bottle, (2) grasp it, (3) place the nipple in your mouth, and (4) drink from the bottle.

The matching process might proceed as follows.

Matching for Identification: Of an Initiating Event. The mother hands the baby bottle to the baby. The child identifies the bottle and the sequence of tasks the mother is performing in handing him the bottle because he has seen them often and has memorized them. They correspond to an image in the baby's mind, so that the baby identifies what is happening as familiar to his past experience.

Matching for Prediction. The sequence of events the baby has identified is matched with the programs in the baby's mind for a prediction. It corresponds to the program that portrays the baby grasping the bottle and then drinking from it, so this program is elicited. The baby then anticipates that events will occur in the order corresponding to the subroutine sequence in the program.

Matching for Identification: To Test the Prediction against Sensory Feedback. The program is executed. The baby reaches for the bottle, grasps it, places the nipple in his mouth, and drinks from it. The program is executed automatically, without concentration, unless a mismatch occurs between the events in the program neuroprint and actual events (too little predictability). At such a time the arousing discrepancy would alert the baby and he would begin to deliberate the problem. For instance, the baby might drop the bottle while drinking from it and become aroused.

It appears that because habits are learned initially through deliberation before they become habits, the individual has an idea of the operation of a habit. Thus the effectiveness of the operation of a habit, such as the program for drinking from the baby bottle, can be monitored on the ideational level. Consequently a habit may be deliberately modified.

Conversely, because autonomic functions of the body are innate and rarely observed, ideas about them seldom develop. Under these conditions there is no basis for modifying the autonomic activity. When ideas about an autonomic function do develop, it is because the operations of the autonomic function have been observed and an idea portraying the function has developed through learning.

Studies of biofeedback show that when individuals are made aware of the autonomic functions of their bodies and continue to observe them they can control these functions. Shapiro and Schwartz (1973) reviewed related research. In studies of the effect of biofeedback on the lowering of blood pressure, the subject is told that a light will go on when his blood pressure lowers. A meter records the time during which the individual is successful in lowering blood pressure or in maintaining it at a lower level. The results show that some subjects are able to lower their systolic blood pressure by 16 to 34 mm. of mercury. (Such results are achieved only when there is no evidence of physical changes in the circulatory system such as hardening of the arteries.)

Another application of biofeedback concerns the treatment of tension headaches. Feedback is provided by signaling the tensing of the involuntary muscles in the neck and head. As the muscles tense the electrical signal produces a higher pitched tone, and the subject attempts to maintain a low signal tone. The studies demonstrate that when individuals are able to observe autonomic processes that usually operate outside of their awareness and control, they are able to control these processes, at least temporarily.

We learn to drive a car by deliberation. We learn to recognize and predict the events we may encounter. At first we learn certain events through memorization in hopes that eventually they may be relegated to habit and executed automatically. Shifting gears is an example—as we begin to learn how to shift gears through deliberation, we memorize the route through the gear box and correct our mistakes as we falter. With more and more practice, gear shifting becomes smoother and is eventually relegated to habit. This frees us to deliberate other problems, such as road and traffic conditions.

Traffic conditions, unlike gear shifting, present us with so many new and dangerous problems that they cannot be dealt with entirely by habit. When we are unable to shift gears by habit, the activities involved become unpredictable. As a result, they will be brought to our awareness for deliberation. We might, then, move the car off the road to deliberate the problem.

It should be noted that when events become too predictable or too unpredictable, deliberation will be directed toward the reinstatement of optimum predictability above all else. Then subordinate decisions may be made through the deliberation of concepts, such as which alternate goals to pursue or which alternate programs to pick as the means of pursuing a given goal.

Above all, we are motivated to predict because prediction is necessary in order for us to function. Once predictability is maintained, we may choose anything we prefer to pursue or any means of obtaining what we wish that we have learned.

The deliberation of concepts is the means of making choices because concepts offer alternatives. In deliberating alternative ideas, the content of the ideas indicates the probability that a prediction will be confirmed.

If you wish to take a trip, it is the content of your ideas that will indicate how long it will take and how much it will cost to reach different possible destinations. You can compare each alternative to determine which will be most feasible to visit. You would not choose a place you could not afford because you could not predict that you would be able to complete the trip. On the other hand, it is the feelings associated with ideas that indicate the relative amount of interest you have in alternative possibilities. You can deliberate the various places you might visit and determine which destinations are of greatest interest.

The deliberation of alternatives in these ways results in a choice indicating a *preference*. A preference may be determined by deliberating the feasibility of taking various courses of action based on the content of ideas and the interest we have in various courses of action based upon the feelings associated with one's ideas. However, it should be understood that the most interesting alternative is not always the preferred alternative. The most interesting alternative would not be preferred if the content of one's ideas indicates that it is unattainable. Something less interesting but attainable would be preferred.

Note

1. As we mentioned earlier, we are not attempting to explain the functions of inherited neuroprints such as instincts and reflexes, although we do make references to them from time to time. It should be mentioned in passing, however, that inherited neuroprints probably operate as automatic thought.

7 Deliberate Thought

So far the examples have concerned automatic thought as it operates to satisfy the prediction motive. We need to consider how the matching process proceeds when boredom or confusion interrupts automatic thought and deliberation is engaged as the means of predicting. When the individual deliberates, not only can an attempt be made to satisfy the prediction motive by reestablishing optimum predictability, but preferences may be pursued as well. To show how the matching process pertains to deliberation, we must expand it in the following way.

Matching for Identification: Of an Initiating Event. In this phase optimum predictability has been violated, boredom or confusion has occurred, and the individual is aroused to deliberate what is happening. The person searches for a match between current events and previously held ideas (concepts and images).

Matching for Prediction: To Determine What Is Going to Happen without Intervention. Once the individual knows what is happening, he or she is inclined to predict what is going to happen if nothing is done. To determine this, the person attempts to match an idea of the sequence of events indicating what is happening with a program idea. If the match is made the individual predicts what is likely to happen. A match for prediction is made because the initiating event is a component of the program and thus corresponds to it.

Matching for Prediction: To Pursue a Preference. At this point the individual is able to deliberate concepts to determine preferred interests: decide whether to let things happen as predicted or intervene and redirect the course of events. It is at this stage that the individual may exercise volition and direct destiny. Volition is discussed by Pribram (1967, 1971).

To redirect events, the individual selects a master neuroprint that leads from a present interest to a goal that satisfies the interest. The master neuroprint contains a program that indicates how the individual must operate on the environment to change events in order to achieve the goal.

If automatic thought was interrupted initially because of too much predictability, the interest would be concerned with confirming the prediction that the boredom would be relieved. The pursuit of the goal is expected to be accompanied by relief from boredom. On the other hand, if automatic thought was interrupted because of too little predictability, the interest would be concerned with confirming the prediction that the confusion would be relieved. The pursuit of the goal is expected to be accompanied by relief from confusion.

Activity

If the choice were made to change the course of events, the individual would execute the program portion of the master neuroprint that leads to the preferred goal. If the individual decided not to attempt to change the course of events, then one of two things could follow: disregard the matter because it is of no consequence, or, if uncertain how events will turn out and the course of events were of some consequence, monitor events to determine whether they turn out as predicted. In the latter case, the person would monitor events, which involves information processing rather than action.

Matching for Identification: To Test the Prediction against Sensory Feedback. If the choice were made to change the course of events and seek a preferred goal, the individual would act upon the environment as the program portion of the master neuroprint indicates. Also, events would be monitored to determine whether or not movement was being made toward the goal. If it were, the program would be continued as prescribed. If not, an attempt would be made to modify the program through deliberation so that the goal could be achieved.

There is evidence that feedback is important for correcting mistakes so that predictions may be confirmed. West (1967) studied the performance of expert typists. When the typist could not see the typewriter or the typewriter roller, West found that there was a sizeable increase in typing errors. Holding (1965) distinguished between intrinsic and artificial feedback. *Intrinsic feedback,* he contends, is related to the correct performance of the task at hand. The typing results cited above show the importance of intrinsic feedback. *Artificial feedback* is external to the task and involves giving an individual a grade or prize for correct performance. Holding concludes that intrinsic feedback is much more effective than artifical feedback. To be effective at all, artificial feedback must be tied to the task. Nutten and Greenwald (1968) showed that informative feedback, such as saying "correct" or "incorrect" with respect to a particular task, is effective only when the subject predicts the need to perform in the future the task he is learning. Correction without the expectation that the performance of a task will be of use in the future produces little learning. The research of Longstreth (1970) confirms this position.

Note that in the matching sequence just described, it is necessary to know what is happening (phase 1). Otherwise, one is totally disoriented. In addition, it is necessary to know what is happening as a basis for predicting what is going to happen (phase 2). If one cannot predict to some extent one is also confused. Further, one must be able to identify and predict in general in order to be able to predict the acquisition of a preference (phase 3). This again illustrates that maintaining predictability is prerequisite to pursuing one's preference.

In summary it may be said that deliberation in the matching process involves first the *review* of ideas to obtain a match for identification of an initiating event. Matching for prediction involves the *preview* of events. Matching for identification to test predictions involves the *viewing* of events to determine whether predictions are being confirmed.

The same matching model applies to situations in which there is too little predictability or too much predictability. In cases of a monotonously prolonged match between events and neuroprints, people seek enough novelty to permit them to escape boredom. In other words, they seek a situation that is challenging and enables them to extend their scope of prediction. Under these conditions individuals might be interested in the challenges that are inherent in games such as bridge or chess, or in solving puzzles such as crossword puzzles. Or they might be enticed by the challenges of research that may lead to discovery and invention.

There is considerable research showing that attention is drawn to novel and complex or unpredictable stimulation. Many of these studies involve the observation of eye movements. It is generally found that attention tends to dwell on novel, complex stimulation. According to the present theory, this is because such stimulation is unpredictable and challenging. Particular studies performed by Yarbus (1967), Antes (1974), Welch (1974), and Thomas (1965) confirm this contention. Travers (1970) and Aitken and Hutt (1974) have reviewed the research on the subject.

When a program prescribes actions that are predicted to lead to a goal, and the actions actually lead to the goal, the individual has gained *control* over the environment. This is because the individual has learned how to take action in the future to control the events that lead to the goal.

The following is an example of the matching process applied to information processing in preparation for dealing with the environment. The example is one of too little predictability.

Matching for Identification: Of an Initiating Event. You are reading automatically as the words on the pages match your ideas and you are receiving meaning from the passage when you encounter a word you do not know. There is a mismatch, reading is interrupted, and you become aroused and aware of the problem.

The new word on the page finds a match with the concept *unfamiliar word*. It is categorized as a word because it is composed of a combination of recognizable letters surrounded by white space. It is categorized on a lower level of the idea hierarchy as an "unfamiliar word" because it is a type of word, a word that does not elicit an idea of an event.

Matching for Prediction: To Predict What Is Going to Happen without Intervention. The abstraction "unfamiliar word" finds a match with a program predicting that if you do not find the meaning of the word you will not be able to continue to read.

Matching for Prediction: To Pursue a Preference. You deliberate whether you prefer to stop reading or to find and understand the meaning of the unfamiliar word. You choose to continue reading, so a match is made with the master neuroprint that contains your interest in continuing to read and the program for finding the meaning of an unfamiliar word in the dictionary (assuming that the master neuroprint has been learned); the goal is to find and understand the meaning of the word.

Activity

You execute the program portion of the master neuroprint and proceed through the dictionary accordingly.

Matching for Identification: The Testing of a Prediction against Sensory Feedback. As you follow the program you monitor events to determine whether they are proceeding as indicated by the program. If they are, you would find the word and understand its meaning, thereby achieving the goal.

There has been some interesting research that applies to the process just described. Collins and Quillan (1970) contended that a word has stored with it a number of pointers to other words in memory. Therefore, the meaning of one word is represented by a configuration of relationships to other words, with special emphasis given to class-inclusion relations. Economy in storage is obtained through the assumption that specific properties such as "yellow" (found in a dictionary definition of canary) would be stored at the node with canary while more general properties such as "capable of flight" which apply to all birds would be stored at the hierarchical level of bird. Even broader properties such as "breathes, consumes food" would be stored at the even higher level of "animal."

Collins and Quillan assume that a search of memory can begin with any word that has been designated, for example *bird,* and may proceed either upward in the hierarchy toward the superset concept *animal* and its properties or downwards toward examples *canary* and their specific property lists. The results of their experiment show that it took longer to respond when the statement to be analyzed involved retrieval of properties stored several levels away rather than at the same level in the hierarchy.

Conrad (1972) verifies the hierarchical organization, with some properties stored at each level, but he questions the economy-of-storage hypothesis.

It should be understood that the information processing involved in matching for identification and matching for prediction may or may not include interactions with the environment. Suppose you are executing a program to solve a multiplication problem. If in executing the program you use a paper and pencil to process information in order to arrive at an answer, then interaction with the environment is involved. However, if you multiply "in your head," interaction with the environment is not involved.

After a match for prediction is achieved and a program directs activity, information processing continues. Environmental events are compared to the predictions contained in the program to determine whether events are occurring as predicted. Thus environmental interactions may be a part of information processing in preparing to deal with the environment, and information processing is involved when action is taken to test a selected master neuroprint against environmental events in an attempt to obtain something from the environment.

As indicated, optimum predictability will be maintained automatically. However, when there is either too much predictability or too little predictability arousal will be generated and the problem will be brought to awareness for deliberation. It appears that when deliberation is the mode of thought, more than arousal is involved. Although arousal and activation were once thought to be the same, recent advancements in our knowledge of brain functions indicate that they are distinct processes. Activation appears to be related to deliberation. After too much or too little predictability triggers the arousal mechanism bringing the problem to awareness, the activation function is elicited and serves to ready the individual for deliberation. When the activation function is elicited, arousal is reduced and concentration is heightened in preparation for the mental effort that is expended in deliberation.

Arousal is associated with stimulus set and activation is associated with response set. Broadbent (1971) discusses the distinction between stimulus set and response set.

As Pribram (1975) explains:

Three neurally distinct and separate attentional systems—arousal, activation, and effort—operate upon the information-processing mechanism. . . .

The orienting reaction [to stimulus] involves arousal but no activation . . .
when neither arousal nor activation is present, behavior is automatic, that
is, stimulus-response contingencies are direct without the intervention of
any of the control mechanisms of attention (p. 133).

Thus there appear to be three brain mechanisms—arousal, activation, and
the mental effort expended in deliberation.[1]

Deliberating Preferences

In deliberating alternatives, one attempts to form a master neuroprint by
choice. This involves deliberating one's interests, programs, and goals.

Newborns react impulsively to the dictates of their instincts. As they
grow older and learn alternative ways of behaving, they can react to the
same stimulus in different ways and are able to choose their reactions. As
their deliberate choices lead to the confirmation of their predictions, they
will tend to restrain their impulses and deliberate more often.

Deliberating One's Interests

Individuals are often beset with a number of interests. They may be hungry,
sexually aroused, short of money, late in delivering a document to the boss,
and so on. The first decision to be made through deliberation is which interests shall be attended to and in which order. This amounts to establishing
preference priorities of one's interests.

Deliberating Goals

Once interests have been deliberated and priorities have been set, goals must
be deliberated for each interest that was assigned high priority.

If several goals can be identified the individual must learn to arrange
them in a hierarchy of preference. The first criterion which must be met for
a goal to be placed high in the goal hierarchy is *attainability*. In order for a
goal to be attainable, at least one program must be identified that can be
predicted to lead to the goal. The determination of attainability is based on
the content of ideas. The individual would learn to determine by mentally
reviewing the content of a program whether or not a program (or many programs) can be predicted to lead to a goal. If so, the goal may be regarded as
attainable.

Second, the individual must learn to deliberate the *desirability* of
achieving goals in order to assign them a place in the goal hierarchy. The

desirability of achieving a goal is evaluated on the feeling level. If alternative attainable goals will result in the satisfaction of interests, the individual can determine the relative satisfaction anticipated in achieving each of them.

The placing of goals in a hierarchy may be said to represent the individual's goal *preferences*. A preference is based on the content of ideas, which is used to determine the attainability of goals, and the feelings contained in ideas, which are used to evaluate the desirability of goals. The resultant hierarchical arrangement represents preferences. Remember that a preference is not determined on the basis of feeling alone but on the basis of deliberating content and feeling. A goal would not be preferred if it were regarded as unattainable, regardless of how desirable it might be.

Stotland (1969) defines "hope" as a shorthand term for an expectation about goal attainment, and distinguishes persons as either "hopeful" or "hopeless." Perceived probability of goal attainment and perceived importance are two factors.

Wise (1970) concluded that both paired-comparison judgments and subjective-probability estimates reflect subjects' underlying subjective expectations about statements, but the estimates were a more efficient measure. He found few circular trends when choice was limited to two alternatives, evidence for rationality.

The initial arrangement of goals into a hierarchy is tentative. Final decisions are made after programs are deliberated. Then programs and goals are evaluated together for the purpose of forming a preferred master neuroprint.

Lewin et al. (1944) raised the question of how a person's successes and failures affect his goals. Atkinson and Feather (1966) suggested a simple ratio of previous successes to previous trials determines the expected probability of success on the current trial. Peterson and Beach (1967) claim that man is an "intuitive statistician," and his methods of dealing with statistical events and those of formal statistical models correspond.

Jones et al. (1968) added personal variables to the simpler ratio with varying weights for previous trials depending on performance expectations. Support for the weighted average model has been obtained by Friedman, Carterette, and Anderson (1968), Anderson (1969, 1974), and Lopes (1976), the last adding a variable for number of previous trials attended to.

Deliberating Programs

Once goals are arranged into a tentative hierarchy, programs can be deliberated for selection. Programs also are deliberated on the basis of preference, that is, on the basis of content and feeling. The *content* of a program indicates the efficiency of the program, for example, the time, work, and money it would cost to follow the program. The *feelings* associated with the events in the program indicate the desirability of following one program or another. It is on the basis of content and feeling that the individual must learn how to arrange programs into a hierarchy representing preferences.

Selecting a Master Neuroprint

After goals and programs are arranged in tentative hierarchies, the individual is in a position to relate programs to goals in the final selection of a master neuroprint. This involves, for instance, the evaluation of the relative merits of pursuing a highly preferred goal by means of a program that is not preferred, as opposed to pursuing a less preferred goal by means of a more highly preferred program.

The procedure for conceiving a prediction through deliberation may be diagrammed as follows:

Perhaps an example will clarify the procedure. This time we shall consider an example of too much predictability or boredom. Suppose an eighteen-year-old girl is bored with school and interested in overcoming her boredom. After this interest is compared with others in her deliberations, she decides to try to overcome her boredom. She would deliberate alternate goals, and in her deliberations she would attempt to determine her preferences by considering the attainability and desirability of the goals. One goal might be leaving school and going to work; another goal might be remaining in school and changing to a more interesting program of study. After deliberating alternative goals, she would deliberate the various programs for achieving the goals in an attempt to determine her program preferences. This would be accomplished by evaluating the efficiency and desirability of the various programs and might involve considering the various courses of study (programs) that lead to graduation and considering the various ways of obtaining employment. Finally, she would relate programs to goals in order to select a master neuroprint to direct her actions.

Game theory, which was introduced in chapter 1, emphasizes the rational side of human nature and the importance of deliberating alternatives to solve problems. According to game theory, a rational person faced with a choice of alternative actions would do the following (Rapoport, 1960, 1964):

1. consider all possible consequences of each and every action;
2. rank order the consequences according to preferences;
3. choose the action which leads to the most preferred consequence;
4. consider the preferences of other persons who influence the consequences; and
5. impute rationality to the opponent.

Game theory assumes that games of strategy, such as chess or checkers, provide a good deal of rational behavior because there are:

1. conflicts of interest;
2. a number of alternatives open at each phase of the situation;
3. people able to estimate the consequences of their choices, taking into consideration the fact that outcomes are determined not only by one's choices but also by the choices of others; and
4. rules.

Research on Deliberation and Hypothesis Testing

The research on concept learning has contributed a great deal to show that mature problem solving is a process of deliberating and testing alternate hypotheses rather than a process of building responses or habit hierarchies as the stimulus-response theorists have contended for a long time. The Kendlers (1959, 1962, 1975) and Kendler and D'Amato (1955) provide substantiating evidence in a series of studies involving shifts in the rules for determining the attributes for inclusion in categories. Typically, the subject learns criteria for inclusion in a category by being presented pairs of stimuli, guessing whether or not they belong to the category in question, and being told the correct answer by the experimenter. Now suppose that in this manner the individual learns that the terms black-small and white-small are correct and black-large and white-large are incorrect. The rule for inclusion in the category that is learned is small. This rule can then be switched in two ways. A reversal shift can be imposed such as the two small ones becoming incorrect and the two large ones becoming correct. Or a nonreversal shift can be imposed such as calling black correct and white incorrect. Now, if concept learning involves strengthening single S-R associations, then the reversal shift should be more difficult to learn because it requires changing four associations, whereas the nonreversal shift requires changing only two associations. On the other hand, if concept learning involves deliberating alternatives and hypothesizing rules that mediate between the stimulus and response, then in a reversal shift the same dimension mediates and only new labels need be added while in the nonreversal shift a new dimension must be found as well as new labels. Thus the nonreversal shift should be more difficult.

In a series of studies it was found that the reversal shift was easier for college students and children over five years of age, but the nonreversal shift was easier for children under five and lower animals to learn. Kendler and Kendler concluded that as age increases the learning of concepts tends to occur more by the hypothesizing and testing of rules than by individual associations.

The Kendlers' explanation is in accord with the explanation of mental development in chapter 4. That is, early learning is the learning of images and the formation of concepts through the association of the common characteristics among images. Early learning is essentially inductive—it involves the building of concepts and concept hierarchies through association. Once concepts form in the mind, the rules or criteria for identifying an item as a member of a concept category are known and the individual can deduce the hypothesis that an item containing the attributes of the category is a member of the category. In short, early learning appears to proceed inductively through association. Later learning, past the age of five, involves deliberating alternatives, deducing hypotheses, and then testing the hypotheses.

The Kendlers' finding that laboratory animals as well as children under five solve problems by means of association rather than through hypothesis testing of a sign of superior intelligence and greater experience in older humans.

Osler and Fivel (1961) add support to this implication. They noted that high school students with IQ's above 110 seem to learn through hypothesis testing, while students with average or below average intelligence learned by means of association.

Bower and Trabasso (1963; Trabasso and Bower 1964, 1968) added evidence to support the contention that older people solve concept problems through hypothesis testing rather than through individual associations. They gave college students a concept-learning task in which they were presented stimuli one at a time and asked to indicate to which of two classes a stimulus belonged. The researchers then indicated whether they were right or wrong. The researcher noted that the pattern of performance remained at a chance level for some time, then the students suddenly performed with 100 percent accuracy. This sudden accuracy could not be the result of a slow build up of associations. It is more likely the result of suddenly confirming the right hypothesis. Bower and Trabasso went further to demonstrate the point. They changed the solution while the students were still performing at a chance level. The associationists' position proposes that the switch would impair learning because it interferes with the build up of associative strengths. The hypotheses testing position proposes that the switch makes no difference since the student has not yet determined the correct classification rule. The results clearly supported the hypothesis testing point of view. Subjects exposed to the shift learned the correct classification rule as rapidly as subjects who retained the same rule throughout the experiment.

The work on reflective and impulsive cognitive styles sheds additional light on the value of deliberate, systematic hypothesis testing on problem solving. Reflective problem solvers proceed by slow deliberation. They systematically scan alternative hypotheses before selecting a potential solution. Impulsive problem solvers select alternatives quickly. In problem situations of high-response uncertainty, the reflectives consistently make fewer errors. This suggests that problems that cannot be solved automatically by habit require deliberation to produce accurate solutions (see Kagan and Kogan 1970; Ward 1968; McKinney 1974; Kagan 1966.)

The impulsive child who fails to concentrate and think through a problem shows poorer achievement in arithmetic (Cathcart and Liedtke 1969), in reading (Kagan 1965), and in school in general (Messer 1970).

There also is evidence that reflective thinking is an index of mental maturity. Ault (1973) and McKinney (1974) found that younger reflectives used strategies that were comparable to older impulsives.

It seems evident that the deliberation and testing of alternate hypotheses is a problem-solving mode used by older individuals and individuals of superior intelligence. The speculation now revolves around how hypotheses are conceived and tested.

As was mentioned in chapter 6, Bruner, Goodnow, and Austin (1956) suggested that individuals create and test hypotheses. Restle (1962) and Bower and Trabasso (1964; Trabasso and Bower, 1968) conceived a model of the process of hypothesis testing, and Restle and Greeno (1970) refined the model somewhat. A more recent explanation of hypothesis testing comes from Levine (1974) whose views were introduced in chapter 3. Levine contends that to deal with a current problem situation, the individual must first categorize or type the problem. Once the problem is classified, the individual deliberates and samples ideas from the category and hypothesizes solutions and then tests the hypotheses in an attempt to confirm them and solve the problem. Each hypothesis generated from the problem category represents a possible alternate solution. Levine's (1966) study lends support to his theoretical formulation. The experiment of Wicken and Millward (1971) also supports the model.

Although the description of the deliberation and prediction process extends beyond the present data, it is clear from the evidence that mature problem solvers deliberate alternatives and select and test predictions to solve problems.

Note

1. We have delineated three brain mechanisms in the rostral portions of these control systems: (a) The first centers on the amygdala, which regulates the monitoring or "arousal" neurons and becomes organized into a "stop" or re-equilibrating mechanism. (b) A second is centered on the basal ganglia and involves the *activation* of "go" mechanisms—expectancies (perceptual) and readiness (motor). (c) Finally, a third mechanism comprising the hippocampal circuit has been identified, which uncouples the stimulus from the response by coordinating the amygdala and basal ganglia mechanisms so that appropriate changes in the central representation can occur, a process that entails *effort*. (Pribram 1975, pp. 131-132) Reprinted with permission.

8 Discovery through Deliberation

Discovery and invention highlight the higher mental functions responsible for human excellence and are achieved through the deliberation of concepts.

When predictions are based on images, the individual will predict that events will turn out in the future as they have in the past. Concepts permit predictions to be made about events that have not occurred before in the individual's experience. Remember that identification is prerequisite to prediction and that a totally unfamiliar event cannot be identified at the time it appears. The event must be memorized before identification can take place.

Concepts permit unfamiliar events to be predicted because images of objects have been categorized on the basis of their common characteristics to form concepts, and a somewhat novel stimulus has characteristics that match the characteristics of a concept. In short, it is the match between the elements of an unfamiliar stimulus and the elements of a concept that permits novel events to be identified and predicted. When an unfamiliar event has been matched with a concept, the individual has discovered that the unfamiliar event has the same characteristics as the concept and the same predictions can be made about the unfamiliar event that can be made about other members of the concept category based on their common characteristics. For instance, suppose a child sees a strange creature in a tree and matches it with the known concept bird because the creature has wings, feathers, and is found in trees. The child has discovered that the strange creature has the same characteristics as other birds and that the same predictions can be made about the creature that can be made about birds in general. For example, the child can predict that the creature will fly.

Discovering the nature of unfamiliar events by matching them with known concepts is common place as the following examples illustrate.

Identifying a strange

1. person as a person because characteristics match the category *person*.
2. vehicle as a helicopter because it has a rotor and hovers.
3. object as a balloon because it is made of elastic and floats in the air.
4. food as a fruit because it is with other known fruits in a supermarket.
5. activity as a ball game because there are two teams competing for control of a ball.

There is another type of discovery that involves learning a new concept category. When individuals learn on their own that various items have common characteristics and that common predictions can be made about them, a new concept has been discovered. For instance, when a child observes kites, birds, airplanes, and butterflies and notes that they all are able to fly, the concept *things that fly* may be learned, constituting a discovery. Or a child may continually observe the parents in the kitchen working with the stove, refrigerator, sink, pots and pans to prepare food and the concept *objects used to prepare food* might be discovered. Or the concept *things to eat* may be discovered by a child as a result of noting the various food items provided by the parents. It is possible that a child can understand the essence of a concept such as food long before the concept is formally taught to the child.

The previous examples illustrated how new concepts can be discovered from the observation of concrete objects and events. New concepts also can be discovered utilizing previously learned concepts. For example, suppose a child knows that the concept *mother* is defined as women with children and that the concept *father* denotes men with children. The child can recognize that the two concepts have common characteristics and discover a new concept. The child might note that both mothers and fathers are adults with children and understand the essence of the concept parent long before it is taught to the child.

The above example involves inductive reasoning. New concepts also can be discovered deductively. Individuals examine the characteristics of a general abstraction category for differences. If they find subgroups within the more general group, they have deduced new concept categories at a lower level of an idea hierarchy. Such would be the case if individuals discover on their own that mothers and fathers are subcategories of the more general category *parent*.

Thus discoveries are made when individuals learn a new concept on their own and when they use a previously learned concept to identify and predict a novel event. Discovery through conceptualization is what psychologists usually refer to as *insight*.

Insight   .

The Gestalt psychologist Kohler (1925, 1929, 1969) introduced the concept of insight to explain why the apes in his experiments solved problems suddenly rather than by trial and error in small graded movements. Wertheimer (1959), Maier (1930, 1931, 1933, 1945), and Katone (1940) discuss further the comparison between trial and error and insightful learning.

Insight often is characterized as an eureka experience in which we suddenly grasp a relationship we did not see before. Insight refers to the moment in the matching process when a match is achieved between a novel sensory event and a concept, or when individuals learn new concepts on their own.

Insight, then, is a form of discovery, and concepts provide the basis for discovery. Any insight is a discovery, even though an individual's discovery is common knowledge. The difference between personal discovery and general discovery is that in a general discovery the insight is new to all people.

The Gestalt Law of Closure can be interpreted within this framework. Individuals achieve closure in two ways. They achieve closure when, in deliberating a problem, insight occurs and they predict a solution. Subsequently they achieve closure when they test and confirm the prediction.

In chapter 7 two research references were cited in which the researchers reported that subjects who solved problems through the selection and testing of hypotheses arrived at a problem solution suddenly. The Bower and Trabasso study (1963) reported that the subjects in the study who were forming and testing hypotheses performed at a chance level for a long time, then jumped suddenly to 100 percent correct response. In the study by Osler and Fivel (1961), it was also noted that in hypotheses selection and testing high school students went through a period of chance performance and suddenly reached 100 percent correct performance when the correct hypotheses were finally chosen. On the other hand, the students with average or below average intelligence who learned by association displayed a pattern in which the rate of correct response for each subject rose gradually. This suggests that learning through hypotheses selection and testing is insightful learning whereas learning through association in small graded increments is trial and error learning.

As noted earlier, the prediction motive induces the comparison of stimuli and neuroprints for similarities and differences and the consequent formation of concepts. The comparison for similarities and differences is the basis for matching and prediction.

We are able to make more predictions concerning unfamiliar events as a function of reorganizing and refining concepts. That is to say, concepts are formed because similar images have been categorized on the basis of certain criteria. These concepts may be reorganized and refined through experience (and directed educational procedures) so that the images are organized by other criteria. This naturally results in a single image being a member of several (perhaps hundreds) concept categories (for example, a *red ball* that *bounces* that is *mine*, and so forth).

Transfer of Knowledge

When a match for prediction has been achieved through ideation, transfer of knowledge has occurred because ideas in the mind representing stored information are being applied or transferred to predict a current event. Thus the only time that transfer cannot occur is when there are no ideas in the mind corresponding to a current event. Then the event is totally unfamiliar and it must be memorized to be predicted.

When transfer is based on images, the event to be predicted is familiar. The master neuroprint used to predict the event has usually been used before in similar situations, so its application is also familiar. Often when transfer is based on image, it involves the execution of a habit, such as the automatic fanning away of a fly, and habits are used to predict familiar events. Moreover, when transfer is based on image, it is implicit that the individuals will deal with the new situation the same way they dealt with similar situations in the past.

Concepts can be used to transfer knowledge in order to predict a novel event through insight. Concepts permit the individual to combine and recombine memories in a myriad of ways. A given event or program may be associated with many different concepts, enabling a given program or event to be used in many different ways. Moreover, insight gained through concepts allows events and programs to be used in new ways to make predictions, which lead to discovery and invention.

Osgood (1949) formulated a graph that is known as transfer surface and is used to predict transfer of learning. In general, the graph proposes that maximum positive transfer occurs when two tasks present similar stimuli and call for similar responses. Maximum negative transfer occurs when two tasks provide similar stimuli but call for opposite responses. Martin (1965) and Shea (1969) support this conclusion. The graph is relatively accurate for predicting the solution of motor skills problems that are solved by means of simple association.

On the other hand, research cited shows that Osgood's principles do not hold true for adults and older children solving concept problems through hypotheses selection and testing. Kendler and Kendler (1962) and Kendler (1964) found that in concept learning older children and adults perform a reversal shift more readily than a nonreversal shift. The research on the selection and testing of hypotheses by Bower and Trabasso (1963) also refutes the Osgood formulation. The shift in the classification rule during concept learning did not impair learning.

It becomes increasingly clear that the primitive problem solving of young children, lower animals, and people of lower intelligence follows the gradual inductive trial and error pattern of learning through stimulus-response associations, whereas the problem solving of older humans and higher primates, who have an inventory of concepts and concept hierarchies in their minds, proceeds deductively through hypotheses selection and testing more closely resembling insightful learning.

Discovering from Context and Structure

One reason discoveries are made is because the familiar features of an unfamiliar event are matched with a concept. Familiar features of an unfamiliar event may be identified in the structure of the unfamiliar object, that is, its composition, and familiar features may be identified in the context or surroundings that contain the unfamiliar object.

In learning how to abstract meaning from the structure of a word, a person learns that a word such as *cat* does not break down into meaningful component features. Therefore, if the word *cat* is unfamiliar, its meaning cannot be derived by abstraction from its structure and must be found in the dictionary or from another authoritative source.

On the other hand, a person may learn that a word such as *semiannual* does break down into component meaningful features. Therefore, if a person knows that the prefix *semi* means half and the word *annual* means year, then the word *semiannual* has familiar features that convey its meaning even though the word has never been encountered before.

In analyzing context, an unfamiliar group of words may or may not have familiar features that convey the meaning of a word. For example, one may determine the meaning of the missing word in the following sentence from context through abstraction. The color of the summer grass was dark _____. The familiar features of the sentence convey the meaning of the unknown word. So if the word *green* were in the blank space and the reader had never seen it before, the reader could still decipher its meaning, knowing beforehand that grass is green in the summer.

However, there may not be enough familiar features in a group of words to convey the meaning of an unfamiliar word in the group from context. If the blank space in the following sentence represents a word that the reader does not know the meaning of, there would not be sufficient familiar features in the group to convey its meaning: The girl was _____. If the features of which a word is composed do not convey its meaning and the group of words in which the unfamiliar word is contained do not convey its meaning either, then the meaning of an unfamiliar word must be found in the dictionary or from some other authoritative source. So the meaning of a word may be inferred by abstraction from its structure, that is, in knowing the meaning of the prefixes, suffixes, and simple words of which a complex word is composed, or the meaning of a word may be deduced from the context in which it sits, that is, from the external features or words that surround the unknown word, or both.

The Gestalt psychologists remind us that relationships can be understood by observing a figure in contrast to its ground. From this point of view, the structure of an object or figure should be analyzed in the context or ground that contains it. In the preceding example, the meaning of a word can be derived through abstraction by analyzing the structure and the context. If both structural and contextual analyses reveal the same meaning of a word, then one approach buttresses the other and one can be more certain that the derived meaning is correct.

Another example of how contextual and structural cues complement each other in identifying and predicting pertains to unfamiliar foreign currency. Suppose a wallet is found and the person who finds it opens it and tries to identify the contents. The individual sees paper currency in it but does not recognize the currency because the person has not seen such currency before. However, the strange object is made of paper and has numbers and a recognizable name of a foreign country on it. In addition, it is approximately the size of other paper money the person is familiar with. So the structural composition of the strange object gives clues to its identity. The fact that it is found in the paper money compartment of a wallet provides contextual clues to its identity.

Making Discoveries and Inventions New to All People

We explained how insight leads to discovery when the familiar features of an unfamiliar event are matched with a concept or when new concepts form. We said that a discovery may just be new to the discoverer or may be new to everyone. Here we will explain how one can learn to discover and invent something new to all people.

The discovery and invention of something new to everyone occurs because the item to be discovered or invented is identified as an *intervening variable*, or a missing part within a conceptual framework. To understand how discoveries and inventions are made, it is necessary to understand how complex concepts are organized and how a blank space within a conceptual framework identifies a discovery or invention that can be made. To illustrate we shall use *public-conceptual frameworks*, which are often called taxonomies or classification systems.

A *taxonomy* may be defined as a publicly identified set of concepts that describe the relationships among a class of events. In terms of prediction theory, a taxonomy is a public-idea hierarchy. For example, the phylogenetic scale is a taxonomy that classifies living things and is composed of conceptual levels, each of which describes a type of living creature (for example, fish, amphibians, reptiles, birds, mammals). Another example of a public-conceptual framework is the periodic table, which classifies the elements.

These elaborate taxonomic systems represent our current knowledge of the similarities and differences among events. What many individuals could but do not learn about taxonomies is that because concepts permit predictions to be made about novel events, they can be used to discover things that may advance not only individual knowledge but the knowledge of all of us. If a taxonomy represents what we know about a class of events, it may be used to deduce what we may discover about the class of events.

A discovery pertains to a gap, or missing part of the taxonomy. Because a taxonomy is a set of concepts, it portrays relationships and it is the knowledge of relationships that allows predictions to be made. When a missing part of a taxonomy is identified, its relative position in the taxonomy denotes its characteristics. The missing thing in the taxonomy is more like the things adjacent to it and less like the things farther removed from it. For this reason, the characteristics of the missing thing may be deduced from the taxonomy, and a new concept may be defined based on these characteristics. In addition, it may be predicted that entities can be found that possess the characteristics of the new concept category.

For example, not too long ago missing parts of the phylogenetic scale were deduced in the category *mammals*. It was deduced that mammals existed at one time that fit into the scale between apes and humans as "missing links." Some missing links were subsequently found. These deductions were made by recognizing missing parts of taxonomies and deducing their characteristics by conceptualizing the relationship between the parts and the whole of the categorical arrangements. (It should be noted, however, that the identification and discovery of missing links is by no means a settled matter.)

In a similar manner the periodic table has been useful in discovering chemical elements. When the table was completed initially, it showed the relationships of the elements that were known at the time. In addition, there were blank spaces in the table that represented the existence of elements yet to be discovered. On the basis of the information in the taxonomy, new elements were defined as concepts, sought, and discovered.

In making a discovery, the matching process would proceed as follows.

Matching for Identification: Of an Initiating Event. The motivation to improve one's ability to predict arouses the interest of individuals in discovering new things. Therefore, they are prone to search through taxonomies for blank spaces that indicate and define the items to be discovered.

The idea of a missing category is matched with the various categories of a taxonomy, say the phylogenetic scale, and a match is found between humans and apes denoting a missing link. Because of the location of the gap within the taxonomy the characteristics of the thing to be discovered can be deduced and a new concept can be defined. The concept might be given the label ape-human and the characteristics that define the concept would be noted by considering its location in the taxonomy. For instance: (1) stood more erect than the ape and less erect than humans; (2) possessed a larger forebrain than the ape but a smaller one than humans; and so on. At this point, a discovery has been conceived and its characteristics have been identified.

Matching for Prediction: To Predict What Is Going to Happen without Intervention. The identification of the new concept ape-human elicits a program that predicts that the discovery of examples of the concept will not be made unless someone puts forth the effort to make it.

Matching for Prediction: To Pursue a Preference. Because scientists prefer to verify the prior existence of an ape-human, a master-neuroprint idea must be formed to accomplish the mission. The goal of the master neuroprint would be the discovery of fossil remains that conform to the characteristics of the ape-human. The interest is the concern of the scientists in finding the fossil remains. What needs to be conceived to complete the master neuroprint is a program that can be predicted to lead to the goal.

The conception of such a program is achieved by working backward from the goal: first, the final prerequisite task for achieving the goal is determined, then the task that is immediately prerequisite to the final task is determined, and so on.

The following program might be derived:

6. Test the fossil remains to see if they conform to the characteristics of an ape-human.
5. Find fossil remains.
4. Dig for fossil remains.
3. Travel to the excavation sites.
2. Prepare for the expedition to the sites.
1. Identify probable locations where fossil remains may be found.

Working backwards from a goal to derive a program to achieve it has been formally defined as *task analysis.* We are suggesting that we have thought in this way long before task analysis was defined as a public procedure. Task analysis is one information-processing program that is used in preparation for obtaining something from the environment.[1]

Each subroutine of the program can form a concept providing for alternatives. The first subroutine might be labeled *promising excavation sites* and a list of such sites that conform to the criteria for inclusion established for the concept would be made.

The match for prediction is finally made when the idea of the ape-human is matched with a master-neuroprint idea that prescribes a way that can be predicted to make the discovery.

Activity

The program is executed. Subroutines 1 through 6 are followed in that sequence. First, promising excavation sites would be identified, and so on.

Matching for Identification: The Testing of Predictions against Sensory Feedback. As the program portion of the master neuroprint is executed, events are matched with the master neuroprint to see if they are happening as predicted. If not, corrections are made. For example, if fossil remains of an ape-human are not found at one excavation site, an alternative site may be chosen.

The same mental process leads to invention. Except if we consider invention the creation of a new product, the objects in the environment must be manipulated and molded to conform to the idea of the product. Here is an abbreviated, oversimplified example of how an invention would be made.

Matching for Prediction: Of an Initiating Event. The initiating event is again the idea that a blank space in a taxonomy can lead to discovery and invention. In this example, we will presume how Edison might have invented the electric light.

The concept *light* might be defined as anything that illuminates. It might include oil-lamp light, kerosene-lamp light, sunlight, and so forth.

A match for identification might occur when a blank space within the taxonomy is found indicating that light can be caused by electricity and that electric light might be invented. The characteristics of such a light would be defined as light caused by electricity, identifying the new concept *electric light*.

Matching for Prediction: To Predict What Is Going to Happen without Intervention. The identification of the new concept *electric light* finds a match with the program that predicts that unless experimentation is done the invention will not be produced.

Matching for Prediction: To Pursue a Preference. Edison prefers to develop an electric light, so he attempts to organize a master neuroprint that will accomplish this interest.

The goal is producing an electric light, and the interest is Edison's propensity for doing this. What remains to be conceived is a program that leads to the goal.

Again, to derive a program one works backward from the goal.

5. Test the electric light to see if it works.
4. Construct the light
3. Obtain the materials.
2. Select materials that will conduct electricity.
1. Arrange for electrical current, space and money to buy materials.

Activity

The subroutines of the program are executed in order from 1 to 5.

Matching for Identification: The Testing of Predictions against Sensory Feedback. As the program portion of the master neuroprint idea is performed, events are matched with the prescriptions of the program to see if they are occurring as predicted. Different materials are combined in different ways until a combination is found that produces light.

It is the location of intervening variables, such as ape-human, and inferring their characteristics from their relationships with other things that permit concepts to be discovered that are new to all of us. It is the discovery or invention of instances of a new concept that validates the concept.

Taxonomies are static representations of categories. They represent only one basis for identifying intervening variables. Programs are dynamic because they represent activity sequences. Intervening variables in programs also can be identified as a means of pursuing discoveries. An intervening variable in a program would represent the deducing of an activity needed to complete a dynamic sequence of activities.

It should be pointed out that we are only illustrating some of prediction theory's implications for discovery. We are not dealing comprehensively with discovery. *Discovery* might be defined as broadly as any learning without instruction. It would be beyond the scope of this book to pursue all of the implications of such a definition.

The matching process that leads to discovery and invention is one instance in which the initiating event or *cause* that directs mental activity and behavior happens within the mind. Mental activity is the initiating force, not environmental stimulation. The desire to improve one's predictions induces the individual to make discoveries and invent.

Discovery and invention are initiated in the mind when an intervening variable is found and a new concept is created. Once the new concept is defined, the prediction motive impels attempts to validate the hypothesis that instances of the new concept can be found, or made in the case of invention. Therefore, the prediction motive is the underlying cause of discovery and invention; and conceptualization is the beginning of the procedure.

The contention that environmental stimulation causes all behavior is not tenable.

Finally, as we indicated earlier, boredom fosters discovery and invention because boredom initiates excursions into novel and unfamiliar areas.

Correspondence in Matching

In the matching process, a match is made on the basis of correspondence. The closer the correspondence between events and neuroprints, or between two neuroprints, the more probable it is that a match will occur between them. Correspondence is sought on two dimensions of the idea hierarchy, which both contribute to the accuracy of prediction: the horizontal dimension and the vertical dimension. Achieving correspondence on the horizontal dimension contributes to *validity* of the match. Achieving correspondence on the vertical dimension contributes to the *precision* of the match.

Precision involves the tightness of fit or degree of detail of the match. Greater precisions can be achieved at lower levels of the idea hierarchy. Therefore, if a match can occur at a lower level it will tend to be made there. The fact that greater correspondence can be achieved at lower levels of the idea hierarchy can be illustrated by comparing an image with a concept. An image represents a specific event in detail, whereas a concept is a more general representation. It corresponds to no one event in particular but to the general features of a class or category of events. It is as if an image was a key that was made to fit a specific lock in every detail, whereas a concept was a master key, which fit a number of similar locks because it has a general profile that is common to all of them but fits none of the locks in every detail. Precision in the matching process seems to promote adaptation because a match for identification obtained at a lower level of the neuroprint hierarchy will probably lead to a more accurate prediction than a match achieved at a higher level.

Consider the following clarification of this point. First, the event is matched with a neuroprint at some level of the idea hierarchy in order for the event to be identified. If the event is matched at a lower level of the idea hierarchy, it will be identified in greater detail for the reasons given.

Second, in matching for prediction, the neuroprint representing the event is matched with a master neuroprint. If the neuroprint representing the event is on a lower level of the neuroprint hierarchy, it will be defined in greater detail. Therefore, it has the potential of fitting a master neuroprint in greater detail. For example, an image defines an event in greater detail than a concept and, consequently, when an image represents an event, it has the potential of matching a master neuroprint in greater detail when a match for prediction is attempted.

When a match for prediction is achieved in greater detail, there is a greater potential for predictive accuracy. This is because when there is greater correspondence, the prediction can be in a sense more specifically tailored for the event. For instance, if an item is matched for identification with an image of an apple, it is because an apple has been seen before. When the image of the apple is matched for prediction with a master neuroprint and as a result the apple is eaten, it is because apples have been eaten before. The prediction generated by the master neuroprint indicating that the apple will satisfy the individual's hunger, without serious side effects, most probably will prove to be accurate.

On the other hand, when an unfamiliar object is matched for identification with the concept food and that concept is matched for prediction with the master neuroprint that governs the eating process, when the match is achieved and action is taken, there is less probability that the object will satisfy the individual's hunger, and a greater probability that the person will be poisoned.

Garner (1974) explains that more precise identifications are made as individuals are presented with clues that prompt them to be more discriminating. Present someone with the following card and that person will respond that it is the letter "B":

B

The stimulus calls for a general categorical identification. Afterward, if you show him the following card,

b

the individual will now say, "I see a small letter 'b' " or perhaps "a lower case 'b.'" The presentation of the second card requires more precision in identification and the person refers to a subcategory that includes only lower-case letters. If you then show a card with a very large lower-case "b" printed on it, the person might then say, "I see a large small 'b.' " This identification refers to a smaller subcategory which includes large lower-case b's. The more precise the identification of an object, the smaller the subset to which it is assigned.

Validity is another factor that contributes to the accuracy of prediction. The search for validity may be considered as horizontal movement across the categories of the idea hierarchy. As one moves across the horizontal dimension of the idea hierarchy, one encounters the categorization of different kinds of events. If in attempting to predict an event correspondence is not achieved along the horizontal dimension, then the resulting prediction will be inaccurate because the individual will not be predicting the prevailing event. That is, the resulting prediction would be invalid, therefore inaccurate, even if precision were achieved along the vertical dimension.

To clarify the point, in the previous example concerning the eating of food, it was said that an imprecise prediction could lead to the taking of poison. It also may be said that an invalid prediction could lead to the taking of poison. To explain, presumably poison and food would be categorized at different positions along the horizontal dimension. If the individual were attempting to acquire food, but a match was made within the category poison instead of within the category food, the resulting prediction would be invalid, therefore inaccurate, and the individual would be poisoned as a result.

Now that the distinction between validity and precision has been made, another example will clarify the relationship between the two. Suppose an individual were looking through a telescope attempting to make some prediction about the moon. If the person were indeed looking at the moon, the match would be valid. On the other hand, if Mars were being viewed, the match would be invalid, and the resulting prediction would also be invalid. Now, suppose the individual were making a valid match by focusing on the moon, but the telescope were out of focus, yielding a fuzzy, unclear view of the moon. The match would be imprecise, and the resulting prediction would tend to be inaccurate because of the imprecision of the match.

So it can be seen that both validity and precision contribute to the accuracy of prediction. If a match is invalid, it matters not how precise it may be because the wrong event is being predicted. If a match is imprecise, there is not tightness of fit. This lack of correspondence also will affect the accuracy of prediction. This interpretation is consistent with the scientific interpretation of accuracy.

There is a second, subordinate factor that determines whether a neuroprint will be selected when one neuroprint is matched with another or a neuroprint is matched with an event. That is the prediction of the satisfaction of one's interests. Accuracy of prediction is superordinate in the selection process because predictions must be accurate to be confirmed, and they must be confirmed to satisfy the basic prediction motive. Predictions must also be accurate to satisfy one's interests.

The behavior of young children, typically, is governed by automatic thought. They react impulsively, prompted by instincts and habits. As they grow older and more concepts form as a result of learning, their idea hierarchies expand and they are better able to predict through the deliberation of concepts. Kuhn and Phelps (1976) demonstrated that competence in distinguishing causal direction—certainly prerequisite to prediction—is acquired rapidly during the sixth year. In order to predict accurately and efficiently through deliberation, children should learn first to seek a valid match for identification at the highest possible level of an idea hierarchy. They should seek a match at the highest level first because if they do not find a valid match there, they will not find a valid match at any lower level. For instance, if an item does not meet the criteria of the general abstraction *food,* it will not be identified as a particular type of food on a lower level of the idea hierarchy. Ashcraft and Kellas (1974) showed how retention of categorized photos is enhanced when children are given clustering instructions; but even with such instructions, comparable (with regard to mental age) retarded children were unable to benefit from the instructions and responded randomly. Noninstructed normal children seemed to be acquiring the strategy by themselves (see Kellas, Ashcraft, and Johnson 1973).

Second, children should learn that a match for validity should be made before they match for precision. If a valid match cannot be achieved, then precision is of little consequence. If an item is incorrectly identified as food instead of poison, increased precision will not compensate for the mistake. To make a valid match, the individual must know the necessary and sufficient criteria for including items in abstraction categories.

After a valid match is achieved at the highest level of the idea hierarchy, individuals should learn to work down the hierarchy to increase the precision of the match. They should learn that more accurate predictions can be made about an animal, for example, if it is identified more specifically as a bear at a lower level of the idea hierarchy, than more generally as an animal at a higher level of the hierarchy.

Deliberation and Mental Process

Deliberation has been discussed at length in chapters 6 and 7. We now consider the mental processes involved in deliberation.

As long as optimum predictability is not violated, the servoprogram (described at the beginning of chapter 6) will match neuroprints and events automatically requiring little, if any, attention on the part of individuals. The mode of thought will be automatic. When optimum predictability is violated and boredom or confusion occurs, denoting a psychological problem, the servoprogram triggers the arousal mechanism and a search for an image of the initiating event is begun automatically. This is an attempt to match for the identification of the initiating event. If an image is not elicited, then the servoprogram automatically directs mental process to find a match between the initiating event and a concept. As noted, a match is sought with an image first because images permit more precise identifications that result in more accurate identifications.

If an image or concept of the event is elicited, individuals become aware of the event and their interest in confirming the prediction that the attendant boredom or confusion will be relieved. If the event is identified by a concept, then, in search of greater precision in matching, an attempt will be made to identify the event as a member of a subconcept category and such membership is deliberated. For instance, if the initiating event is identified first as an animal, deliberation will ensue to determine what type of animal it is. In preparation for the effort required in deliberation, the activation function is elicited, arousal is reduced, and concentration is heightened.

Once a match for identification is made, the servoprogram directs a match for prediction to find a match between the image or concept representing the interest and a master neuroprint indicating the means of satisfying the interest. In pursuit of precision, a match is sought first with a master-neuroprint image. If a match is found, action is taken to test the prediction that the master-neuroprint image will lead to satisfaction of the interest. If a match is not found, then a match is sought with a master-neuroprint concept.

If a match is found with a master-neuroprint concept, the activation mechanism is engaged, arousal is reduced, and concentration is heightened in preparation for the mental effort needed in the coming deliberation. The master-neuroprint concept contains goal and program images associated with the satisfaction of the interest. Deliberation involves selecting or composing a master-neuroprint image from the content of the master-neuroprint concept that will lead to the satisfaction of the interest. Again, precision is sought to maximize the probability that the interest will be satisfied. However, attainability of goals as well as the desirability of pursuing goals by means of particular programs is considered in selecting a preferred master-neuroprint image.

When a preferred master-neuroprint image is selected it is tested as an hypothesis to determine if it satisfies the interest. If not, another preferred master-neuroprint image would be selected from the master-neuroprint concept, after further deliberation based on feedback from the previous trial. This procedure of sampling and testing preferred master-neuroprint images from the master-neuroprint concept may be continued until the interest is satisfied and the boredom or confusion is relieved (see Levine 1974).

On the other hand, if a match for the identification of the initiating event of interest is not found, an image or concept of it could not be brought to mind. In this case the servoprogram would switch mental process to the memorization mode and a search would be made for the initiating event. It would be identifiable as the source of the boredom or confusion. If it were located it would be memorized, an image of it would form, and it subsequently could be identified.

Also, if an image or concept of the event of interest is elicited, but in matching for prediction a match with a master-neuroprint image or concept is not made, the interest cannot be satisfied. In this case, too, the servo-program would switch mental process to the memorization mode to find a way to satisfy the interest.

The memorization mode involves a predisposition to learn the source of the boredom or confusion, if an identification of it cannot be made. Or, if an identification of the source can be made but there is no known way to predict relief, then there is a predisposition to learn a master-neuroprint image that indicates a way to find relief.

Deliberation involves both the deliberation of alternatives and memorizing. Both thought modes require prolonged concentration when compared to automatic thought.

Note

1. The procedures for systems and task analysis are described by Corrigan and associates in their manual, *Systems Analysis for Education (SAFE),* and in books written by Leslie Briggs (see Briggs, L. *Sequencing of Instruction in Relation to Hierarchies of Competence.* Palo Alto, Calif.: American Institutes for Research, 1968).

9 Defensiveness

In the preceding chapters dealing with mental process, the focus was on thought directed toward making and confirming specific predictions in an effort to relieve boredom and confusion. However, there are times when boredom and confusion are not overcome by deliberating events. Either individuals are not aware of the source of their boredom or confusion, or they are not aware of a satisfactory way to find relief, or they cannot deliberate all of the boring or confusing events confronting them at the time. The individuals are overwhelmed. Under such stressful conditions, defensiveness is engaged to overcome boredom or confusion. The purpose of defensiveness is to relieve mental stress so that the individual may maintain a predictable relationship with the environment and make specific predictions effectively.

Defensiveness is a type of compensatory reaction to too much or too little predictability. *Defensiveness* is the shutting out of environmental stimulation for the purpose of maintaining or restoring predictability.

Individuals' desire to improve their ability to predict prompts them to face the events they can manage. However, when they cannot manage events and mental stress becomes excessive, defensiveness is engaged.

Most of us are aware that we have a tendency to deal with traumatic experiences by shutting them out of our minds. The children who are being told something they do not wish to hear may say, "Don't tell me that," or may cover their ears with their hands to shut out the distasteful message. A wife may refuse to talk with her husband about an upsetting day at the office because she wants to forget it.

Pribram's (1967) view of defensiveness is a similar one. He states that "the clinical and experimental literature is replete with examples of preparatory processes. Concepts such as 'repression,' 'suppression,' and 'perceptual defense mechanisms' can be interpreted as preparatory processes for they are forms of defensive 'gating out,' that is, ignoring or repudiating those aspects of the situation that initiated the disruptive emotional state" (p. 36).

Festinger holds a compatible view. In discussing how individuals deal with cognitive dissonance, Festinger (1957) suggests that cognitive dissonance is psychologically uncomfortable and that one way to deal with a dissonant experience is to ignore it or shut it out.

In addition to theoretical positions that support our definition of defensiveness, there is some neurophysiological evidence that attentional processes include a capacity to block out disruptive stimulation. Hernandez-Peon, Sherrer, and Jouret (1956) recorded the impulses from the auditory nerve of a cat as it was presented tone signals. The electric potentials from the nerve registered distinctly and corresponded accurately to the presence of the tone. Then the cat was presented with a distracting visual stimulus—a mouse. Under these conditions, presentation of the tone stimulated little or no activity in the auditory nerve of the cat. The auditory stimulus was screened out from the central nervous system. Broadbent (1958) concluded that attention must function as a sort of filter screening out unwanted signals. Bacon (1973) found that arousal narrows the range of cues processed by actually diminishing the subject's sensitivity.

There also is evidence that induced stress during an industrial task is accompanied by a shutting out of environmental cues from the worker's sphere of attention. Bursill (1958) found this to be true when stress was induced using heat as an environmental stressor. Hockey (1970a, 1970b) arrived at similar findings using noise as the stressor.

When there is too little predictability and individuals become defensive, they ignore the variable and novel events that are confusing to them. When there is too much predictability and individuals become defensive, they ignore the redundant and familiar events that are boring to them.

Defensiveness is adaptive in that it contributes to the maintenance of a predictable relationship with the environment by stabilizing mental process and, therefore, preparing the individual to make specific predictions effectively. On the other hand, defensiveness is maladaptive because in the process certain environmental stimuli are ignored. Thus defensiveness falsifies experience which in turn interferes with the individual's ability to predict events.

Carver, Coleman, and Glass (1976) found that coronary-prone patients put through a "tiring but challenging" physical test put forth more effort than noncoronary-prone groups, but subjectively related their fatigue as less. They hypothesize that the patients suppress their fatigue as an instrumental response for attaining mastery over the environment.

According to Veevers (1974), voluntary childless couples in his study perceived negative sanctions by society, but were able to remain unperturbed by adopting a varying world view that involved selective perception, differential association, reaffirmation of biases, and interpretation of disapproval as envy.

Chandler (1975) contends that adolescents who feel isolation and estrangement use abstract thinking—which they have just mastered, if one accepts the formal operations theory—to lop off awkward differences of opinion, accept an ironclad consensus with small peer groups, and impose an elegant if somewhat contrived consensus.

The effect of defensiveness on adaptation can be understood if we realize that it is necessary to maintain predictability before it is possible to predict specific events.

There are two general modes of defensive thought: thought directed toward the prevention of unpredictability and thought directed toward the restoration of predictability.

Preventive Defensiveness

Preventive defensiveness is initiated before arousal reaches the threshold level (mentioned in chapter 1), when we become disoriented and are unable to predict and negotiate the environment.

When too much predictability is anticipated, preventive defensiveness involves ignoring familiar events, which have become monotonous, and pursuing novel events to escape boredom and prevent mental instability. For example, a person with a monotonous job may defensively attempt to escape boredom by ignoring the routine tasks being performed and seeking novelty in the environment. Filtering out the demands of the repetitive task to prevent the mental instability the worker anticipates falsifies events, which in turn increases the probability of an accident.

When too little predictability is anticipated, preventive defensiveness involves ignoring novel stimulation that has become confusing and pursuing familiar events that are readily predictable. Thus mental process is aimed at insuring that the next prediction is confirmed.

Suppose we have been thwarted in numerous love affairs. We would tend to predict that we will be thwarted in a subsequent affair. On the other hand, we prefer to be loved. According to prediction theory, if we anticipate unpredictability, that is, uncertainty about the outcome, we will arrange our relationship with the environment to confirm the prediction that we will be thwarted, even at the sacrifice of love and affection because we believe that this prediction (thwarting) will be confirmed. Perhaps we will become overpossessive or overaggressive because we anticipate the loss of love and affection once more. However, as a result, we are likely to confirm the prediction that we will be unloved in the future as we have been in the past. Thus we are able to maintain predictability at the expense of achieving love.

Preventive defensiveness against too little predictability leads to a vicious circle. Whenever the unpredictable stimulation emerges, defensive individuals try to prevent unpredictability at the expense of achieving their preferences. Consequently they learn neither to acquire their preferences nor to improve their ability to predict.

The programs employed in such preventive defensiveness are likely to represent primitive programs, which are remnants of early childhood, because primitive programs are well established and easy to execute success-fully. For this reason, such defensiveness is generally regressive in nature.

An interesting feature of preventive defensiveness is that it explains why some people are inclined toward failure. Because a prediction of failure is usually easier to confirm than a prediction of success, we may tend to predict failure and contribute to its achievement in order to confirm the prediction.

One way to exercise preventive defensiveness is to avoid contact with undesirable stimulation. Brayfield and Crockett (1955), in their review of the research on job satisfaction, concluded that job dissatisfaction was positively correlated with avoidance behavior such as tardiness and absenteeism. Herzberg et al. (1957) came to the same conclusion in their review of job-satisfaction literature. They concluded that there is a correla-tion between negative job attitude and both turnover and absenteeism, with some data showing that negative attitudes correlate with incidents and psychosomatic illness.

Restorative Defensiveness

When preventive efforts fail and unpredictability occurs for any extended period of time, we become disoriented and unable to negotiate the environ-ment. In addition, arousal will exceed the threshold level mentioned in chapter 1. In this state of mind we resort to defensive modes of thought to restore mental stability and our ability to predict and negotiate the environ-ment. Such defensive modes of thought are autistic—the individual tends to ignore external stimulation and resorts to an autonomous mode of restoring predictability.

We will define *autism* as an idea and/or program that operates divorced from environmental events. Following are examples of autism representing too little and too much predictability.

If we are aroused by hunger, for instance, and panic is induced before we can acquire food from the environment, we might suck our thumbs for temporary relief or fantasize about eating food. In the case of thumb suck-ing, the autistic mode represents the operation of a motor program, and fantasizing represents an ideational autistic mode. Both are examples of autism generated when there is too little predictability.

We have said that we are seldom placed in a situation in which too much predictability is so prolonged that our mental process becomes unstable and events become unpredictable. However, the Chinese water torture (the con-stant dripping of water on the individual's forehead) is an example of men-tal instability induced through monotonously redundant stimulation. Also, research that involves the imposition of monotonous white noise on subjects for extended periods provides insights into reactions on too much sameness.

Heron (1957) reports that individuals subjected to boring stimulation began to hallucinate and have impaired judgment. They also expressed tendencies toward belief in the supernatural. This research suggests that the defense against boredom may cause individuals to conjure mental images of novelty and variability.

We are hypothesizing that in the case of too little predictability autism would be directed toward creating familiar stimulation. In the case of too much predictability, autism would be directed toward the creation of novelty.

The point is that these types of autistic activities are means of restoring predictability without relying on the environment. In essence, what happens in this matching process is that a match for prediction is achieved between the neuroprint of the event inducing boredom or confusion and a master neuroprint that portrays a means of relieving the boredom or confusion autonomously. So, for example, when panic results because the individual is unable to get food from the environment, a master neuroprint may be elicited that directs thumb sucking or fantisizing about eating food.

It appears that all forms of autism attempt to restore mental stability so that the individual may again relate effectively to the environment. Autism, therefore, is adaptive; although, if an individual is in an extended state of autism, he or she is psychologically disturbed. This may be regarded as a prolonged desperate and final attempt to restore predictability and is therefore an attempt to adapt. It would also follow that while a disordered individual is in a psychotic episode, autism has not yet been effective in restoring predictability sufficiently to enable the individual to relate to the environment again.

Psychiatrists are not in agreement as to the causes of autism though the syndrome is well documented. It seems to occur in all parts of the world, at birth or shortly afterward, over a wide distribution of social class and personality factors (Ornitz and Rituo 1976).

Autism is a defense and the disorder it may generate may be regarded as defensive insanity. There is a type of insanity, however, that may be a result of defenselessness, resulting from the individual's inability to utilize defenses to stabilize mental process. It would be associated with a dysfunction of the defensive operation of the mind. Environmental input would be admitted indiscriminately and the individual would be unable to predict it.

Such mental reactions may be compared to the lens openings of a camera. When the individual is dealing with the total environment within the perceptual field, the lens opening is wide open and stimulation is selectively admitted. When preventive defensiveness is employed, the lens opening is partially closed and input is restricted and biased. When restorative defensiveness is used, the lens opening is closed and stimulation is shut out during these psychotic episodes. In the case of defenseless insanity, the lens opening does not adjust the input and stimulation is admitted indiscriminately.

Studies of the behavior of acute paranoid schizophrenics and chronic nonparanoid schizophrenics suggest that the latter exhibit defensive behavior while the former exhibit defenseless behavior. (However, this is by no means a settled matter.) McGhie and Chapman (1961) quote the experiences of acute schizophrenics as follows: "It's as if I am too wide awake—very alert. I can't relax at all. Everything seems to go through me. I just can't shut things out" (p. 104).

"Things are coming in too fast. I lose my grip of it and get lost" (p. 104).

In contrast, Broen (1973) describes chronic schizophrenic behavior as a defensive limiting of stimulus input. He states that "a life style dedicated to limiting stimulation is seen as a protective deficit—a defense that increases the likelihood of *chronic* inability to monitor the environment and adjust to its changing demands" (p. 189).

Studies comparing normal people with acute and chronic schizophrenics give evidence that chronic schizophrenics filter or shut out stimulation while normals and acute schizophrenics do not (Feeney 1971; Kristofferson 1967).

Defensiveness is maladaptive because it falsifies experience. Ignoring either novel or familiar stimulation prevents the individual from dealing with existing events. Any predictions made will be based on incomplete information and probably will be inaccurate.

The reason that primitive defenses based on too little predictability tend to become permanent is that when they are employed, the defensive reaction is automatic and subliminal and deliberation tends to be bypassed. We said that deliberation is employed to predict the unfamiliar. However, when a situation arises that generates defensiveness involving too little predictability, the novel aspects of the situation are not deliberated. They are shut out or ignored, and the most familiar elements of the situation are predicted automatically. Perhaps defensive modes of thought operate without awareness because, when deliberation is bypassed, the unfamiliar features of a defense-looking situation tend to be ignored repeatedly and, therefore, remain unpredictable.

In a sense, then, defensiveness short-circuits the adaptive complementary relationship between automatic and deliberate thought in which automatic thought is employed to predict familiar events and deliberate thought is employed to predict novel events. This is unfortunate because an unpredictable situation, which is traumatic for a child and results in automatic defensiveness, might easily be predicted in adulthood if the unfamiliar aspects of the situation could be deliberated.

The research of Kogan and Wallach (1964) shows that low-anxiety, low-defensive subjects are most situation sensitive. The researchers imply that these subjects deliberated to produce the predictions necessary to solve the problems confronting them. The subjects are termed *reflective risk-takers*.

Although early defensiveness tends to be automatic, once the individual matures and becomes artful at deliberation, deliberation can be used defensively. In defensive deliberation the individual avoids dealing with a problem by excessively considering alternative solutions and not making a selection. With maturity the individual gains mastery in predicting the environment, which in turn predisposes the person to encounter the same situations repeatedly. This development may lead to boredom and defensive deliberation. Moreover, when automatic defensiveness is used repeatedly, it becomes ritualized and contributes to boredom and the probable employment of defensive deliberation. The obsessive personality provides an example of defensive deliberation—the individual deliberates excessively, being afraid to act. When the individual does act the actions are as likely to be based on automatic thought as they are to be based on deliberations.

Young children cannot distinguish between the consequences of thought and action. They tend to feel that thinking about something bad has the same consequences as doing domething bad. However, action elicits consequences from the environment; thought does not. There need be only one consequence of thought and that is action.[1] The defensive individual is not able to deliberate effectively, is unable to consider the various possible consequences of actions before acting, and is unable to act in accordance with deliberations.

The more mature individual who has experienced deliberating effectively is able to preview events before deciding on a course of action and select a program to direct actions on the basis of deliberation. Such an individual would be aware that thought may precede and provide an effective basis for action.

Defensiveness was described as a part of the preparatory process in that it prepares the individual to predict and negotiate the environment. There are other mental states which are a part of the preparatory process but which do not falsify experience as defensiveness does. These include mental states of relaxation, such as sleep and reminiscing, that preserve mental stability by reducing fatigue and providing diversion from the work of conceiving and validating predictions. Reminiscing involves the review of past experiences as a pleasurable pasttime without the need to predict.

Note

1. It should be acknowledged that when an action is taken, the thought that led to the action may be considered in determining the consequences that shall be invoked for the act. For example, the consequences are more severe for premeditated murder than for unpremeditated murder.

10 Play and Games

An important influence in growing up is the learning that occurs through play and games. In both cases children learn relationships that enable them to make and test predictions to improve their ability to predict. Erikson (1950) said, "I propose the theory that the child's play is the infantile form of the human ability to deal with experience by creating model situations and to master reality by experiment and planning . . ." (p. 209).

In the earliest years, play is self-centered. Children explore the parts of the body to determine how they function and what they may do with them. Play varies from the manipulation of the head and trunk to the extension of the limbs, from which infants learn the relationship between one part of the body and another.

Soon children become able to understand that their environment is separate and apart from them and they begin exploring the objects in the crib and playpen. They may play with the bottle after their hunger has been satisfied sufficiently to allow room for less demanding impulses, such as interest and curiosity in the world around them. Between meals they may reach out and touch the side of the crib and grasp its bars, or they may investigate a toy or rattle that an adult has thoughtfully placed in the crib.

Cowell (1949) states that motor abilities are "highly related to the emotional feature of a child's behavior. Without participation in play and games, the child has few opportunities for experiencing thrills, risks, failure or success, which make for moral and mental health. From these experiences such mental factors as hope, confidence, zeal and sociability are derived" (pp. 198-199).

The concepts of risks, failures or success, moral and mental health, confidence, and so forth relate well to the theory under discussion. Kelly (1955) observes that an important development in peoples' lives is the ability to experiment, predict, and control events in order to find avenues for extending the range of one's construct systems. In childhood this is the function of play. "Play is adventure. Its outcomes are always veiled in some delightful uncertainty" (p. 998).

If children are nursed or cuddled when they are fed, they are able to explore the body of the mother and learn about the form of another person. Once they learn that they will be fed when the mother brings a bottle, they are able to predict the relationship and, in anticipation of being fed, may stop crying immediately upon being picked up.

The earliest evidence of the infant's ability to predict can be found in a review of the literature on mother-infant relationships among primates by Stone, Smith, and Murphy (1973). As early as four weeks, it appears the infant has learned to make eye-to-eye contact with the mother and has learned to predict what the mother will do next from observing her eyes. Bell (1970), in his discussion of the infant's understanding of the permanency of objects, gives evidence that the infant predicts the mother's return when the mother is absent, showing knowledge of her continued existence. Later the infant shows the same understanding of other objects.

Bower (1974) states that almost at birth infants engage in a swiping movement of arm and hand that brings them into contact with objects. As this movement becomes coordinated, the hand improves in its ability to grasp and hold. First, the hand opens in expectation of contact with an object and then the extent to which the hand is opened becomes adjusted to the size of the object.

In our culture when infants learn to sit up and crawl they are usually allowed to spend more time in the playpen and play with a greater variety of toys. The toys they are given initially challenges them to reach, grasp, hold on, and perhaps shape them. The second level of toys they get challenges them to do more. A toy car or truck familiarizes them with wheels and vehicular locomotion. They also get objects that teach them to distinguish sizes and shapes by challenging them to put pieces together and take them apart or to fit one thing into another.

In the early years, toys serve to provide concrete representations and examples of the words parents are trying to teach them. Although children learn language primarily by listening to adults and talking with them, using toys to illustrate the meaning of words facilitates the teaching of language. Showing a picture of an object to children may help them learn the meaning of a word that stands for the object. But a toy is a more helpful representation than a picture because, while children can only look at a picture, they can feel and manipulate a toy as well as look at it. Also, certain ideas and words can be more faithfully represented by pictures and toys than by natural examples. For instance, a square or a triangle can be illustrated better by a toy or a picture than in nature. (See Gramza 1976; Shotick et al. 1976; Dornbush and Winnick 1966; Etaugh and van Sickle 1971; and Falk 1968, for discussions on the relative merits of pictures and manipulative objects for young children.)

However, as children grow older, looking at pictures has certain advantages over playing with toys. More complex relationships can be shown in picture form. Sequences of pictures, such as the comics, tell stories about people and the things they encounter in their lives. This challenges the child to learn more about transitions in life over time, as events change over time in the stories, and, the learning of transitions and trends enhances prediction.

Toys are becoming increasingly varied and ingenious. Even though some of them perpetuate violence and are otherwise detrimental, others are becoming more instructive and better correlated with the development of the child. They help children learn music, tell time, build things, and improve their coordination.

Eichorn (1973) summarizes three important longitudinal studies on intellectual outcomes of childrearing practices. The studies were The Berkeley Growth Study, The Guidance Study, and The Oakland Growth Study. These studies followed subjects from early childhood into adulthood, and the results show that spontaneous interaction of children with toys and play facilities has a substantial effect on their intellectual growth. The effects become especially evident in adolescence and adulthood.

Dolls provide an unusual opportunity for children to learn human relations by pretending their dolls are people and using the dolls to act out their understanding of the way people relate to each other. Playing house is an example in which family relations are acted out.

As the children grow older, they become less involved with dolls and more involved in playing with people. As this happens unstructured play is replaced with a greater involvement in games. Seagoe (1971) surveyed 1,650 children in the United States, Norway, England, Spain, Greece, and Egypt and found in all societies except Greece (due, she conjectures, to political upheavals) a positive relation between age and play socialization.

Games require a more formal and controlled interaction among people and objects because games are played in pursuit of some specified goal according to prescribed rules. A *rule* is a program that specifies appropriate behavior. In order to play the game, children must learn the rules and how to pursue the goal according to the rules. The transition from play to games is rather subtle and gradual because in playing with a complex toy the child must follow an orderly procedure to get the toy to work even though rules for operating the toy are not explicitly stated. For example, in order to operate a phonograph, children must follow certain procedures in a prescribed sequence, which they are usually taught by an adult. Thus, in some play, rules must be followed although they tend to be implicit rather than explicit. Regarding the transition from play to games, Bettelheim (1972) has observed that depending on a child's success with a game and that child's needs of that moment, a child will alternate between the "rigidity" of games and the laissez faire of unstructured play. For example, a child may be happy playing "by the rules" as long as winning, but may toss those rules aside when the complexities of them result in losing.

One view of play therapy suggests that it is a process in which the psychotherapist first makes events more predictable for the clients and then teaches the clients how to make things more predictable for themselves. As stated in the *Langly Poster Child Psychiatry Series* (Szurek and Berlin 1969):

One individual may control the behavior of another in a way that benefits both. If inner controls are chronically unreliable, as in chronic offenders, the application of consistently reliable controls are adopted by the offender himself because he learns that they help him to feel better and to live better. Controls from without become converted to controls from within. Thus, an important integrated learning experience occurs. The modification in behavior is not the result of fear of consequences, a dubious deterrant; nor does the individual feel coerced. Destructive behavior simply becomes less necessary when it is perceived as a futile effort to escape from internal turmoil. (p. 66)

Thus, when applied to therapy, the therapist can aid in control of alternatives until the client takes over. If the counselor encourages the confused client to choose more predictable activities, the predictability of the environment is being controlled to reduce confusion. The counselor may have to make suggestions as to what activities appear confusing and unpredictable for the client at first. Hopefully the client can then apply the same principles of predictability alone.

In true games such as chess, cards, Monopoly® , and charades the rules and goal of the game are explicitly stated and individuals must learn them before they begin to play. Some games can be played alone, such as solitary card games and crossword puzzles. However, most games involve a number of people in competition with each other.

Most sports are games. Football, baseball, basketball, and the like require goals to be pursued according to specified rules.

The popularity of game shows on radio and television is evidence of our interest in games. In most cases the contestant is attempting to guess or predict the right answer and we observers are attempting to outpredict the contestants. In one television game ("The Price Is Right") the contestants attempt to predict the price of various commodities. In another game ("Hollywood Squares") the contestant must decide whether the answer given by a celebrity is right or wrong.

Although games may be considered recreational, they include many ingredients of real life and in that sense they represent rehearsals for living. In any society citizens are required to regulate their behavior according to prescribed rules, which we call laws. Gamesmanship in life involves the pursuit of goals within the confines of the legal structure of the society. If the rules or laws are violated, the violaters may be penalized or expelled from the game. They may be fined or put in jail. Thus there is a remarkable similarity between playing recreational games and gamesmanship in life.

Bettelheim (1972) has pointed out that chess is a game that can symbolically teach us to recognize our own stance in society while showing consideration and respect for those around us. It is said that, fully recognizing his stance in society, Napoleon, a notoriously bad chess player, used to suspend the rules to allow himself to win a game. Or, perhaps, he was merely applying the rules of true warfare more realistically than anyone else.

A most beneficial aspect of games is that in defining rules of conduct they prescribe an orderly relationship for the actions of the participants. Because learning relationships is the basis for making predictions, games provide a singular opportunity for individuals to improve their ability to predict. Once people learn the rules and goal of a game, they know how they must act to win. In playing the game they can conceive and test their predictions in an effort to win more often.

The review of research by Seidner (Gage 1976) shows quite clearly that games and simulations that are organized to provide optimum predictability for students and involve them in making and testing predictions generate high student involvement in the learning task. And high involvement in the learning task increases learning. Optimum predictability in this case refers to organizing the game to provide the players with a situation that is familiar enough to be understandable and manageable, yet novel and challenging to them. Underachievers especially showed a marked increase in involvement. *Underachievers* have been traditionally defined as those students with necessary cognitive skills for achievement but who do not become sufficiently involved in the activities of the classroom and subject matter tasks to master them.

One reason we seem to organize activities according to rules, whether in recreation or more serious purposes, is to bring order and avoid chaos. In real life, events tend to be highly variable and random. By organizing activities according to rules we define relationships which in turn makes events more predictable. The whole fabric of society rests on the need for one person to be able to predict the actions of another. Without this there could be no cooperation or sharing among people.

Unfortunately, in defining rules of conduct, we are inclined to over-simplify relationships, thereby making them unrealistic. For recreational purposes, we can make the rules of a game as simple as we like so that the players may not be unduly tormented as they try to predict the actions of participants. In real life, however, if we oversimplify the rules of conduct for the members of a society, it will not permit the degree of flexibility that is required to conduct the variety of affairs that life requires.

For instance, in sports such as football, baseball, and hockey, the rules of the game regulate the activities of the players. It is easy to distinguish one team from the other by the different uniforms they wear and determine who is winning and who is losing because it is relatively easy to keep score. Moreover, in any given tournament the rules are arranged so that there can be only one winner. As a result, both the players and the observers can understand what is happening and the predictions that are required.

However, we seem to have tried to apply the rules of games such as football and hockey inappropriately to real-life situations. A notable example is war. It appears that war strategy was conceived as a game and that those who were involved in wars played them as if they were team sports. Each side wore a different uniform so that it was easy to distinguish friend from foe. Battle lines were formed, and it was the strategy of the game to drive the enemy into retreat until he was forced to surrender. This made it simple to tell who the winners and losers were.

In recent years, since guerrilla warfare has become more prevalent, as in Viet Nam, the character of warfare has changed. It is more difficult to distinguish one's allies from one's enemies because uniforms are less distinct and battle lines are less prominent. As battle lines became less distinct, the capture of territory in itself could no longer be used as a sign of advancement or victory. Thus, in Viet Nam for example, they began counting the bodies of dead enemies as a sign of victory. However, this became confusing because it was not only difficult to distinguish friend from foe but to tell civilians from soldiers. Robert Thompson (1969), an expert on guerrilla warfare, states that, "It is interesting to note . . . that the line of advance in 'Peoples' Revolutionary War' is exactly opposite to what it would be in conventional war" (p. 34).

To add to the dilemma, there has been a growing apprehension of intimidating the enemy in any way that might spread the war and make the use of atomic weapons more likely. This, of course, places a restraint on forcing an enemy into surrender. But if you cannot force an enemy to surrender, how can you determine that you have won the war?

Another problem with applying the rules of classic war gamesmanship to modern warfare is that it is difficult to determine what the loser has lost and what the winner has won. In olden days "to the victor belong the spoils." The victor subjugated the loser and ravaged the loser's territory. In modern warfare there seems to be some obligation for the victor to contribute to the rehabilitation of the loser. The movie "The Mouse That Roared" was about a small country that tried to declare war on the United States so that it might lose and demand reparations. Looking at our World War II enemies, Germany and Japan, it is hard to determine now what they lost in the war—they are two of the most economically powerful countries in the world. It is even harder to tell what we won from them.

There is obviously order in the universe and this permits us to make predictions about events. There also seems to be reason to create order in the universe by establishing rules of conduct so that people may live in peace and cooperate for their mutual benefit. On the other hand, it is of no benefit to create rules that overregulate conduct. This simply gives the impression of orderliness when in fact the circumstances being regulated are not nearly so orderly.

We seem to have a need to organize to make things more predictable for ourselves. However, if we try to overorganize relationships, we are being unnecessarily restrictive and actually falsifying reality. For instance, the activities of children can be regulated realistically within limits. If we establish too many rules for them, they will not be able to follow them and we will be promoting insubordination and delinquency. We must pay attention to the rules we invoke and make sure that they are realistic. Bettelheim (1972) has stated that if children were allowed to participate fully in "childish" fantasy, "they would not feel compelled later to attempt to recover and re-enact their lost childhood through drugs. . . . In earlier times when adults were partners in play with their children, no generation gap could be revived in adolescence simply because it had not previously existed in childhood" (p. 3).

Our need to organize experience into gamelike structures in order to make life more predictable may be responsible for a great many of our social problems. This is especially true when we create "sides" as we do in team sports. Our compulsion to stipulate who is friend and who is foe may be responsible for many of our prejudices. We seem to organize the world by boundaries and regulations. On one hand, there are those who are like us, the "good guys," who look like us, act like us, and dress like us. We refer to them kindly. Then there are those who are not like us, the "bad guys," who do not look like us, act like us, or dress like us. We refer to them unkindly. Soon we become concerned about their influence on us, which we feel we must restrict lest be become like them. We begin to defend ourselves against them, restrict our association with them, and attempt to triumph over them. We claim that "right" is on our side and that we must prevent them from turning good guys like us into bad guys like them.

It may be all right to fill this psychological need for order that we seem to have through our participation in and identification with team sports, but to try to fit reality into unrealistic, tight organizations is to falsify experience. In essence, although this penchant is an attempt to increase predictability, it does not. It falsifies events by oversimplifying them and therefore making them less predictable. In this rapidly changing world, we must learn to live with ambiguity and novelty without regarding them as threats. It is in learning to live with and predict the unfamiliar that we gain self-confidence and security and improve our ability to predict.

Michener (1976) feels that we are guilty of oversimplifying real-life situations with sports and gaming concepts. He points to our use of sports and gaming phrases, such as referring to the president of the United States as "the quarterback" and to his advisors as "the team," when we discuss such important events as war.

When individuals find themselves in an unfamiliar milieu, they generally are impelled to test the situation to improve their ability to predict. For instance, suppose a child is told by the parents that a new babysitter is coming. It is most common for the child to test the babysitter in order to find out the constraints and allowances the babysitter will permit. After all, to feel secure in the care of the babysitter, the child must be able to predict that the sitter is able to manage the situation.

Play and games provide the opportunity for individuals to test their relationship with the environment, usually without dire consequences. It is safe to be a loser in games. On one hand, we tell children who become overzealous in a game to "calm down; it's only a game." On the other hand, it is important to realize that play and games are rehearsals for life and that success in life is related to success in play and games. The problem is that in our society success is defined as winning. From the present theoretical position *success* is defined as learning to predict accurately. If you can predict accurately, you can win or lose as you choose; and it is possible for a person to prefer to lose. For example, a mother playing checkers with her young daughter may prefer on occasion to lose to her daughter.

Prediction theory enhances our understanding of play and games, a pervasive aspect of human behavior. Prediction theory explains that people become involved in play and games to satisfy their interests in predicting and improving their ability to predict. For the young, play and games provide a means of developing their ability to predict under safe conditions, as they learn and prepare for the responsibilities and risks of the adult world. Adults continue to play games because predicting without serious risk is recreation, and while having fun, they can hone their predictive powers.

Play and games also provide respite for either boredom or confusion. Bored individuals can find challenge in games. Games such as bridge and chess challenge the predictive abilities of the most intelligent persons. If individuals get bored with a game they have been playing for a long time, they can learn a new game.

People who are confused by the contingencies and unpredictability in their social or work life can find relief in play and games. They can choose to play a simple game which they are thoroughly familiar with. They can feel secure because most occurrences in the game are predictable to them, even if they should happen to lose. In addition, people reduce the confusion inherent in the exigencies of daily living by organizing activity into gamelike structures. They bring order and regularity into life by prescribing rules of human conduct.

So, it appears that prediction theory provides a cogent explanation of why people spend so much of their time engaging in play and games.

Part II
The Group

In part I we posited the basic assumption of prediction theory that individuals are primarily motivated to predict their relationship with the environment. We explained that the pursuit of preferences is a secondary motive because it is necessary to maintain a predictable relationship with the environment to acquire one's preferences, whatever they may be at the moment. Part I was devoted to the explanation of the behavior of individuals from the perspective of prediction theory.

In part II we will apply prediction theory to the explanation of groups. We will explain that groups form and are maintained to satisfy the prediction motive. That is, people form and maintain groups primarily because group membership improves predictability in general and facilitates the confirmation of particular predictions of interest at the moment.

In chapter 11 the nature of social groups and social rules are explained from the perspective of prediction theory. Chapter 12 explains how three basic types of social rules—rules of language, rules defining group values, and rules defining group status—are interpreted in terms of prediction theory. Then chapters 13, 14, and 15 deal with group interactions. Chapter 13 considers the relationship between the group as an entity and its members; chapter 14, the relationship among group members, and chapter 15, the relationship among groups. We propose to show that for both intragroup dynamics and intergroup dynamics prediction theory offers a fresh and convincing explanation of group behavior.

As we proceed, we will discuss fundamental social issues and relate them to prediction theory. However, we will not probe social issues in depth—only to the extent necessary to elaborate prediction theory.

11 The Social Group

In this chapter we will attempt to establish the nature of social groups as viewed from the vantage point of prediction theory. We begin by building on our discussion of rules in chapter 10.

In chapter 10 we defined a *rule* as a program that specifies appropriate behavior. Because a rule is a program, it facilitates prediction. You will remember in chapter 4 we defined programs as neuroprints that represent sequences of activities. We indicated further that programs are the mental equipment for making predictions because predictions are inherent in them. They describe if-this-then-that relationships and prompt individuals to predict when this occurs that will follow. Because rules are a type of program, rules facilitate prediction.

There are two kinds of rules that can be distinguished—personal rules and social rules. A *personal rule* refers to an individual's opinion of appropriate behavior. For instance, a person may believe that the program for brushing one's teeth should be executed twice daily. Personal rules may be publicly disseminated. Such is the case when a person publishes a book of recipes.

A *social rule* is a rule of public record that has been created through social agreement. Social rules are concepts that exist by virtue of social agreement. When a group of people agree to define appropriate behavior in a certain way for themselves and publicly record it, a social rule has been created and a group norm has been established. The Ten Commandments, civil laws, and the Boy Scout motto "Be Prepared" are examples of social rules. Arithmetic is a social rule for dealing with numbers, and music as a discipline has social rules for writing and playing musical compositions. Social rules, then, are agreed upon directions for programming behavior and, as such, are public consensual manifestations of programs.

Social rules also are concepts. Humans use symbols to represent complex categories or types of things, define the criteria for inclusion in the concept category, and disseminate the definitions among group members through public records so that the group has common references to classes of items. Dictionaries, encyclopedias, and textbooks are examples of how humans standardize, record, and disseminate references for members of their groups. Most words are symbols for concept categories, and the definitions in the dictionary provide criteria for inclusion in the categories that a word symbolizes. This will be elaborated in chapter 12.

Sherif (1966) tells us that there is considerable evidence from research that concepts have a categorizing effect. He states that language produces the highly organized character of human perceptions.

Social rules are concepts because they express appropriate or inappropriate types of conduct. The biblical rule, "Thou shalt not kill," is a statement indicating that a class or type of behavior is wrong. Similarly, arithmetic rules are rules for dealing with a class of things we call numbers. Rules of grammar govern the way we deal with the class of items we call words.

All programs facilitate prediction; therefore, all rules facilitate prediction. Personal rules enable people to routinize their lives making their lives more predictable to themselves and to others who are aware of the personal rules that are followed. However, social rules enhance predictability even more because social rules are the foundation of social groups, and within social groups people are more predictable to one another.

A *social group* consists of people who accept the same social rules and expect conformity to the social rules. The acceptance and expectation of conformity to the group's social rules makes it more probable that group members will behave as the social rules specify. As a result, group members become more predictable to one another. Group membership enhances predictability for another reason. Group rules standardize behavior. Therefore, members of a group are more likely to behave the same way under the same conditions. For instance, Americans can be expected to stand and salute the American flag when it passes by. Thus rules enhance prediction. Social rules adopted by social groups enhance prediction even more.

Social rules become public when group members mutually agree upon them and adopt them as modes of appropriate behavior. Social rules are publicly disseminated through language; they are expressed both in writing and orally. In either event, they are of public record and have an existence external to and independent of the existence of individual group members. It is because of the public recording of group rules that groups can endure despite the demise of individual group members.

The members of a social group may have created their rules or they may have inherited them from their ancestors. In either case, the current members accept the rules and expect conformity. In some groups conformity to group rules is voluntary while in other groups conformity is enforced.

Because social rules are disseminated to group members as specifications for appropriate behavior, the members tend to learn the rules as a guide for appropriate behavior. Conformity is encouraged when arrangements are made to teach formally the group's rules to the members. This ensures dissemination of the rules and emphasizes the importance of conforming to the rules. Conformity is ensured further when the group enforces its rules. The teaching and enforcement of rules by the group along with the members' dependence on the group for the confirmation of their predictions ensure that group members will conform to group rules.

The vital function of social rules for group cohesion has been recognized since the beginning of sociological writing. Emile Durkheim, who is commonly credited with being one of the founders of modern sociology, wrote about social rules as early at 1895 when, in his *The Rules of Sociological Method* (1938), he defined a *social fact* (rule) as ". . . every way of acting, fixed or not, capable of exercising on the individual an external constraint; or again, every way of acting which is general throughout a given society while at the same time existing in its own right independent of its individual manifestations" (p. 13).

Durkheim was not the only sociologist who emphasized rules. The founder of American sociology, W. Graham Sumner, in his classic work *Folkways* (1940), deals with the importance of written and unwritten rules of behavior, through his exploration of the folkways and mores that underlie society. He states that the interests of people in groups are served most by folkways.

Another of Sumner's works *The Science of Sociology* (1946), while dealing with how folkways become mores, explicitly expounds the importance of rules. He says that people believe certain folkways are indispensable once they have practiced them for an extended period of time. Sumner and Durkheim are concerned with how these rules come into being, starting from a large number of individual actions satisfying individual interests and moving toward greater consensus and coercive force.

Another of the pioneers of sociology who was concerned with the same process was Max Weber. In his outline of interpretive sociology *Economy and Sociology* (1968), he explains how an informal rule, which he calls a *custom,* becomes formalized. First, he explains that custom can be differentiated from both law and convention. A *custom* is a rule that has no external sanction. The transition from a custom to an enforced and valid convention to a law is a gradual one.

The importance of rules to the social group is firmly entrenched in the field of sociology. It is mentioned prominently in most introductory sociology texts. Everett Wilson (1966), in his text *Sociology: Rules, and Relationships,* describes rules as the cultural matrix of society. Paul Sites (1975) in his book *Control and Constraint: An Introduction to Sociology,* defines *culture* in terms of the tools used by society to control the behavior of its members and the agreed on rules for the use of these tools. Most of the cultural tools are either rules, in our terms, or other concepts such as roles and status which are essentially defined by rules. In another text (Cuber 1968) the importance of rules to the understanding of how individual behavior is interrelated with the behavior of others is made most explicit.

Having defined a group as people who accept the same social rules and expect conformity to them, let us explore in the remainder of this book how group memberships influence human behavior. That is, we will attempt to determine how people who share common rules of conduct relate to each other.

Others have distinguished types of groups and discussed how members of different types of groups relate to each other in distinct ways. We will focus on what all groups have in common and how sharing common rules influences human behavior in general. To understand group behavior we must determine first how membership in any group affects behavior. Once we understand the fundamentals of group behavior, we can become more definitive by exploring how memberships in different types of groups affect behavior differentially.

In science we search for laws that are broadly generalizable if not universally applicable. This attempt to identify the most basic elements in all social groups is an effort to find the roots of social influence that are generalizable to all human groups.

This approach will allow us to draw examples and research from different social disciplines, such as sociology, business, and political science, in search of a basic understanding of groups. We will discuss intergroup behavior only to determine how groups with differing rules interact, regardless of how the rules differ. Hereafter, we will use the term *group* to refer to the social group.

Let us begin by delving into the enforcement of rules.

Some enforcement of rules is informal; a mother may reprimand her child for violating a rule. Enforcement may also be formal. Rules may be established defining appropriate conduct, and a group official may be selected to enforce the rules. For instance, rules are established specifying traffic violations—policemen give tickets to people who violate these rules and the violator is punished.

Sherif (1966) says that ". . . we find that an important difference between groups distinguished as to their solidarity is the extent to which the membership actively participates in correctives for deviating behavior" (p. 179). Sumner (1946) suggests that the enforcement of rules can be formal or informal, and positive or negative, as follows.

	Formal	*Informal*
Positive	Nobel Peace Prize	Teacher orally praises
	Letter of recommendation	student's deportment
	B+ grade on report card	Boss says to employee,
	Pay	"Keep up the good work."
Negative	Speeding ticket	Ridicule
	"Pink slip" indicating that	Gossip
	employment is terminated	Oral reprimand

Social rules must be disseminated and enforced to affect the lives of group members. When they are enforced, social force is exerted because there are consequences for violating the rules. On the other hand, physical forces provide their own consequences. When children are burned, they understand the harmful consequences of playing with fire; when they see a tree uprooted by a strong turbulent wind, they witness a consequence of wind. The laws of nature enforce their own consequences. Social rules have no consequences unless they are enforced by the group.

However enforcement takes place, what is crucial is that it does take place. As Weber (1968) wrote, ". . . the means of coercion are irrelevant. Even a 'brotherly admonition' is law provided it is regulated by some order and applied by a staff" (p. 10). As Durkheim (1938) points out, a social rule (or fact, as he calls it) is recognized by the coercive power it can exercise over people.

Social rules exert force only in the groups that adopt and enforce them. For example, traditional Japanese people are compelled to remove their shoes before entering a dwelling; occidentals are not. On the other hand, Japanese men and women use a common public restroom, much to the dismay of the American tourist on a first trip to Japan.

When the consequences for violating a rule are known to be the same for every member of the group, the members will probably regard the treatment they receive for a violation as impartial and fair. Consequently they will be less likely to rebel when they violate a rule and the rule is enforced. If the fine for parking in a no-parking zone is the same for everyone, violators will be inclined to regard the fine as just. However, if rules are not impartially enforced, violators will regard the punishment they receive for a violation as arbitrary and perhaps tyrannical, and their allegiance to the group will be strained. The impartial enforcement of rules, therefore, contributes to group solidarity and members are prone to support social fairness.

Minority groups complain about the lack of fairness when equal-opportunity laws allowing them access to group opportunities are not enforced in their behalf. Because equal opportunity is a rule for the group, the group as a whole tends to regard the minority group's complaint as legitimate when evidence of the injustice is provided. The group will tend to act to remedy the injustice.

Homans's (1974) statements about "distributive justice" are compatible with our description of fairness. According to Homans, distributive justice pertains to a norm-reference of fair exchange within the group. The group establishes norms of fairness and enforces these norms. Blau (1964) also makes reference to fairness in the treatment of group members. He indicates that social norms demand fair exchange and that third parties in a community will disapprove of unfair treatment of group members.

The need to enforce rules is reduced to the extent that the group members know the rules and are inclined to abide by them. The group facilitates conformity by teaching its rules to the young members and convincing them that conformity to the rules is in their personal interest, as well as in the best interest of the group as a whole. When rules are internalized and endorsed there is increased likelihood that the members will conform to them voluntarily. It is characteristic of social groups to teach their rules to the young, thereby transmitting their culture from generation to generation. This end becomes one of society's main purposes.

It was said that individuals are primarily motivated to predict their relationship with the environment and secondarily motivated to pursue their preferences. Prediction is the primary motive because it is necessary to be able to predict in order to pursue one's preferences, whatever they may be.

It can now be said that people form groups because groups enhance their ability to predict and satisfy their preferences, human interaction being about "mutual confirmation and disconfirmation" (Reason 1980, p. 3). The group enhances the members' ability to predict because in living by common rules of conduct, the behavior of the members becomes more predictable. In addition, one member can help another confirm predictions and improve the ability to predict. As is pointed out by Steiner (1966), the group imputes superiority to individual members because one member may possess resources that other members do not possess. In combination, these resources are more able to produce confirmed predictions.

Group associations are used to deal with confusion and boredom. When members are confused they will solicit the aid of other members to help make events more predictable. When they are bored they will pursue novelty through their associations with other group members.

Group membership also makes it more likely that the individuals will attain their preferences. Individuals can confirm more predictions that they are interested in confirming by cooperating with other group members than by foraging on their own.

The prediction motive is also more universal than the inclination to pursue one's interests—all groups and individuals are motivated to improve their ability to predict. Interests vary from individual to individual and for the same individual from time to time. For example, a hungry individual desires food but when satisfied has other preferences.

In chapter 3 we cited evidence (Levine 1959) showing the importance of hypothesis testing in human problem solving, and, of course, hypothesis testing involves risk taking. There is evidence that group participation increases an individual's willingness to take risks. Clark (1971) found that "individuals advocate greater degrees of risk taking following participation in a group than they had previously advocated privately" (p. 251).

It is important to realize that when we focus on the individual as an individual we tend to view people as selfish and acquisitive. Theories that posit desire as the primary motive describe people as selfishly striving to satisfy appetites. Even when you subscribe to the psychological motive posited in prediction theory, people must be viewed as selfish and acquisitive. The difference is that in prediction theory, people are, above all, selfishly trying to predict. Secondarily they are selfishly striving to satisfy their preferences, which may involve attempts to satisfy an appetite of the moment.

Once we consider the social dimension of human nature, we realize that membership in a social group improves the potential for prediction and the satisfaction of one's preferences. These advantages accrue because the group member learns the rules of the group. Consequently each member is able to share with other group members and they are all able to help each other satisfy motives.

Humans are capable of sophisticated social sharing because they create and live by rules. Newborn infants cannot survive without the care of ministering adults, so young humans are imprinted early with the importance of social sharing for survival. Although social sharing is a learned motive, once it is learned it becomes powerful.

With this in mind, social sharing may be introduced into the stream of human motivation as follows:

Level 1 The prediction motive

Level 2 The pursuit of one's preferences

Level 3 Social sharing; social acquisitiveness

Prediction, the primary motive, is shown on the first level, and the pursuit of one's preferences, the secondary motive, is shown on the second level. You will remember that a preference is determined as a result of deliberating alternatives. Individuals may deliberate the various things that interest them in choosing their preferences. After social sharing becomes an interest through learning, it takes its place alongside the various selfish interests individuals may have on the third level. Then individuals may deliberate social sharing as well as selfish interests in choosing a preference. Once individuals become motivated toward social sharing, they may prefer it equally to or even more than they prefer selfish acquisition.

The psychological view of humans as primarily selfish has been responsible for one of our most profound dilemmas. In contrast, people have recorded rules that require them to share with other people. The Ten Commandments and civil tax laws are examples of rules that require humans to share. However, we have been prone to believe that these rules were needed to counteract and constrain our basic selfish nature. Often the impetus to share was said to come from our spiritual nature, reflected in our abstract religious and philosophical pursuits, as opposed to selfishness, which is a part of our psychological nature. Thus humans have been tormented by the proposed conflict between spirit and mind. Spiritually, we are our neighbor's keeper; psychologically, it is dog-eat-dog.

It is unnecessary to perpetuate this conflict between spirit and mind if we regard both selfishness and sharing as potent psychological motives. Humans are predisposed to satisfy both motives. The satisfaction of one motive does not exclude the satisfaction of the other, nor is the satisfaction of one more psychologically natural for humans.

We are not contending that humans do not have a spiritual side to their nature. Rather, we are saying that selfishness and social sharing should both be regarded as psychological motives. It is counterproductive to contend that selfishness is our psychological motive and social sharing is our spiritual motive, and our lofty spiritual motive to share must exert constraint over our base selfish psychological motive. It may be that in religion or philosophy there is reason to consider which of the two motives is more noble and more entitled to predominate. But in psychology both motives should be regarded as causal agents having impact on human behavior.

Finally, both our selfishness and our tendency toward social sharing can be addressed scientifically within the domain of psychology because both are psychological motives. There is no need to consider humans as being continually pushed by external forces, supernatural or otherwise, to share with each other. Once the rules of the group and the necessity for social sharing are imprinted in children they are compelled toward social sharing.

Social Power and Dominance

Power, in general, refers to the capability to confirm or prevent the confirmation of predictions. The more power we have the more likely we are to be able to make events turn out as we choose or assure the achievement or defeat of a goal. Although Max Weber (1964) has a definition of power that is not oriented to prediction, it is compatible with our definition. He defined *power* as the probability that one actor within a social relationship will be in a position to carry out his own will despite resistance, regardless of the basis on which this probability rests.

Power may be due to superior physical strength. One person may exercise power over another by physically forcing him or her into submission. Power among animals, attributable largely to physical prowess, is exhibited in the pecking order of animal groups.

Power may also be attributable to the control of resources. A person may be able to control the confirmation of predictions through possession of great wealth and property. Having wealth and control of resources may sometimes enable a person to avoid the enforcement of laws.

It is important to realize that a person may control the confirmation of predictions and therefore have power without using physical strength or abundant personal resources to control outcomes. Often such people influence people's minds and conduct through persuasive argument and ideology. Patrick Henry, Martin Luther King, and Billy Graham are examples. As Weber points out in his discussion of types of power and domination, charismatic grounds are as legitimate for the assumption of dominance as are traditional and rational grounds.

Industrial psychologists use the term *incremental power* or influence to refer to the power of a leader that is not attributable to prescribed power or reward-punishment power but rather power that stems from personal magnetism or charisma. Student (1968) found that incremental power was positively related to four of eight production measures.

Now *social power* pertains to the control of the confirmation of predictions as a result of controlling the enforcement and establishment of rules. The exercise of physical force, the use of wealth, or persuasive argument may be used to influence the environment or establishment of rules. A gangster may influence law enforcement by threatening physical violence to the family of a legal official. A wealthy person may influence law enforcement by bribing a public official or by contributing to the campaign funds of legislators to influence them to modify the law. On the other hand, the enforcement of rules may be influenced without the use of physical force or material wealth. Martin Luther King influenced law enforcement by directing marches and sit-ins in the South. These led to a more equitable enforcement of laws involving blacks and to the eventual writing of new laws that further protected the rights of blacks and other minority groups.

Groups as well as individuals have social power to the extent that they control the establishment and enforcement of rules. A group such as a legislative body has social power because it enacts laws. A group such as a labor union has social power in that it can influence the Congress to enact laws. A labor union may also influence the enforcement of rules by influencing the police to permit a strike to continue even though some of its members have broken the law by provoking physical violence.

The example of the labor union influencing Congress to enact laws is an illustration of the social power one group may have over another. A group may also have social power over individuals. For instance, a labor union enforces rules when it influences its members to pay dues. The union may also change its rules by raising the dues the members are obligated to pay.

Social power is most inherent in people who hold social offices that entitle them to enact and enforce rules within the social system. State and federal legislators have the right to enact laws by virtue of the offices they hold. Policemen have the right to enforce laws because of the social position they hold. Internal Revenue agents have the right to enforce income-tax laws because the office they hold so empowers them. Thus social power is most directly exercised by social officers; others who exercise social power do so most often by influencing social officers.

Americans are quick to recognize the power of physical prowess and wealth and slow to recognize the power of persuasive argument and ideology. When America was first founded, physical prowess was needed to win the Revolution and fight the elements of nature in order to establish a foothold in this land. Daniel Boone and Davy Crockett epitomize the early American hero. Then with the onset of the Industrial Revolution emphasis was placed on materialism and wealth, and moguls such as Cornelius Vanderbilt, Henry Ford, and Horatio Alger characters became heroes of this era. The exercise of free enterprise in the pursuit of material wealth tended to submerge the importance of earlier ideology. It has become difficult for us to give credence to the power of persuasive argument and ideology, yet Christianity grew despite the lack of physical power and material wealth. We find it hard to understand how the ideology of communism can be preferred by many developing nations to the American offering of material wealth through free enterprise. It is well to remember that "there is nothing more powerful than an idea whose time has come" and that people often are willing to suffer material deprivation for their ideology. It is also well to remember that power in our courts of law is largely the power of a lawyer to influence a judge or jury through persuasive rhetoric.

Social Dominance

Dominance is the ability to control the confirmation of another's predictions, including preventing the confirmation of another's predictions.

Patterns of dominance are common in primates. Lorenz (1966) argues that dominance is an organization principle necessary to the development of advanced social life in higher vertebrates. DeVore (1965) states that dominance interactions are basic to the behavior of primates and are particularly prominent in Old World monkeys, apes, and humans.

One may dominate another by physically forcing submission, by controlling the resources needed by the other, or through convincing rhetoric. Our primary concern is with social dominance.

Social power may be spoken of in general as the ability to enact and enforce rules. *Social dominance* is particular to the relationship between two or more social bodies (groups or group members). When one social body can enact rules that govern the activities of another body and can enforce the rules it can be said to be *socially dominant,* and the body subject to the rules and their enforcement is *socially subordinate.* As physical force and material wealth can contribute to social power, so can they contribute to the social dominance of one social body over another. However, social dominance concerns the ability to impose and enforce rules on another. One group may dominate another group, as the federal government in the United States is dominant over the states because the states are subject to the laws enacted and enforced by the federal government.

To summarize, a group dominates its members when rules are enacted by the group governing the members and the rules are enforced. An individual dominates another individual when rules governing that individual are enacted and enforced. An individual dominates a group when that person enacts rules for the group and enforces them.

In conclusion, social power is the general ability to establish and enforce rules. Social power implies the ability to be socially dominant to some extent. Social dominance is the exercise of social power by a more socially powerful entity over a less powerful entity.

Let us now summarize and relate the topics in this chapter to prediction theory. People form and maintain groups because groups enhance predictability and the confirmation of particular predictions that are of interest at the moment. Group membership facilitates prediction because group members accept and conform to the same rules. Thus their behavior is standardized and more predictable to one another. When rules are taught to group members and enforced, conformity to group rules and, therefore, predictability within the group are ensured. When the consequences for violating rules are known to be the same for all members and the rules are impartially enforced, voluntary conformity to the rules is more likely.

Group membership facilitates the relief of boredom and confusion and the confirmation of particular predictions because group members provide assistance for one another. When group members are bored or confused and are interested in confirming a particular prediction to find relief, they can seek assistance from other members.

Prediction theory also provides a cogent explanation of power and dominance. *Power,* according to prediction theory, is the ability to confirm or prevent the confirmation of a prediction. *Dominance* is the ability to control the confirmation of another's prediction. People seek power and dominance because with them people can be more assured that their own predictions will be confirmed.

12 Social Rules

This chapter considers three fundamental types of social rules: rules defining group referents—language; rules defining group values; and rules defining group status. An understanding of these three types of rules is crucial to the understanding of groups.

Rules Defining Group Referents: Language

The most fundamental social rules that are established by a group are the rules for sharing perceptions. The group defines common referents for group members to use in referring to events. It is the definition of these referents that structures the languages of the group. The use of these common language referents permit group members to agree about the events they witness. For example, defining the word *water* allows members of the group to agree that rain is water, and defining the word *cold* permits group members to agree that ice is cold, and so on.

Rules defining group referents or rules of language must be established so that group members can share perceptions because if individuals cannot share perceptions, there is little else they can share. Without being able to share perceptions, each individual is held to his or her own subjective impressions and individuals cannot have their impressions confirmed by others. Under these conditions, people can provide negligible assistance for one another. They can do little to help each other to acquire their preferences or predict. In short, to form a group in the first place, rules must be established defining common language referents.

The term *language* is being used broadly to mean any signals, signs, or symbols with definitions that permit individuals to make common references to events and therefore to share perceptions. Thus group languages include all modes of sharing such as gestures, words, music, art, mathematics, and rituals.

Language defines objective reality for the group. It is necessary to have common language referents in order to make objective observations. Through language people can agree about an event and establish its existence as an objective fact. When people agree that the sun is hot, the hotness of the sun is established as an objective fact. However, the group's ideas of reality are specific to the group and sometimes are biased. If it is said that disease is caused by germs, then that is the conception of causality the group members will hold. If the cause of disease is commonly said to be evil spirits, then this is the conception of reality to which the group will subscribe. The language of the group conveys the ideas the group shares about reality, and language is the means by which its ideas are communicated from generation to generation.

Language not only reflects the group's ideas; it also acts as an active structure of these ideas. Whorf (1940) points out that the grammar of a language shapes ideas and guides mental activity. In support of what Whorf says about the function of language as it relates to structuring reality is an article by Dorothy Lee (1950). She observes similarly to Whorf that how reality is perceived is directly influenced by one's language and social rules. This does not mean that language changes reality but that one's conception of reality is changed by how it is perceived. She reports on a study of the people of the Trobriand Islands, who see the world differently than we because they do not tend to perceive events, time, or motion in a linear manner. This is not automatic in them as it is among Western people. They indulge in patterned activity rather than linear activity. They can perceive lineal behavior and when they do, they despise it. The reason, according to Lee, that they perceive in a nonlineal manner is because they value pattern perception more highly than linear perception. An example of how this works is that for the Trobriander, a path is not going to or from but is *at*. There are no symbols in this language for *to* or *from*.

Through language the dead are able to contribute to the education of the living, and the group is perpetuated even though individual members live and die.

The primary languages of the group are denotative, especially the verbal languages. They are constructed to permit members to aid each other in predicting and pursuing preferences. Because identification is prerequisite to prediction and the pursuit of preferences, group members are taught first to use their language to identify events. The members learn the language symbols for the events they experience so they can make the same identifications as all the other members. In part I of this book we considered how individual ideas pertain to (1) images of concrete events, (2) concepts of categories of events, (3) the hierarchical relationships among events, and (4) programmatic relationships among events. We can now consider how group language provides common references for these ideas.

Some words refer to concrete experiences and bring images to mind of the tangible events they represent. Proper nouns are such words because proper nouns are labels or names of specific concrete events that can be experienced through the senses. Each person has a name that represents that person. When you meet someone for the first time you introduce yourself by giving your name and she introduces herself by giving her name. Thereafter you attach the name to the person and she to you. When you meet again you greet and call each other by name. Proper nouns can represent tangible objects other than people. The *Queen Mary* is a name representing a particular ship, Spectacular Bid is the name of a horse that won the Kentucky Derby, Louisville, Kentucky is the name of the city and state where the Kentucky Derby can be witnessed each spring. The main section of the dictionary includes relatively few proper nouns. However, most dictionaries contain sections that list names. For example, the names of famous people and their trade, occupation, or historical significance can usually be found in the section entitled Biographical Names. There are also sections listing names of places. Personal pronouns also represent concrete events, simply because they may be substituted for proper nouns. Instead of referring to particular people by their names we may refer to them as he or she.

Most words in the dictionary refer to concepts. Earlier we defined *abstractions* as the process of making identifications based on limited features or attributes. The process of abstraction is used to group concrete events into concept categories based on their common characteristics. A public concept is created when the common characteristics of concrete objects are enumerated and a word label is designated to refer to the category. For instance, the word *mother* is a word label for a category. The common characteristics of members of the category are (1) female (2) with a child or children.

Concepts are abstractions because they refer to only a limited number of features of a concrete event. For instance, the word *mother* as we have defined it refers to only two features. Although any mother has these two features, a particular mother has many other features that make her distinct from other mothers. A mother may be tall or short, heavy or lean, and so on.

It is important to realize that most words in the dictionary are labels for concepts. When we look up a word in the dictionary we are given definitions. Each definition specifies features or criteria for inclusion in a category the word represents. To be a member of a category, the person or item must meet the criteria for inclusion in the category.

As already indicated, personal pronouns and proper nouns are words that nearly always refer to concrete tangible things. However, sometimes a personal pronoun is used to refer to an abstraction category. This is the case in the sentence, "The dog is a he." The word *he* in this instance refers to the category male, and the sentence indicates that the dog belongs to that category. Proper nouns also sometimes refer to categories of things, as the name Buick refers to a category or type of car.

It is also important to realize that while most often proper nouns and personal pronouns refer to concrete things, other words do not. The name Jimmy Carter stands for a person who can be seen. The name is a proper noun representing a concrete entity. The proper noun southerner is a label for a category of people who were born and raised in the South and does not stand for a concrete entity. Only examples of the category are tangible. You cannot see "southerner." You can see a concrete example of a southerner, such as Jimmy Carter.

Words not only represent concepts, they are often used to convey the hierarchical relationship among concepts. Organizing concepts into class-inclusion hierarchies facilitates the understanding of the concepts and the relationship between them, as well as the vocabulary used to describe the concept.

Ausubel (1963) states that "an individual's organization of the content of a particular subject-matter discipline in his own mind consists of a hierarchical structure in which the most inclusive concepts occupy a position at the apex of the structure and subsume progressively less inclusive and more highly differentiated subconcepts of factual data" (p. 79).

He also states, "Now if the human nervous system as a data processing and storing mechanism is so constructed that both acquisition and new knowledge and its organization in cognitive structure conform *naturally* to this principle of progressive differentiation, it seems reasonable to suppose that optimal learning and retention occur when teachers *deliberately* order the organization and sequential arrangement of subject matter along similar lines" (p. 79).

Consider the example of a class-inclusion-representational hierarchy (figure 12-1). Each word in the class-inclusion-representational hierarchy is a label for a concept or abstraction category. However, the categories prose and poetry are subcategories of the more general category literature. The categories novel and short stories are subcategories of the more general prose. And the categories ode and sonnet are subcategories of the more general category poetry. This is a representational hierarchy because the lower levels are represented in the higher, more general levels of the hierarchy. An ode is a representation of or a subtype of poetry, and poetry is a representation of or a subtype of literature. Prose is also a representation of or a subtype of literature.

In mathematics we might arrange concepts in a hierarchy such as in figure 12-2. In science we might organize the content hierarchy in figure 12-3, and in social studies we might define the class-inclusion hierarchy in figure 12-4.

The arrangement of concepts into class-inclusion hierarchies tends to facilitate the learning and understanding of the concepts. As indicated earlier, Bower et al. (1969) demonstrated that students recall two or three times more words if the words are presented to them in the form of a class-inclusion hierarchy. Preusser and Handel (1970) showed that given words and pictures of objects, students tend to organize them into class-inclusion

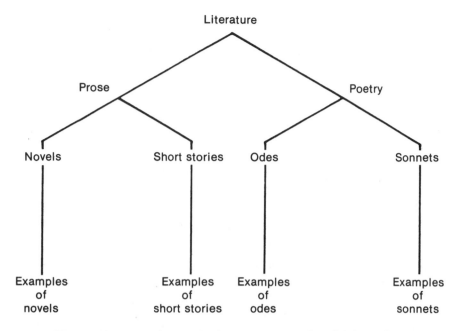

Figure 12-1. A Class-Inclusion-Representational Hierarchy

hierarchies. Bower's findings indicate that information is more easily retrieved and remembered if it is presented in that form. These findings suggest that people tend to organize and store information in the form of class-inclusion hierarchies.

Public information is organized in this same manner. The information in the library is stored in the form of class-inclusion hierarchies for easy retrieval. Books and references are listed according to types and subtypes. Also, the table of contents of a book forms a class-inclusion hierarchy as in figure 12-5. In addition, the chapters of a book are often subdivided by headings into subtopics of the chapter. A table of contents is nothing more than a topic outline. All topic outlines form class-inclusion hierarchies.

Finally, words may be programmatic references. Such words refer to a sequence of events. All names for methods and procedures are references to programmatic sequences. The term *scientific method* represents a program for conducting scientific inquiry, the terms *addition, subtraction, multiplication,* and *division* are words representing mathematics programs.

When programs are designated by the language of the group, they allow members to make common predictions. When the mathematical language of the group is learned, members can make such common predictions as one plus one will equal two. When the verbal language of the group is learned,

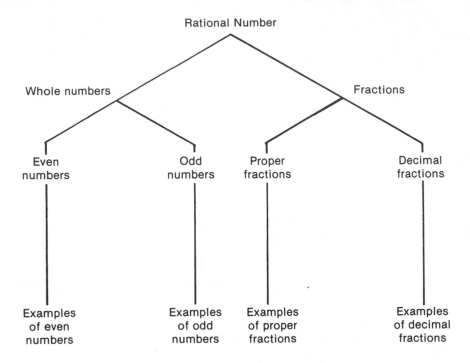

Figure 12-2. Hierarchy of Mathematical Concepts

members can make the common prediction that a sentence will contain a subject and a predicate. In short, language defines if-this-then-that relationships for the group. When members learn these relationships, they can make common predictions. As a result they are able to support each other's interpretations of probable outcomes, and they can agree that one event will lead to another.

The programs used by a group to predict are transmitted through language and include the technologies for dealing with the environment. Hunting cultures describe programs for hunting, farming cultures transmit programs for farming, industrial cultures describe programs for manufacturing.

Languages are also used to establish group identity—they permit members to predict who belongs to the group and who does not. These language functions we can call *rituals*. Rituals such as the style of dress and the songs and dances of the group enable an individual to identify other group members and know that they will have common perceptions. The group members tend to feel close to them and secure with them because they are able to assist in predicting and acquiring preferences. Goffman (1967)

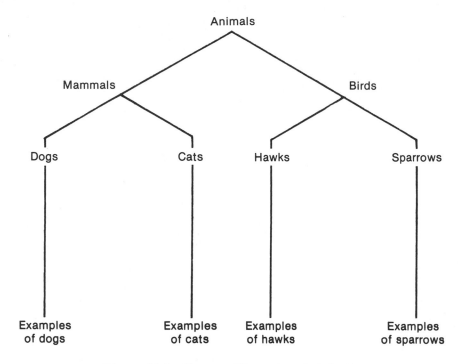

Figure 12-3. Content Hierarchy of Animals

emphasized the importance of social rituals when he stated that we sometimes refer to particular gestures as being empty when they may be the fullest of all things.

Rituals are also used to identify an individual's position in the group. In the army, a commissioned officer dresses differently from a noncommissioned officer, and a noncommissioned officer is expected to salute a commissioned officer. Rituals are often used to identify transition from one position in the group to another, for example, graduations.

An example of how our language defines relationships between superiors and subordinates and what happens if this relationship is ambiguous can be seen in a paper presented to the American Sociological Association (Little and Gelles 1972). The study was concerned with how graduate students address faculty members. Using a questionnaire, graduate students in the sociology department of a small university reported on how they addressed each faculty member. The forms of address ranged from formal through informal to no interaction. It was shown that graduate students respond to rank and age when picking a form of address. Moreover, it was shown that although postmasters students tend to be less formal than

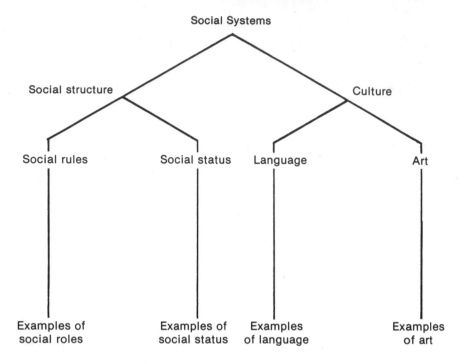

Figure 12-4. Sociological Class-Inclusion Hierarchy

premasters students, they also tend to show greater ambiguity in choosing a form of address. This supported the hypothesis that they were subject to increasing conflict in choosing a form of address as they approached collegial status with faculty. This is an example of a situation in which relationships are not adequately defined by rituals. In this instance, because of inadequate rituals to govern the situation, anxiety is created in the group member.

It may seem that we are arbitrarily avoiding common social referents such as customs, mores, and folkways or reducing their importance. This is not the intention. Instead, we wish to emphasize that it is through the rules of language that the character of the group is overtly expressed. Language provides group referents and conveys the customs, mores, and folkways of the group. It is through the group's languages that its characteristics are made known.

Rules Defining Group Values

Groups not only establish rules of language to make common identification and predictions of events, they establish rules for assigning common values

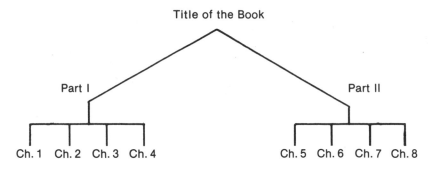

Figure 12-5. Example of a Class-Inclusion Hierarchy

to events. A *value* is a common preference of group members. A value of Americans is to abide by the Bill of Rights; a value of the Boy Scouts is to abide by the Boy Scout laws. Attitudes are distinct from values in that an *attitude* is expressed as a personal idiosyncratic preference, such as a personal preference for the color blue.

Hogan (1973), in summarizing the traditional approaches of sociologists, social psychologists, and anthropologists, contends that all social behavior occurs within a rule system and that social behavior is basically a rule-regulated system of behavior. Second, it is traditionally held that human rule systems have associated with them ethical standards of right and wrong conduct. Goffman (1959) expresses his belief that shared values are the social glue by which society is held together. There is a brand of theory that emphasizes value conflict as the primary course of group behavior. Karl Marx was the most influential advocate of the theory, and George Simmel and Ludwig Germplowicz also were prominent contributors.

All groups value the things that support their survival and propagation. They value health and the commodities that support health, such as food, shelter, and clothing. They value conformity to the group's rules, languages, and particular values. Groups also value their leaders because their leaders are in a position to contribute to the common good. A member who rejects the social rules of the group to pursue selfish desires will probably be punished by the group. In addition, groups usually value maintaining good relations with the supernatural. However, each group may have a different conception of the supernatural, ranging from monotheism to animism, as well as its unique way of placating supernatural forces. Most groups value wealth, but each may have its own conception of wealth. In one, wealth may be considered as the possession of money, stocks, and real estate, while another group may measure wealth in terms of the number of sheep or cattle owned.

Groups value certain interests. A group will value becoming aroused by an enemy and reacting hostilely toward the enemy because this is necessary for group preservation. However, the group will dislike overly hostile posture within the group.

Groups also assign value to programs in the pursuit of goals. Each group has its own way of waging warfare. However, with the advancement in weapon technology, modern warfare becomes more similar across groups. In addition, each group tends to value particular child rearing, education, and religious practices, as well as methods of producing and preparing food, shelter, and clothing. In the literature there are numerous examples of how the group's values and opinions can influence and control the opinions and values of the individual members.

An example of how an individual can be influenced by group opinion can be seen in an experiment done by Sherif (1937). When studying the phenomena of autokinetic movement (how a single light in a dark room seems to move about), he decided to see if the range of variation on individual assessments of the amount of movement was affected by the presence of a group. He observed that the amount of variation was smaller when a group was present than when the same subject was exposed to the phenomena individually.

Another study that follows a similar track is the study of Asch (1951). He demonstrated how the individual shifts convictions and decisions to conform to group consensus when confronted with an incorrect majority decision about the length of a line.

Allen and Levine (1971) showed that individuals shift their preferences for art to conform to group opinion. Steiner (1964) demonstrated that, in contrived situations, when a subject felt group pressure toward consensus with which he disagreed, he manifested anxiety.

The research of Sherif (1937, 1956) and Asch (1951, 1956) support a basic tenet of the present theory; that is, group membership is valuable to individuals because they rely upon the group to help them maintain predictability. The Sherif and Asch studies show that greater conformity to group opinion occurs when the individual is presented with unpredictable or ambiguous stimulation.

The above studies show how the group in experimental situations can affect the individual's opinions. In another study, it was demonstrated that acceptance of group rules was a function of how much one felt a part of the social group. Festinger, Schacter, and Beck (1950), in a study of college housing units, found that conformity to the rules (norms) of a particular housing unit depended on how many friends the individual felt he had in that unit.

Brainwashing provides an example of how values can be changed. During the Korean War, American prisoners of war were subjected to highly organized, systematic brainwashing. What was washed out was the set of values that the prisoners had at the time of capture. Although numerous techniques were employed to accomplish this change in values, according to Schein (1957), the one most significant feature was the systematic destruction of the prisoners' formal and informal group structure. The object was to isolate totally the individual from the group support that he needed to maintain his value system. While this was going on, a new value system was being indoctrinated into the individual.

Rules Defining Group Status

Groups create rules that define group roles and the relationships among them. Each role is defined by rules indicating the characteristics of those qualified to occupy the role and the appropriate behavior for anyone holding that role. For instance, groups create the role of father when they define the appropriate behavior for people acting in that role and the characteristics that qualify a person to occupy the role, in this case males with children. Thus a *role* is a concept that exists independently of the particular person occupying it. When the role of father is defined it exists independently of the many individuals who may be occupying that role at the time. So roles are perpetuated even though the individuals who occupy them come and go.

Roles are not defined in isolation. Rather, they are defined in relation to other roles thus creating a network of roles that provide group structure. The role of husband is defined in relation to the role of wife.

In addition, most roles are defined to be reciprocal to one another, so that occupants of related roles are obliged to confirm each other's predictions. This provides for group cohesiveness. In role definitions cooperation rather than competition is emphasized. Competition is expressed in contests with outsiders who threaten the group and in controlled contests within the group, such as sports and games, that do not disrupt the work of the group. The roles of husband and wife are defined so that husbands and wives will cooperate and reward one another.

Within the family there are at least three sets of roles describing its social structure: (1) husband and wife, (2) mother and child, and (3) father and child. When two roles intersect, such as father and husband, it is referred to as a position. A *position*, then, is a location in a social structure that involves the performance of a set of roles.

Rules are defined that organize positions into a hierarchy creating domination-subordination relations among the positions. For example, in a family the positions of wife and mother and husband and father are dominant over the position child and sibling. Government and corporate bureaucracies provide examples of groups with extensive and elaborate hierarchical organizations. The hierarchical arrangement of positions within the group describes *group status*, and a person who holds a higher-status position is dominant over a person who holds a lower-status position.

A person who holds a higher-status position may also be said to have authority over a person in a lower-status position because that status has been authorized by group rules. For this reason, *authority* may be thought of as power and dominance legitimated by social rules. Woodward (1966) states: "The subordinate has his work allocated to him by his superior, is accountable to him for end results, and refers back to him the problems which he cannot overcome himself. Spheres of influence and authority and the size or importance of the task over which he has discretion become greater as an individual moves up the hierarchical pyramid" (p. 44). Sherif (1937) tells us of numerous sociological studies that support this analysis.

Group members seek status because status gives them the authority to control the confirmation of predictions and the attainment of preferences. Groups give status and authority to members as a reward for supporting the common good. Here we are referring to *achieved status*, that is, status awarded on the basis of performance. It should be noted that there also is *ascribed status*, wherein the individual is given status because of birth or physical endowments. In monarchies members of the royal family are given status as a birthright. In a society that includes a caste system, one's caste is an ascribed status based on the family one is born into.

There is a great deal more social mobility in societies that award status on the basis of achievement. In modern technological cultures most status positions are awarded because of achievement.

A *social institution* may be considered to be a group with a formal status structure that is defined by social rules. In illiterate primitive societies the rules governing the tribe and the positions within it are communicated and perpetuated by word of mouth. In advanced societies the rules are often written on record in a public office. For instance, in the United States a child's birth and family membership are usually published on a birth certifiate of public record. Government and corporate laws are also published and of public record. Burns and Stalker (1961) found that organizations in stable industries tend to be more "mechanistic." They define mechanistic, in part, as dependency on formal rules and regulations.

The publication of rules facilitates sharing because it provides a ready reference for interpreting events in a standard way. The dictionary provides a ready reference for the correct sharing of perceptions, while the Bill of Rights is a reference for the shared values of citizens of the United States. The publication of rules also enables an individual to identify appropriate behavior when not in face-to-face contact with knowledgeable group members. Finally, the publication of rules facilitates the transmission of culture from one generation to the next.

Let us now summarize the relevance of prediction theory to rules defining language, values, and status. It was said that social rules enhance predictability because they standardize behavior and group members can be expected to behave in similar ways under similar conditions. Rules of language are the most fundamental type of rules because they standardize perception and communication. Language provides the basis for sharing and is the vehicle through which one member confirms another member's predictions. It was said that images permit predictions about familiar events and concepts about novel events. Because words, such as proper nouns and personal pronouns, represent images, these words enable group members to have their predictions about familiar events confirmed by other group members. Because words also represent concepts, these words allow group members to have their predictions about novel events confirmed by other members. When members derive a discovery, they can describe it to another member using word concepts. By doing so, they can have their discovery confirmed. In many cases, rules of language enable group members to predict friends and foes. Group members can be predicted to be agreeable, while outsiders can be predicted to be disagreeable.

Rules defining group values enhance prediction by prescribing standards indicating what should be sought and what should be avoided. When members seek things that are positively valued by the group, they can predict that other members will regard their behavior as correct and issue positive sanctions or rewards. Conversely, when members seek things that are negatively valued by the group, they can predict that other members will regard their behavior as incorrect and issue negative sanctions or punishment. Thus, the definition of group values enables people to predict when they are likely to be rewarded or punished.

Rules defining status facilitate prediction because they standardize the use of power and dominance. They indicate who in the group has the authority (legitimated power and dominance) to confirm or prevent the confirmation of predictions and the conditions under which the authority may be exercised. This tends to regulate and limit the exercise of power and dominance, making the exercise of power and dominance more predictable.

People seek status so that they may have the authority to control the confirmation of predictions. People seek assistance from group members of higher status because members with higher status have more authority and can be more influential in helping them confirm predictions.

13 The Group and Its Members

To begin our discussion of social dynamics, it is important to extend our interpretation of motivation because motivation provides the dynamic force that directs behavior. When we considered the individual in part I there were two motives of concern. The motivation to predict was given as the primary motive, and the pursuit of personal preferences was given as the secondary motive. In part I we dealt primarily with the individual's interests in satisfying desires such as hunger, thirst, and sex. It usually turns out this way when we look at people from a psychological perspective. It seems that because of tradition and Freudian influence we tend to focus on the individual's interest in satisfying inherited, impulsive, appetitive predispositions. Since discussing groups in part II, we must add three other interests, all of which are learned. Through group membership the individual learns the importance of conforming to group values. As a result, one becomes interested in leading the "good life" according to the values of the group. In addition, one learns the benefits of group status and becomes interested in achieving status. Also, the group's language is learned, which becomes part of one's personal identity and develops an interest in supporting the group.

With these additions in mind, we must elaborate human motivation as follows:

Basic Motive: Prediction
Individuals are motivated to predict (an innate motive). When bored they will attempt to predict novel events, and when confused, familiar events.

Secondary Motives: Interests
Individuals will pursue their preferences. They will deliberate alternative interests to determine their preferences from among the following:
1. the pursuit of their appetitive desires, such as food and sex (an innate interest);
2. the pursuit of status (a learned interest concerned with social sharing);
3. the pursuit of what the group values (a learned interest concerned with social sharing); and
4. support of the group's languages (a learned interest concerned with social sharing).

People in general will be interested in satisfying all of these interests. However, individuals will vary in their inclinations. One person may be more interested in catering to desires, another may spend most of the time seeking status, while a third person may think it most important to pursue the good life according to group values. A fourth person may be concerned primarily with language and ritual.

At least three forms of social dynamics must be considered: (1) the relationship between the group and its members, (2) the relationship between one member and another, and (3) the relationship between one group and another. Let us consider these in sequence in this chapter and chapters 14 and 15.

The group and its members are in a reciprocal relationship. The group needs the support of its members to endure, and the members need the support of the group to satisfy their motives. If the group does not satisfy the motives of its members, the members will not support the group and the group will disintegrate. If the group does satisfy the motives of its members, the members will support the group and the group will thrive.

We may now consider how the group may provide for the satisfaction of its members thereby encouraging them to support the group, and how the members may support the group thereby contributing to its survival and cohesiveness.

The importance of group support can be seen in a study of the success of a program for the hard-core unemployed. Friedlander and Greenberg (1971) found that the sole correlate of performance was degree of perceived organizational supportiveness.

In the following analysis we first consider the *prediction motive*, that is, the maintenance and improvement of prediction. Then we consider the *secondary motive*, the *pursuit of preferences* with respect to the individual's interests in appetites, language, values, and status. We discuss these motives from the group's perspective and from the members' perspective. The statements we make are intended to apply to groups in general. We will offer a wide variety of examples pertaining to many different types of groups.

The Maintenance and Improvement of Prediction

The group gains support from its members when it makes provisions for the reduction of confusion, so that members will not become confused in the first place, and, if they do, they can find relief. Confusion is reduced by providing for the maintenance of predictability.

In a field study, Cohen (1959) found that telephone operators were more highly motivated, felt more secure, and worked more efficiently when the path to the goal was relatively clear and predictable than when it was ambiguous and unpredictable. A laboratory study by Raven and Rietsema (1957) generally agreed with these findings.

The importance of the group in helping its members to avoid and reduce confusion was pointed out by Bales (1950) in his first book *Interaction Process Analysis*. Bales identified prediction as one of the basic tendencies of human behavior and views group organization as operating to satisfy the prediction motive. He states further that the practical goal of observation is prediction and an increase in ability to control events. It is interesting to note that not only are Bales' point of view and our point of view in accord, but he seems to understand implicitly the relationship between abstractions and prediction (Bales 1970).

Predictability is promoted by the group when conformity to rules leads to the confirmation of predictions. The prescription of rules, in itself, promotes the confirmation of predictions because rules specify appropriate behavior and inform the members of acceptable and unacceptable behavior. Therefore, a member knows what to expect when behaving in a prescribed way. The prescription of rules according to the master-neuroprint format insures that those who conform to the rules will have their predictions confirmed. For instance, the rule may convey that if you want to drive a car (interest) you have to obtain a driver's license (goal). You obtain a driver's license by making application and passing written and driving tests (program). Writing rules according to the master-neuroprint format aids the confirmation of predictions because the if-this-then-that relationships inherent in the master neuroprint will direct a member to the goal being pursued.

In addition, rules promote predictability because they are common references that allow one member to assist another in the confirmation of predictions. Because the rules for obtaining a driver's license are public knowledge, one member can help another attain one. A major advantage of group membership is that members can assist each other to confirm predictions. Peter B. Hammond (1959) explains how indirection is sometimes used to promote communications such as may exist between in-laws who dislike each other but find it mutually profitable to avoid outright conflict. Indirection describes forms of verbal and social interaction which by circuitousness or evasion minimize the potential for conflict inherent in a relationship. This does not make these forms any the less rules, it is just that in some societies the use of indirection in communication is "negatively sanctioned." According to Hammond, in situations with a high potential for conflict, the society minimizes potential conflict by (1) reducing tension through catharsis; (2) evading tension through avoidance; (3) communicating the cause of tension, thereby permitting its removal; and (4) preserving the positive elements of the relationship. These rules are useful for allowing the individual to predict in situations that would otherwise be intolerable. Hammond gives some specific examples of how these useful conventions work in non-Western societies where they are positively sanctioned as well as examples of Western societies where they are used and considered underhanded.

The confirmation of prediction is facilitated further when the group provides for the teaching and interpretation of its rules. Obtaining a driver's license is facilitated when the group's rules pertaining to traffic regulations and the correct operation of a car are taught to the member. This can be done personally or through publications. One value of publications is that they provide a ready reference for the proper interpretation of rules which a member can read at leisure.

The enforcement of rules also promotes predictability. Issuing drivers' licenses only on the successful completion of driving tests insures predictability because the rules state, and therefore it is expected, that a person must pass a test to obtain a license. Further, impartial enforcement of rules enhances the confirmation of predictions. It would be confusing if the rules state that tests must be passed to obtain a driver's license, but some people received licenses without passing the tests. This may explain, in part, why impartial or fair enforcement of rules is endorsed by group members.

Predictability is not only promoted when members assist each other to confirm their personal prediction but also when they work together to confirm consensual predictions. Consensual predictions are supported because each member believes that personal predictions are more likely to be confirmed through agreement with the group. Consensual predictions are made to pursue the goals that the group values. Seeking to win a war or to land on the moon represents goals that groups have wanted to achieve.

The confirmation of predictions is often enhanced when the group works together as a team to achieve a goal. Group effort is more effective than individual effort in achieving many goals. And, in fact, a group effort is essential to the achievement of certain goals. For instance, it took the cooperative efforts of the NASA team to arrange for a landing on the moon. However, we should also be reminded that in the pursuit of some goals the adage "too many cooks spoil the broth" may apply.

Predictability is facilitated further when the group focuses on its common interests, those prescribed by group rules. The mutual support of the language, values, and status structure of the group focuses attention on mutual concerns and results in group cohesiveness. Further, it foments cooperation and, therefore, the confirmation of predictions.

The fact that cooperative effort and group cohesion are important and reciprocal aspects of the group, which helps its members to predict accurately, can be illustrated by referring to a Dutch study of group cohesion on volleyball teams (Vos, Doerbecker, and Brinkman 1973). This study was an attempt to replicate a previous study which asserted that members of volleyball teams that had achieved objective success were less likely to move on to other teams. They defined *objective success* as the status level the team achieved in national competition. *Subjective success* was defined as the combination of the level of aspiration and expectancy minus the objective success. They also hypothesized a similar relationship between subjective success and player mobility. The findings of this study show that there is a high negative correlation between subjective success and player mobility. By inference, it would seem that these results support the contention that group cohesiveness is a function of the members' confirming consensual predictions. When group members concentrate on the pursuit of their personal desires, individual differences are emphasized and members tend to pursue different goals. This diversity contributes to unpredictability and strains group solidarity. A number of studies showed that cooperation in the confirmation of predictions enhances group morale and productivity. Among these are studies by Deutsch (1949), Shaw (1958b), Willis and Joseph (1959), and Blau (1954).

There is another subtle factor that prevents the group from achieving its goals: the prediction of failure. During a particular group task the goal will be pursued as long as its achievement is predictable. When the group believes a goal cannot be achieved, it will predict failure and act, maybe unwittingly, to confirm its prediction of failure. For instance, the goal of a basketball team is to win games. However, if they believe they cannot win (they predict failure), perhaps because they are on a losing streak, they will be prone to stop trying. This, in turn, will serve to contribute to the confirmation of their prediction of failure. Consider another example: societies pursue prosperity as a goal. However, if a depression is predicted (failure) people may withdraw money from the bank, refuse to make investments, and avoid long-term financial commitments, all of which snowball to contribute to the confirmation of the prediction that a depression is coming. Examples of these self-fulfilling prophesies abound. Such prophesies and the propensity to fulfill them undermine the achievement of group goals and group cohesiveness. In part I we saw how the defensiveness of individuals prompts them to act to confirm failure when that is their prediction. We presently are describing defensiveness as it is manifested in group behavior. Zander (1968; Zander and Newcomb 1967), in researching attitudes among members of United Fund organizations, found that failing organizations, those that do not collect the goal amounts, do not pay enough attention to the probability of success when they select a campaign goal. This may be because these organizations are predicting failure.

It is necessary for the achievement of status to be predictable, too. The group can assist the members to understand and obtain status by stating rules that describe the relationship between one status position and the next in the hierarchy, the means of improving one's status, and the authority and responsibility of each status position. It is important for the continued cohesion of the group that members be able to predict the achievement of status. Lott and Lott (1960) showed how this may become a divisive factor to the group's cohesion. In their study they predicted that members of a three-person group who are rewarded for their performance in front of the other members will have more positive attitudes toward the other members than when public rewards are not given. This prediction was clearly confirmed.

In order for members to believe that the achievement of higher status is predictable, they must be able to maintain predictability in their present positions. This may be achieved by specifying the rules for successful performance on the job and the people who will judge the performance. In addition, the authority of the officeholder must be sufficient to carry out responsibilities. If in performing one's job, the outcomes of one's actions are unpredictable, one cannot successfully fulfill responsibilities. In such a case, failure may become more predictable than success, and if one must continue the effort, the officeholder may predict failure and act to confirm this prediction.

Although provisions for maintaining predictability are necessary to promote group cohesiveness and satisfy group members, these provisions are not sufficient. The group must also provide for the improvement of prediction. From the group's perspective, conditions keep changing and its rules become obsolete because they do not realistically direct the behavior of group members. In such cases the enforcement of existing rules alienates group members and they withdraw group support. This can be counteracted by changing the rules. For example, laws in the United States prohibiting abortions have been changed in many states to allow abortions. This change of rules is realistic because despite legal prohibitions, abortions became common practice. So one reason for changing laws is to keep them in tune with common practice. Legalizing the possession of small amounts of marijuana is another case in point. Such rule changes amount to catching up with the past because they simply legitimate existing practice. Based on his theory and some empirical evidence, Brehm (1966) contends that there is a tendency to desire marijuana and other illegal commodities when the individual feels that the law is an unwarranted infringement on personal freedom. The individual becomes aroused to regain that freedom.

There is also a forward-looking approach to the changing of rules. In this case rules are changed to bring about a beneficial change in practice in the future. The rules define goals that the group is committed to achieve in the future. Passing laws that required automobile manufacturers to reduce the emission of noxious gases in the cars of the future is an example. This was not legitimating common practice; rather, it was an attempt to create a future practice that is for the common good. This approach to the changing of rules is preferred because it represents an attempt to direct changes purposefully in group practice (instead of legitimating existing practice). Passing laws to change practice in the future is especially important in modern technological societies because of accelerated change. For these societies it is necessary to direct change to prevent intense confusion.

Provisions must also be made for members to improve their ability to predict. Members who are not satisfied with their status want to be able to predict ways to achieve a higher status position. This can be accomplished by providing for continuing education so that they may keep up with the times and project goals for themselves. They can learn how to proceed in the present to achieve the goals in the future.

Providing for career advancement also serves to prevent boredom because members are meeting new challenges. However, those members who are engaged in monotonous work need to find daily relief from boredom. The group can provide relief by planning recreation and allowing the members to take breaks during their work day.

The improvement of one's ability to predict and provision of relief from boredom can be facilitated by providing opportunities for members to improve their status, encouraging them to try, and preparing them for higher-status positions through education. Status seeking provides a continuing challenge for many people.

Work groups characteristically are primarily interested in maintaining predictability during work. This is necessary in the production of a product. Novelty and the confusion it may bring is avoided except during coffee breaks.

In the elaborate status structures of large bureaucracies, the positions near the bottom of the hierarchy usually require the execution of routine tasks: assembly-line workers and fruit pickers are examples. In such jobs predictability is monotonously maintained in the performance of the task at hand. The employees in these jobs search for novelty and the relief from boredom when they leave work.

The positions near the top of the hierarchy are discretionary, executive positions. The executives are expected to use their discretion to maintain predictability when confusion emerges, threatening to interfere with production. Consequently they must deal with novel circumstances much of the day. When they leave work they probably search for familiarity and continuity for relief.

Although the relationship between work and leisure is by no means a settled matter, the work of Wilensky (1960) and Snyder and Spreitzer (1974) point to a compensatory relationship between work and leisure. Snyder and Spreitzer found a marked inverse relationship between leisure and work orientation. Wilensky (1960) identifies the compensatory leisure hypothesis as a major hypothesis to be tested.

Recreation and play depend on the eye of the beholder. For those who work at monotonous jobs recreation seems to involve novelty and variability. For those who work to restore order out of inclement chaos, recreation involves stability and harmony.

The Pursuit of Preferences

In addition to satisfying its members and promoting its own cohesiveness by providing for the maintenance and improvement of prediction, the group can further these ends by helping its members obtain their preferences. The master-neuroprint format is the key to understanding the acquisition of preferences. The interest represents the preference the individual wants to satisfy; the goal is the outcome that is proposed to satisfy the interest; and the program is the proposed means of pursuing the goal. Let us consider how provisions may be made for obtaining what one prefers in the areas of language and ritual, values, status, and appetites.

One preference that is often overlooked is the choice by group members to be expert in the language and rituals of the group. Some become involved with the verbal language of the group and attempt to improve their ability to write or speak well. Others are interested in knowing the rituals or group lore that give the group its character and identity. Such people attempt to improve their understanding of the folkways and mores of the culture.

These members become the interpreters of the culture. They learn the correct use of language and the appropriate practice of ritual. The group benefits by assisting them because they clarify group referents for other members and propagate language and ritual as teachers. Those concerned with verbal language write such books as dictionaries and grammar texts or they may teach language in school. Those concerned with ritual and lore write and teach about the cultural identity and evolution of the group.

The group contributes to its own cohesiveness by encouraging these people and employing them as interpreters and teachers of group language and ritual. Because group referents are never isolated from group values, these people become interpreters and teachers of group values as well.

To serve its members and own interests, the group provides public facilities for interpreting and teaching its culture. Public libraries and authorized experts can be provided to clarify traditions. In addition, public schools can be maintained to teach the culture to the members.

A second preference group members may have is to live the good life according to group values. They may find satisfaction in filling particular positions in the group, or they may have status aspirations. In either case, they would support and play by the rules. Such people tend to be conformists and encourage others to conform. They often serve as missionaries encouraging other group members to conform to group values and may attempt to convert outsiders to adopt the rules of the group.

By encouraging people to conform to group values, the group is promoting cohesiveness and stability. The endorsement of the common preferences of the group serves to unite members in the pursuit of group goals by means of procedures that are valued by the group. As George Homans (1974) puts it, conformity to group norms tends to result in a reward called a collective good which enhances further conformity and solidarity. On the other hand, conformists are sometimes a hindrance when the group wishes to change its rules, since they tend to be conservative and resist change. If they are for change of any kind they usually will support new ways of gaining conformity to existing rules rather than to support a change in the rules themselves.

For the benefit of the group and the satisfaction of these members, conformists are employed to pursue traditional goals by traditional means. They are probably more comfortable with too much rather than too little predictability and would probably balk and be ineffective when confronted by ambiguity and change.

A third preference is status seeking. When members learn that status provides authority and authority legitimates the control of the confirmation of predictions, they become interested in improving their status.

Competition for status indicates that the members believe that success in the group is worth pursuing. It is an indirect endorsement of the group by the members and should be encouraged by the group. The group encourages status seeking by offering opportunities and defining rules for being promoted. In addition, the relationship between status positions in the hierarchy must be defined as well as the authority and responsibility of each position. The army, the federal government, and some large corporations publish descriptions of their status hierarchies, rules for being promoted, and job descriptions. Most often they encourage their members to seek promotion, provide opportunities for them to be promoted, and prepare them for promotion through in-service training. Some bureaucracies subsidize the education of members in public schools.

Leadership positions in groups are highly valued. Research by Fu (1979) has shown that even kindergarten-aged children value leadership. While leadership is of high value, the qualities of leadership always have been puzzling and it is difficult for a group to determine who to promote. The type of leadership exhibited in a group is of importance in determining the outcome of group goals and the effectiveness of group process. Peteroy (1979) has shown that expectations of leaders can also affect the self-esteem of group members. Within the context of the present theory the qualities of leadership are the ability to (1) maintain predictability within the group, including the support of group rules; (2) confirm the specific consensual predictions of the group; and (3) change the rules for the benefit of the group. It is these qualities a group should look for when considering a member for promotion.

In the armed forces, such as in the navy, in order to receive a promotion, an enlisted man must first demonstrate that he is a "real navy man" and that he accepts unquestionably navy dogma (maintains predictability and supports the rules of the group). Second, he must demonstrate that he is competent in directing others in the navy tradition (confirms specific consensual predictions). If he continues through promotions, meeting these criteria each time, he may arrive finally at a policy position at which he is encouraged to recommend changes that will improve the service (changes rules for the benefit of the group). However, he may not be trained to change the rules beneficially, in which case he is unable to make this contribution. Too often groups support conformity to existing rules and neglect the other leadership qualities.

If a group awards status primarily because of the first leadership quality, the group will tend to be more rule-oriented than mission-oriented. Members will regard obeying the rules and their superiors as the way to succeed. Under these conditions, each member may dutifully obey superiors and the group may not progress toward any goal. Members may also regard the changing of rules as deviancy and the group may not modify its rules to keep up with changing times.

The research on leadership shows in general that those who attempt leadership tend to be ascendant or upwardly mobile and sociable (Bass et al. 1953). Those who become leaders are assertive (Borg 1960), dominant (Cattel and Stuce 1960; Stogdill 1948; Megarger, Bogart, and Anderson 1966; Smith and Cook 1973; Scioli, Dyson, and Fleitas 1974; and Watson 1971), participate in group activities (Shaw 1959b), and are empathetic (Bell and Hall 1954). These findings tend to conform to our general impressions of leadership characteristics.

The research also supports the particular leadership traits we propose. With respect to providing for the maintenance of predictability, Haythorn (1953) shows that leaders promote group cohesiveness. Stogdill (1948) found that leaders are cooperative and dependable. Based on the work of other researchers (Grant 1955; Roach 1956), Bass (1966) presented a model for assessing leadership behavior. The model includes promoting compliance to group rules and group loyalty as leadership traits. Heizer (1972) found that planning was a trait of the effective leader. All of these leadership characteristics contribute to the maintenance of predictability within the group.

There also is support for the second leadership trait we propose, that is, leaders are influential in gaining confirmation of group predictions. Shaw (1959b) showed that individual prominence in the group correlates positively with influence on group decisions. Meyer (1961) found a positive relationship between leadership and social judgment, while Stogdill (1948) found social insight and skill to be related to leadership. More pertinent to our proposal, there are a number of studies that show leadership to be related to contributing to the achievement of specific group goals (Bass et al. 1953; Palmer 1962; Maier 1950; Sheritz 1955; and Shaw and Penrod 1962).

Our final proposal contends that leaders change the rules for the benefit of the group. The evidence supporting this point is indirect. Borg (1960) found leaders to be assertive and creative and to vary their behavior from role expectations. McDavid and Sistrunk (1964) found dominance to be inversely correlated with conformity, and Cattel and Stuce (1960) showed that dominant group members offer negative social-emotional remarks. We can infer that although leaders are cooperative, dependable and loyal, and support group cohesiveness and rules, they are creatively challenging the status quo and existing rules.

Although the research on leadership is far from conclusive, there is enough congruence between our proposals and existing evidence to warrant additional research to test the proposals.

There is an interesting connection between the three qualities of leadership and *social prominence*. Prominence may be achieved by exhibiting these qualities, but the display of each quality in itself leads to social prominence via a distinct route.

The person who supports the group's rules (the first leadership quality) gains prominence by systematically moving up in the status structure. That person supports group language and ritual, group values, and the rules for achieving status, and is mindful of the authority and responsibilities of the people in the various status positions. That person is also considerate of subordinates, friendly and helpful to peers, and deferent to authority, never bypassing immediate superiors. That person is considered loyal, dutiful, and respectful by the members of the group, is rewarded by being given their support whenever eligible for higher-status position, receives regular promotions, and unobtrusively moves to the top of the status structure.

The person who directs the confirmation of the group's predictions (the second leadership quality) is mission-oriented and uses talents to mobilize resources in pursuit of the common good. This is the person who is most typically thought of as a leader. Examples are numerous. Generals, like Washington, Grant, McArthur, and Eisenhower exhibit this quality because they directed the winning of wars; empire builders such as Henry Ford and John D. Rockefeller also qualify.

It is important to realize that this quality of leadership is not stated as "directing the achievement of group goals." This is because a leader directs the confirmation of group predictions whether or not their goal is achieved. For instance, we might say that prior to World War II, Britain's goal was to maintain peace. This defined success, and Chamberlain was the leader who claimed to his countrymen after visiting Hitler, "I bring you peace in our time." However, when Hitler violated one treaty after another it became evident that war was inevitable, and this became the consensual prediction. After war began Chamberlain was forsaken for the leadership of Winston Churchill, who had been predicting that war was inevitable. Churchill then directed the confirmation of the prediction that Britain, with her allies, would win the war.

The person who changes the rules for the benefit of the group (the third quality of leadership) changes the way people look at their affairs. These are the revolutionaries. Among them are Moses, Buddha, Christ, and Mohammed in the area of religion. Newton and Einstein are examples in the physical sciences and Freud and Skinner in the social sciences. In political affairs Thomas Jefferson exhibited this quality more than George Washington. The rule changers are ahead of their time, and acceptance of their ideas is often slow. If their ideas concern new ways to regard the environment, acceptance is faster than if their ideas require people to change their views of themselves.

Glaser and Skills (1966), when reviewing the role of change in groups, indicated an article by Paul R. Lawrence which deals with resistance to change. Lawrence's general conclusion about overcoming resistance to change, after relevant research was reviewed, was that the way to overcome this resistance was by getting group members to participate actively in making the change. This is a function of this third type of leader.

A fourth preference may be the satisfaction of one's appetites. Appetites are a personal matter and vary from one individual to the next and for any given individual from time to time. However, no matter how variable a person's appetite may be, some people are prone to be more concerned with them than anything else, and the group must then deal with hedonism.

It was said that group cohesiveness is enhanced when group members work together to achieve a common goal. The pursuit of the satisfaction of personal appetites creates diversity and disrupts group activities. Therefore, the group must prevent such pursuits from interfering with the common good. This may be accomplished by prohibiting the pursuit of the satisfaction of personal appetites at times when the group is operating in accordance with rules. This might be during work when members are cooperating on an assembly line to produce a commodity or during recreation when a group is playing a game according to rules such as bridge, football, or Monopoly® . At such times the expression of personal sentiments intrudes and interferes with the coordination or concentration that is needed to follow the rules.

On the other hand, members will attempt to satisfy their appetites, and the group must deal with this tendency. Members can be encouraged to pursue the satisfaction of their appetites on their own time as a private matter. They can be taught that group activities are for the common good, and private activities should not interfere with conformity to rules when there is a conflict.

We have characterized four different types of people depending on whether their preferences were the support of language and ritual, the support of group values, the pursuit of status, or the pursuit of the satisfaction of personal appetites. Although there are some people who resemble these stereotypes, you should be reminded that all members are involved to some extent in each of these pursuits. However, the extent of involvement in each pursuit varies from member to member.

Children are born into the family group. It is the first and only group they know for a while. Eventually, they learn that they and their families belong to other groups, such as the church and the community. As adults they may be members of many groups, especially if they live in a large industrialized society. Each of these groups provides an avenue for them to pursue their preferences—if they do not succeed in one group they can try in another. In addition, they have allegiances to their groups and they are expected to assume their responsibilities in each of them. Most adults belong to multiple groups, which provide them with multiple opportunities and impose upon them multiple obligations.

14 The Relationships among Members

Maintaining and Improving Prediction

Because of an interest in maintaining predictability, a group member solicits other members to assist in the formulation of predictions and afterward in attempts to confirm predictions. This is because members learn that feedback improves the accuracy of prediction in the first place and assistance often is needed to enhance the confirmation of a prediction.

On the other hand, our self-esteem depends on our ability to predict. Therefore, we are reluctant to admit that our identifications and predictions are wrong. This inclination often is exacerbated by cultural influence. In our culture and others, mistakes are equated with failure. The fault is that it is necessary to admit to a mistake before we can correct it. If we do not correct our mistakes we cannot proceed to confirm our predictions. Some parents always regard mistakes on the examinations their children take in school as an indication of failure rather than as feedback from the teacher that allows the child to correct mistakes.

Festinger (1957) illustrates the importance of the group in helping the individual to confirm predictions. He posits the existence of a state of tension within the individual in the face of dissonant (inconsistent) cognitions. That is to say that when there exists an occasion in which an individual is saying one thing and believing another, an unpleasant tension state exists. In order to reduce this tension, the individual is impelled to seek social support. If in the seeking of *social support* (confirmation of the accuracy of an identification or prediction), the individual in fact finds that this support is not forthcoming, there is dissonance between his or her belief and that of the group. Festinger posits three basic ways that the individual can reduce this dissonance or better confirm predictions. One could change one of the dissonant elements, add new elements consonant with cognitions, or decrease the importance of the elements that are involved in the dissonance. Hence, in order to get beliefs back in line with the group so that they will again confirm's one's predictions, the individual will change beliefs or get the group to change. One could also repress cognitions or change the social group to one that would be more predictable.

An example of this process is found in a study by Kipnis (1961). He identified a dissonant situation—male college students who on initial contact perceived themselves as either better or worse than their new friends.

Within six weeks the students shifted their self-ratings so that they became congruent with those of their friends. Festinger, in his own writing and Aronson (1968), offer experimental evidence showing how groups can arouse dissonance in individuals as well as how groups can reduce dissonance. According to prediction theory, people seek confirmation from others to increase the accuracy of their identifications and predictions.

Although people would rather be right than wrong, their inclination to improve their ability to predict prompts them to seek help from others to correct their mistakes. Whether we take golf lessons, driving lessons, or courses in school, we want our teachers to correct our mistakes so that we may improve. Remediation is an important part of teaching, and it is more easily accepted if the group does not stigmatize those who need remediation.

When one individual remediates another, correction for violating a rule is usually involved. A golfing instructor teaches rules of good golfing, a driving instructor teaches rules of good driving, and so forth. When their students err, they are corrected for violating a rule. Remediation often involves restating the rules and working toward conformity.

Sometimes a member is corrected without wanting remediation—corrections are often enforced. Children are captives in school until they are of legal age to withdraw. Their teachers enforce the rules of deportment and the subjects they learn. Students may be required to redo an arithmetic problem when they derive the wrong answer, and remediation may involve correcting the inappropriate use of an arithmetic rule.

Remediation is often accompanied by punishment. A teacher may punish a student for violating a rule governing pupil conduct, or a driver may be fined for violating a traffic law. People, in general, are not prone to reveal their mistakes to those who are expected to issue punishment for an infraction.

Feedback from other members is necessary to confirm that we are maintaining predictability and correct our mistakes so that we can improve our ability to predict.

We also seek the company of others to find relief from boredom. Whatever our daily routine is like, we leave it to seek contrast. A bookkeeper who ritualistically posts numbers into a ledger all day may find the aberrant behavior of his children pleasing. On the other hand, an executive who is trying constantly to smooth disruptions at work may ask her husband to make the children behave. She might prefer to listen to music. In a review of the literature on the subject, Fox (1971) concludes that background music played to industrial workers benefits performance when the worker is performing simple, routine, or boring tasks. However, there is no evidence that music has any benefit when the worker is performing complex tasks.

Entertainment in general is conceived to bring relief from boredom. As work becomes more specialized and routine in modern industry and relaxation during retirement wears thin after a while, entertainment leans more and more toward the unusual, often the bizarre. However, traditional excursions into adventure find resolution before they are over. Most stories in books, movies, and on television bring adventure, but predictability is restored by the end of the story. The bad guy is caught, the sick person is restored to health, the young girl finds a mate. The jokes of a comedian involve us in surprising situations, but we expect to be given a punch line at the end of the joke that will make us laugh. If the comedian is talented our expectations are fulfilled.

Pursuing Preferences

In addition to being interested in maintaining predictability and improving one's ability to predict, the group member is motivated to pursue preferences. We solicit other members to assist us, and to encourage their assistance, we help them. Preferences are usually obtained through the exchange of goods and services between members. Peter Blau (1964) states that reciprocation serves as a starting mechanism of social interaction. Continued reciprocation builds trust and integration.

Members will assist each other in the interpretation of group languages. It is not uncommon for one member to informally correct another's use of verbal language. (Dictionaries are at hand to settle disputes.) A request for clarification is automatic when one member does not understand what another is saying. Communication is a necessary part of sharing and members are prompted to restate their remarks until they are understood by the receiver.

Group members participate in group ritual to satisfy their common identity, and they teach their rituals to the young. These exercises emphasize unity and harmony among group members rather than competition. Durkheim (1951) contends that ritual and ceremony play an essential role in holding society together. Through ritual worship of a common totem, members of primitive tribes reaffirm their mutual commitment and collective solidarity. Goffman describes a number of interpersonal rituals. Presentation rituals (Goffman 1956, 1967) include acts such as invitations and compliments through which an individual shows appreciation of a group member. Avoidance rituals (Goffman 1963) show respect for the privacy of members such as maintaining distance and avoiding eye contact when encountering a stranger. Maintenance rituals (Goffman 1971), such as family reunions, serve to maintain and strengthen bonds. Ratification rituals (Goffman 1971), such as congratulations at marriage and condolences at divorce, mark the passage of an individual from one status to another. Access rituals (Goffman 1955, 1967), such as hellos and goodbyes, are used to indicate transition from more intimate to more remote access to one another.

Members will express to one another their endorsement of group values. Because the support of the family, work for the common good, and education are values of most societies, people in every culture will support these values. Most Americans will openly state their support for the Bill of Rights and the Constitution, although some may offer their interpretation of these documents. Communists pronounce their support of the Marxist doctrine.

Whether or not people conform to the values of their group they are prone to express their endorsement. Those who protest against group values tend to be regarded as heretics with whom it is dangerous to associate. Guilt by association is something to worry about in many societies. The careers of many Americans were ruined during the McCarthy era when they were found guilty of being communist sympathizers because they were associated with communists.

A person demonstrates an endorsement of group values when working with other members to achieve group goals. A member of the Shrine fraternity shows that he shares group values when he contributes to the construction of a children's hospital.

Members also enforce conformity to group rules. Members of a service organization who are reluctant to make an adequate contribution may be hounded by others until they do so or embarrassed by public exposure if they do not.

If members want to achieve higher status it behooves them to show their endorsement of group values. As Hamblin, Miller, and Wiggins (1961) showed, the power and influence of the group leader is dependent on the ability to help the group achieve its goals. Sherif, White, and Harvery (1955) note that, in order to enhance that position, a leader must show support of the group's purposes and goals and act consistently with the internal norms and values. Blau (1964) indicates that an aspirant to leadership gains obligation and support from group members when contributing to the achievement of group goals.

The pursuit of status presents status seekers with a puzzling problem. They must show a willingness to cooperate with group members while they are competing with some for higher status. A delicate balance must be maintained between expressions of comradeship and the need to triumph over competitors. They must show their willingness to support persons of higher status while seeking a higher-status position for themselves so that they do not need to. They must seek the support of those capable of elevating their positions by convincing these people that they merit their support and that they can benefit them if they achieve the status they seek.

A person running for office needs financial support for a campaign. To obtain funds the candidate is likely to indicate to potential contributors how they can benefit. If the candidate is in a primary election and is too insulting in declamations toward opponents, some support may be lost because the party may see an unwillingness to support an opponent should the bid for the nomination be lost. If one is too insulting toward one's peers, one's allegiance to one's group comes into question, hence the phrase "the loyal opposition." One must show the tendency to cooperate with one's competitors.

An experiment by Hollander (1960) shows the relationship between status and conformity. In this experiment, researcher confederates were acting as group members in problem-solving situations. Nonconformity on the part of the confederate was introduced at various times and his influence was measured by the number of times the confederate's recommended solution was accepted by the group as their choice. Hollander found that there was a significant increase in his influence as the trials progressed. This was presumably a function of past evidence of competence. Another factor was revealed as well: past conformity of the confederate was found to be related both significantly and positively to the acceptance of his influence.

The satisfaction of personal desires within one's group is also a sticky business. The group endorses the support of its common interests and considers excessive attempts to satisfy personal desires as exploitation, contrary to the common good. An architect who belongs to a social club may attempt to use the club as a vehicle for obtaining clients. This may be regarded as exploitation, particularly if attempts are too open and aggressive. On the other hand, helping the social club achieve a common goal would please the members. The architect, for example, could volunteer services in designing a new facility for the club. Although people are inclined toward satisfying their desires, they must do it discreetly without giving the impression that they are subverting their group.

To maintain and improve prediction and pursue preferences, there are three types of individuals a member relates to: members of higher status, members of lower status, and peers. Each is courted with different tactics.

Relating to Members of Lower Status

Maintaining and Improving Prediction

To maintain predictability, authorities must understand the goals they are to achieve and the programs they may use to achieve the goals. They must also understand the part that each subordinate is to play in the execution of the program and the idiosyncracies of these subordinates. Some may have traits that interfere with group progress, such as tardiness, absenteeism, or rabble-rousing. Others may be cooperative, diligent, and talented and contribute to the achievement of group goals. Knowing the characteristics of the members helps an authority figure to direct effectively the activities of the group. The authority can control aberrant behavior more efficiently and assign tasks that suit them best.

To maintain predictability further, the authority figure does not let aberrant behavior interfere with the group mission. Subordinates are informed that they are to satisfy their personal desires privately. While they are at work, they are to contribute to the group's mission. However, knowing that individuals are prone to pursue their desires, one may allow them to express their desires within the framework of the group's mission. A principal may permit a teacher some latitude in choosing instructional methods and materials. The authority figure may also arrange for informal social associations where members may be encouraged to forget about the group goals for the moment and relate to each other on a personal basis. Group parties, bowling leagues, softball teams, and coffee breaks provide time for the satisfaction of personal desires and cement group loyalties. Breaks during the workday also serve to provide respite from boredom.

The Ohio State University studies of work relations conducted in the early 1950s (Fleishman 1967; Fleishman and Harris 1962; Fleishman, Harris, and Burlt 1955) describe leadership behavior on two dimensions; consideration, which is people-related activity and initiating structure, which is task-related activity. They found that if a leader is described as considerate, increased structure will increase turnover and grievances. These findings have been upheld by later research.

In order to maintain predictability, it is important for the authority to make certain that subordinates know the rules and can execute them. Education must be provided when it is necessary to teach rules and the proper execution of them. The authority must make provisions for clarification of the rules should a subordinate be in doubt. To accomplish this, rules can be published and group officials can be assigned to interpret the rules. In addition, the rules must be enforced impartially. This assures that the rules will be followed and that members will regard enforcement as fair treatment. Persistent violators of rules are dismissed.

Sherif's (1966) studies at a boys' camp support this position. The group, at the initiative of its leader, had instituted a standard penalty for "getting out of line . . . which was administered by the leader with the consent of the entire membership" (p. 81). He found that at the end of the group-formation phase, "most behavior in the group was in accord with the customary modus operandum with very little need for correctives" (p. 81, 82).

A superior must also be careful not to favor subordinates who are personally pleasing since this could lead to partiality in the enforcement of rules. A factor analysis conducted by Roach (1956) showed impartiality to be an important ingredient of supervisory behavior.

An authority figure must be prepared to make changes that will facilitate the achievement of group goals and improve the predictive skills of all involved. There may be a need to change personnel if a member is not doing a job well. Further, the authority must be prepared to change the rules if they are inhibiting the group effort and modify their enforcement if it is extreme or unfair. Chapter 13 furnished evidence that effective leaders possess these characteristics.

By providing for an exchange of views with subordinates the authority can make changes that are in keeping with the subordinates' desires. For instance, a minister may seek the advice of the congregation to improve services. An authority can request recommendations in rules and their enforcement as well as changes in personnel. To reduce fear of retaliation, insurance of anonymity for those making recommendations can be given. Roach (1956) also found "approachability" and "open-mindedness" to be important factors of supervisory behavior.

A study by Coch (1948) indicates that group members who participated in decision making were more productive than those who did not. Three groups were used. In one group members participated directly in decision making; in a second group participation was through a representative; and the third group did not participate in decision making. The members of the first and second groups were more productive on the job. The research findings of Medow and Zander (1965) suggest that people who have more important roles in the work of the group may have a greater sense of responsibility.

Pursuing Preferences

An authority will be more effective by making certain that the languages of the group are used correctly so that communication among members may be facilitated. This is a matter of providing references for the interpretation of language. In addition to the folk language of the society there are professional languages that are used. Mathematicians converse in the language of mathematics, computer programmers and operators use computer language, and some psychologists speak "Freudian."

It is not only imperative that the symbols of a language mean the same thing to the members who use them, but it is also important that the symbols make reference to empirical events. They should refer to events that can be identified in the real world. Otherwise, they cannot help us deal with reality. For example, there are no known counterparts that have been located in the real world for the Freudian symbols id, ego, and superego.

Further, we would not know where to look for them if we wished to find them. Such symbols are abstractions that are given meaning through definition. However, an abstraction is useless if we cannot find examples in reality that fit into the category. Humans are inclined to create jargon that does not denote events in the real world, and such jargon can cripple our efforts to improve our ability to predict.

The authority creates unity and comraderie in the group by utilizing group rituals to focus the members' attention in their common identity. It is necessary to emphasize their similarity and their differences from outsiders to improve the rapport among them. Hence, colleges have their school songs, cheers, and colors. Their sports teams wear the school colors and, during sports contests, the members sing the college songs and shout their cheers. In addition, it would be difficult to tell one's team from the opponent if different uniforms were not worn.

An authority must convey to subordinates that they all share common values and that the group is to strive together to achieve what the group values. The authority is to provide leadership in the common good and assert that neither the authority nor the subordinate shall subvert the group values. It is the authority's duty to clarify and enforce rules so that the values can be maintained. It is in this vein that solicitations are made for the support of subordinates. If taking an initiative or changing a rule, the authority must explain that arbitrariness is not intended by showing how the change in the state of affairs will uphold group values. This is essentially the creation of one or more superordinate goals for the group. There is much empirical research that shows how influential a superordinate goal can be in promotion of group solidarity.

The responsibility for the morale of subordinates is a charge that is often given to an authority figure. Sometimes the maintenance of group morale is interpreted as making members happy. Then the happiness of each group member becomes the responsibility of the authority figure. This perverts leadership responsibility because first it is impossible for one person to insure another's happiness. Whatever happiness is, it varies from one individual to the next. By focusing on the personal desires of the members the authority figure is catering to individual differences instead of concentrating on the achievement of group goals.

In one of the first experimental studies to measure the influence that group cohesion has on group members, Schacter (1951b) investigated the hypothesis that a group's power to influence its members is positively correlated with group cohesiveness. In this study, increases or decreases in group productivity were taken as an indication that the group had success in influencing its members. The findings of this study were inconclusive in terms of high productivity but did indicate that high-cohesive groups were more receptive to negative induction than were low-cohesive groups.

Berkowitz (1954), following Schacter's lead, further investigated the relationship between productivity and cohesiveness in the group. Using a sample of thirty-four college males, he randomly assigned them to four experimental groups having four conditions: high productivity and high cohesiveness; high productivity and low cohesiveness; low productivity and high cohesiveness; and low productivity and low cohesiveness. In all the groups, the coworkers were the experimenter's assistants. In each condition and for different time periods there was a consistently significant interaction between the standard that the group set and the amount of group cohesiveness. These results supported their major hypothesis. A member of a cohesive group "will tend to conform to the perceived group standard—by raising production if the standard is high for high production or by lowering it, or not increasing as rapidly, if the standard is for low production—even after overt pressure to conform to the group standard is discontinued" (Berkowitz 1954, p. 519). This strongly supports Schacter's earlier position that the greater the group's cohesiveness, the greater the group's influence on its members. Another study supports this point. Throughout and after World War II, Janis (1968) along with others collected and analyzed information from the American, British, and German armies about morale. He deals at length with the role of external threat in developing group cohesion and how the extremely cohesive group may develop internal systems of rules which are particularly strong.

It may be all right to play music to members to soothe them or to provide attractive work conditions, but a leader must try to create group morale by generating enthusiasm in the achievement of group goals. The morale of assembly-line workers can be improved by instilling pride in their work. Their morale can be high because they cooperate to build quality products efficiently.

Great leaders insist on personal sacrifice for the common good. Morale is maintained because of devotion to the team effort and the achievement of the group's goal. Generals Eisenhower and Patton are examples of such leaders, as well as President Kennedy, who said, "Ask not what your country can do for you. Ask what you can do for your country."

By obtaining advice from other group members, subordinates, superordinates, and peers and insuring them that they will be considered in making decisions, an authority figure is likely to gain group support in efforts to be promoted to a higher station. One's associates are more likely to support a person for promotion who flatters them by seeking and considering their advice. This is because they are inclined to regard the solicitation as a cooperative overture and feel that they have an indirect vote in decisions that may affect them.

Because an authority is endowed the responsibility of providing leadership to attain group goals, the authority will not be supported through conveying the impression that the achievement of status is held above group values. Sometimes it is suggested that for people of high status, conformity is a sham since leaders set the rules they conform to. While this may be true to some extent, in actual situations there is some experimental evidence that leaders do conform to rules imposed on them. Emerson (1973), in a study of the relationship between power and conformity, found that leaders conformed to norms set by the experimenter.

It would seem that those who possess the qualities of leadership are the ones who would be supported for higher-status positions. But this is not always the case. An authority figure gains support by supporting the group rules and helping confirm the group's consensual predictions. Richard Nixon lost favor by violating the first quality of leadership when he disregarded the fundamental laws of the nation. He gained favor when he exhibited the second quality of leadership—he removed us from Viet Nam, helping confirm a consensual prediction.

However, exhibiting the third quality of leadership—changing the rules for the benefit of the group—does not always gain support. It must be handled delicately, lest the authority figure's actions backfire.

There are always conservatives in the group who resist change. Conservatives are usually older members who have attained higher status that they want to hold and, in general, any change in rules is resisted by them. They support the status by seniority and the status quo which at least entitles them to their present position.

It is less controversial to advocate new ways of conforming to existing rules than to advocate a change in the rules. However, an authority figure is occasionally compelled to try and must first convince other authority figures that it is for the benefit of the group and introduce the rule change as unobtrusively as possible. Otherwise, resistance will build and the authority figure may be dubbed disloyal.

In his efforts to bring the United States out of the Depression, Franklin D. Roosevelt advocated changes that were recommended by Karl Marx—the organization of labor, income tax, and inheritance tax. These changes are in fact part of the communist doctrine, which is alien to the American belief in free enterprise. Because we were in a depression and there was a need to redistribute the wealth, Roosevelt was able to convince legislators to pass laws bringing about these changes. However, the rhetoric used by Roosevelt to gain support for the new legislation was sugar coated and the proposed laws were never associated with communist doctrine.

To change rules in a democracy, tact and persuasion must be substituted for the muscle of authority. Authority figures may satisfy their desires by directing subordinates to supply what they want. However, because the pursuit of personal desires interferes with the common mission of the group, they are setting a bad example and subverting their effectiveness. It is not acceptable to advocate that other members sacrifice the satisfaction of their desire to the common good while the authority figures selfishly indulge themselves. This will cause the authority to lose the support of group members. Authority figures, like other group members, should pursue their desires privately. Richard Nixon was accused of exploiting the nation because he spent large sums of money to satisfy his personal desires. The use of funds and federal employees to improve his San Clemente residence is a case in point. There is evidence which suggests that advocating the importance of satisfying group interests rather than one's personal interests is a way to gain influence in a group. Walster, Aronson, and Abrahams (1966) demonstrated, in an experimental study, that persons of low prestige could increase their persuasiveness in the group by assuming such a posture.

Blau (1964) notes that the dynamics of leadership and the exchange of services with group members pose a dilemma. Stable leadership rests on power over others and their legitimating approval of that power. The attainment of power and the attainment of social approval make opposing demands. To achieve power one must furnish services that make others dependent while remaining independent of any services they offer in return. To legitimate this power, the leader must earn social approval of followers; hence, it is impossible to maintain complete independence of them. An individual who refuses to accept offers of favors from those who owe favors and who insists on independence from them is experienced as rejecting and evokes their disapproval. The leader's best course is first to mobilize power, then be magnanimous in its use. With much power, the leader can make moderate demands and eliminate fear. The leader who gives services but takes nothing from the others gains their respect—but also fear (xenophobia) and hostility. To achieve social approval and legitimation, the leader should let the followers give something in return but of less value than the leader gave. After the initial establishment of power, the leader can lead the organization better with the social approval and willing cooperation of the others, based on demonstrated approachability (humility, modesty, humaneness, openness) as well as service for the common interest.

Relating to Members of Higher Status

Maintaining and Improving Prediction

For subordinates to succeed in their group it is necessary for them to remain in the good graces of authority figures as long as the authority figures prevail. Therefore, they must be able to predict the actions of these authority figures. At first it would seem sufficient to learn the rules of the group. However, authority figures have the prerogative to interpet and change rules. As a result, the subordinates can better predict the actions of the authority figure if they know their superior's priorities and interpretation of the rules. This knowledge also is used so that the subordinates can make themselves predictable to the authority figure. Superiors are antagonized by unpredictable members and tend to regard them as deviants. So subordinates are better able to predict a superior and make themselves predictable to the superior when they know the superior's views of the rules.

Making one's self more predictable to one's boss requires one to be open and announce one's plans ahead of time. The plans are offered as tentative subject to the boss' approval and modifications. Making one's self predictable does not require surrendering to every whim of the boss. Groveling at the feet of a superior is demeaning in the eyes of others, and such behavior is regarded as that of a sycophant or apple polisher.

It is more impressive for a subordinate to express loyalty to a boss while offering suggestions for improvement in the pursuit of the common goal. Such suggestions are regarded as attempts to help. Subordinates who do nothing but agree are not contributing to improvement and are often not believed because it is unlikely that one person can agree with everything another says. However, Byrne, Rasche, and Kelley (1974) indicate that flattery and positive statements are liked, even when the person receiving them knows they are probably not true.

To improve their ability to predict, subordinates may learn the views of an authority figure by asking questions. This is regarded as the legitimate prerogative of any subordinate. It is advisable when asking questions of one's boss to convey the impression that you have done your homework. This amounts to conveying the impression that you have studied the rules and want clarification. Also, if it is necessary to take exception to a rule, it is safer for the subordinate to receive permission from the authority. Violations of the rules are not considered acts of deviancy when they are permitted by one's boss.

It is inadvisable for members to convey to their superior that they are bored carrying out their duties. Members should express to the boss enthusiasm in pursuing the group's mission under the boss' leadership.

In an experimental attempt to investigate the relationship between upward mobility and behavior toward superiors, Cohen (1958) created an artificial hierarchy. In this hierarchy, rank was defined both as status and the power to fulfill need satisfaction. (In terms of the present theory, power amounts to the ability to help another predict successfully and obtain their preferences.) Cohen found that those with low rank who have the ability to move upward communicate in a way designed to protect and enhance their relationships with those higher up. This is not the case with those who were experimentally frozen into the low rank, who did not try to protect or enhance their relationships with higher ups. Upwardly mobile subjects made fewer critical comments about superiors, indicated less attraction toward their peer group, and spent more time on task.

Pursuing Preferences

To insure that they are predictable to an authority figure and that the authority figure is predictable to them, subordinates must know the language of their group. Otherwise they are not able to communicate. In addition, they should know if there are any particular meanings a superior assigns to language symbols. In many instances, subordinates are required to learn particular language symbols to conduct their work. Electricians must learn electrical symbols so they can read circuitry on a blueprint. In addition, parliamentary procedures are often used at group meetings. Members must learn how to use the appropriate language to express themselves so that they can participate. The superior would need to know parliamentary procedure and might be antagonized when a member violates the procedure and must be ruled out of order.

Subordinates must also conform to the group rituals to ratify their group identity or face a possible reprimand from a superior. Allegiance to one's group is verified by attendance and prayer according to the ritual of the religion. Membership in a club often is verified by wearing the club pin or ring. Members demonstrate that they subordinate themselves to the greater good when they make their allegiance to the group visible by practicing group ritual.

In some instances the practice of ritual is considered good form, while in other instances conformity is enforced. In the armed services and in the Girl Scouts inspection is held to see that members are dressed properly. Violators are reprimanded and sometimes punished.

To maintain the support of an authority figure, subordinates indicate they support group values and that they believe the actions of the authority figure are for the common good. When subordinates are accused of not contributing to the achievement of group goals, it is advisable for them to claim that it was inadvertent and offer to mend their ways. When superiors explain their actions to subordinates, discerning subordinates indicate that they believe it was for the common good, even though the outcome may not have been desirable.

When a football team loses a game, the coach may explain his actions to a player who was benched most of the game. The player must try to understand the coach's reason for benching him, whatever it may be, and concede that it was for the good of the team. He must also show confidence in the coach's leadership by telling him that he is a master strategist and that the game was probably lost because of the "breaks" or other factors beyond the controls of the coach. Failure is more obvious than the reasons for it. It is easier to tell that you have lost the game than to determine the reasons for the loss. Loyalty to one's boss must not be fickle.

Subordinates can support a superior in these ways without appearing to be too fawning. These tactics do not prevent them from making their own recommendations for improvements.

Although subordinates are considered disloyal when they do not support the superior, they may suggest improvements for achieving group goals. Such suggestions are more discreetly made to the superior and should not come to the superior as behind-the-scenes carping that can be construed as a complaint. Spies are everywhere. Suggestions are offered to the boss as an attempt to help the boss succeed, and, of course, it is not discreet to go over the boss' head to make suggestions. This can be interpreted as dissatisfaction with one's immediate superior and as disloyalty.

One ploy in pleading one's case is to cater to the superior's presumed sense of fair play. Indicating to a superior that there are precedents for granting your request is helpful, that is, to point out that similar requests have been granted in the past. Fair play can also be pleaded when subordinates believe that they have been unfairly treated and can document the contention with precedents. Otherwise, they may be considered to be paranoid.

Subordinates are not in a position to change group values, and it is usually not tactful for them to suggest rule changes to superiors. Authority figures tend to regard this as their domain, and unless they provide procedures for making such recommendations subordinates are better off being indirect in their approach to a superior.

A suggestion for a change in a rule is best implanted in a superior's mind as the superior's thinking. Subordinates can give the impression that they have inferred from what the authority figure has said that the authority figure may wish to change the group rules in a certain way and that they, the subordinates, were prompted to give the matter serious thought. Then the subordinates can extol the benefits of changing the rule in support of the idea introduced by their superior.

Subordinates have little leverage in encouraging an authority figure to satisfy their personal desires, and superiors often prevent subordinates from getting personal. Personal desires are regarded as a private matter that subordinates should pursue on their own time. A superior may be offended by overtures to satisfy personal desires, viewing them as an encroachment on both the superior and the group.

Subordinates are asking a favor of a superior when they request the superior to grant a personal request. However, superiors do get involved in the personal problems of their subordinates. Their penchant for displaying power and their concern for their subordinates make them approachable. The subordinates are in a sense appealing to the charitable nature of the superior, admitting that they may have no right to impose. The subordinates might suggest that they come to the superior because of the superior's ability to solve problems of this sort and the superior's expressed interest in the subordinates. They may also suggest to the superior that they have come to the superior to prevent their personal problems from interfering with the group's mission.

It is advisable to attempt to socialize with the boss and to get the boss to accept favors because this obligates the superior to bestow favors on the members. However, it is ill-advised to forget that the boss is the boss even in a social setting. One's posture must always be deferent to a superior.

Relating to Peers (Members Who Are Neither Dominant Nor Subordinate)

Maintaining and Improving Prediction

Peers are concerned with maintaining prediction in order to cooperate with each other so that they may achieve their common goals. Peers clarify and interpret rules for each other and enforce them for this purpose. When people voluntarily sit down to play games such as bridge, checkers, or Scrabble® , often there are no domination-subordination relations to contend with. So one player is not obligated to tell another what to do nor is one player required to defer to another. Rules must be enforced simply because the game cannot be played unless the rules are followed. At the moment their common goal is to play the game.

Even when peers are interacting within a status hierarchy, they enforce rules primarily so that they may cooperate with each other to achieve the group goal. Assembly-line workers operate as a team to produce a product. They cooperate with each other and depend on each other to produce the product, and the rules they follow serve to direct their cooperation. The members of the peer team will enforce conformity to the rules specified in the blueprint. Members who deviate will be corrected so that production may proceed efficiently and effectively. In short, peers in work groups enforce rules to maintain predictability because the benefits of a cooperative division of labor cannot be reaped without conformity to the rules. Schacter (1951a) showed that deviants who fail to conform to group norms are rejected by the other group members. Haythorn (1953) found that unconventionality is interpreted by other group members as a disinterest in the group's tasks and consequently leads to lowered group productivity.

Authority figures enforce rules for the same reason. However, rules are also created to clarify and ritualize the domination-subordination relations in a status hierarchy. The rules directing a noncommissioned officer to salute a commissioned officer in the army is an example. Such rules do not govern directly the productivity of the group and it is not clear when such rules benefit group productivity. In any event, authority figures enforce these rules and peers generally do not. A commissioned officer will reprimand a noncommissioned officer for not saluting. A noncommissioned officer will not attempt to enforce this rule on a fellow noncommissioned officer. However, one might call attention to the infraction to make sure that the peer is aware of the infraction and the consequences for the violation.

Unless a rule violation affects the productivity of the team, one peer will be sympathetic with another's infractions because they are both subordinate. Burke (1967) developed evidence that supports this last point. As long as the task has a "low task legitimation" it will not give rise to tension and hostility. But if the task has a high legitimation (is considered important by the group), then tension and hostility will be generated. The enforcement of rules by a superior reminds peers of their common subordination and creates empathy among peers. Since subordinates are themselves in an "us" and "them" situation, this feeling of empathy is often very strong. The contention that an outside force promotes group cohesion is well documented by the work of Sherif and Sherif (1956) and others (Zander 1968).

A baseball pitcher may be fined by the manager for violating the team curfew. The other players will tend to be sympathetic with the pitcher's plight, unless his pitching is affected. If he loses his control and begins to walk too many batters, his teammates will pressure him to stop dissipating. They will be more concerned with the effect of his dissipation on the team effort than with his violating the curfew.

Peers will help each other to improve their ability to predict, especially if the assistance helps the group achieve its goal. It is not uncommon for one group member to work with a peer that is having a problem that can affect seriously the group effort. Soldiers will help each other improve the performance of their duties when the group as a whole is affected. This includes preparing for barracks inspection as well as preparing for war.

The boredom one feels is more likely to be understood by a peer because it is usually a peer that is subject to that same monotony that you are. Two equals performing the same boring tasks are more likely to understand each other's boredom. In addition, it is not probable that confessing boredom in the pursuit of a group goal to a peer will bring recriminations as confessing boredom to a superior might.

Pursuing Preferences

Peers are interested in language primarily so that they can cooperate in the pursuit of common goals. In order to play a game the language of the game must be learned. To play poker one must know what the terms full house, straight, and flush mean. To play chess one must know what the words pawn, rook, and checkmate symbolize.

In addition, to work together members often must use a professional language. In the construction industry tradesmen must learn how to read a blueprint in order to coordinate their duties in building a house. Doctors use medical language, lawyers use legal language, and there are medical and legal dictionaries to clarify the terms. Because language denotes common referents, language is necessary for social cooperation of any kind.

Peers verify their allegiance to their group and to one another by practicing group ritual. At work group ritual is performed as part of the daily work routine. But other group identifications are not validated without taking measures to practice them intentionally. To validate one's fellowship with other Catholics, a Catholic must go to a Catholic church and participate in the services. The paid officers of a church practice their religion as part of their employment—not so for the layman. To identify themselves with their religion, they must take the time to perform the religious rituals with their fellow laymen at an appointed time and place.

A member may seek verification and clarification of the group's language and rituals from peers with less vulnerability and embarrassment than from authority figures or subordinates. It is necessary for a superior to retain the respect of subordinates in order to provide effective leadership. The superior is expected to be more expert in language and rituals of the group than other group members. An admission of ignorance or doubt can result in a loss of respect.

Peers discuss group values with each other to reevaluate them. Employees discuss their common goals in their labor-union meetings. Management discusses group values at management meetings, such as the board of directors meetings in large corporations. At these meetings peers attempt to use persuasion to get others to subscribe to their views.

Peers have a voice in officially changing values, if group rules give them the voice. In many groups, such as democratic and communistic groups, the greatest good for the greatest number is the referent for establishing group values. However, in a democracy the rules specify that the people shall decide what the greatest good for the greatest number is through agreement. The town meeting is one way of democratically seeking agreement to establish group values. In this case consensus hopefully emerges with discussion. Voting is another way of democratically establishing agreement among peers. In some instances a simple majority determines the values of the group.

The establishment of group values is a policymaking function. When peers set policy, authority figures cater to peers. Such is the case in a republic. When peers do not establish policy, authority figures tend to ignore them, even though the authority figures may claim that their decisions are for the benefit of the citizenry.

A member seeks the support of peers to fulfill status aspirations, if one's peers influence status assignments. In a democracy and a republic, peers elect members to status positions. In an autocracy peer support is not as important since it is often a superior that appoints people to status positions.

To obtain the support of peers it is necessary to convince them that you support group rules, mainly for the purpose of achieving group goals. Empathy can be built with peers by showing acknowledgment of common persecutions imposed by authority figures and acknowledgment of the lack of understanding, appreciation, and cooperation of subordinates.

A member's personal desires can be expressed to one's peers in informal settings when one is not infringing on group activities. Personal desires are told to a *confidante*—a peer who you think cares and understands and who is not apt to use the information to cause you problems with other members. A member does not confide in an authority figure who may levy recriminations. Nor does a member usually confide in a subordinate because superiors wish to retain the respect of subordinates and not become vulnerable to them. For these reasons superiors remain aloof.

Peers are more free to satisfy each other's personal desires. The exchange of favors in an authority-subordinate relationship encumbers and interferes with the duties of each to the other. The authority is supposed to repress the pursuit of personal desires and not to become obligated to use the office to repay a favor. The subordinate may be punished by an authority as a result of asking a personal favor that subverts the common good.

George Homans (1974) contends that, in leisure, members of the small group tend to express favorable sentiment for and associate with members who are equal rather than their social superiors or inferiors. Equals seek each other out in a nonwork situation so that they can exchange activities in which they can return the same sort of reward as they get—activities that range all the way from exchanging jokes to exchanging hospitality.

In conclusion, it should be acknowledged that adults have complex peer, authority, and subordinate relations, as well as complex group memberships. However, it is necessary to extract basic analytic units from these complex relations in order to simplify and understand them. Most unitary member relationships are either with peers, authorities, or subordinates, and each is different.

In this chapter we discussed many aspects of the relationship among group members. The following is a summary of the major issues in the chapter and their relationship to prediction theory.

In maintaining predictability, group members seek confirmation of the accuracy of their identifications and predictions from other group members. Members learn that feedback and often objective judgment enhance the accuracy of identification and prediction. In addition, members solicit assistance from other members when they are attempting to confirm predictions because assistance often is needed to facilitate the confirmation of a prediction. Feedback from others also is necessary to identify mistakes and assistance often is needed to remediate mistakes in order to improve one's ability to predict. Further, assistance from other members is sought to relieve boredom and confusion. When confusion occurs, the company of familiar, predictable people is sought. When boredom occurs, the company of new and entertaining people is sought.

In pursuing preferences group members seek assistance from one another. Members help each other in the interpretation of group languages. You will remember that language standardizes perception and communication. It is the basis for social sharing and the provision of mutual assistance. Thus, although members may prefer engaging in group language and ritual, language serves as the basis for utilizing others to assist in the confirmation of predictions.

Members express to one another their endorsement of group values, and they will provide mutual assistance in enforcing conformity to group rules. In addition, one member will assist another in pursuing the good life in accordance with group values. Although living by group values may be a preference of members, it should be remembered that conformity to group values facilitates prediction. As we said earlier, group values are standards that indicate acceptable and unacceptable behavior. Consequently they enable members to predict when punishment and reward are likely to be forthcoming.

Seeking status is another preference of group members. Members often are in competition for status because status provides authority and legitimates control over the confirmation of predictions. Members may assist other members or attempt to prevent other members from achieving status, depending on their own interests. In addition, members may or may not assist each other in pursuit of the satisfaction of personal appetites. They would be prone not to provide assistance, if the pursuit prevented the group from achieving its goals or conflicted with other members' achieving their preferences.

In relating to members of lower status, authorities maintain predictability by enforcing the pursuit of group goals by means of group rules. To improve prediction, authorities must see that rules are changed when present rules impede the confirmation of predictions. With respect to the pursuit of preferences, authorities must enforce the group's rules of language, values, and status and provide for clarification of these rules to minimize misinterpretations and confusion.

In relating to members of higher status, subordinates contribute to the maintenance of predictability by assisting authorities in the pursuit of group goals in accordance with group programs. Subordinates contribute to the improvement of prediction by suggesting needed rule changes to authorities. Subordinates improve their own ability to predict by learning group rules and the authorities' interpretation of them. This includes rules of language and ritual, values and status. They can openly pursue their preferences in accordance with these rules. However, in pursuing the satisfaction of their appetites, they must do so without interfering with the achievement of group goals.

In relating to peers members contribute to the maintenance of predictability by voluntarily cooperating with them toward the achievement of group goals. Peers will help each other to improve their ability to predict by clarifying and interpreting group rules, helping each other on the job, and cooperating in the relief of boredom. In pursuing preferences, peers conform to rules of language and ritual voluntarily because these rules provide the basis for sharing and cooperation. Peers will use each other as sounding boards to reevaluate group values and seek each other's support to fulfill status aspirations. Also, members can more freely express their interests in satisfying their appetites to their peers and seek their help in satisfying them.

When members pursue language and ritual, value, or status preferences according to group rules, predictability is enhanced. This is because all social rules tend to standardize behavior. Thus group members who follow them are more predictable to one another. The occasions on which the pursuit of preferences countervenes predictability are when preferences are idiosyncratic, as is often the case when members pursue the satisfaction of personal impulses.

15 The Relationships among Groups

In this chapter our discussion of social dynamics focuses on the relationships between one group and another. Group relationships, like the relationships of individual members, are for the purpose of maintaining and improving predictability and confirming particular predictions that are preferred at the time. In addition, a group may pursue these ends in associations with other groups of higher status, other groups of lower status, and other groups of equal status.

Maintaining and Improving Prediction

Because one group influences another, one group must be able to predict how another will act in order to deal with it. The first problem in predicting the actions of another group is to establish lines of communication with it—one group must know what another is doing currently as a basis for predicting what it may do in the future.

Once lines of communication are established, representatives are appointed by the groups. A representative should be expert in the rules of the group and must learn the rules of the other group and how they are enforced. Only then is the representative equipped to discharge the responsibility of predicting how the other group will act.

William Gamson (1961) proposed and tested a theory of Coalition Formation. His theory posits that if we know the payoff for each possible coalition and the decision points, resources, and nonutilitarian-strategy preferences of the possible coalition members, we will be able to predict their behavior.

One factor that makes another person or group more predictable is to know what they predict will happen. Knowing what another anticipates makes the other person more predictable because that other person can be expected to take action to confirm those predictions. We are suggesting that to predict another's behavior it is important to know that person's expectations as well as the goals being pursued. This is because if one is pursuing a goal and expects to achieve it, the probability is greater that one will achieve it than if one is pursuing a goal and does not expect to achieve it.

You can increase the likelihood that your prediction will be confirmed by convincing an opposing person or group that it will be. This plants the expectation in their mind, and they are more likely to act to confirm the expectation. Saaty and Vargas (1980) studied behavior in competition among chess players and found that the outcome of games in chess is determined in part by the player's expectation to win, lose, or draw against the opponent. Suppose a mother wants her daughter to learn something difficult. The mother can increase the probability that the daughter will learn the material if the mother tells the daughter that she can learn it and that she will learn it. So if you are dependent on another to help you confirm your prediction, convince that person to make the same prediction that you make.

The same strategy prevails in dealing with an opponent. Convincing opponents that they will lose in a contest with you will enhance your chances of winning. In a game or sports contest the opponent may not try as hard. In wars enemies sometimes surrender without a fight when they believe their defeat is inevitable—some European countries surrendered to Hitler without a fight. Since no one can be certain about the future and each of us wants to maximize the probability that our predictions will be confirmed, it behooves us to convince others that our predictions will be confirmed. This is the purpose of propaganda.

Hans Morgenthau, in a section of *Politics Among Nations* (1967) entitled "The Struggle for the Minds of Men," explains the purpose of propaganda in foreign policy: ". . . [T]he ultimate aim of foreign policy is always the same: to promote one's interests by changing the mind of the opponent. . . . All foreign policy, then, is a struggle for the minds of men . . . " (p. 325). He states further that "No exact correlations exist between the truth of a political philosophy and its effectiveness as political propaganda" (p. 326).

Lee and Lee (1972) describe a number of devices that are used by propagandists. In summary they are:

1. Name calling: giving an idea a bad name to prevent closer examination of its merits;
2. Glittering generality: associating an idea with a "virtue word," such as democratic, to gain its approval without examining the evidence;
3. Transfer: assigning the attributes of something respected and revered to an idea;
4. Testimonial: having a prominent person testify for or against an idea;
5. Plain-folks play: presenting one's self as "plain folks" and indicating that one's ideas are "of the people";
6. Card stacking: presenting numerous arguments in favor of one's position, whether one's arguments are half-truths or falsehoods, and not presenting opposing views; and
7. Band-wagon play: creating the impression that everyone is in favor of an idea and that it is inevitable that the idea will be accepted.

The aim of propaganda devices is to persuade the audience to predict the acceptance of one's idea as a means of persuading them to accept the idea.

To confirm your predictions it is necessary also to make yourself unpredictable to an opponent. If opponents cannot predict what you will do they cannot take steps to prevent you from achieving your goal. For this reason it is sometimes advisable to give misleading information to an opponent. In sports one team scouts another to be able to predict their tactics, so most teams vary their strategies so that they do not become too predictable.

However, there are times when becoming too unpredictable to an opponent is dangerous. For instance, if there is a threat of war between nations and one wishes to prevent war, when one nation becomes too unpredictable to the other, the other will take steps to restore predictability. One way of restoring predictability is to take the initiative against the other nation. Then the other nation can be predicted to react to the aggression and their actions become more predictable. If the goal is to avoid war, it becomes dangerous to make one's actions too unpredictable because this becomes threatening to an enemy who may attack to restore predictability. The hot line between the USSR and the United States serves the purpose of reducing the probability that a lack of mutual predictability will cause an attack to occur. So if one's goal is to prevent enemy aggression, one does not make one's actions too unpredictable. On the other hand, if the goal is to beat an opponent in a contest, one makes one's actions as unpredictable as possible.

An example of the type of situation that will become so polarized that it will generate a breakdown in communications and a concomitant increase in unpredictability can be seen in the following win-lose situations. First, in many labor-management situations, the interests of the two groups tend to be on a win-lose basis. This is what strikes and lock outs are all about. Gersuny (1967), in a study of grievance records of a large union local, found that a system of rules developed over the years by the union and management mediated against a polarized win-lose relationship. However, a code of rules does not always develop. As Morgenthau (1967) points out, *diplomacy* (the mediation of conflicts between groups) cannot proceed in the face of two diametrically opposed conflicting doctrines.

It is generally true that taking the offense makes circumstances more predictable than reacting defensively. You at least can predict what you will do as well as predicting how the opponent may counteract your offensive. When you are on the defensive you have more difficulty predicting an opponent's actions and you must await those actions before deciding how you will defend against them. Hence the adage, "the best defense is a good offense."

Opposition between groups emerges as a natural part of group process. Different groups have different rules. Members of one group can distinguish their own members from members of other groups because members of different groups exhibit different behavior when conforming to the rules of their groups, thus marking their distinctiveness. Pood (1980) found that groups that confronted conflict in a more predictable, regulated manner were more likely to develop more accurate decisions than groups who used unpredictable, unregulated responses.

The noticeable differences between groups make members of one group identify members of the other group as outsiders and aliens. The need to maintain predictability encourages the members of each group to reinforce the idea that their group rules are superior to those of the other group. What begins as the noting of differences becomes subject to the other's influence. Then each group tends to fear that the other group will impose its rules. When this happens the other group is regarded as an enemy who must be resisted to preserve "our better way of life." One group begins to restrict its associations with the other, defends against them, and attempts to triumph over them. Hostility, conflict, and often violence emerge as the groups contest each other. As Morgenthau (1967) points out, ". . . ideologies render involvement in that contest for power psychologically and morally acceptable . . . " (p. 84).

Sherif and Sherif (1953) point out that although the development of attitudes toward out-group members can be affected by experiences and frustrations suffered in dealing with the out-group, this is not typically where these attitudes come from. They make and document the point that these attitudes are an integral part of the earliest socialization processes. Therefore, it is important to remember that the development of opposition between two groups is a natural process as is the development of norms and stereotypes that accompanies it. The very process of becoming an in-group member means that one internalizes the prevailing rules of the group.

Weidner (1960) studied the values of members of various governmental agencies. He found that the members identified with the goals and values of their particular agency, and the values within each agency could be differentiated from those of the other agencies of the bureaucratic structure. Siegel and Siegel (1957) studied the influence of changing one's group membership on one's values. They found the greatest change in values among subjects who changed from a group they preferred to a group not of their preference. The evidence that groups can instill their values in their members is compelling. Etzioni (1964) points out that one way a group can insure cohesiveness and conformity to its values is to admit members who already subscribe to its values and convey to those admitted to the group that they possess exclusive and admirable attributes.

In an examination of the variables affecting the development of group hostility (particularly ethnic hostility), Bettelheim and Janowitz (1949) illuminated some of the basic roots of intolerance. They contend that hostility in a group member stems from the individual's feeling that he or she has suffered deprivation in the past and from anxiety at the anticipation of future tasks. They also showed that individuals tended to blame out-groups for their personal failing and to attribute to the out-group member those characteristics which they would deny in themselves. This was accomplished through the formation of stereotypes. It would seem that a compensatory relationship exists between the individual's success in life and the level of hostility to out-group members. It might be that when unsuccessful at dealing with life, the individual may withdraw into stronger in-group identification and correspondingly stronger out-group hostility. This may well be a factor that helps explain individual variations among group members in terms of how strongly they identify with the in-group and its set of rules.

Sherif, White, and Harvery (1955), in examining the development of norms and stereotypes, conducted a study of intergroup behavior. The experimental groups were introduced to activities that were competitive and mutually frustrating. Hostile attitudes and unfavorable stereotypes developed among members of each group toward the other groups.

The development of win-lose situations seems to increase strongly the potential for intergroup conflict. As Sherif (1966) says, "The sufficient condition for the rise of hostile and aggressive deeds . . . was the existence of two groups competing for goals that only one group could attain" (p. 85). This effect has been documented by a number of investigators. Blake and Mouton (1972) and Blake, Shepard, and Mouton (1964) reported on the formation of group structures and development of intergroup hostility and unfavorable intergroup stereotypes following a series of competitive encounters. They also reported heightened in-group solidarity and increased in-group glorification.

Sussman and Neil (1960) found similar conditions with children rather than adults. This experiment was conducted in a camp where competitive games were instituted between cabins. After a win-lose outcome, friendship preference moved almost entirely within the group. A study by Roy (1954) in an industrial setting observed the workings of in-groups acting in opposition roles. Roy found that in a factory a combination of work teams worked together, controlling production to protect their own interest, when they thought that management rules worked against them. The management (the out-group) working against the work teams' interest contributed significantly to cooperation and group identification in the in-group.

The above research together with a series of studies conducted by the Sherifs (1953) highlight the fact that one way to generate group cohesiveness is for the group to identify a common enemy. The Sherifs demonstrated further at a boys' summer camp that intergroup hostility can be reduced if the competitive groups find a common superordinate goal.

Pursuing Preferences

Because groups interact with each other, one group can attempt to attain its preferences in transactions with another group. In addition, the representatives of a group can pursue and attempt to obtain their preferences in their transactions with another group. And they can attempt to use their transactions with the other group to get what they prefer from their own group. Their own group will reward them for effectively representing it.

It is natural for a group to enforce conformity to its language and ritual in its own members and resist the imposition of another group's rituals in order to maintain predictability. In addition, a group is prone to influence another group to use its languages and rituals as the groups interact. The preservation of one's own language is tenaciously pursued because, as we have said, language provides common referents for group members. Common referents permit people to share perceptions, and the sharing of perceptions is prerequisite to all other sharing. It is the basis on which people are able to have the accuracy of their predictions ratified by others and are able to acquire assistance when attempting to confirm their predictions. In addition, group language and ritual are jealously guarded because they give the group its identity which enables members to predict friend and foe. Consequently when groups interact, each group will support its own language and ritual and resist adopting the language and ritual of the other group. An example may serve to illustrate how fundamental language is to group identity. The government of India, realizing that language could be a unifying factor, tried to impose the Urdu language as the main language for the entire country. This was the only one that was to be taught in the public schools. As soon as the plan became public, it caused a massive upheaval throughout the country. Another example of this can be seen in the negative attitude many French Canadians have to the English language.

However, a group may become fascinated by the rituals of another group as an art form and find them entertaining. Viewing the dances and pageantry of another culture provides variety and escape from the boring rituals of one's daily routine. For this reason, one prominent form of entertainment is the presentation of exotic rituals of foreign cultures.

In order to represent their group representatives must learn the language and ritual of the group with which they are transacting. To some extent the language and ritual of the other group will be different from theirs, if only in idiom. Any indication on their part that the rituals of the other group are peculiar will be counterproductive because the representatives will convey to them a lack of understanding, which will in turn tend to break down communications. People do not feel that they can communicate with anyone who does not understand them. They must feel that they are understood and accepted despite their differences. If representatives cannot communicate with another group they cannot transact with them.

Brown and Lennenberg (1958) point out in an article on linguistic relativity that we cannot predict all the things we want to with the desired precision and therefore the work of categorization needs to go on. Different languages often supply new and different categories. The representatives of a group, in order to communicate with another group, must be able to look through their window. Moreover, they must not cloud their judgment with the moral rules of their own group. As Morgenthau (1967) reminds us, a political realist does not identify the moral aspirations of a specific country with universal laws.

Representatives must also honor the ritual of another group by conforming to it when the occasion arises. An ambassador visiting a foreign country must practice their protocol or risk offending them. Language and ritual are seldom the major issue in the transactions between groups unless they are negotiating a cultural exchange to promote a better understanding. A breach of protocol can prevent representatives from fulfilling their primary mission.

The major issue between groups is usually a matter of conflicting values. Labor values higher wages; management values lower wages. Nations value their influence over other nations and compete to preserve and extend their influence. Industries value the production and distribution of commodities and profit and compete with each other for a larger share of the market. Competition of this type is normal. When the goal of winning has been accepted by a group, this goal can spontaneously mobilize the group and give it direction. Blake, Shepard, and Mouton (1964) point out, in their chapter on win-lose struggles in industrial life, that often labor and management prior to negotiation will prepare and then check out the support within their group for lists of demands. This has the effect of hardening the bargaining positions and increases the feelings of righteousness. When this happens, it intensifies the conflict. The conflict is further intensified by the conviction that because they are right, the other side will back off.

Representatives of a group will attempt to maintain and acquire what their group values in their transactions with other groups. A religious missionary attempts to influence members of another group to adopt the doctrine of that religion. A negotiator for a labor union attempts to get higher wages and better working conditions in negotiations with management. If representatives do not preserve and acquire what their group values, they will lose favor in the group and be discharged from their duties as their group's representative.

For this reason, representatives are reluctant to concede their group values in their transactions with other groups. This makes it difficult for competing groups to make concessions to each other in attempts to reconcile differences and reach agreement. Often when representatives meet to negotiate, they find that their positions are fixed. They cannot change their objectives. Blake, Shepard, and Mouton (1964) point out that group members are reinforced when they provoke members of another group. This serves to further arouse mutual suspicions. A study by Deutsch and Krauss (1960) showed that the presence of threat as a factor in bargaining (experimental) inhibited concession. Yielding in the face of threat becomes a matter of losing face and not upholding the honor of the group.

Blake, Shepard, and Mouton (1964) found that union leaders who lose in transaction with opposing groups are in trouble when reelection time comes. Similarly, management officials who lose share a negative fate as well. This replicated the experimental finding of Blake and Mouton. As Morgenthau (1967) very aptly puts it: "Public opinion, while dreading war, demands that its diplomats act as heroes who do not yield in the face of the enemy, even at the risk of war, and condemns as weaklings and traitors those who yield . . . " (p. 534).

March and Simon (1958) described four ways in which conflicts might be resolved when adversaries hold different beliefs:

1. Problem-solving approach: The parties focus on their common beliefs and embark on a search for a solution. Information gathering is emphasized.
2. Persuasion: The adversaries recognize that their beliefs may be different. However, they do not consider their beliefs to be fixed. A solution is pursued by an exchange of viewpoints and a search for areas of agreement.
3. Bargaining: The parties accept the fact that their beliefs are different. Problem solving involves threat, falsifications of position, and gamesmanship.
4. Political: The adversaries accept the fact that their goals are different and fixed. They attempt to increase their influence by forming coalitions and detentes. Power bases are identified.

The groups may be related in the same status hierarchy, in which case the groups are components of a larger group and subject to its rules. In this case the interactions of the subgroups do not have sovereignty. The organization of major-league baseball is an example of groups within a group. Individual teams belong to a larger group, the league. Teams enforce their own contracts, regulations, and strategies on their members, but transactions between teams such as player trades as well as their competitions are subject to the codes of their league and the commissioner. In addition, player contracts and franchise sales are subject to the restraints of the civil laws of the states and the nation.

It is not simply that the subgroup follows the rules of the higher collectivity but also that it accepts the superordinate goals of that macrogroup.

This fact has been demonstrated empirically a number of times and is at the very fulcrum of the labor-management relations of this country (Blake and Mouton 1972; Blake, Shepard, and Mouton 1964). This recognition of a superordinate goal helps the two groups to agree on a common set of rules. In terms of collective bargaining, these rules might well be the rules of conduct in the industrial setting. This process is also important in the interdepartmental transactions of organizations. Lawrence and Lorsch (1961) reported an instance. Here there was friction between a developmental-engineering department and an industrial-engineering department over the manufacture of a new product. Plans for the production broke down because of the dispute. This common threat created a superordinate goal, saving the product, and provided the basis for cooperative effort. The branches of the armed forces is another example of groups within a larger group which are subject to the rules of the larger group.

Groups that are a part of the same status structure may compete with each other to improve their status. This is achieved by following the rules of the larger collectivity. In baseball a team's status depends on the number of games it wins. In other cases, the rule for improving group status is not as explicit. In the armed forces a group's status is related to its contribution to national defense, a primary group value. The air force began as components of the army, navy, and marines. It was later given equal status with the other three branches because of its increasing contribution to the national defense. So it appears that a subgroup achieves higher status by contributing to the achievement of the values of the larger group.

However, the status positions of groups tend to be more stable than the status positions of individuals. The hierarchical organization of the status system must be restructured in order to change the status positions of the groups within it. Individuals move from one status position to another without affecting the status structure.

Peter Blau (1964) makes the distinction between the dynamics of *microstructures*, which are smaller groups whose members are in frequent face-to-face contact, and *macrostructures*, which involve the interaction of microstructures in a larger collectivity. Group members do not normally come in contact with the leaders of the macrostructure. We seldom have the privilege of seeing the president of the United States face-to-face. Blau contends that unlike the microstructure, where people can understand each other's values from face-to-face contact, a macrostructure needs a formalized, public statement of rules as mediating links. Mediating links include laws such as the Constitution and media of exchange such as money and defined status relationships. Transactions among organized collectivities may result in dominance of a few coalitions or huge corporations, and only two major parties, and one or two labor unions. Then an overall political organization is needed to maintain order, ensure distribution of benefits, and protect against violent overthrow.

When two groups are not part of the same status structure, they interact voluntarily as sovereign powers without being subject to the same rules. In this case the influence one group has over another is not based on status in that there are no rules authorizing one group to control another. The influence that one group has over another depends on the relative power of the groups, that is, the ability to confirm or prevent the confirmation of predictions.

A professional baseball and football team from the same town are not a part of the same status structure in the sense that they do not belong to the same league. They may voluntarily share the same stadium. In this case, intraleague, intrasport, intragroup competition is absent. The teams are not subject to the same rules. Presumably, the team with the greater power over the stadium owner would be able to reserve the stadium on the dates and times they preferred.

Also, because nations are not part of the same status structure, they compete with each other as sovereigns. In their transactions the nation with the greatest power will tend to dominate.

When groups are not a part of the same status structure, the representatives of a group gain the advantage for their group by convincing the people they are attempting to influence that their group is capable of confirming their predictions. This is especially important in the areas where the two groups are in competition.

To continue the previous example, suppose the representatives of the baseball and football teams are negotiating with the stadium owner to reserve the stadium and both teams want to reserve it on the same dates. The stadium owner is compensated by receiving a percentage of the gross sale of tickets. The representatives of both teams are competing to convince the stadium owner that their team will draw the bigger crowd resulting in more profit. This is the prediction the stadium owner would like to confirm. The representative who can convince the stadium owner that one team will confirm this prediction is more likely to influence the stadium owner to reserve the stadium for that team on the dates desired.

When groups are a part of the same status structure, the representatives of a group accomplish their group's mission with the same strategy suggested above, except that they must operate through the appropriate channels according to the rules of the larger collectivity. They must convince the representatives of other groups within the status hierarchy that their group confirms its predictions and that it can direct the confirmation of the predictions of the larger group. It is in this way that representatives may improve the status of their group. A branch of the armed forces can achieve higher status when its representatives convince the secretary of defense and other officials in the Department of Defense that it accomplishes its missions and that it is most capable of contributing to the national defense, the mission of the larger body.

The rules set down by the superordinate group are important in determining how the subgroups behave toward each other. If the range of behavior allowed by the rules is too wide or not clearly defined, predictability is impaired. This may lead toward poor adherence to the rules and eventually a more powerful subgroup taking advantage of a less powerful subgroup. An example of this is the racial integration in the public schools. Although more than twenty years have elapsed since the rules were changed, large portions of the country are still not in adherence with these rules. If superordinate groups are aligned as equals, the benefits derived from the cooperative effort are generally distributed in accordance with the distribution of power in the organization (Morgenthau 1967). But, then, democracy has not generally been considered a particularly efficient way of running an organization. Since this is true, most organizations are run in a more autocratic pattern. How elaborate and centralized this system is depends on its size and function (Etzioni 1964).

Representatives of a group enhance the fulfillment of their status aspirations whenever they are able to direct the confirmation of their group's predictions.

A group member may pursue personal preferences in interactions with another group. Business executives who deal with confusion in their daily routine may vacation on a serene tropical island where things happen in a quiet, routine, predictable fashion. Persons who are bored with their daily routine may find the exotic events of another culture satisfying. They might enjoy the bullfights in Mexico or pursuing commercial interests in foreign trade. Etzioni (1964) states that when tensions build up in one area, they can be released in a different area.

A group may relate to three types of other groups in its efforts to confirm its predictions and pursue its preferences: a dominant group, a subordinate group, and/or an equal group. The tactics used to deal with another group depend on the type of group it is.

Relating to Subordinate Groups

Maintaining and Improving Prediction

A dominant group is often able to persuade a subordinate group to conform to rules, thereby making the activities of the subordinate group more predictable. If the two groups are part of the same status structure, the dominant group is authorized to direct the affairs of the subordinate group and issue punitive actions against the subordinate group should it violate the rules of the larger collectivity. For instance, the Department of Defense is authorized to direct the affairs of the army, navy, and marines. These branches are subject to the rules of the department and the department enforces the rules. The Department of Defense prevents the conduct of the service branches from becoming too unpredictable. Similarly, the National Football League establishes and enforces rules for the member teams to follow. The teams' activities conform to the league rules, therefore, the conduct of the teams remains relatively predictable.

When two groups are a part of the same status structure, they are subject to the rules of the larger body. Thus, to some extent, they use the same language and ritual, which makes their behavior somewhat predictable to one another. When two groups are not part of the same status structure, they are not subject to the same rules, and the language and rituals of the group are more foreign to each other. Thus the conduct of the two groups is less predictable to each other. In this case the dominant group will more likely impose its rules on the subordinate group, as Caucasians imposed their rules on the American Indian.

In general, it can be said that groups in the same status structure will be more predictable to each other. However, whether or not a dominant and subordinate group belong to the same status structure, the subordinate group will be more predictable to the dominant group than vice versa. This is because the dominant group has greater control over the activities of the subordinate group.

Pursuing Preferences

The dominant group will eventually influence the subordinate group to use its language and ritual. However, unless the groups have facility in each other's language, as a practical matter each will use its own language, and interpreters will be used for communication. As communications continue, the subordinate group will tend to learn and use the language of the dominant group.

The dominant group also is in a position to impose its values on the subordinate group. As the relationship continues the subordinate group will adopt more of the values of the dominant group. Such a transition occurred in Brazil. The influence of the white Catholic missionaries in Brazil caused the African slaves living there to modify their religious beliefs to accommodate Catholicism. The resulting religion is present-day Macumba.

If groups are arranged in a status hierarchy, the groups higher in the hierarchy are authorized by rules to control groups lower in the hierarchy. The groups higher in the hierarchy have authority to dominate groups lower in the hierarchy as well as responsibility for enforcing the rules of the larger collectivity on the subordinate groups. The federal government has such authority over the states as provided by the Constitution. The states have authority over the counties within them as provided by the state constitutions. General Motors has authority over its subdivisions, such as Chevrolet and Buick, as provided by its corporate charter and bylaws. And, of course, the branches of the armed forces are arranged in a tight status hierarchy.

The authority that a dominant group has over a subordinate group depends on the rule specifications. The rules of the status hierarchy specify the responsibility that the dominant group has for monitoring the activities of the subordinate group and the consequences for violating rules. The Internal Revenue Service is authorized to inspect the financial records of corporations and levy a fine against any corporation that does not pay sufficient income taxes.

When a subordinate group is found guilty of violating a rule and penalized, the subordinate group often takes punitive action against the person whom it holds responsible for conforming to the rule. The corporation that paid a fine for not remitting sufficient income taxes might fire the accountant responsible for computing and filing its tax return. However, this would depend on the seriousness of the infraction. If the corporation was accused of fraudulent income-tax evasion, they would be likely to discharge their accountant. On the other hand, if the accountant simply claimed too many expense deductions, he might not be penalized at all, especially if the deductions were for the entertainment expenses of high corporate officials. In this case the corporation might take action against the high corporate officials. It might ask the officials to repay the amount that was disallowed by the Internal Revenue Service, or it might discharge an official.

The status of members of the dominant group is affected by the way in which they represent their group in transactions with subordinate groups. Representatives of the dominant group may improve their status by imposing their group's rules on a subordinate group and confirming a prediction their group values. A revenue agent of the Internal Revenue Service is apt to be promoted if in the inspection of financial corporate records a sizable number of income-tax violations are found which result in increased collection for the Internal Revenue Service.

Individual members of the dominant group will exploit the subordinate group to fulfill personal desires. Soldiers in armies of occupation often help themselves to the wares of the defeated country. After the Civil War, carpetbaggers from the North came South to ravage and feed on the defeated Southerners.

Relating to Dominant Groups

Maintaining and Improving Prediction

A subordinate group is more predictable to a dominant group than the dominant group is to the subordinate group because the dominant group takes the initiative and controls the confirmation of predictions in their interactions. In general, the subordinate group acquiesces to the rules imposed by the dominant group and the subordinate group must learn the rules of the dominant group so that the actions of the dominant group may be more predictable.

The Freudian defense mechanism called *identification with the aggressor* helps us understand a result of the domination-subordination between groups as well as between individuals. In the case of the individual we can consider as an example a child who is afraid of ghosts, so he pretends that he is a ghost to allay his fears. The defense mechanism conveys the implication that when you deal with foes "if you can't beat them, join them."

In the case of the domination-subordination relationships between groups identification with the aggressor involves the subordinate group adopting the rules of the dominant group and thus taking on the traits of the dominant group.

Excessive indulgence in the defense mechanism identification with the aggressor is pathological. It suggests that a person or people who feel the inferiority imposed by their subordinate position cannot stand to live with it and have little pride in being what they are. They try to rid themselves of their feelings of inferiority by becoming like the dominant group. They shed their own identity and try to take on the identity of the dominant group.

In recent years the suppression of minority groups has subsided in the United States, and there has been a noticeable reduction in the use of the defense mechanism. Minority groups display less identification with the aggressor and an increased pride in their own special identity. Fewer blacks are trying to be like the whites. Instead, they are resurrecting and manifesting their own identity with increased pride and pleasure.

Pursuing Preferences

Although the dominant group imposes its language and rituals on the subordinate group, the subordinate group prefers to preserve its own language and ritual. It must do so to instill pride in its members and survive as a group. The language and ritual of a group are the bases for its identity, cohesiveness, and intragroup predictability. The intimidation of the dominant group notwithstanding, to survive, the subordinate group must continue to practice its own rituals, at least in the privacy of its own intragroup communications.

The United States is a pluralistic society. When it was founded most immigrants were pleased to support the Constitution and Bill of Rights. However, they clustered together in neighborhoods and communities with people of their own kind so that they could preserve and practice the language and rituals of their heritage. In many sections of this country communities still display prominently the rituals of the national and religious heritages of the people who live there. There are the Mormons in Utah, the Amish in Pennsylvania, and in large cities there are neighborhoods of various national and religious denominations. The French Canadians preserved their culture despite the dominance of Canadians of English extraction.

The values of the subordinate group cannot be separated from its language and rituals. However, the confrontations between dominant and subordinate groups crystallize in the differentiation of values. We can enjoy the expression of rituals by another group, such as their song and dance, and often find them entertaining. It is the contrast in the beliefs and values of different social systems that is antagonistic. At the beginning of World War II it was difficult to get Americans to regard Germans and Japanese as enemies because we are a pluralistic society and are accustomed to being friends with Americans of various heritages. For the most part German and Japanese Americans shared the same national values as other Americans. Exceptions were regarded as opinions of individuals not the beliefs of total ethnic groups.

In order to build in Americans the necessary animosity toward Germans and Japanese, we embarked on a propaganda campaign that emphasized the difference in national values. In the United States suicide is against the law and most religious doctrines, so we showed the Japanese committing hara-kiri and Kamikaze pilots with maniacal grins crashing their airplanes into American warships. Of course, the men on the warships were shown as clean-cut-looking Madison Avenue types. These Japanese suicide rituals displayed a value that is unacceptable in American tradition. Americans were propagandized to picture the Japanese attempting to occupy the United States in order to impose their unacceptable values on us, consequently destroying predictability in our lives. This, of course, built in us fear of the Japanese and we became committed to fighting them to the death. (In passing, it should be acknowledged that for humans the desire to survive does not always predominate. We may be willing to give our lives for our country. Humans, like other creatures, are born with the instinct to survive, but once the values of one's group are learned and imprinted, members may be willing to give their lives to preserve their group's values.)

Although the dominant group will impose its values, the subordinate group can maintain cohesiveness and intragroup predictability if it supports its own values in the privacy of its own intragroup associations. In *The Teahouse of the August Moon*, the Okinawans were subject to the impositions of their dominant American captors. The Americans tried to impose their values on the Okinawans. The Okinawans gave lip service to supporting American values and ostensibly bowed to American demands. However, in the privacy of their own group, they rejected American values and practiced their own. They wanted a teahouse with Geisha girls and they, through deception and camouflage, were able to have one, despite American resistance. Examples of experimental studies that showed that cohesiveness could be maintained and even increased during periods of conflict were cited in the work of Blake and Mouton (1972) and of Blake, Shepard, and Mouton (1964). Thibaut (1950) showed that if the hostility felt by the subordinate group remained unexpressed, the group cohesion increased.

Whether or not subordinate groups are captives of dominant groups, they will work surreptitiously in support of their own values. In openly rejecting the values of the dominant group, the subordinate group would invite the dominant group to block its efforts. A local political group may give lip service in support of an expressed value of their political party, such as the forced busing of school children, while working within their own city for the support of neighborhood schools.

If the dominant and subordinate groups are subgroups of a status structure, the subordinate group can use the rules to protect its own interests. Within a status structure of groups, rules may indicate the limitations of authority of domination-subordination relationships. If there is a higher authority than the dominant group and the rules permit, the subordinate group may appeal to the higher authority to seek relief from unlawful persecution by a dominant group. Otherwise, the subordinate group must appeal to the dominant group and beseech it to abide by the rules.

Black citizens in the United States used the legal system to gain equal educational and employment opportunities. They appealed to the authority of the courts to gain their ends. In addition, the blacks appealed directly to the consciences of the dominant whites. They continuously reminded the whites of their constitutional rights for equal educational and employment opportunities and gave them examples of flagrant violations.

Where there are no rules governing the relationship between a dominant and subordinate group, the dominant group can and often does tyrannize the subordinate group. The railroadmen tyrannized the Chinese laborers they employed in our nation's westward expansion. England was said to have tyrannized the American colonies. The colonies claimed that "taxation without representation" was tyranny, but there were no rules legitimizing the rights of the colonies and no higher authority to appeal to.

When there are no rules governing the relationship between a dominant and subordinate group, the subordinate group cannot claim entitlement to receive what it wants from the dominant group. Anything the dominant group does for the subordinate group is done as a favor. For instance, war reparations are sometimes given by the victors to the losers as a benevolent favor.

In such cases, when groups are not related in a status hierarchy, a dominant group bestows favors on a subordinate group to gain an advantage over a competing group. The USSR and the United States compete to proffer favors on underdeveloped countries in their efforts to expand their ideologies and realm of control. However, favors are most often offered by a dominant group in exchange for something the dominant group wants. The United States gives industrial equipment to subordinate nations in exchange for air bases. If a subordinate group has something that competing dominant groups want, the subordinate group can gain more in its negotiations by playing one dominant group against the other. An underdeveloped nation can negotiate with dominant nations such as the USSR and the United States who want to establish military bases in its territory. It can conduct its negotiations in the fashion of an auction and allow the higher bidder to establish the military bases.

Representatives of a subordinate group may, through their transactions with a dominant group, gain status in their own group by preserving the group's prerogative to act in accordance with its own rules, thus ensuring the maintenance of predictability. An ambassador from a subordinate nation may successfully prevent either the United States or the USSR from dominating his country, in which case he stands to be promoted in his own country. He may accomplish his mission by declaring that his country is neutral. When the USSR begins to impose he uses the United States to prevent interference, and when the United States begins to impose he uses the USSR to prevent further interference. Sweden and Switzerland preserved their independence over the centuries through ticklish negotiations and maneuvering.

Members of a subordinate group may seek to fulfill their personal desires by trading favors with members of the dominant group, if the subordinate members have anything to offer. A soldier in a prison camp may make deals with his captors to gain what he wants. However, if members of his own group learn that he is consorting with the enemy and relinquishing what his group values, he will lose status within his group and perhaps be ostracized. Such was the case with Benedict Arnold. Here is a less extreme and contrasting example. In the 1920s the general manager of the Boston Red Sox, Harry Frazee, settled huge debts he had incurred in the operation of his baseball club by selling his superstar players. He sold the legendary Babe Ruth to the New York Yankees. Bostonians considered the big-time trader quite a traitor.

Relating to an Equal Group

Maintaining and Improving Prediction

When two groups are not in a domination-subordination relationship, they may still vie for control over the confirmation of each other's predictions. This occurs when the two groups compete for the same thing. They may be in direct competition over something specific. For example, two nations may compete over fishing privileges in the ocean where fish are abundant. Competition may arise also because two groups are expanding their realm of control and, although there is no immediate confrontation, the groups regard each other as threats. This is the threat of empire building, and in international affairs it is called the threat of imperialistic expansion.

If competitive groups are mutually interested in avoiding violence, they may agree to establish communication to enhance predictability and prevent the need for immediate emergency action. Hot lines and ambassadorial exchanges are arranged for the purpose of improving predictability.

In addition, to make an opponent more predictable, a group will seek information the opponent does not wish to disclose. So each group will attempt to establish a spy system. In sports the procedure is legitimated and is called scouting an opponent. In international affairs the consequences for spying can be severe. In commerce there also is a good deal of spying among business competitors.

Pursuing Preferences

In general, equal groups cannot impose their languages and ritual on each other, but some infection occurs through voluntary cultural exchanges. Voluntary exchanges are given impetus because of people's common interest in art and music and because they find foreign culture novel and intriguing. It is seldom regarded as threatening to be exposed voluntarily to the language and ritual of a foreign group, and learning their language and ritual makes the foreign group more predictable.

In addition, each group has representatives who know the language of the other group so that each can be informed of the other's activities. In the United States, people who are to interact with Russians must be taught to speak Russian because there are few native Americans who speak Russian fluently.

In sports and in international affairs, codes are created to prevent an opponent from understanding a group's communications. Football signals provide an example of a sports code. Also, each nation transmits its secrets to its members in code.

Equal groups in competition with each other learn each other's values so that they can predict better each other's behavior. They are prone to accept each other's language and ritual more readily than differences in values. This is because the languages and rituals of groups merely are different. The values of one group may not only be different from the values of another group, but, in addition, they may be contradictory and mutually exclusive. One does not believe in both free enterprise and Communistic government, nor does one believe in both democratic and autocratic government.

So equal groups may compete with each other to win and still remain relatively friendly because their values are not contradictory—for example, two baseball teams. However, if losing to an equal carries the threat of being required to adopt the contradictory values of the other group, the antagonism between the groups will be pronounced because predictability is threatened.

When equal groups are not part of the same status structure, they are not subject to the same rules but are sovereign. They transact with each other voluntarily, and they compete with each other because they both want to confirm the same predictions. Such is the case with the transactions and competition between nations such as the USSR and the United States.

On the other hand, if two equal groups belong to a larger group that has the authority over them, their sovereignty is abridged by the rules they are subject to. In this case they may be forced to relate to each other as the rules indicate. Labor and management are subject to the laws of the United States. They must transact and compete with each other within the framework of the laws or be penalized. A labor union must suspend a strike if it is ordered by the federal government to do so.

In some status structures the larger collectivity is unable to enforce its rules to any great extent. The penalty for violating a rule is of no great consequence. In such instances where the larger group cannot coerce the member groups to comply with its rules, it must use persuasion. It must try to enforce its rules by soliciting member groups to pressure a group who has violated the rules to conform. Such is the case in the United Nations.

If an individual is an official representative of his or her group in a transaction with an equal group, that person can gain status by preserving and obtaining what the group values. General Eisenhower attained the presidency chiefly because he led the United States to victory in World War II. The status and salary of a college football coach is raised when he wins games. He might be made athletic director in his school as well as coach.

Members of a group may transact with an equal group to satisfy their personal desires, provided the groups permit exchange. Farmers were permitted to sell their wheat to the USSR in 1975 after the U.S. government negotiated the arrangements. However, members must be careful not to violate the rules of their group in their transactions lest they be penalized and lose status within their own group. Americans who illegally buy contraband from foreign countries and sell it in the United States are subject to stiff penalties.

Many facets of intergroup relationships have been discussed in this chapter. Let us summarize the key points and their relationships to prediction theory.

To maintain and improve predictability in relationships with other groups, it is necessary to determine the rules that govern their behavior, that is, the goals they are pursuing and the programs employed to achieve the goals. It also is beneficial to know what they predict will happen and convince them that the outcomes you are predicting will be confirmed. To confirm your predictions, it is helpful to make yourself unpredictable to an opponent, to take the offensive whenever possible, and not to forsake the rules of your group. On the other hand, to avoid violence, it is not advisable to make yourself too unpredictable. It is advisable to maintain communications with them and provide for perturbations to be dissipated before problems become too volatile.

Groups pursue their preferences in their relationships with other groups. In interaction with other groups, the group's rules must be maintained and imposition of another group's rules must be resisted. Otherwise, intragroup predictability will be weakened. Language is the vehicle through which people confirm the accuracy of each other's predictions and assist each other when help is needed to confirm predictions. Learning the language and ritual of another group enhances the prediction of their conduct.

Conflicting group values usually are at the core of problems between groups because group values define what the group holds sacred. What is acceptable to one group may well be unacceptable to another. Groups become seriously disturbed when they believe unacceptable values of another group may be imposed on them. Such anticipation threatens predictability and generates intense hostility toward the other group.

When groups are related in the same status hierarchy, subgroups are regulated by the rules of the macrogroup. Such regulation enhances predictability within the macrogroup. When groups are not part of the same status structure, they interact voluntarily as sovereigns. To enhance predictability in their associations, they must establish rules, through negotiations, governing their interactions. A group gains dominance in group relations when it convinces another group that it controls the confirmation of the other group's predictions.

Dominant groups often are able to impose their rules on subordinate groups making the conduct of the subordinate groups more predictable to them. Conversely, events become less predictable for the subordinate groups. When groups are organized in a status hierarchy, the groups of higher status have authority to control the confirmation of the predictions of groups lower in the hierarchy.

When a dominant group imposes its rules on a subordinate group, the subordinate group must learn the rules so that the actions of the dominant group may be more predictable. With continued subordination, members of a subordinate group will tend to adopt the rules and identity of the dominant group to facilitate the confirmation of their predictions. However, to maintain intragroup predictability, the subordinate group will make an effort to preserve conformity to its rules, at least in the privacy of its own intragroup associations.

Representatives of groups, through their transactions with other groups, gain status in their own group by preserving their group's prerogative to act in accordance with its own rules because such an accomplishment preserves predictability.

When two groups are not in a domination-subordination relationship, they may still vie for control of the confirmation of each other's predictions by competing for the same thing. To make an opponent more predictable, they will seek information the opponent holds secret. On the other hand, to make each other more predictable, equal groups may agree to establish communication and cultural exchange. The more compatible the values of the two groups, the more apt they are to establish amicable exchanges.

Epilogue

At the beginning of part II we indicated that our primary intent was to introduce social factors and issues to explain the application of prediction theory to the understanding of groups. There has been no attempt to cover all of the subject matter pertaining to groups. One of the major issues covered was the explanation of status relationships. It might be helpful to summarize the status relationships discussed.

Figure 15-1 shows a parent group represented by the large triangle that contains three subgroups. Subgroup A is of higher status than subgroups B and C and dominant over them. Groups B and C are equals. In each group member 1 is of higher status than member 2 and member 3 and dominant over them. Members 2 and 3 are equals or peers.

Although relationships are more complex than this, these are the essential status relationships we have discussed.

We can now attempt to unravel and simplify the complex relationships discussed in previous chapters by relating the individual to groups in part III of the book. Before doing so, however, it behooves us to pause in order to clarify prediction theory by contrasting it to other theoretical views of social behavior. This will help evaluate the potential of the given explanations of social behavior. These explanations will be contrasted to two other types of social theories—*exchange theory* and *role theory*. We will use the theory of Peter Blau as an example of exchange theory and the theory of Talcott Parsons as an example of role theory. The theories will be contrasted with respect to four fundamental questions.

Why Do People Form Social Groups?

According to prediction theory, people form groups because they believe that group membership will help them maintain and improve predictability and confirm a particular prediction of preference at the time. The satisfaction of the prediction motive is the primary director of group activity as well as the actions of individuals. The attainment of personal preferences is secondary because it is necessary to maintain predictability in order to confirm a prediction of preference, whatever that preference may be.

Blau (1964) indicates that social attraction is the force that induces human beings to establish social associations on their own initiative and expand the scope of that association. He adds that processes of social attraction lead to processes of social exchange. However, Blau does not indicate why people are attracted to each other in the first place. So the fundamental motivation towards group activity is not explicitly stated. We state explicitly

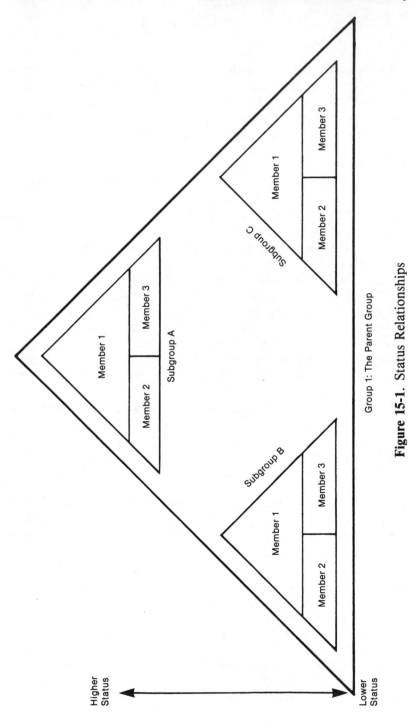

Figure 15-1. Status Relationships

that people are attracted to others because others contribute to the confirmation of their predictions. Blau (1964) also states that groups form because of some interest or standard of values. Yet he does not indicate the nature of the common interests that bind them into social groups.

Nor does Parsons (with Shils 1951) explain why individuals form groups. From his point of view, people participate in groups because they are born into groups and from the beginning they are coerced by their groups to conform to group rules (also see Black 1961).

In a concise review of Parsons' theory, Szemanska (1954) recalls five important components. First, people must be socialized into the prevailing value system in order to preserve the dominant system of order. Second, those who remain unsocialized are managed by "second-line defense mechanisms" such as social ostracism and police control to avoid social disruption. Third, the "core value system" is the fundamental determinant of the organization and change of social systems. Fourth, each major institution functions to enhance the stability of the system as a whole. Fifth, social systems tend to gravitate toward the development of the value of universalism, specificity, law, equality, democracy, and freedom. Szemanska criticizes Parsonian sociology, stating that the terminology is obscure and the system is incomprehensible.

Why Do People Interact?

According to prediction theory, people interact to pursue the confirmation of their predictions. One person interacts with another person because the other person exhibits the ability to confirm or prevent the confirmation of one's predictions—whether or not the other person contributes to the confirmation of a particular prediction at a particular time.

This theoretical position is in contrast to Blau's theory, which proposes that people will continue to interact with each other when they receive their preferences (tangible or intangible favors) from each other. The present theory contends that people interact to pursue the confirmation of their predictions and will continue to do so as long as they believe another person controls the confirmation of their predictions. This would hold true whether or not a person received a preference in an exchange with another person.

The prediction motive is more basic than the inclination to exchange with others. Another person may control more than the confirmation of a preference you are pursuing and may control the confirmation of the way you perceive the world. Without this confirmation you may question your understanding of the way things are, even your sanity. Infants learn early that ministering adults can confirm or withhold the confirmation of their predictions. Most fundamentally, adults confirm through language that infants' perceptions of the world are correct and they correct mistakes. The confirmation of their ability to communicate accurately is prerequisite to their being able to request their preferences from adults or to enter into any sort of social exchange with them. Whether or not children receive their preferences from adults, they will continue to interact with them because adults control the confirmation of their predictions. Similarly, one adult will continue to interact with another as long as she or he believes that the other controls the confirmation of predictions, whether or not the other adult bestows favors.

From the perspective of Parsonian theory (Parsons and Shils 1951) it appears that people interact with one another because of the expectations of the roles they occupy and to satisfy personal needs. Interactions because of role expectations are the result of social pressure rather than inherent, internal motivation. Interactions to satisfy needs are similar in nature to pursuing one's preferences. From the point of view of prediction theory, all interactions are for the purpose of confirming predictions whether they emanate from social expectations or personal needs.

Why Do People Establish Rules?

According to the present theory people establish rules to enhance the confirmation of predictions. When another person controls the confirmation of your predictions, group rules are helpful in at least two ways. First, linguistic rules enable you to communicate with another for the purpose of influencing that individual. Second, rules obligate group members to cooperate with each other. They provide the conditions under which the other person is obliged to help you.

Blau (1964) contends that rules or norms provide common referents for group members and differentiate between proper and improper conduct for group members in pursuit of common objectives. Blau does not indicate why people establish rules. He specifies only that they do so based on common values and that the rules or norms give the group its character. Once rules are established, they serve as common referents of proper conduct for the members and serve functional purposes as well. As Blau suggests, if a group has no common goals, an aspirant to informal leadership would have to obligate each member separately. If a group has common goals, however, the superior contribution toward the achievement of the goals obligates all members and becomes a source of power over them. In short, Blau does not explain why people establish rules in the first place.

Parsons with Shils (1951) suggests that social institutions establish rules to preserve, perpetuate, and stabilize the functions of the institution. Here again, Parsons gives us no inkling as to why the institutions originated or why people continue to institutionalize their relationships. A given social institution may disband, but people continue to form new social institutions through the establishment of rules.

Why Do People Conform to Rules?

Our theoretical position indicates that people conform to rules to enhance the confirmation of predictions. If you conform to the rules of the group, group members are more likely to assist you in confirming your predictions.

This theoretical position is more fundamental than Parsonian theory. Parsons proposes that individuals conform to role expectations (rules) to gain group approval and avoid disapproval. Our theoretical position suggests that people conform to role expectations because group members will approve and be more likely to help them confirm their predictions. It is the confirmation of their predictions that people are ultimately after. A more severe interpretation of Parsonian theory would suggest that individuals are coerced into conforming to rules, with the threat of being ostracized from the social institution hanging over their heads.

For Blau, conforming to group rules is the means of gaining collective approval, which legitimates leadership and power into authority. If conformity to rules represents the common good, then one gains collective approval by conforming. Although Blau offers other reasons for conforming to rules, he seems to emphasize conformity as the primary basis for achieving group status. To gain social status in exchanging with group members, one gives something of greater value with respect to group norms and accepts in return something of lesser value.

We do not propose to do justice to the theories of Blau and Parsons. Our purpose is to clarify the position of prediction theory by contrasting it to theirs. In short, our position is that people are attracted to one another, interact with one another, establish rules, and conform to rules in order to increase the probability that their predictions will be confirmed. Because a social group consists of people that establish rules and conform to the rules they establish, people form and perpetuate groups to enhance the confirmation of their predictions.

**Part III
The Individual in Groups**

16 Living in Social Groups

Now that we have considered both the personal and social forces acting on the individual, we can relate them to get a better idea of why people behave as they do. We will do this by considering, as we have throughout the book, that there are two motives driving the individual: the basic motive to predict, and the secondary motive to confirm particular predictions of interest at the moment.

Programs

Looking at prediction from a psychological point of view first, we find that the mental equipment people have to make and confirm predictions is the program called a neuroprint (or coding of the mind) that represents a sequence of events. It is the mental coding of sequences that allows people to predict one event from another because the programmed coding indicates that one thing leads to another.

The individual's mind is coded with program neuroprints at birth. Each person is "wired" with certain instinctive programs that direct the automatic functions of the body and maturation processes. Predictions are inherent in these programs even though the individual is not aware of them.

Some social anthropologists such as Tiger and Fox (1971) make the point that a species is programmed to grow and develop in a highly specific way, and they claim that humans are programmed to learn because instinctive programs to perform cannot cope with the complexities of social life. They state that the basic human needs are space in which to move about, participation in the activities of the group, a chance to rise in status, an opportunity to make deals and exchanges, recreation and grooming services, and an opportunity to contribute to the community of which one is a part.

Our interest in predicting motivates us to learn programs. We memorize sequences of events that we see and are taught to improve our ability to predict. As we execute programs, we check to see if the predictions contained in them are confirmed. If not, the programs are modified or discarded.

Kelly (1955) contends that all behavior can be construed as anticipatory in nature. Behavior is our way of posing questions about life. "Man looks at life, notes a series of events which seem somehow repetitive and then places an interpretation upon this predictable aspect of his experience" (p. 50).

In an intriguing study of coloured (mixed white and black parentage) clerical workers in South Africa, Orphen (1973) found a significant association between subjects' tendency to support militant violence in pursuit of human rights and the extent to which subjects perceived themselves as able to control events in their own lives and their future. An adaptation of the Rotter I-E (internal-external control) scale was used to measure perception of ability to control one's life and future. The tendency to support militant action was assessed two ways: (1). Subjects were asked if they would be prepared to engage in violence in order to improve the general position of the coloured in South Africa. A "yes" respondent was classed as a militant. (2). A synthetic newspaper account of a recent riot between coloureds and whites in South Africa was presented to each subject, and the subject was asked if he or she agreed that the riot was justified. A "yes" caused classification as a militant.

Subjects whose Rotter-scale score revealed them to believe that their life and destiny lay in the hands of an external agent were significantly less militant. Could it be that perception of internal control ensues from successfully predicting one's environment? As such, a high I score would be associated with high predictability. People with high I scores might seek the novelty provoked by a militant posture. Those whose lives are perceived to be controlled externally may live with a high level of novelty and thus be unwilling to invest in more.

Once memories are formed into concepts we can deliberate the programs contained in concepts and choose the ones we prefer. This further improves our ability to predict because in deliberation we can preview in our minds the probability that one program or another will lead to our goals. This increases the probability that the programs we choose will lead to the confirmation of our predictions.

It is the programs we are born with that allow us to predict in the first place—the programs we learn from ideas that permit us to be aware of the predictions we can make and improve our predictive ability. Our predictive powers culminate as programs are formed into concepts and we learn to deliberate concepts. This allows us to increase the probability of predicting novel events we are encountering for the first time and enables us to make discoveries.

Rules

Society contributes to the improvement of prediction because it provides and teaches its rules to the individual. The rules are expressed in language and many contain a sequencing of events. When these rules are learned, they are coded as programs in the individual's mind. The learning of rules improves prediction because the group enforces the rules and members abide by them. This makes their behavior more predictable. In addition, conformity to rules is the basis for sharing and providing mutual assistance because rules make it possible for members to communicate and cooperate. Consequently one group member can help another confirm a prediction. This assistance often increases the probability that an individual's prediction will be confirmed.

When rules are not clearly defined, manageable, and consistently enforced, group members become concerned because predictability is lessened. Buelow (1974) states that socialization is learning the consequences of breaking a rule. In discussing rule theories, Clammer (1973) indicates that Levi-Strauss contends that rules ensure continuity of the social group by restricting the number and range of moves possible. Totman (1973) discusses how individuals will persist in finding rules that make events in their life more predictable. The theory seems to play up the importance of rules as organizational. When rules are "broken," one does not usually perceive them as such, but looks instead for another rule that is being followed.

The rules that provide the foundation and social matrix of group activity are the rules of language and ritual that give the group its identity. They allow members to predict who belongs to their group and those with whom they can communicate. Leap (1974) offers the particular form of English used on reservations by American Indians as an example of the role of language in maintenance of social and cultural identity.

The values and status structure of the group are expressed through the group's language. However, the status structure and values of the group make their own contribution to the improvement of prediction.

The specification and enforcement of rules that define group values improve prediction because these rules distinguish good and bad conduct, and, generally, group members can be expected to exhibit good rather than bad deportment. Conforming to the group's language and ritual and seeking status within the group is highly valued and encouraged by the group. These group values make it more likely that members will seek status and conform to the group's language and ritual. Conversely status is often awarded to those who conform to group language and values, making it more likely that they will. In this way the rules of the group reinforce each other.

Hippler and Conn (1974) describe how the Eskimos, in the years 1920 to 1950, developed uniquely suitable (for their culture) legal mechanisms. When outside influences in the form of state magistrates and district courts came in, lacking understanding of the culture, disorder resulted.

The rules defining the status structure of the group enhance prediction because they allow the members to predict success. They know they are succeeding when they are within the status hierarchy. In addition, group rules help them predict how to succeed because they indicate what they must do to be promoted.

Looking at the pursuit of preferences from a psychological perspective, we find that the mental equipment that people have to satisfy their interests is the master neuroprint. You may remember that a *master neuroprint* is a coding of the mind that represents an interest, a goal predicted to satisfy the interest, and a program predicted to lead to the goal. Thus rules that follow the master-neuroprint format satisfy preferences. The mental coding of the interest indicates a particular motivation and reflects what is predicted to satisfy the interest. The coding of a program indicates the steps that are predicted to lead to the goal.

The individual's mind is coded with master neuroprints at birth. The programs that govern the autonomic functions of the body are connected to the arousal mechanisms of the mind (the ARAS) so that when the predictions contained in the program are not confirmed, the individual becomes aroused and interested. For instance, when the individual inhales and does not take in oxygen as inherently predicted the individual will gasp and become concerned with the problem. Then the goal is to restore normal breathing, and programs are enlisted that will lead to the goal.

The master neuroprints that are inherited and the master-neuroprint ideas that form as a result of initial learning tend to be linear and inflexible. They connect single interests with particular goals that satisfy the interests by means of specific programs.

Once alternates are learned, concepts form and behavior becomes more flexible. The individual has the equipment for deliberating among the alternatives in a concept in order to choose one and is no longer bound to a fixed automatic way of responding. Concepts may form categorizing different interests, which enables the individual to deliberate events of interest at the moment to determine which to deal with and in what order.

Concepts form categorizing different goals. These include different ways of satisfying a particular interest. Concepts also form categorizing programs. Then the individual can choose a program from among alternatives to achieve a particular goal.

Concept formation involves generalizing. As one finds new examples to add to the concepts already acquired, one is increasingly able to generalize. Rafky (1971) describes how such generalizing underlies socialization.

> He (self as subject) takes on the role of mother and commands himself (self as object) to wash. In either case, the child learns to act in the manner expected by significant others. In taking on the role of the child, the child has also internalized the roles of his significant others; it is this which allows him to interact or relate to these significant others. The internalized roles of the significant others are synthesized within the child and make up the role of the generalized other. This enables the child to relate to people in general, to those who are not his significant others, even to people he has not encountered. (p. 13)

Payne, Platt, and Branch (1974), in a study of inner-city children, showed how increased generalization can lead to socialization.

As we mature and our experiences broaden and extend, we become aware of an ever-increasing number of choices we can make. Society provides us with many of these choices through its teachings. However, it is our inclination to confirm particular predictions of interest that directs our attention and determines goals we will pursue. The extent to which we will support our group's rituals and values or seek status or the satisfaction of personal desires depends upon which interests us most and whether we can identify goals to satisfy the interest and programs to reach the goals.

Adults can deliberate the things that interest them and goals and programs. They can set priorities as a result of their deliberations. Although there are an enormous number of choices a person may consider in deciding preferences, the deliberation of alternatives is the key to understanding preferences and how they are determined.

We prefer the language and ritual of our own family because these are the first rituals we learn at our most impressionable time of life. The language and ritual of our own family are regarded as essential for survival by us since we are dependent on our family to insure our survival, and the family's language is the vehicle for obtaining their assistance. Further, our family teaches our language to us, encourages us to use it, and shows us that we can obtain their assistance in confirming predictions if we learn to use their language correctly.

Pickering (1974) sees rituals that involve the family as those which persist, however "illogically": baptism, marriage, death ceremonies, as opposed to those open to the whole society or membership. Kitahare (1974) comes to much the same conclusions regarding ritual in general.

Our family languages are at the very foundation of our being. They are at the root of our identity and we are not likely to give them up, no matter what group affiliations we develop later on. As we grow and become involved in additional groups, we learn their languages. However, the new languages we learn seldom replace our commitment to our family language because, for one thing, later learning tends to build upon early learning rather than replacing it.

The adolescent revolution brings with it a reexamination of one's family teachings. Hopefully, the adolescent emerges from this soul searching with a unique mind and lifestyle. The adolescent is much like the molting snake which sheds its skin so that it can continue to grow, but it remains very much the same creature that it was before. If adolescents disclaim their heritage completely, they are in trouble. One cannot reject one's heritage completely without rejecting one's self. Although we are constantly changing, we are in part what we have been.

Adolescents are more likely to reject their family values than their families' language. Their families' language serves as the vehicle for sharing and acquiring their preferences initially. Besides, one is less prone to attack a communication mode than a value because communication modes are the vehicles through which people obtain assistance from others in their efforts to confirm their predictions. Adolescents may discount a family value as being old-fashioned; the belief may be contradictory to the values of the peer group with which they are identifying.

The family has always been the initial and major influence on the individual. However, with the emergence of modern technological society, mobility increased and the opportunity for a person to belong to a number of groups increased. As people tended to belong to greater numbers of groups this brought with it a potential for value conflicts, which made it more difficult for a person to determine value preferences. Each group has its own values. When a person belongs to many groups, there are more values to consider and compare before deciding what to believe is the good life. Not only must one contrast family values with the values of more peripheral groups, one must compare the values of one peripheral group with another.

This can become confusing. There are too many alternatives to consider and the values of one group may be contradictory to the values of another group. One's church group may teach that we are our brother's keeper, while one's business group may teach a dog-eat-dog philosophy. Since developing a personal identity and lifestyle is mainly concerned with adopting one's own values from among alternatives, the modern adolescent has an enormous problem selecting preferences from a host of alternative values.

In olden days there were fewer alternatives and fewer conflicting values, and families lived in communities in which other people's values were similar to their own. Modern people have the curse of selecting their own values from so many alternatives, some of which conflict. However, when they do they can claim a more individualistic set of beliefs and lifestyle.

Selecting one's status preferences is usually not so confusing as selecting one's value preferences. A person who is upwardly mobile would normally prefer to rise as high as possible in the status hierarchy as soon as possible. Multiple group memberships make it possible to pursue status in more than one status structure. If a conflict arises because receiving a promotion in one group prevents one from being promoted in another group, one must deliberate the problem and make a choice.

As Freud and Freudians remind us, we will pursue the satisfaction of our appetitive impulses, such as food, thirst, and sex. These impulses direct us to survive and procreate. As we mature and learn, we come to understand that we can satisfy our appetites better if we do not react impulsively to their urgings. We learn to deliberate the pursuit of pleasures, along with the pursuit of status and the good life according to group values. Seldom do we need to deliberate group language and ritual as an alternative because most often the group's language and ritual merely serve as a vehicle for pursuing status, values, and appetitive pleasures.

Although we are tempted to think that our survival impulses are predominant, this is not always the case. It may be the case with the young, but an adult who has adopted a set of values which codify a lifestyle may risk death to preserve these values.

17 Socialization

This chapter examines human nature from a different perspective, the socialization of human beings over time. This will allow us also to integrate, summarize, and highlight many of the ideas presented previously. We do not pretend to account for all socialization in this and chapter 18 with respect to psychological, social, or physical development.

Inherited neuroprints are the givens at birth and set the scene for human development. They program the individual to pursue particular things in the environment, such as food, safety, shelter, and associations with members of the same species. They underlie and direct psychological and social development. Instincts govern the autonomic functions of the body and are directed toward the survival of the individual. Since humans are so helpless at birth, their survival seems more dependent on learning than does the survival of most lower creatures. Therefore, humans seem to be more heavily committed to learning and have more uncommitted brain cells at birth, which become connected through learning. Thus humans are not as preprogrammed to behave in given ways, and they have the potential for learning a greater variety of behaviors than infrahumans.

The earliest learning is self-centered. Infants explore the parts of their bodies to determine how they function and they move their arms and watch them. They touch and feel themselves and suck their fingers. As a result, they learn the relationship of one part of the body to another. When they learn that sucking their fingers is pleasing, they can make that prediction.

Soon children become able to distinguish their environment from themselves and begin exploring the objects around them. They may play with clothing or a diaper or a toy left in the crib. Or they may flail their arms and shake off their shirts and learn to make that prediction. In a short time they learn to manipulate a bottle.

Their experiences with family members permit them to learn about other people. Once they learn that they will be fed when the mother brings a bottle, they are able to make that prediction. When they see the mother with a bottle of formula, they will anticipate that they will be fed and stop crying before food actually is received.

Social indoctrination begins when children are taught the spoken language of their group. They learn to associate sounds with the ideas they have of the events they have experienced. When this happens a word sound will bring the event it denotes to the child's mind. Once children are able to use their group's language correctly, they have shown the first semblance of being members of a social group. This is because they have learned and abide by a group rule—a rule of language.

The first words children learn are nouns as they learn to pronounce "ma-ma" and "da-da" and connect the word sounds with the mother and father. Of course, as their parents teach them spoken language they continuously correct the pronunciation of the words and make certain they associate a word with the event it denotes by saying the word and showing the event it denotes. This may be the first experience with the enforcement of group rules. If the word stands for a particular person, the parents would say the word and point to the person. If the word stands for a concept they might say the word and show pictures of a number of examples of objects that fit the category. If the parents are teaching the meaning of the word *bird* they might say the word and point to numerous pictures of birds until the children get the idea.

What should be made clear to children is that most words are labels for concepts. Concepts do not denote specific events but a category of events with common characteristics. What one experiences is examples of events and objects that fit the concept category. Only proper nouns and some applications of pronouns stand for specific events and objects.

As children learn concepts, they can make choices and identify and predict novel events. As they learn alternate ways of performing the same task, the programs they can execute form concepts, and as they learn to deliberate alternatives, behavior becomes more flexible.

After children learn the meaning of individual words, they learn the meaning of word combinations and are able to understand the phrases and sentences that others use and to express ideas to others in sentence form. Once children understand sentences, they understand how words convey relationships. When they learn that sentences can express the transition from one state to another, they understand that words can contain information about predictions that can be made. For example, when they learn the meaning of the sentence, "When the sun sets it will become dark outside," they understand that the words denote a transition that informs them of a prediction they can make.

As children learn the meaning of word combinations, they become able to inform others of the predictions they wish to confirm and solicit their assistance in attempts to confirm predictions. They can tell the parents that they are hungry and ask for food. So it is the understanding of the word combinations of the group that is the basis for sharing predictions and for cooperation in attempts to confirm predictions. The ability to use language to make common identifications and predictions is the first evidence of social membership. Children are eager to learn the language of their group because they realize that the use of language enhances the confirmation of predictions.

Children learn that words are used for family identification when they understand that the family's surname is common to all members of the family and identifies family membership. They also learn that certain rituals, such as saying a prayer before eating, are characteristics of that family.

Children not only learn that the linguistic rules of their group are enforced; they also learn that the family has certain values and they enforce conformity to their values. They may be punished for taking a sibling's toy without permission and learn the family's rules for respecting the rights of others. The family may insist that they say "please" before requesting something they want.

The learning of group values is a civilizing influence on children. They learn that there is more to life than the satisfaction of one's impulses and that to get what they want, they must conform to group values and learn to curb their impulses. Children conform to group values because conformity is made a condition for the confirmation of their predictions. They learn that they are dependent on adults for survival and welfare and that to insure that their interests will be fulfilled by adults, they must conform to adult values.

Children learn to test their predictions very early in life. We are aware that children ask questions to increase knowledge. However, when they have an inkling that they know the answer to a question they make a prediction and ask an adult for confirmation. A child might say, "That's a dog. Isn't that right?"

Once children learn that conforming to rules increases the likelihood that one's predictions are confirmed, they seek to understand the rules and their enforcement. It is not long before children learn that the adults must enforce their rules in order for predictions to be confirmed. Children tend to relax when they know the rules and know that they will be enforced, because events are predictable. They become anxious when they cannot depend on an adult to enforce the rules because without enforcement many events do not turn out as the rules stipulate. Thus outcomes are unpredictable.

It is not unusual for children to ask an adult for a ruling on behavior before acting, and then to test the adult to see if the adult will enforce the rule. This is especially true when children find themselves in a new and unpredictable situation. For instance, they may ask a new babysitter what the babysitter will do if they go outside to play by themselves. If the babysitter forbids it, the children may start to go outside to see if the babysitter will stop them. This ritual is enacted on an official level with "test cases" in court. No one knows what a law really means until someone has broken it and a judge has to rule.

As children observe the relationships among the family members, they learn a conception of power. They discover that certain family members have greater control over the confirmation of predictions than others.

Children also come to understand domination-subordination relationships by observing family relationships. They learn that their parents are dominant over them because they control the confirmation of predictions and that parents also are dominant over any siblings.

As children make acquaintances outside of the family, they learn of groups other than the family group. As they find playmates they learn that they belong to different families that have different surnames and different rituals. If the family takes the children to church, they become aware of a type of group, a church group, that is different from a family group. They find out that members of this group have common characteristics in that they all choose to worship in the same way.

The child's first understanding of *authority* (power legitimated by rules) may come through finding out that a policeman has legal authority to prevent people from breaking the law and arrest them if they do. Or if the family goes to church, it may be that the minister has some authority over the congregation.

Children learn what status means when they observe relationships in a status hierarchy and learn that there may be a number of status positions within a group and that a person in a higher-status position has more authority than a person holding a lower position. In observing a television serial, they may learn that on the police force a captain has higher status than a lieutenant and a lieutenant has higher status than a sergeant. When they attend school they learn that the principal has higher status than the teachers and that teachers have higher status than the students. In addition, when children learn that someone in the family graduated from school, was given a diploma certifying the graduation, and that there was a graduation ceremony and celebration, they learn that rituals are sometimes used to confirm status.

When children enter school, the first thing they learn is the written language of their group so that they can transmit and receive communication without speaking to other people. They are taught that through writing they can make ideas known and that through reading they can tap the wisdom of the ages that has been accumulated in the libraries of society. Through reading they can learn without assistance from others and find enjoyment.

In school children are also taught technological rules that society uses to predict and control events. They learn mathematical rules for computing quantities and scientific rules for predicting and controlling physical and social events. The students also learn rules for classifying things. They learn to place plants, animals, and minerals into their appropriate concept categories based on their common characteristics.

The students also are taught vicariously about other groups through reading, lecturing, and visual illustration. They learn that their family group is part of a community group; the community group is part of a municipal group; the municipal groups are in counties; counties are in states; and the states comprise the United States, which is a nation. They also learn that there are other nations with people of different characteristics.

In social studies the students learn about the values of the nation when they are taught about the Bill of Rights and the Constitution. They also are taught that people of other nations have different values. (See Conner [1974] for a summary of "traditional American values" derived from the works of numerous historians.)

The social structure of the school may allow students to hold offices to which they are elected. If so, this gives the youth direct experience with formal authority and status. They learn that members of the Student Council discuss school problems and can make recommendations to the school administrators. There may be a Safety Patrol made up of elected students who gain authority and status.

This alerts the students to the fact that they can achieve authority and status and can gain control over the confirmation of the group's predictions if they do. They then become interested in achieving status and authority in their peer group. The parents taught previously that they can gain popularity within the family by curbing the fulfillment of personal desires in favor of conforming to family values. They now learn that espousing and conforming to the values of peers and the larger society instead of being selfish will increase popularity and the probability that they will be supported for public office, Student Council, and the Safety Patrol.

At this point the youths have an inkling of the various preferences from which they can choose: the pursuit of personal desires, group language and ritual, status, and what the group values. (See Boocock, [1973] for a review of the effects of school on socialization from Durkeim and Weber to modern times.)

The school supports what the youth learned earlier from the family. The successful person shares and cooperates with members of the group. This is the way of increasing the confirmation of predictions. Violent impulses are to be directed toward members of enemy groups, the bad guys. In addition, children learn that violent impulses may be expressed in some sports within the framework of the rules of the game. During the game the opposition is regarded as an enemy, but when the game is over the opposition is regarded as fellow sports participants.

In high school adolescents' horizons expand. Upon receipt of a driver's license, the first civil certification of approaching adult status, they gain a great deal of mobility. They drive to ball games at other schools, and they explore the community with friends in search of excitement and first-hand knowledge. Adolescents attempt to learn for themselves about the things they learned from the family and in school which formerly they had to accept on faith.

In high school and in explorations, adolescents learn a great deal more about authority and status. In high school there are many more opportunities to gain status. In addition to being elected by peers to a position in student government, adolescents can join clubs and try out for school teams. If they make a team, they gain status within the school. They also learn that the coaches of the teams have authority over the members of the team.

By this time adolescents have learned to work domination-subordination relationships to their advantage. They cater to people of higher status, become friends with peers, and direct the activities of people with lower status. Because people of higher status have more control over the confirmation of predictions, they become status conscious and interested in achieving status. They also correlate the achievement of authority and status with becoming successful adults.

As their interest in status increases, adolescents become attuned to the qualities of leadership. They learn that those who achieve status support the rules of the group, help the group confirm its consensual predictions, and contribute to rule changes for the benefit of the group. They also may become sensitive to the fact that proposing rule changes is a very delicate matter that can meet with substantial resistance.

As adolescents approach the legal adult age, they become more conscious of the adult responsibilities they must assume soon. They become interested in learning more about career opportunities and the preparation that is needed for them. They become acquainted more thoroughly with the status structure of business organizations and government agencies, and they become concerned with the adult responsibilities they are expected to fulfill in the community. Because they will soon be old enough to vote, they inquire further into the voting process and the status positions to which candidates seek to be elected.

Adolescents also find out that they are expected to contribute voluntarily to social-welfare groups in the community. They are expected to make charitable contributions and give time and effort to public service. This acquaints them further with public service and nonprofit organizations.

As adolescents' scope of experience expands, they begin to learn some of the distinctions between smaller, more intimate microgroups. As they grow older and their exposure broadens, their membership in groups expands. First, they identify themselves as members of the family group, then memberships extend to religious, peer, and school groups. In all of these groups they are in face-to-face association with the members.

As they find that they are automatically a member of a community, state, and nation, they become aware that some of their group identifications are with members who they seldom or never see. They may have on occasion seen the mayor of the town, but most of the other officers that represent members of their group are seen on television, seldom in person. These may include the governor of the state and the president of the United States.

From these experiences adolescents learn that publically recorded rules allow members to interpret the group's values when members are apart from one another. In addition, they learn that public records earmark the social institution and are the means of transmitting the rules of the group from generation to generation, despite the death of individual group members.

Through television and other news media, adolescents learn that the macrogroup to which they belong transacts with other macrogroups. This makes them aware that an official representing their group whom they have never seen in person is transacting with an official of another group. They have probably never seen the official or members of the other group in person. Yet they are aware that these transactions, which are remote to them, affect their lives. If the transactions are between the secretaries of state of their nation and another nation the exchange could lead to war, and they might have to fight for their country.

The adolescent crisis is intensified because in addition to the surge of strong sex impulses and the rapid transformations in physical form, adolescents become aware of an overwhelming number of social alternatives and opportunities among which they must choose. With the responsibilities of adulthood facing them soon, success seems unpredictable, and they become confused with the choices they do not feel equipped to make. Also, they are seeking intimacy with peers on a one-to-one basis, especially with members of the opposite sex. Yet they are aware that officials who are remote to them can commit them to serve their group.

Adolescents learn more about values other than those of the family group. Their peer group's values are in many ways distinct from the family's values. In school and from television and other news media they learn about the values of other nations and subgroups within the United States.

The adolescent crisis centers around a search for personal identity. Adolescents must attempt to decide who they are and who they aspire to become in the future so that they can make preparations for adulthood. They must find ways of satisfying their personal preferences within the social framework of their groups and select a pursuit from among the opportunities provided by their groups.

To become unique individuals, adolescents must reexamine the values propagated by the family and the values proffered by peers, school, church, and government. They must sort through the array of values, some of which conflict, until they can say, "This I believe; this is what I stand for." Otherwise, the journey into adulthood will continue to be confusing, life will have little meaning other than the gratification of impulses of the moment, and they will despair.

The literature, Gove and Herb (1974) claim, shows that young boys show more stress than young girls, in part because of social expectations and differential rates of biological development. This difference decreases with age, until by late adolescence, girls exhibit as much stress as boys or more. Data for treated mental illness for ages five through nineteen show similar results. In preadolescence, boys show more stress; by late adolescence, girls overtake them.

Mature adults have reduced their confusion by selecting from among the alternative values of their groups. They have sifted their own identities and lifestyles, eliminating those identifications that are alien, no matter how laudable they may be. They have found positions in their groups, mates, and careers that are satisfying. They have made their lives predictable enough so that they are not confused. They seek sufficient novelty to improve themselves and keep themselves from getting bored. And they have made a choice of the goals they prefer to pursue, whether the goals involve personal pleasure, status, group rituals, and/or the pursuit of group values.

Moral Development

Of the various aspects of socialization, one that is being given considerable attention currently is moral development. *Moral development* can be regarded as the learning and adoption of rules for valuing objects and events. Individuals learn concepts for valuing their experiences which members of their group endorse. The endorsement and enforcement of the rules make the behavior of group members more predictable. Therefore, group members are motivated to learn and live by the rules, the rules become internalized as a guide to behavior, and problems are associated with the violation of the rules.

The rules represent the values of the group. Individual members adopt the rules because living by the rules makes their lives more predictable. In addition to satisfying their primary motivation to predict, group members learn eventually that they are more likely to obtain their preferences if they conform to the rules of the group. That is, they are more likely to get what they prefer if they do what the group prefers.

Moral development training was first given impetus by John Dewey. In works like *Ethical Principles Underlying Education*, he first presented a progressive or developmental conception of moral education. He proposed that intellectual education is the stimulation of the child's development of an active organization of his or her own experience. Dewey also stressed the central role of *thinking* or active organization in morality. He further stressed that *development* is moral education's critical aim and that this development takes place in *stages*, hence a *cognitive-developmental* perspective on moral development (see Kohlberg and Turiel 1971, p. 413).

Piaget introduced a two-stage sequence of moral development in his work *The Moral Judgment of the Child.* The first stage is the stage of "moral realism" in which the young child adheres to a predominantly authoritarian moral code of conduct. In this stage morality is associated with the edicts of parents and other authority figures. The second stage is the stage of "moral autonomy or relativism." In this stage the child develops a morality of social concern and cooperation with others. Research to date provides some support for Piaget's two-stage sequence (see Ginsburg and Opper 1969, p. 6).

Since Piaget, Lawrence Kohlberg has been a central figure in the formulation of moral development. Kohlberg (1971) posits three levels of moral development with stages within the levels. The first level, or *preconventional level*, is one in which children lack understanding of rules. The first stage in that level is called the *punishment and obedience orientation stage*, where painful or unpleasant consequences of behavior cause that behavior to be perceived as "bad." The second stage in the first level is called the *instrumental-relativism stage* in which individuals are guided merely by their own desires.

Kohlberg's second level is called the *conventional level* and is comprised first of the *interpersonal concordance stage* (stage 3) and then the *authority orientation stage* (stage 4). In the former stage, behavior is based on whether or not another individual would approve of the behavior and label it as being "good." In the latter stage, doing one's duty and respecting authority are the primary emphases.

The third level of moral development according to Kohlberg is the *postconventional level*, in which individuals define their own moral principles and values without needing verification from other persons or groups. Stage five within this level is termed the *social contract orientation stage* where actions are viewed in terms of authority structures balanced by individual rights and fairness. Stage six within this level, *universal ethics orientation stage*, is the highest level stage in which one defines right behavior in accordance with one's own abstract and ethical principles.

Kohlberg's theory is based on data which are collected by first presenting a person with a hypothetical moral dilemma, asking the person what is the right thing for the actor in the dilemma to do, and then trying to draw out with a series of probing questions the structure of the person's reasoning which forms the cognitive basis of his or her judgment. Whether a person judges a given act to be right or wrong is not that important; rather, what is important is why the act is judged right or wrong (see Boyd 1977, p. 70).

The universality of the stages is documented by findings by Kohlberg and Turiel (1971) in villages and cities in the United States, Taiwan, Great Britain, Turkey, and Mexico. In all of these cultures were found the same basic moral concepts used in making judgments. Each of the basic concepts or values develops through six stages (p. 431).

In addition, religion was considered as a variable. However, Kohlberg's research indicates that moral principles are not dependent upon a particular religion, or any religion at all. He and his associates found no important differences in development of moral thinking between atheists, Buddhists, Catholics, Jews, Moslems, and Protestants (Kohlberg 1971).

Transition from the earlier stages of development to the later stages is marked by the increased personal predictability of one's affairs. At the preconventional stage, children do not understand rules. Hence, rules cannot improve their ability to predict. At the conventional level, children first understand rules as edicts imposed upon them by authority figures such as parents. By learning these rules they become able to predict the behavior of the authority figures. However, predictability in a child's life is subject to the whims and interpretations of the authority figures. So the learning of rules at this stage provides only limited predictability for children. Predictability stabilizes further as individuals progress in level 2 and learn rules that are superordinate to the authority figures who have immediate control of their affairs. By adopting the rules of the social order to which they and the authority figures belong, the authority figures become more predictable to them, as well as are all of the other members of the particular social group.

Predictability increases still further as individuals arrive at level 3, the postconventional or principled level. At level 2, the predictability reference is the rules of the particular group with which one is in contact at a particular time. However, as one grows older one's group memberships increase and predictability varies from group to group. The rules are different for one's religious, work, family, educational, and social groups. Further, when one is confronted with a new group, one must learn that group's rules so that its members will be predictable.

At level 3, individuals adopt their own code of conduct that maintains across the boundaries of the various groups to which they belong. In establishing their own identities they become more predictable to themselves. And by sharing personal rules of conduct with others they become more predictable to them. The rules that govern behavior are less subject to time and place and are broadly generalizable. They emerge from the incorporation of more specific rules the individual has learned in experiences with a variety of groups.

It is important to realize that Kohlberg's stages describe not the content of people's moral opinions or values, but the structure of their moral reasoning. Two people who are at the same stage may use the same form of reasoning to arrive at opposite conclusions, while two people at different stages may arrive at the same conclusion using different forms of reasoning (see Reimer 1977). Thus although the content of one's deliberations may change, predictability is maintained by using the same structure for reasoning about moral issues.

There is evidence that people at the highest level of moral development, those who exercise principled moral judgment, tend to act consistently according to their moral convictions, making them more predictable. Experiments (such as the famous obedience experiment conducted by Stanley Milgram) demonstrate that principled persons act more honestly and live up to their beliefs in the face of authority and inconvenience more so than do those at lower stages.

An important study at the University of California at Berkeley lends empirical support for Kohlberg's contention. Students were interviewed after student demonstrations to determine whether there was any correlation between a student's stage of moral development and the decision to join a sit-in protest against the administration's decision to bar political activity on campus. The researchers found that while few students at the stage 3 and stage 4 conventional levels of moral judgement joined the protest, a majority of students at the preconventional stage 2 and the postconventional stage 6 levels did protest. The students at the stage 2 level explained that they had protested out of a sense of anger at the power play of the administration against the students. Those at the stage 6 level had protested against the administration's having violated the students' right to exercise their freedom of speech. Thus each grouping of students had pursued a course of action consistent with its moral world view. What distinguished the stage 6 students from those at stage 2 was that they were protesting an infringement of civil liberties and not simply acting out against an authority figure.

A study of Krebs and Kohlberg found that only 15 percent of students showing some principled thinking cheated as compared to 55 percent of conventional subjects and 70 percent of preconventional subjects.

Kohlberg (1960) gives credibility to the ability to predict as a determinant of moral conduct when he describes his construct *ego strength*. He claims that ego strength and the child's level of moral development determine moral conduct. One attribute of ego strength is the intelligent prediction of consequences.

Although Kohlberg's stages of moral development have, in general, been supported by research, critics see a difficulty in distinguishing between stages 5 and 6 (see Beck, Crittenden, and Sullivan, 1971; and Gibbes 1977).

In addition, Rest (1975) takes issue with Kohlberg's interview procedures as a means of accurately measuring moral development. However, Rest devised his own test and has substantiated some of Kohlberg's stages of moral development using his test, the Defining Issues Test. Finally, Maschette (1977) feels that more work must be done to connect the reasoning in hypothetical moral conflict situations with a person's actual behavior.

Education

A most important aspect of socialization is formal education. Schools have received increasing criticism in recent years because their graduates have not adequately acquired basic skills such as reading, writing, and arithmetic and are not prepared to adjust to society and the world of work. A recent study funded by the U.S. Office of Education and conducted through the University of Texas has indicated that from 13 to 30 percent of the adults in this country cannot adequately perform tasks like addressing an envelope, determining the "best buys" from quantitative information on products, or reading a paragraph stating their rights under the Constitution. Clearly, new approaches to education should be explored in hopes that we can remedy these problems.

Prediction theory has unique implications for education which presently are being investigated by a number of researchers. First, from the perspective of prediction theory, educators should primarily be concerned with teaching thinking skills that are applicable to all content areas and aspects of life. The implication is that if people learn to think effectively they can solve the problems that confront them in school and daily living. The Educational Policies Commission (1961) gave highest priority to teaching students to think. According to prediction theory, there are a limited number of thinking skills that need to be taught and applied in and out of school. People will be able to learn and live effectively if they acquire these skills.

In addition, prediction theory advocates that the most effective way for these thinking skills to be acquired is in an optimally predictable learning environment. In short, prediction theory has implications both for what should be taught and how it should be taught. The what of instruction should be the teaching of thinking skills and their applications. The how of teaching involves providing an optimally predictable classroom environment to enhance the learning of the thinking skills. Let us first consider the thinking skills that are to be acquired and then the optimally predictable learning environment.

You will remember that much of the discussion of learning in part I revolved around the learning of prediction skills and the identification skills that support prediction. Here is a summary outline of major identification and prediction skills that should be taught followed by a short discussion of each.

    I. Identification Skills
        A. Identifying concrete events: remembering
        B. Identifying through abstractions: using limited cues
           1. identifying similarities and differences
           2. identifying through concept categories
               (a) categorical identification
               (b) programmatic identification
               (c) hierarchical identification
   II. Prediction Skills
        A. Predicting coming events: based on trends
        B. Predicting the consequences of intervention
           1. predicting the consequences of intervention as a passive observer
           2. predicting the consequences of intervention as an active manipululator: pursuing preferences

Identification Skills

Identifying concrete events simply involves remembering a past experience recorded in an image. This skill often is referred to as literal comprehension or the remembering of facts. Of all of the thinking skills in the outline, this skill is the one most taught in schools. Several studies point to the inadequacies of instruction beyond the literal-comprehension level. Gallagher (1965) reported the results of a study designed to assess the level of comprehension most often dealt with in the teaching of social studies. He found that literal understanding was the process observed most often. Davis and Tinsley (1967) conducted a study to determine the range of cognitive objectives assessed in secondary school social studies classrooms from questions asked by student teachers and their pupils. The results revealed that both teachers and pupils asked more questions involving remembering literal statements than all other questions combined. Similarly a study of Pfeiffer and Davis (1965) revealed an overwhelming emphasis on the acquisition of facts in the analysis of ninth-grade social studies examinations. In a study by Hogg (1973) it was found that 87 percent of the questions of student teachers probed for factual knowledge. Hunkins (1974) demonstrated that by changing the emphasis of questions on instructional materials to probe higher levels of thought, pupils' achievement in these areas can be increased. The evidence indicates that although teachers tend to dwell mostly at the level of literal comprehension, involving students at higher levels of thought is beneficial to learning.

Identifying through abstraction involves making an identification based on limited attributes of an object or event. In chapter 5 abstraction was defined as the identification or prediction of an event based on a limited set of its attributes. We also reviewed research and showed that individuals abstract and remember only a set of attributes of an experience. Thus the ability to abstract is a crucial skill in itself and underlies other thinking skills. It can be taught and tested for by providing students with only partial information and asking them to make an identification. For example, students may be asked to identify a picture of George Washington with a portion of the picture covered.

Identifying similarities and differences among events is the basis for discriminating and generalizing about events. Finding differences enables discriminations to be made. Finding similarities identifies relationships and enables one to generalize about related events. It is important to realize that identifying similarities and differences is based on abstraction because events are similar only with respect to a limited number of their attributes. All compare and contrast questions require students to identify similarities and differences. For instance, compare and contrast Judaism and Christianity requires students to identify the similarities and differences between the two religions.

Throughout part I of the book the importance of concepts for identifying and predicting was stressed. In particular, concepts provide the opportunity for deliberation because they contain alternatives from which selections can be made. In addition, concepts provide opportunity to identify novel events. When some of the features of an unfamiliar event can be matched with a known concept category, the novel event can be identified. There are three primary identification skills based on concepts: categorical identification, programmatic identification, and hierarchical identification.

Categorical identification entails determining whether an event belongs to a concept category. The student learns the word label and critical attributes of a category and learns to distinguish examples from nonexamples of the category. For example, students may be given the word label *kitchen* and the critical attributes of kitchens, say, stoves, refrigerators, sinks, pots, pans, and so forth. Then they are shown rooms that are examples of kitchens and rooms that are nonexamples of kitchens and are asked to distinguish between the examples and nonexamples. There are many subskills associated with this basic thinking skill. If students master the basic skill, they should be able to detect missing elements of a category. For instance, shown a picture of a kitchen with a stove missing, they should be able to determine that the stove is missing. They also should be able to detect incorrect elements of a category. Shown a picture of a kitchen with a bathtub in it, they should be able to determine that the bathtub does not belong.

It should also be pointed out that evaluation is a categorizing skill. The critical attributes for categorizing in evaluation are criteria for determining whether or not an event is desirable. Comparisons are made to the criteria. Those events that meet the criteria are considered desirable and vice versa. For instance, an evaluation may involve determining whether or not students pass or fail a course. The criterion of desirability might be earning an average of 70 on the course tests. Those who meet the criterion belong in the category *pass*. Those who do not belong in the category *fail*.

Programmatic identification involves sequencing. There are two kinds of sequences that need to be learned—static sequences and activity sequences. The learning of static sequences involves learning how to rank order events with respect to various inherent characteristics, such as rank ordering objects on the basis of their size or length. In addition, rank ordering static events imparts the meaning of relative and absolute degrees of relationship. A knowledge of sequencing enables students to determine which of two objects is larger or which among a number of objects is largest. Further, in understanding sequences, students can detect the underlying basis for sequencing. For instance, shown a picture of lines sequenced by their length, students can detect that length is the basis for sequencing. Also, students learn to detect an incorrect element in a sequence. If a line does not fit properly in a picture of lines sequenced by their length, a student can detect it. In addition, knowledge of sequence enables students to supply a missing element in a sequence, such as filling in the length of a missing line in a blank space, given a sequence of lines of progressively increasing length.

The identification of activity sequences underlies the ability to predict because activity sequences indicate changes or trends over time. It is on the basis of an understanding of activity sequences that students learn to project what may happen in the future. In learning the rain cycle, students learn the sequence of events leading to rain and have a basis for predicting rain. There are a number of types of sequences discussed in chapter 5 that students can learn; sequences that include sets, series, or both. This provides the basis for distinguishing fixed linear sequences and sequences that provide for some flexibility in their execution. We cited the sequence of starting a car in which entering the car and driving it must occur in that fixed order. However, some activities performed in preparation for driving, such as adjusting the seat and fastening the seat belt, can be performed in any order. A most important kind of activity sequence is the cause-effect sequence because it is in understanding cause-effect sequences that students learn that certain causal agents can be manipulated to produce specific effects. In learning that combustion produces heat, students are prepared to cause combustion when they wish to effect heat.

Of course, when activity sequences are understood, students are able to detect missing and incorrect elements in the activity sequences.

Hierarchical identification involves learning the relationships in an idea hierarchy. Knowing such relationships, students are able to distinguish more general from more specific identifications. For instance, after learning the following idea hierarchy, students know that *animal* is a more general identification and that *dog* and *cat* are more specific identifications because they are subcategories of *animal*.

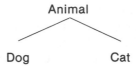

It is in learning the properties of idea hierarchies that students learn to make deductive identifications, as illustrated in chapter 8. In knowing the concept *animal,* students can deduce the subcategories *dog* and *cat*. Conversely, knowing the concepts *dog* and *cat*, they can induce the concept *animal*. Thus knowledge of the constitution of idea hierarchies is the basis for inductive and deductive reasoning. When the properties of idea hierarchies are known, students can identify incorrect and missing elements in a hierarchy. Knowledge of the following hierarchy would enable students to detect that the term *dog* belongs in the hierarchy where it is entered, should it be missing. In addition, should the term *plant* be entered instead of *dog* the mistake can be identified. Finally, knowing the relationship among concepts in an idea hierarchy enables students to arrange them in the appropriate hierarchy, should students be given the names of the concepts on different cards.

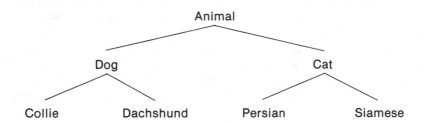

Prediction Skills

Predicting coming events involves noting an activity sequence and projecting into the future what is expected to happen based on the activity sequence. Predicting coming events was dealt with in chapters 6, 7, and 8. When we read who-done-its we attempt to predict the guilty person based on the trends we uncover in the plot. We also can predict the next stage an animal is going to enter, based on knowledge of the life cycle of that animal.

Predicting the consequences of intervention was dealt with in chapters 7 and 8 on deliberation, when we discussed "Matching for prediction: to pursue a preference." However, here we make the distinction between predicting the consequences of intervention as a passive observer and predicting the consequences of intervention as an active manipulator. Both require an understanding of cause-effect relationships and the ability to predict the effect when a causal agent is introduced. In the former case, one observes the introduction of a causal agent. In the latter case, one deliberates and introduces a causal agent to produce a preferred effect. Predicting the consequences of intervention as a passive observer occurs while reading a who-done-it. We may need to change our prediction of the guilty person as the author introduces additional information that has new implications for the story. Predicting the consequences of intervention as an active manipulator involves deliberating the goal we wish to pursue and then selecting a program or procedure predicted to lead to the preferred goal. A number of examples of this thinking skill were offered in chapters 7 and 8.

Of the thinking skills outlined and discussed here, it appears that the identification of concrete events, which involves nothing more than memorizing, is the skill emphasized most. More advanced identification skills are taught and tested for much less frequently. Further, it is difficult to find evidence that prediction skills are taught in schools on any systematic basis. One exception is in the field of reading. Some reading exercises require students to read a passage and then predict what will be said in the coming passage.

With the heavy concentration on memorizing and the neglect of teaching more advanced identification and prediction skills, it is no wonder that the graduates of our schools are ill prepared for productive living. In neglecting to teach prediction skills and the relationship between identification and prediction, schools lose an important opportunity to motivate students to learn. If students could see the relationship between what they are learning and the improvement of their ability to predict, they might well be much more interested in learning and less inclined to drop out of school.

Providing for Optimum Predictability in Learning Situations

To maximize learning, the learning situation should provide for optimum predictability. The material to be learned should contain enough new elements so that students will be challenged and have the opportunity to improve their ability to predict. If the material is too familiar, students will have little to learn and they will become bored. In addition, once they have learned the material, they must not dwell on it too long lest they become bored. They must soon advance to meet new learning challenges. On the other hand, learning material should contain sufficient familiar elements so that new learning can be built on what students already know. If everything in the material is new, students will not have the foundation necessary to learn the material and they will become confused. Also, the introduction of new material must not occur too rapidly or students may not have sufficient gestation time to learn it. Even though students may begin learning without confusion, proceeding through material too rapidly may engender confusion. Confusion also can be generated when the learning background is too noisy and distracting and when learning objectives and directions are not clear and complete.

This short explanation of the summary outline of thinking skills introduced the thinking skills and shows their relationship to basic propositions of prediction theory presented earlier in the text. In addition, the importance of providing optimum predictability in learning situations has been explained briefly. For more information on these thinking skills and how they can be applied to the learning of various kinds of subject matter as well as prescriptions for providing for optimum predictability in the classroom, see *Teaching Reading and Thinking Skills* (Friedman and Rowls 1980). However, it should be apparent from this brief summary that prediction theory has important implications for what should be taught and how it should be taught.

18 Boredom, Confusion, and Rules

Since rules specify appropriate behavior, they influence the attitudes and preferences of group members and often generate boredom, confusion, and defensiveness. Although people seek situations that are optimally predictable, society sometimes impairs their quest. Let us consider some illustrations that pertain primarily to American culture and subcultures.

Boredom: Too Much Predictability

The cause of boredom, as we have said, is too much sameness or predictability, which usually occurs when stimulation is redundant, repetitive, and in a word, monotonous.

When humans, like lower creatures, spent the major portion of their time battling the elements of nature for their survival, there was little time to be bored. However, as survival is insured, the luxury of leisure time emerges and boredom becomes more prevalent. Some causes of leisure are familiar—the shorter work week, retirement, and increased longevity.

A person may, in the beginning, find work satisfying because it is new and there is satisfaction in learning how to master the job. However, for many people, once the job is mastered it becomes routine and monotonously repetitive. New challenges seldom arise from such work and we become bored. The monotony of the work routine makes us irritable and, in a desire to find novelty, we might become inattentive and be diverted from the task at hand. The desire to seek diversion may interfere with work and, in the case of a machine operator, might cause an accident.

Kunce (1967) found that industrial employees who score high in interests related to adventuresome occupations, such as aviation, have twice the accident rate of those whose interests are related to more cautious occupations such as banking. Perhaps those who are interested in adventurous occupations are bored and attempting to find relief from boredom.

Although some bored workers may be tempted to find a more interesting and challenging job, they might be reminded of the security provided by such things as seniority and fringe benefits which increase with longevity of employment. They also might be prone to think of themselves as indulging their selfish impulses if they were to seek adventure and excitement in a new job.

A woman may look forward to fulfillment in marriage because this traditional promise was part of the American dream. But after she is married she may become very disappointed and seriously disturbed because marriage did not measure up to her expectations. This may be partly because she had idealized marriage and her mate and is suffering from an abrupt letdown because of her unrealistic expectations. Any number of other conditions could have contributed to her problem, but, again, boredom may often be a serious contributing factor. Vanek (1974) demonstrates that women not in the labor force spend as much time at housework as their mothers, despite social and technological advances.

The aging probably are the most trapped victims of boredom. The vast sum of knowledge they have accumulated over the years makes most new experiences seem familiar to them. The elderly seem to be inclined to deal with new experiences by relating them to their past and espousing how they dealt with them in the good old days. This tendency to reminisce, instead of meeting challenges that the novel elements of a new situation impose, is understandable if we realize that their energy is ebbing and they are losing the power to control and shape the world to their wills. This realization prompts the elderly not to attempt new challenges because they would be prone to predict failure. Finally, when the elderly become unable to care for themselves, they are often committed to a nursing home where the routine and lack of stimulation can cause boredom.

According to Shanas (1980), since 1900 the number of people aged sixty-five and over has increased eightfold, and their proportion in the population has increased threefold. The status of the aging, however, has decreased rather than increased. As the result of some of her research, Shanas suggests that "old people and their families are the new pioneers of our era" (p. 14). They must find new ways to establish relationships and deal with the world.

Shanas and Hauser (1974) predict that if the slowdown in population rate increase now underway reaches zero growth by 2028 as predicted, the ratio of over-sixty-five citizens to those younger will increase from 5:1 to 4:1. Moreover, each of these elderly will have fewer children and grandchildren to contribute to their support. Therefore, more government aid for care and housing of the elderly will be needed. Although the authors do not make this point, this is an argument for keeping the aged self-sufficient as late into life as possible.

One danger of boredom is that is induces the individual to take unnecessary risks. The adolescent especially tends to court danger in order to escape boredom.

In addition to the serious problems caused by basically boring lifestyles, there are boring little things that occur in everyday living: listening to someone tell you about things you already know, driving a car on a straight road across a desert, ironing, adding numbers, collating, and shifting gears in a car. Perhaps the most punitive thing about putting a prisoner in solitary confinement is the boredom. Boredom also is induced as punishment when a teacher makes a student write 500 times "I will not talk in class."

Boredom generates feelings of worthlessness because individuals who engage in repetitive tasks do not feel that they are accomplishing anything. It is only when we extend ourselves to master new tasks that we feel especially worthwhile. Learning and growing are inherent in all of us; to do the same things over and over is to stagnate. People who feel stagnant do not hold themselves in high regard and feel equally that others have no reason to hold them in high esteem. It is important that we meet new challenges and extend our ability to predict.

Standardization

A factor that contributes heavily to boredom is standardization. The development of industry and the machine led to the standardization of operations that in turn generated monotony and boredom. Machines repeat the same operations and each product is the same as the last. Quality control mandates that deviation be avoided and that products that vary too much from standard specifications be rejected. As people tried to coordinate their own activities with the machine, their actions became more standardized and repetitious. Although the machine was originally made to serve humans, people became more like machines as they began to integrate their activities with the machine. In a sense, we became enslaved by the machine that was created to serve us.

As industry began to dominate our way of life, we came to believe that standardization was synonomous with the good life. So we began to standardize everything. Streets were laid out in standard rectangles. The houses in many subdivisions are extraordinarily similar. Fashion in clothes meets the standards set by the fashion industry, and, despite the many options that are offered, automobiles look very much alike.

As products became more standardized, our behavior became more standardized as well. Standardized rules of conduct have become more prevalent and we have come to reward conformity and reject deviance. This reached its peak with the Madison Avenue, man-in-the-gray-flannel-suit stereotype of the successful corporate man. A symptom of this stereotype is what some have come to call the Willie Lowman complex. Willie Lowman was the central character in *Death of a Salesman*. He said that his claim to fame was, "In my day I was not only liked, I was well liked," as if this were the earmark of success. Now it seems that many of us have found middle-class mores too confining and frustrating and have rejected them for something more satisfying.

The irony seems to be that instead of becoming more individualistic, many of us have traded middle-class rituals for other fads that are equally standardized. A clear example of this trade was evidenced by the hippie and yippie movements. Adolescents are so compelled to be unlike the ruling adults that they fail to see that in their rebellion they have, in certain respects, adopted even stricter standards within their peer groups. There are few things more stereotyped than the behavior of adolescents at a rock concert.

But trading middle-class standards for other rigid standards is not limited to adolescents. Many adults, feeling the frustration of middle-class conformity, have chosen other equally restrictive cults. The difference seems to be that middle-class standards are fundamentally materialistic; the new standards tend to be more spiritual and occult. Nevertheless, they are often more rigorous. Zen Buddhism, yoga, transcendental meditation, and the like require highly ritualized behavior. Mingle and Roll (1974) provide one example of the "trade-one-cult-for-another" phenomenon, bringing us examples of aggression in the self-proclaimed peaceful hippie culture. Eister (1972) contends that one of the factors in the formation and maintenance of cults seems to be the failure of established organizations to deal with the modern information explosion that contributes to confusion.

One factor that had contributed heavily to the detriment of individuality is the standardized test. Standardized tests show how an individual compares to others in a group by establishing *norms*—or average performances—for a test and comparing members of the group to the norm. The standard person performs at the average and it is supposedly to one's credit to perform above average. The more above average an individual performs, the more outstanding that person is said to be. To perform below the average is interpreted as failure.

The IQ test, presumably a measure of overall intelligence, is an example of a standardized test. If we obtain an IQ score on an individual, we can compare that IQ score to others in the nation. This is to say, we can determine the percentage of people in the nation who have IQ scores higher than that individual and the percentage that have lower scores.

We have become so accustomed to using these tests to appraise people that we have come to believe that above the average is an index of a person's quality. Many of us consider it an affront when our children score below average on a standardized test. But many people do not seem to understand that it is inherent in the notion of test standardization that half of the population must score below the average.

Standardized testing also contributes to the standardization of behavior, and we test standardized teaching by giving students standardized tests. If they have learned all of the material they will offer standard responses and receive a grade of 100 on the test. Implicitly we also suggest that the principles students learn are generally applicable in the world and will be of general benefit to all of the children in the class.

Aside from the boredom that this lock-step method of teaching perpetuates, this overgeneralized approach is phony and falsifies the world for the student. The general principles that are taught, at best, are applicable to certain limited situations and within time these facts will become obsolete because circumstances are changing at an accelerated rate. Furthermore, these general principles are not equally beneficial to the individual students. To some they may be meaningful, to others they may be totally irrelevant.

Not only do we teach these general principles as if they represented immutable truth, but we teach them over and over again, year after year, until the students are thoroughly bored. For instance, we are taught English from the time we are born to well into college. English grammar is taught year after year. However, when we reach the college level we are often told that we are still unable to express ourselves well in English, and our teachers continue to hammer English at us.

One thing that contributes to boredom is the irrelevancy of what is being taught. Not only is English grammar taught repeatedly, but students tend to forget it after it is taught each time because they are unable to see the connection between their speaking and writing and the rules of grammar they are being forced to learn. They simply do not help much.

What seems sad beyond the boredom and inequities that standardization creates is that we have become so used to it that we are unable to tell the difference between becoming individualistic and trading one standard way of behaving for another.

The problem with boredom is that it is seldom taken seriously and is often overlooked as a source of trouble. We should recognize that trading one set of boring rituals for another solves nothing in the long run. In the beginning, new rituals will be stimulating because they are novel. But soon, when they become habits, boredom will emerge again.

A mistake we often make is to believe that retreating from uncertainty to boring stereotyped rituals provides security. It is dangerous, however, to confuse boredom with security. The truly secure individual has learned how to face and accept the unfamiliar and deal with it as it comes. Because of the accelerated change, transcience, and diversity in our technological society, we are forced to deal with novelty whether we like it or not. Impermanance and change is very much a part of our lives.

Boredom has one important value that we should emphasize again—it is when people are attempting to escape boredom and pursue novelty that they are most likely to discover and invent new things. Suedfeld (1977) supports this idea in his discussion of the benefits of boredom.

Confusion: Too Little Predictability

In the beginning infants find everything unpredictable. They learn how to predict from their parents and their own experiences. At this earliest stage of development when babies have little control over their own survival, they must be able to predict that adults will minister to their needs or there will be too little predictability and therefore frustration.

As babies grow older, they become aware that their parents want them to be toilet trained. It is at this time that they may predict that they can take autonomous action in controlling body processes to affect their parents' reactions to them. If at this stage they were unable to predict their parents' expectations, or how to satisfy them, there would be too little predictability and they would become confused.

At the next stage children begin to learn how to take care of themselves. They learn to feed and dress themselves, and they learn about the many things in daily life that are dangerous. Some hazards they can learn to predict as a result of the consequences of their own explorations.

On the other hand, they are not allowed to confirm for themselves many of the predictions they learn to make. These predictions are taught by parents to prevent serious harm. For instance, they may be told to stay out of the medicine cabinet. They must accept such predictions on faith because it would be disastrous to confirm the predictions. For this reason, it is of great importance that children have confidence in parents that results from previous experience in taking their advice. If the predictions parents taught were refuted by experience, children would not have confidence in them. Under these conditions children might become seriously disturbed.

Many social rituals are taught to a child that do not involve danger but which must be accepted on faith because the consequences are subtle and not directly evident to the child. These include the moral teachings of the parents. The parents tell the child that it is wrong to behave in a certain way, to which the child responds with the classic question—why? In many such instances the parent is at a loss to describe the consequences of wrong actions in a way that is clear to the child. The child is told not to do something and is prevented from testing the consequences of acting. Or if the child should disobey, there is unlikely to be any direct natural consequence that the child would regard as objectionable. In cases of morality, the parent might provide the objectionable consequences by spanking the child.

So it appears that activities that are physically dangerous for children and activities that are considered wrong by the parents are taught in the same way. Children are taught to regard both as dangerous and that harm will come if they disregard parents' objections. That is, people are taught to predict consequences that they cannot confirm for themselves. Therefore, they must take the word of their teachers that the consequences will occur. This is detrimental to learning because it prevents the testing and confirmation of predictions. It engenders defensiveness to some degree because if confirmation cannot be achieved, the outcomes remain unpredictable to the individual. Conceiving the prediction is the first step in learning. Testing the prediction follows. If the prediction is not tested, there is no way for the individual to confirm that the conception is valid. Of course, in child rearing it is often necessary to instill such superstitions. Similarly, children are taught that certain actions are forbidden because they are illegal. They can eventually confirm for themselves that people who violate laws are fined or sent to jail.

Quite often rules of conduct for a particular group, such as a family or a religious group, pertain to that group alone. The consequences for violating a rule may also be specific to that group as well as the issuing of punishment for a violation. In this case, the individual will find out eventually that the rules are not applicable in the broader community. This implies that children should be taught that certain predictions will be confirmed in certain milieus but not in others. There are also predictions that can never be confirmed by the individual.

Unpredictable consequences are especially troublesome to the chronically guilt-ridden individual. Many people feel guilty and expect to be punished for their behavior without knowing what kind of punishment to expect or when to expect it. They wait impatiently for their punishment until they can tolerate the delay no longer. To relieve their guilt and their preoccupation with the retaliation they expect, they seem to arrange for their own punishment. The chronically guilt-ridden individual is preoccupied with this dilemma to an inordinate extent.

We do not mean to imply that morality is harmful. On the contrary, the individual needs moral standards to give value and meaning to thoughts and actions. It is only when the individual is unable to determine the source of feelings of guilt and the means of relieving it that debilitation occurs. Individuals who feel guilty because they have not contributed to an important charity, for example, know the cause of their guilt and how to relieve it. They need only to make a contribution to the charity to gain relief.

One way to avoid the instilling of defensiveness is to make certain that children are free to think about anything they choose. To the extent that children are taught not to entertain certain thoughts, defensiveness is being instilled because they are being taught to shut out certain events from consideration. As children are taught to exclude more and more events from their deliberations an increasing portion of their world is relegated to unpredictability, and they must necessarily become less effective in coping with the environment.

Children should be taught that action should be based on thought and that under most circumstances it is action that brings consequences from the environment. They should be encouraged to deliberate freely before acting, and in these deliberations assess the consequences of various courses of action for themselves and others. When they decide on the course of action that they predict will bring the environmental consequences they prefer, they should take that action. In addition, they should be taught to monitor progress toward a chosen goal so that they may correct their errors and maximize their chances of achieving the goal.

This prescription has benefits other than the prevention of defensiveness. Children are learning to appraise and direct their own destiny and seek the goals they prefer. This should make them more prone to accept the consequences of their own actions and should make them more autonomous.

Social taboos institutionalize defensiveness in that groups of people are taught not to think certain thoughts. One example is the teaching about sin. It is, of course, restrictive when groups are taught that certain actions are sinful. The Ten Commandments offer ten examples of sinful actions that can be committed. However, the Ten Commandments themselves do not instill defensiveness because defensiveness involves thought. When a group is taught that it is sinful to think about violating a commandment, then defensiveness is institutionalized in that culture.

The distinction between thought and action is also important with respect to civil law. Laws are passed and communicated so that people may know how to predict the consequences of their actions and the actions of others, and how to live with other people. Most legal penalties are for illegal actions, but penalties are also based on thought. For example, the penalty for committing murder is greater if the murder was premeditated. Laws that penalize conspiracy or the planning of a crime, whether or not the crime is committed, legislate systematically against certain thoughts. However, it is often unclear whether planning a crime mentally is of itself a crime or whether to be considered illegal the planning must involve actions taken to prepare for the crime. Such vagueness and subtlety do not make it easy for the child to see clearly the relationship between thought and action.

At the age of five or six children are sent off to school to learn social tools such as reading, writing, arithmetic, and the foundations of society. The American way is taught in history, social studies, and the like. The trauma involved in this transition centers around weaning children away from parents and introducing them to substitutes such as a teacher and principal. Since they now must rely on these substitutes to teach them how to predict in the world, they become apprehensive about getting involved. This apprehension increases considerably in the new and unpredictable environment that they find at school. School is different from home, and it is strange and confusing at first. There are now more choices to make, and, as Starr's (1980) work has shown, when there are more alternatives available, one tends to cling loyally to one of them. We often see a child who is entering school for the first time grasping and holding on to something familiar as the child faces a new and unpredictable situation.

As children begin to adjust to the school environment and it becomes more predictable, they can concentrate more on the subjects being taught.

They may regard much of the teaching they receive as the teaching of superstition because they are unable to test many of the concepts and confirm the truth for themselves. There may be some notable exceptions, however. For instance, children may be allowed to test certain scientific principles in a laboratory course. The problem is not so much that other things in school cannot be made relevant, but that children are usually forced to accept the validity of a concept on faith.

We are aware that children ask questions to find out about the world. However, many of the questions they ask are for the purpose of determining whether or not their predictions are correct. They make assertions and then ask whether they are right or wrong. We are suggesting that what we often take as a question is in fact a child's attempt to determine whether or not a prediction is correct. This type of question is distinct from other types of questions.

By the time children become adolescents, they become bored with the rituals of home life and school and are eager to test their abilities in the real world. They now begin to question the relevancy of things they have been taught. Much of their knowledge was presented in the abstract. Some examples were offered to clarify the meanings of the abstractions, but, at best, they were able to derive meaning from these examples vicariously. They did not receive much opportunity to test their relevancy themselves, and too many things remain unpredictable. Also, many teachings were offered as generalities, as if they applied to all people. So the question arises, "What meaning do these general principles have for me? How can I apply them to pursue my own interests?"

To find answers for themselves, adolescents are prompted to move out into the world on their own, in spite of the threat of unpredictability that confronts them out there. They are more concerned with escaping the boredom of a ritualized life and with seeking relevancy than they are with the threat of too little predictability. Unfortunately, the teachings of home, school, and church have been so abstract and generalized that adolescents are ill prepared to cope with the specifics of life on their own. The gap between education and life may be so wide that adolescents must find life very unpredictable when they set out to face it. This venture is almost always traumatic, and the chance for success much too limited.

We must live as we learn, instead of learning before we start living, and the learning we acquire must be relevant to our life in the here and now. Adolescence is a transitional period between childhood and adulthood. If we think that schooling is only preparation for the transition to life and that we cannot begin to live before we finish school, then we are fostering a dangerous and destructive practice. We are keeping people in a perpetual state of adolescence well into their adult life. For example, the psychiatrist may attend school until into the middle thirties in order to be certified for that profession. However, because the psychiatrist spends so much time in school, worldly experience may be quite limited.

Adolescence is a relatively unpredictable stage because it is transitional and rapid changes are taking place. The rapid growth of adolescents' bodies reminds them that they are not the same as they were yesterday. Adolescents continue to outgrow their clothes, they become gangly and uncoordinated, and their sexual impulses become more active and unmanageable.

We seldom consider that the propensity of adolescents for hero worship and their tendency to be idealistic may be attempts to stabilize a very unpredictable stage of life. By idealizing conditions, one in fact is simplifying them. Life is quite variable, and the adolescent predicament makes it even more variable. In idealizing their outlook, adolescents assert their own viewpoint and identity while at the same time simplifying life for themselves.

One way for adolescents to try to escape the boredom and the unpredictability inherent in this stage of life is to attempt to assume adult roles. Adolescents generally complain that they are given responsibility with no authority, and in many ways this complaint is justified. To assert themselves they seek any authorization of adult status they can find. The first authorization for which they qualify is a driver's license, which represents not only adult status but increased freedom and greater opportunity to escape boredom. A car becomes a worthwhile challenge, and, because adolescents have been deprived of testing their knowledge, they use a car to show that they can master unpredictability. They may take unnecessary risks to demonstrate that they can manage cars under the most hair-raising conditions.

Alcohol and drugs provide the same kind of opportunity as the automobile. They provide a challenge and a chance to prove adulthood. Imbibing introduces risks, but "holding your liquor" is a sign of adulthood. It shows that they can predict how much they can hold and still navigate. After all, although many frown on drinking, intoxication from alcoholic beverages is a socially legitimated adult mode of escape.

One reason adolescents form gangs is that the gangs provide a bridge across the wide gap between their dependence on their family and the independence they hope to achieve eventually. Peer groups help adolescents to test and confirm many predictions, which they must do to gain confidence. Adolescents feel they must take chances to prove themselves. Such risks might well be regarded as wrong, foolish, or dangerous by parents.

Condry and Simon (1974) show that peer-orientation arises often from "passive-neglect" parents and that those choosing peer orientation are usually anxious and unsatisfied with their socially undesirable behavior. Their conformity to the peer group is of necessity, not enjoyment.

The adolescent dilemma is distressing. They are ill prepared to handle adolescence. In pretending to be an adult they are often ridiculous.

However, unless we can make adolescence and the transition from adolescence to adulthood more predictable, these problems will remain. Not so long ago in the agrarian culture, a youth of seventeen often was ready to assume adult responsibilities of making a living and starting a family and was usually prepared for it. Now youths are prepared for neither a prolonged adolescence nor the adult responsibilities they must assume in order to make the transition to adulthood.

The family suffers because of the confusion generated by the conflict among daily values. Another factor that causes confusion is the middle-class notion that one should sacrifice in the present to pursue a more important goal in the future. This outlook makes the prediction of satisfaction impossible because if one should achieve an important goal, one is predisposed at the time to consider the pursuit of a subsequent goal as more important. This, of course, prevents one from savoring the satisfaction of the moment. For the fanatically upwardly mobile middle-class person, there is no satisfaction in the present.

To make matters worse, it is impossible to predict success in either the role of the adult male or the adult female in our society. Further, the staggering divorce rate reminds us of how difficult it is to predict success in marriage.

Wiley (1973) observed that traditional sex roles in American society indicate that males should be aggressive, assertive, domineering, and task-oriented, whereas females should be passive, submissive, nurturent, and person-oriented. The results of a study by Aneshensel and Rosen (1980) showed that occupational and domestic expectations are intricately interwoven for females and are relatively discrete spheres for males. Hoffman (1972) found that women are socialized to seek affiliation rather than mastery as a source of satisfaction. Socialization for affiliation is consistent with the woman's traditional role of housewife and mother. However, there is evidence that boys more strongly prefer the stereotyped male role than girls prefer the stereotyped female role (see Hartup and Zook 1960; Brown 1957; Rosenburg and Sutton-Smith 1960). Saario (1973) concludes that such stereotyping is present in schools at all levels and in nearly all educational materials. In a study of 5,600 graduating high-school seniors Lueptow (1980) found no evidence of change in sex-related socialization patterns over the 1964 to 1975 decade.

The 1974 U.S. census report shows an increase in the number of working women from 1960 to 1973. In 1973 there were 35 million working women in the United States, comprising almost 40 percent of the labor force. Almost three out of five of these women were working and living with husbands, and of the 13 million working mothers, 4.8 million had children under six years of age. So there has been a dramatic change in the woman's role in the past several years. But the emergence of women into the work world has not yet enabled them to achieve equal-employment opportunities. The 1973 census report shows that females occupy low-paying, lower-status jobs when compared to males, and women are promoted less frequently and suffer higher unemployment rates.

Klenmack and Edwards (1973) studied factors influencing women's acquisition of stereotyped occupational aspirations. It increases with "anticipated family size," decreases with increasing "prestige of father's occupation," and increases with "advanced dating status." Two implications emerge as important factors: (1) the transfer of family values, in this case job aspirations, even from father to daughter, and (2) stereotyping of housewife as the typical female.

Although the traditional female role was well defined, as women emerge from this identity some become confused by the number of alternatives available to them and the diffuse expectations imposed on them. The modern woman is expected to be all things to all people. She is expected to be a cook, housecleaner, mother, breadwinner, hostess, lover, teacher of morality, community worker, and chauffeur, just to name a few of the roles. Not only does she lack the time to carry out all of these responsibilities, but in some cases they are in conflict.

The traditional female role in our society is not possible to fulfill because the expectations are too numerous and diffuse. The dilemma of the American male is a little different. He cannot achieve the expectations of the stereotyped role of the American hero, a role that has its roots in American tradition and has been perpetuated to this day. Many of the successful television and movie heroes of today represent this stereotype.

The American male hero is aggressive, instrumental, indestructible, stoic, mission oriented, violent, virtuous, a loner, and persistent. He accepts a challenge, no matter what the odds for success may be. He doggedly pursues his mission with single-mindedness of purpose and right on his side. He resists the temptations of people who attempt to divert and bribe him. His involvement with people is temporary and limited. He curbs his feelings toward them and avoids deep attachments lest he be diverted from the task at hand. With spartan determination, he overcomes all obstacles and always gets his man. However, once he achieves his goal his respite is short because there is always evil lurking and he must continue to fight to conquer it.

The classical western provides a clear picture of our hero. He may be a marshall or merely a soldier of fortune, but it is clear that he is a good guy. The villain is out to exploit the local citizenry and our hero is obliged to stop him because no one else can. He rides to the battle on his trusty steed and, with guns blazing, brings down the bad guy and restores peace and tranquility to the community. The town lady, who has fallen in love with him, offers herself as the prize, but he pecks her fondly on the forehead, chooses his horse to the lady, and rides off into the sunset to seek his next challenge.

We see examples of the stereotyped hero on television in the personification of Wyatt Earp and Bat Masterson. It is interesting that these portrayals much more closely correspond to the stereotype than to the actual lives of these men. This stereotype of a hero may seem unreal and in many ways he is nowadays. However, some of the founders of our country were to some extent this kind of man. They fought their enemies and the fickle natural elements to carve civilization out of the wilderness. The amazing thing is that we have preserved the early American hero as an exaggerated and perverted stereotype for our men to emulate.

The stereotyped American hero is not limited to the western scene. He has been transplanted to modern settings but he is always the same type. Our private investigators and police heroes are cut from this mold. Television gives us Rockford, Kojak, Starsky and Hutch, and others. In books and movies we find James Bond, Mike Hammer, and Phillip Marlowe.

As ludicrous as it may seem, the popularity of this stereotype of the American hero persists and prevails. We have preserved and idealized him and we and our children identify with him.

Unfortunately this identification leads us to great frustration because in modern America the rugged individualist does not have much chance for success. For example, the rate of failure for men starting new businesses is very high and getting higher all the time. Today the demand is for the team man in corporate enterprise and in bureaucratic work. There is not much demand for the loner anymore.

The stereotyped hero on today's scene is a misfit, a deviant, and a troublemaker. The stereotype calls for aggression and violence; today's world calls for peaceful conformity and compliance. The stereotype calls for virtue without compromise; today's world calls for flexibility and negotiation. It is no wonder that today's male is frustrated and dissatisfied and seeks escape from his bewilderment. It is no wonder that he is victimized by alcoholism, ulcers, and early heart disease. The complexities of modern life are unpredictable enough. Our model of a man makes matters worse.

The male and female stereotypes present problems not only to those who are trying to fulfill them; they complicate and undermine the relationships between men and women. If the American woman wants a mate who resembles the stereotyped male, she is in for a disappointment. Instead of a rugged individualist, she must settle for a man who is trying to find a place for himself as a member of some work team. Instead of molding the world to suit himself, he must mold himself to fit into a specialized niche in a corner of the world. In comparison to his dream of becoming an American hero, he is repeatedly reminded of his inability to fill that role.

Komarovsky (1973) concludes that the notion of male intellectual superiority is giving way, and those who refuse to accept this change tend to be anxiety ridden. Raymond (1973) argues that however useful or important it might be to societal survival, the patriarchical family has inhibited self-actualization.

The emulation of the American hero also tends to encourage our men to be stoic and mission oriented and not to allow their feelings to interfere with their mission. However, such a man does not make a good husband. He tends to inhibit his feelings and restrain expressions of warmth. He often regards a show of emotion as a sign of weakness and feminity. Moreover, because he is mission oriented, he may readily neglect his family for his work.

Another factor that interferes with the compatibility between men and women in our society is that many men have subscribed to the notion of the "lady" and the "tramp." This duality leads to what some psychologists call the "prostitute complex." The implication of the malady is that "ladies" are for marriage and raising children, and "tramps" are for sex and pleasure. A man suffering from this complex will marry a lady. He will tend to idealize her in accordance with the virtues and goodness of the stereotype. In addition, he may place her on a pedestal and not regard her as a suitable sex partner. Inevitably, he becomes disillusioned with his marriage when she turns out to be human and unworthy of her place on the pedestal. Furthermore, because of *his* inhibitions, she will not prove to be a satisfying sex partner. In order to enjoy sex, he may be tempted to sneak out to find a tramp who can provide him with sexual excitement.

The American female who traditionally looked for happiness in marriage as the fulfillment of her life may no longer feel safe with this aspiration. The numerous and diffuse expectations that have come to comprise the role of the modern woman have caused her to search in so many directions for satisfaction that it seems there is little stability in her life. It seems that she cannot fulfill all of the various expectations she may have, and, in attempting to pursue too many of them, she may decrease the probability of succeeding at any of them.

In general, her problem is that she is confused. She does not know which alternative to pursue. She may see some satisfaction in working, in family life, and in community service. However, because she cannot pursue everything, she tends to feel that whenever she pursues one goal she will be sacrificing something else. This dilemma leads to a feeling of entrapment if she stays home or a feeling of guilt if she leaves home for extended periods and thinks she is neglecting her family.

In conclusion, it appears that many of our social rules lead to confusion and unpredictability. Social expectations for both men and women in our society make it exceedingly difficult for them to predict success together in marriage. The traditional commitment in marriage of "until death do us part" seemingly is being replaced by the concept of "serial monogamy," one marriage at a time.

19 Coping with Boredom and Confusion

This chapter presents prescriptions for diagnosing and treating boredom and confusion based on research studies that have been completed. Although more research needs to be done, available research results are encouraging and point to a distinctive method of coping with mental stress based on prediction theory. First we will summarize the method of coping with boredom and confusion that people can employ to manage the mental stress in their lives. Then we will discuss research on boredom and confusion in the areas of counseling and psychotherapy. Prediction theory has implications for self-management of mental stress and treating people who need assistance in dealing with their mental stress.

Throughout this book, we have been talking about boredom and confusion and how these are maladaptive states of mental stress. We have maintained that the intermediate stage of optimum predictability represents an adaptive stage in which mental stress is minimal. It should be remembered that the following coping procedures are for persons who have psychological problems but who are not suffering from general psychological disorientation. It is assumed that people who utilize these procedures are able to help themselves.

Optimum Predictability: Preventing Boredom and Confusion

How individuals maintain optimum predictability and thus prevent mental stress is the first consideration. As noted, an optimally predictable situation is one that provides enough novelty and variety to be challenging but not so much that confusion results. In addition, an optimally predictable situation is one that provides enough familiarity to permit predictions to be made but not so much that boredom is caused. To achieve this adaptive state and not experience the maladaptive extremes of boredom or confusion, individuals must be able to recognize and have some control over the parameters of predictable circumstances that influence their lives.

Maintenance of a lifestyle that promotes flexibility without frustration seems essential. It is necessary that one lead a life that has the degrees of interest, activity, responsibility, and challenge that the particular individual is comfortable in handling. There are widely diverse levels of stimulation that are acceptable to different people, and even these change over time and under varying circumstances. Situations that would be entirely too routine for some people are quite acceptable to others. Some individuals seem geared for a lifestyle in which there is a great variety of activity while others would be totally frustrated by such diversity. It can thus be seen that optimum predictability is not an absolute state in itself; it is always relative to the individual and to that person's preferences and physical limitations at the time.

The important elements in an optimally predictable situation are capability and confidence of the individual. Knowing one's levels of tolerance for routine and one's comfortable levels of tolerance for novelty provides for arriving at a balance for that person. Being able to predict to some degree what is going to happen is essential in preventing confusion. The activities that allow prevention of confusion involve planning: scheduling, stabilizing, organizing, and simplifying. One works through an organized plan to reach goals so that the level of predictability among events along the way to the goal is increased. Conversely, when the levels of predictability are too high, boredom results. To combat this one needs to introduce more challenge, novelty, and variety into his or her life.

Whenever people feel stress, pressure, or frustration with their daily lives, they are experiencing either boredom or confusion. Predictability is not at an optimum level. However, once a diagnosis has been made as to which maladaptive state a psychologically distressed person is in, the direction of relief is apparent. Regardless of which extreme of the bipolar continuum of predictability a person is experiencing, the treatment should lead toward the middle, the adaptive position of optimum predictability.

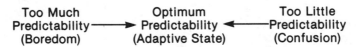

Too Much Predictability (Boredom)	→	Optimum Predictability (Adaptive State)	←	Too Little Predictability (Confusion)

However, for bored individuals, relief from boredom and movement toward optimum predictability is achieved by introducing novelty and challenge into their lives. On the other hand, for confused people, relief from confusion and movement toward optimum predictability is achieved by stabilizing, regulating, and simplifying their lives. Thus boredom is treated in one way; confusion is treated in another way.

Coping with psychological problems has a prerequisite. People have to identify the stress felt as boredom or confusion and then accept the fact that this is the problem for which a solution must be found.

Acceptance of the fact that a psychological problem exists is essential before any progress can be made to solve the problem, whether it involves boredom or confusion. People are reluctant to admit a psychological problem even to themselves. In the past, and to some extent today, a stigma accompanied psychological problems. As a result, individuals become fearful that they will be labeled crazy, loony, a psychiatric case, and so forth. There is a mystery associated with treatment even after identification has been made. Lack of physical evidence of boredom or confusion makes diagnosis less precise than for a bone fracture, for instance, so acceptance is more easily deniable. People find it difficult to admit their own weaknesses and frailties. However, these problems have to be faced. Individuals have to embrace the idea candidly and honestly that they have a psychological problem, whether it be boredom or confusion, before they can alleviate their stress.

Boredom

Recognizing and Accepting Boredom

The first step toward finding relief from boredom is being able to recognize and accept entrapment in a boring situation, a monotonous routine. *Entrapment* means that there are forces holding a person in a boring routine. These forces may be feelings of guilt or the idea that sacrifices would be too great for one to relieve oneself from the boredom.

There are a number of kinds of things that may be entrapping to a person. One's obligations to parents, children, or mate are not usually taken lightly when a person is trying to achieve personal satisfaction or goals. Financial security is also of importance when one is thinking of factors that can cause feelings of entrapment. For example, a person may realize that he or she is in a very boring job but opts for the financial security provided by that job rather than freedom from the boredom. Values and traditions are sometimes entrapping to the extent that one may choose to remain in a boring marriage rather than alter or discard beliefs in traditional religious or civil laws. Also one may be entrapped by feeling personally dependent on someone else. Regardless of age, there is a certain amount of fear of the unpredictable or of making a drastic change in one's life. There is no risk of confusion if one maintains the status quo because a high level of predictability is likely in familiar circumstances.

Conditions that generate boredom involve sameness and lack of novelty. Before people can deal with boredom in a positive way, there must be the realization that their life situations are overly routinized, that is, they may rise at the same time every day, eat the same type breakfast, follow the same route to work, perform the same daily tasks, associate with the same people, maintain the same hair style and dress mode regardless of fashion changes, hear the same sounds, eat at the same restaurants, pursue the same leisure-time activities, and so on. There is little novelty, no variety in personal relationships, no real challenge to meet. There are specific types of boring situations and conditions for persons of different age groups and with different lifestyles but, in any case, there is too much predictability. Housewives are classically considered as likely candidates for boredom because of the nature of their daily tasks and their routinized life pattern. Assembly-line workers may become so bored by the repetition involved in their work that they become careless. Old people and retirees whose lives are devoid of stimulation and challenge may suffer from boredom. They can be fairly certain that today will be very much like yesterday and that tomorrow's major activities will vary little from today's.

How do people proceed to diagnose their own boredom? Individuals who are attempting to determine whether their stress is boredom would benefit by following the sequential plan proposed here.

1. Look for things in their daily lives that are repetitious or things that are too predictable.

2. Examine their feelings about these things. Do they bore them? Does it make them feel tired or disinterested to realize that these things are persistently the same from day to day?

3. Decide whether or not they are suffering from boredom. There are monotonous activities which all people have to perform but the level of boredom experienced is dependent on one's ability to cope with and adapt to these activities.

4. Identify the specific situations that are boring to these individuals.

Seeking Immediate Relief from Boredom

Once boredom has been recognized and accepted, procedures for getting some immediate relief are appropriate; people who have accepted their boredom as a problem would seek immediate relief as follows.

1. Make a list of novel activities or changes that would be desirable.

2. Note which of these things can be done immediately.

3. Determine which of the things are feasible. In other words, consider which of the things could be carried out because the necessary time, money, or other resources are available or could be made available. Consider, too, whether they have the determination or ability to break whatever entrapment may be existent.

After this stage the list should enumerate only novel things that can be done immediately and for which a desire and the means to do are assured.

4. Make arrangements to do some of these things. Plan some alternative activities based on the list. For example, if one's list contained an item involving meeting new people, arrangements should be made to join a club, go to church, enroll in a class, go to a resort. If the list included items pertaining to learning, arrangements should be made to gain additional educa-

tion or to take classes in a new sport or hobby activity. If self-improvement items were listed, an appointment with the beauty salon or getting information about available diet or exercise facilities would be appropriate measures.

5. Do the things that were arranged to do. Planning is therapeutic to some extent but unless the plans are implemented, additional frustrations are likely. So it is important to actually take that vacation, go on the picnic, start taking the tennis lessons, visit the friends, redecorate the room, go on the fishing trip, or do whatever was planned to get the immediately desired relief from boredom.

Seeking Continuing Relief from Boredom

Procedures for seeking continuing relief from boredom are much like those for attaining immediate relief. The major difference lies in the fact that in the case of continuing relief, long-range challenging goals are dealt with rather than short-term activity changes. The following are suggested procedures for persons seeking continuing relief from boredom.

1. First make a list of long-term challenging goals that would be desirable to pursue to relieve the boredom. Goals of this type might include such things as getting a college degree, changing careers, getting a divorce, or building a home.

2. Select the goals that are most interesting.

3. Investigate means of achieving those goals that have the highest priority on the list.

4. Narrow the list to include only those long-term goals that are feasible and of high interest. If the highest priority items are not feasible at the present, discard them and accept those that can be carried out.

5. Make plans to pursue these goals. Devise the means to the goals by scheduling time, money, and activities so the goals can be reached.

6. Proceed toward the goals according to the schedule.

Confusion

Recognizing and Accepting Confusion

The first step in finding relief from confusion is being able to recognize and accept confusion as the stress-causing factor. When people are confused, their lives are fraught with too much stimulation, variation, newness, or strangeness. They feel stress because they are in a state of unpredictability and uncertainty, not knowing what is going to happen.

Conditions that generate confusion include having too many alternative choices or having too much to do in the time allotted. Perhaps there is too much happening at once or a rapidly changing, unstable situation arises. Other confusion-causing conditions are new and strange experiences. Having responsibilities that are unmanageable, for whatever reason, can be confusing. Confusion may be caused by such things as rush-hour traffic, going to a doctor, driving a new car, ordering from an extensive menu or one that contains unfamiliar words, moving to a new city or neighborhood, or meeting future in-laws. Under any of these conditions there is a low level of predictablity.

Before any solutions to the problem of confusion can be reached, a diagnosis must be made. The following procedures for diagnosing confusion are suggested. People who feel that their stress may be caused by confusion should:

1. Look for situations in their lives that may be confusing. These might relate to work, home life, social associations, circumstances that have changed recently.
2. Ask themselves if they have a satisfactory idea of what is going to happen in each of these situations. If there is no idea of what is going to happen, these persons are confused about the situations.
3. Decide whether or not they are suffering from confusion. They must be willing to accept the fact that confusion is the cause of their stress before it can be alleviated. The importance of acceptance was discussed earlier in this chapter.
4. Identify the specific situations that are confusing them.

Once people accept the fact that they are actually experiencing a psychological problem diagnosed as confusion, they can begin to work toward some immediate relief.

Seeking Immediate Relief from Confusion

The procedures for seeking immediate relief are simple. Persons seeking such relief would benefit by following this plan.

1. Make a list of things that are stressful and confusing to them in their own lives. This list-making has value within itself because seeing things written down gives organization to thoughts which lessens confusion.

2. Decide which items can be eliminated. A problem such as inflation on a list should be eliminated; a person cannot cope with any confusing situation that vast and complex. An aspect of inflation that concerns one individually and for which some solution can be found should remain on the

list. For example, if one's noon meal at restaurants is rising in cost and the financial pinch is felt, the problem might be solved by that person's taking a home-prepared lunch to work.

3. Eliminate those items that can be eliminated from the list. Discard the items that cannot be changed or controlled. Deal only with specific stress-causing items, not broad, general areas of confusion.

4. For the remaining items determine how they can be simplified, organized, and scheduled. For example, if coping with confusing rush-hour traffic is a problem decide if it would be advantageous to leave for the destination either earlier or later. Perhaps a desirable activity could be scheduled as an alternative to fighting the traffic at that particular time.

5. Simplify, organize, and schedule the items on the list.

Some healthy alternatives to confusion might be for confused persons to delegate some of their responsibilities if they are overburdened or learn to say "no" when asked to take on new or additional responsibilities. Accept their limitations; plan and work within them. Avoid new situations which may confuse them. Stop doing confusing things that are not absolutely necessary.

Seeking Continuing Relief from Confusion

The procedures for seeking continuing relief from confusion are similar to methods for seeking continuing relief from boredom. However, in setting goals there should be a sequence of enabling goals that lead to a terminal goal. This simplifies and structures the goal-setting process and prevents achievement of goals from becoming too remote. Persons seeking continuing relief from confusion should do the following things.

1. Establish priorities. Those problems most stressful or of greatest importance need goals for solution before some of the other listed items.

2. Investigate means of achieving higher-priority items. Ignorance is a primary cause of psychological problems. Acquiring knowledge often leads to solutions.

3. Consider alternative means of achieving these items in terms of feasibility. What avenues are open in terms of money, time, resources, and changes?

4. Make long-range plans, remembering to emphasize reduction and limitation of complicated activities, keeping activities familiar and within limitations.

5. Carry out the plans. Assume no unplanned responsibilities. Keep things simple, organized, and scheduled. Stay in familiar surroundings and within the realm of the predictable.

Whether individuals are attempting to cope with boredom or confusion, the importance of having knowledge cannot be overemphasized. The procedures listed in this chapter all included investigation or learning about possible courses of action when seeking relief from psychological problems. Learning new things alleviates boredom. Learning is equally important in the prevention of confusion.

Whenever it is feasible or when there is intense interest in learning individuals can get knowledge by reading, attending lectures or workshops, or taking courses. However, whenever the subject is uninteresting or is highly technical, individuals may choose to utilize the professional assistance of others rather than attempt to become personally educated about that subject. Individuals cannot be specifically knowledgeable about all the stressful conditions or circumstances affecting their lives. Therefore, they seek aid from others who have expertise in particular fields. Individuals who are mathematically inadequate often utilize the services of tax assistants and accountants. When people are not relieved by their own medical self-helps, they go to a physician. Most people have to rely on lawyers to handle any legal entanglements.

The more knowledge people possess the more capable they are of making accurate predictions. The more capable people are in their predictive abilities, the less likely they are to find themselves in the maladaptive states of either boredom or confusion.

Counseling and Psychotherapy

One advantage of using prediction-theory procedures to relieve mental stress is that they can be learned and employed by almost anyone to prevent and control boredom and confusion. Procedures derived from other theories are designed to be administered by trained counselors and psychotherapists. One claim is that individuals are too subjective about their problems and are unable to get a clear view of them. They need the objectivity of a trained counselor or psychotherapist to reveal to them the nature of their problems. Freudians contend that psychological problems are unconsciously based and by definition, individuals cannot be aware of these problems.

Counselors who use procedures derived from prediction theory assist people by diagnosing them as bored or confused and guiding them through the stages previously summarized to relieve boredom or confusion as the case may be. When they achieve success in treating their clients, they teach the clients the procedures to reduce dependency on the counselor and show clients how in the future they can prevent and control their own boredom or confusion. Liu (1980) constructed a test that indicates whether individuals have learned the principles of prediction theory sufficiently well to apply them effectively in managing their own mental stress.

Albert Ellis (1976) gave impetus to the application of prediction theory to counseling and psychotherapy. In a review of *Rational Behavior* (Freidman 1975), Ellis stressed the importance of the theory and its compatibility with rational emotive therapy.

Savitz (1979) designed the first diagnostic and counseling procedures based on prediction theory. She tested it successfully on a population of outpatient clients who, after being interviewed and examined by a physician for physical problems at a family practice clinic, were diagnosed as suffering from psychological problems. However, the clients were not regarded as disoriented or potentially dangerous to themselves or others. The clients volunteered for psychological diagnosis and counseling. Fourteen of the clients were diagnosed as confused and nineteen as bored. Of the fourteen confused clients, eight were assigned to a control group and received no counseling. Six were assigned to a treatment group and were counseled for four weeks to relieve their confusion. The results showed that five of the six clients in the treatment group changed to an adaptive state of mind, while there was no change in the control group. (The difference between the groups was statistically significant beyond the .005 level based on a Fisher exact test analysis.)

Of the nineteen bored clients, nine were assigned to a control group and received no treatment. Ten were assigned to a treatment group and were counseled for four weeks to relieve their boredom. The results showed that nine of the ten clients in the treatment group changed to an adaptive state of mind, while only one of the nine in the control group changed to an adaptive state of mind. (The difference between the groups was statistically significant beyond the .001 level based on a Fisher exact test analysis.)

The results show that both bored and confused clients will recover to an adaptive state of mind as a result of such counseling. The counseling procedure consisted of guiding the clients through stages similar to those summarized earlier in the chapter. The diagnostic procedure consisted of categorizing clients as bored or confused based on their responses to six interview questions. The way in which responses are categorized is presented followed by an explanation of the responses in the context of prediction theory. This will acquaint you more fully with the behavior of people suffering from boredom and confusion and the interpretation of such behavior. Technical aspects of the development of the diagnostic interview schedule are presented in a research report (Savitz and Friedman, in press).

The Diagnostic Interview Schedule

The following is the interview schedule used to diagnose individuals as bored, confused, or adaptive. The questions followed by typical responses for the three categories are presented.

Question 1: Why Are You Here?

Adaptive Responses. Individuals admit they came because they have a problem. They are able to identify the situation that is troubling them and the aspects of the situation that are causing them a problem. In describing their problem, the individuals are able to describe their feelings toward the various people in the situation as well as the behaviors that need to be changed to alleviate the problem. For example, a person might say, "We have a new baby, my husband is gone all day, and I stay in every minute. I love my baby, but I need to make arrangements to get out of the house a couple of times a week."

Maladaptive Responses. Bored individuals indicate that they came for help on their own initiative. They display a keen awareness that they have a problem. They indicate that they are emotionally upset and express a desire for relief. For instance, they might say, "I am frustrated and don't know what to do about it. I'm in a rut—do the same things every day."

Confused individuals indicate they came for help because others prompted them to. Although they can identify their problem situation, they indicate that others are more aware of their problem than they are. For example, they might say, "People say I'm just spinning my wheels and need help. I can't seem to get anything accomplished at work, but I don't know why."

Question 2: What Has Been Happening to You?

Adaptive Responses. Individuals describe their activities and their feelings about them in relating their problems. They describe their own contributions to the problems, and their responsibility for contribution to the solution. For instance, they might say, "My difficulty is mainly housework and raising kids. I get angry with my husband because he spoils the kids. I need to control my temper and work out a plan with him."

Maladaptive Responses. Bored individuals express a general lack of interest in their activities and a lack of energy to carry them out. They complain that they are not motivated to do anything. For example, they might say, "I used to do a variety of things, but now I do the same things over and over. I'm tired most of the time." When they discuss their problem situation they describe the routine, repetitive tasks they perform without understanding specifically that they suffer from boredom. For example, they might say, "I get up at 6:15—I bathe, I cook breakfast, I clean up, and so forth,—through the whole day."

Confused individuals describe how others view the events in the problem situation and how others interpret the factors creating the problem. For example, they might say, "My friends tell me I'm handling my boss all

wrong. They think I should assert myself more. I wish I knew what to do."
In addition, confused people describe the many different things that are
overwhelming them without understanding specifically that they are confused by it all. Their description of events seems detached from their feelings. For instance, they might say, "There's too much to do at the office. I
never seem to get caught up. I do the work of two people, but I can't get the
help I need."

Question 3: What Does the Future Hold for You?

Adaptive Responses. Individuals have no difficulty discussing the future.
They convey what they expect to happen and/or what they hope will happen. They describe their short-term and long-term goals and tell how they
are in the process of pursuing them. For example, they might say, "I am
working now and taking courses at night to qualify as a supervisor next
year."

Maladaptive Responses. Bored people indicate that they expect the future
to be the same as the present. They also express little interest in future
events and complain that they do not have the energy to prepare for the
future or to influence the future. For example, they might say, "I expect
things to stay the same as now—I eat, take care of the house, cook, go to
bed. I can't get with it."

Confused people indicate how others perceive their future. They
describe future events as if they were detached and remote from them. For
example, they might say, "I might want to be a doctor, or a lawyer, or an
accountant. They make good money. People tell me I would make a good
lawyer."

Question 4: Can You Predict What Tomorrow Will Be Like for You?

Adaptive Responses. Individuals describe, in general, what they expect to
happen to them and comment on the things they are uncertain of, without
being troubled by the uncertainty. They communicate a pattern and predictability in their life. However, they describe new and challenging undertak-
ings, the outcomes of which are presently unpredictable. For example, they
might say, "Tomorrow I will get up, and so forth—but what surprises the
day will bring—I'm not sure. It's interesting."

Maladaptive Responses. Bored people provide a detailed description of
their daily routine. They show anger and frustration when they comment on
their routine. For instance, they might say, "I'll get up, wake the children,
shower, feed the family toast and bananas, get the children off to school,
clean the house, fix dinner, and so forth. It's got me down."

Confused individuals provide descriptions that are vague and speculative. They have difficulty conveying details or pattern. They might say, "God only knows; my parents want me to go to school, but I don't feel like it. Maybe I'll join the navy or get a job."

Question 5: What Do You Enjoy Doing?

Adaptive Responses. Individuals enumerate a number of things they enjoy doing, and partake of at least one enjoyable activity weekly. They communicate that they know what they enjoy. They select enjoyable activities and participate in them. For example, they might say, "I enjoy skiing, playing golf, sewing, reading—some I do more often than others. I golf once a week when the weather's right."

Maladaptive Responses. Bored individuals refer to things they might like to do, but they do not see the likelihood of doing them. They do refer to specific situations in the recent past that brought them enjoyment. For instance, they might say, "I used to sing, play golf, and so forth—now I just do my daily chores. I don't have the time or energy for other things."

Responses of confused people indicate that they do not know for sure what brings them enjoyment in the present. The best they can do is refer to a remote situation. For example, they might say, "One thing's as good as another. I used to like to play baseball when I was a kid. Someday I hope to travel."

Question 6: What Are Your Goals?

Adaptive Responses. Individuals refer to specific goals they have set, a time frame and plan for achieving them, and are involved in pursuing them. They refer also to what the achievement of the goals will mean to them. For example, they might say, "I'm going to night school. In two years I'll get my master's degree. Then I'll get a promotion and raise in salary."

Maladaptive Responses. Bored individuals refer to goals they might like to pursue, but make excuses for not pursuing them. They describe little if any movement toward the goals and do not regard the goals as attainable under prevailing conditions. For instance, they might say, "I wish I could go play tennis but I don't have the time."

Confused individuals refer to unrealistic, remote goals or do not define specific goals at all. If they do state a goal, they do not prescribe a way of achieving it. For example, they might say, "One day I will run for political office, I'm not sure which one."

Summarization and Integration of Responses. The following is an attempt to summarize and integrate the responses into the theoretical framework.

The Adaptive Individual in An Optimally Predictable Situation. Although adaptive individuals have problems, they are able to cope with them. They are neither suffering from too little predictability nor too much predictability. Their situation is sufficiently familiar and understandable to enable them to make predictions they can expect to confirm. In addition, their situation is novel enough to be challenging and to enable them to improve their ability to predict. They describe the elements of their problems and their own contribution to the problem. They also describe how they feel about the various elements of their situation. They describe their likes and dislikes and are actively engaged in activities they enjoy. They predict the actions they must take to solve their problem. They describe their goals, when they expect to achieve them, and how they will pursue them. They also indicate how they will feel when they achieve their goals. They describe the uncertainties they face as interesting and challenging.

The Bored Individual in a Situation That Is Too Predictable. Bored individuals are suffering from too much predictability. Although they are not specifically aware that they suffer from too much predictability, in their accounts of current events they describe in detail their ritualistic routine that is the source of their problem. In essence, they are repetitiously making and confirming the same predictions. They indicate further that they are entrapped in the routine. When they refer to their entrapment, they display frustration and anger. They seek help on their own because they are able to predict that therapy may help them. Their anger and feeling of entrapment dampen their motivation and drain their energy. Because they feel entrapped and listless, the future holds no promise for them. They are not actively engaged in working to achieve goals and make excuses for not doing so. The only prediction they tend to make is that the future will be very much the same as the humdrum present.

The Confused Individual in a Situation That Is Too Unpredictable. Confused people are suffering from too little predictability, although they are not aware that their problem is their inability to confirm the predictions they make. They are confused about what is happening to them in the present and their feelings about the happenings. Because of their confusion, they rely on others to interpret and direct their activities. They are unable to predict that therapy may help them. They seek help because others urge them to. Since they are overwhelmed, their descriptions of current events are vague and diffuse and convey that they are uncertain of how they feel about them. Their descriptions lack detail, pattern, and continuity. They are unable to predict the future or to project how they may feel about future events. They refer to how others perceive future events in their lives. They indicate that they do not know what they will be doing in the future and speculate on various remote and often unrealistic possibilities. They are not actively pursuing any of the possible goals they mention and do not prescribe ways of achieving the goals, nor do they show an intense interest in pursuing any particular goal they mention.

In administering the interview schedule, the diagnostician was instructed and trained to establish rapport with the subjects and to reduce their anxiety. Then the diagnostician was instructed to ask the six questions in the order presented here. The diagnostician was to allow ample time for the subjects to answer each question and to encourage them to respond until an adequate answer was given.

Recent efforts to apply prediction theory to relieve mental stress include marriage counseling and the treatment of alcoholism. Research on the application of prediction theory to the treatment of alcoholism is based on the rationale that individuals may be driven to alcoholism by situations that are too boring or too confusing. However, once addicted to alcohol, individuals are in a state of confusion. The slogans of Alcoholics Anonymous pertaining to the treatment of alcoholics indicate the need to simplify and regulate one's life to reduce confusion. These slogans include "first things first," "easy does it," "one day at a time," and "keep it simple."

It appears that the effects of alcohol are more predictable to alcoholics than anything else in their lives. This explains why psychologically the alcoholic is inclined to continue drinking and why treatment should be aimed at reducing the confusion in their lives to encourage them to abstain. This also explains, in part, why the Alcoholics Anonymous treatment claims more success in curing alcoholism than counseling and psychotherapy treatments. The fact that there is agreement between the Alcoholics Anonymous approach and the approach that prediction theory would prescribe suggests that prediction theory may provide a valid explanation of alcoholism and that revised treatment based on prediction theory has potential for improving the recovery rate of alcoholics. However, research is needed to determine this potential.

20 Deliberating by Rules

The ability to deliberate makes it possible for individuals to make and confirm predictions effectively and achieve their preferences. As individuals mature and learn that deliberation improves the ability to predict and acquire preferences, they will control their impulsive reactions and deliberate more often. Deliberation becomes more effective as individuals' inventory of concepts increases and they learn how to deliberate among the alternatives in a concept and make choices. The payoff of effective deliberation is the confirmation of one's predictions. Individuals deliberate to predict what may happen and how they will feel about the happening. If their predictions are confirmed, they have deliberated effectively.

Maintaining and Improving Predictions

Programs

Deliberation contributes to the confirmation of predictions when program concepts are deliberated and a program is selected from among alternatives. Comparing and contrasting alternative programs before choosing one allows the individual to select a program most suited for a particular task. This in turn increases the probability that the program chosen will do the job. For example, a salesman is more likely to make a sale if he deliberates alternative ways of talking to a customer before making his sales pitch than if he impulsively blurts out the first thing that comes to his mind. In addition, the deliberation of program concepts improves prediction because it is the basis for making and confirming predictions about new and unfamiliar events.

Programs are procedures that lead from one place or event to another. They exist apart from personal preferences. A route from one city to another is a program that will permit you to drive between the two cities. The program will get you from one city to the other whether or not you prefer to make the trip. So programs allow you to confirm predictions. Whether or not you prefer to confirm a specific prediction that a program allows you to confirm is another matter. Interstate 20 leads from Atlanta to Augusta, Georgia. Whether one prefers to take the route is another matter. People learn programs because this improves their ability to predict. They use a particular program they have learned when it takes them where they prefer to go.

The more programs we learn, the more predictions we can confirm. The more program concepts we learn, the greater opportunity we have to deliberate alternative procedures. This increases the probability that the procedure we select will lead to the confirmation of a particular prediction. The more routes we learn, the more places we can drive a car. The more alternative routes we learn that lead from one place to another, say from Los Angeles to New York, the greater opportunity we have to select a route that will get us there efficiently.

Also, the more program concepts we learn, the more able we are to predict the unfamiliar. We might have the concept *problem-solving programs.* This concept could contain a program for finding the correct route to a city we have never visited before. When the occasion arises for us to visit a new city, we would deliberate alternative problem-solving programs, choose the program for finding a route to a new city, and use it to find a route.

Rules are public and exist apart from the knowledge of particular individuals. Rules may be learned by individual members of a group and become a part of the individual's inventory of ideas.

Many rules are programmatic. They present sequences of activities that may be used to confirm specific predictions. Members are interested in learning programmatic rules because it improves their ability to predict. Society is interested in teaching these rules to its members. Members who cannot predict are inept and are of little use to themselves or their group.

Draguns (1974) observed that "abnormal behavior represents a continuation by unrealistic and inappropriate means of learned mechanisms of behavior and an application of culturally shared lore of social learning" (p. 117). "Unrealistic" and "inappropriate" behaviors could be regarded as "unpredictable," and explain why such an individual is considered a social misfit.

The programmatic rules that are recorded in libraries and taught in school are how-to rules. They prescribe methods and procedures for accomplishing almost anything humans have accomplished before and recorded. One can learn how to bake a cake, drive a car, fix a car, multiply, divide, and so on.

Rules are also arranged in categories as concepts. Cooking rules are classified in recipe books, language rules are categorized in grammar texts and dictionaries, and driving rules are in driving manuals.

The categorizing of rules enables a person to learn the categories of rules which then form program concepts in the mind. By recording and teaching programmatic rules, the group improves the predictive ability of its members. The more rules that are taught, the more things the members can do, and the more predictions they can confirm.

By recording and teaching categories of programmatic rules, the group further improves the predictive ability of its members. When members learn categories of programmatic rules and concepts form in the mind representing these categories, members have learned alternative ways of doing things. Further, if they are taught a class of rules called problem-solving strategies, they are equipped with a program for dealing with problems they have never dealt with before. If the category problem-solving strategies includes a programmatic rule for making discoveries new to all people and the members learn the rule, they are able to search purposefully for and discover new things. Scientific method is a programmatic problem-solving rule.

Pursuing Preferences

In addition to contributing heavily to one's ability to predict, deliberation is the means of deciding and achieving one's preferences. It is through the deliberation of alternatives in a concept that the individual decides which of the alternatives are preferred. By deliberating concepts, individuals can decide which interest among alternatives they prefer to attend to at the moment, which goal they prefer to pursue to satisfy the interest, and which program they prefer to use to pursue the goal of their choice. To pursue their preferences, the deliberations must result in the formation of a master neuroprint that identifies the interest to be satisfied, the goal to be pursued to satisfy the interest, and the program to be employed to attain the goal.

Whatever events interest individuals at the moment, to determine their preferences they must deliberate them and decide which they will attempt to satisfy and in what order. The decision is tentative until an entire master neuroprint has been constructed.

The next step in forming a master neuroprint is to deliberate the various goals one may pursue to satisfy a particular interest. Whatever goal one may choose, the decision is tentative until programs have been deliberated. In deliberating programs one considers possible ways of achieving a goal. If the goal is to eat a steak in order to satisfy hunger, the individual may consider programs that involve going to a restaurant or cooking a steak at home, as well as different recipes for cooking a steak.

After programs have been considered, the individual deliberates the various master neuroprints and makes a final selection based on the attainability of a goal and the desirability of achieving a goal but, above all, on the goal's attainability. A goal that is considered unattainable probably would not be pursued no matter how desirable it might be to achieve it. A goal is considered to be attainable if a program can be conceived that will achieve the goal.

A group of thirty, nonfarm rural boys and their parents were surveyed by Mueller (1974). The boys who were low achievers in school shared a stable family life, a stable neighborhood, and the same central cultural values as the high achievers. Most of the boys expected they would go to college as their parents wished, but they did not know for sure what that meant. Some of them had unrealistic occupational goals with no knowledge of what the jobs entailed, but a majority wanted jobs like those of the men in their community. The low-achiever group had much greater variability than the high. There seemed to be only one way to succeed, but many ways to fail.

The only variable that differentiated the mothers of the two groups was the mother's satisfaction with her son. The only differentiating factor among the fathers was his satisfaction with himself in the husband-father role. This research relates success, in a small part, to realistic aspirations. Prediction theory suggests that unattainable goals are not pursued by the rational person.

A separate master neuroprint must be formed to satisfy each interest. However, if an individual is interested in more than one thing, master neuroprints can be formed to take care of each interest, and the individual can decide the order in which each goal will be pursued.

From a psychological point of view, we consider an individual's desires in attempting to determine preferences. Considering the sociological dimension of human behavior, we must add conforming to group values and ritual and status seeking as human motives. This complicates the selection of preferences somewhat. However, in coming to any decision, there are always more things to take into account than we can. The challenge is to deliberate systematically so that one can come to decisions that will lead to the confirmation of predictions and the acquisition of one's preferences.

Rules for Deliberation

Deliberation can be simplified by realizing that a series of decisions can be broken down into a number of individual decisions, which can be dealt with one at a time. Furthermore, many of these decisions may be dealt with on a two-alternative basis.

Even decisions that initially involve a number of alternatives can be broken down into a series of two-alternative decisions. Suppose, for example, that you have ten applicants for a job and must decide whom to choose. You might try to determine which applicant most closely meets the job description by comparing them two at a time, discarding the one that is least like the job description. After your last comparison (the ninth comparison), you would decide to hire the one remaining applicant. Or you could go through the same procedure again to check yourself before coming to the decision.

A better way of proceeding on a two-alternative basis in this case would be to first compare each applicant's qualifications to the job description in order to decide whether each one is qualified for the job or not. All of the unqualified applicants would be eliminated from further consideration. Then the remaining qualified applicants would be compared to each other two at a time, eliminating the less preferred of the pair with each comparison. The applicant remaining after all of the comparisons were made would be chosen for the job. In the first instance, there was no screening to decide whether an applicant was qualified or not. If all ten were unqualified, the applicant finally chosen would be the best of the bunch but still not qualified for the job. The second approach would be preferred because a provision is made to guard against this possibility.

Usually only one or two comparisons are necessary in order to make any given decision. For instance, educators may wish to decide whether a student should be advanced to the next learning unit or not. In order to make this decision we may need only to compare the student's score on an achievement test with the preferred performance level on the test. If there is no discrepancy between the two or the discrepancy is not serious, we would probably decide to advance the student.

There are a limited number of comparisons humans can make at one time. Therefore, the fewer comparisons we need to make, the more accurately we should be able to make them. By comparing two things at a time we should be able to make the most accurate comparisons. Computers, on the other hand, can make myriads of comparisons. When we look at a computer printout that displays a maze of comparisons, we are quickly reminded that we can extract meaning from the data only if we attempt to compare no more than three things interacting at one time. No matter how many comparisons a computer can make in an analysis, if the decision maker cannot cope with the analysis, it is of no value. In deliberating one must guard against "information overload."

The next thing the deliberator should be taught is that decisions should be made in a prescribed order. First you deliberate to decide your interests; then you deliberate to determine goals that can be predicted to satisfy the interests; and then you deliberate programs to achieve the goals. The outcome of the deliberation is the formation of a master neuroprint. The deliberation process can bog down if decisions are not made in a prescribed order. Premature decisions must be deliberated again at the appropriate time.

Here is a description of the decisions that are deliberated in order to maximize predictability. Sixteen steps are noted to indicate the prescribed order in which the decisions are made. The steps are in the framework of the matching process to provide theoretical context. The two-alternative decisions to be made are noted. We are proposing that people are taught to deliberate systematically.

Matching for Identification: Of an Initiating Event

Step 1: Identifying Interests. When beset by a problem, we must be taught to deliberate the cause of our problem because it is necessary to determine the source of one's problem before one can predict a solution. Group members should be taught that it is the content of one's ideas that reveals the cause of problems. To identify the cause of a problem, we must determine the characteristics of our problem. Are we hungry, thirsty, ill, in love, hot, guilty, and so forth. Each source has its own characteristics, and we can be taught to distinguish one source from another.

When the content of an idea is not distinct, it may be difficult for us to distinguish the source of our problem. This condition is sometimes referred to as *free-floating anxiety*. However, we must continue to try to determine, as specifically as we can, the nature of our feelings.

Some feelings are specific, and both the locus of the feeling and the feeling itself are readily identifiable. When you prick your finger with a pin, you recognize the resulting feeling as pain, and you know that it is your finger that pains you.

Other feelings are by their very nature more vague. Love is a feeling we discuss repeatedly. However, it is impossible to identify the locus of the feeling and difficult to define its characteristics. Further, there seems to be a variety of types of love; love of one's mate, children, parents, dog, or country are examples.

If we are to manage our feelings, we must be taught to distinguish each with as much specificity as possible. One way of teaching feelings is to relate them to overt behaviors, since different feelings initiate different kinds of action. The feeling of love is accompanied by acts of affection toward the loved one. The feeling of hostility impels one to hurt the object of hostility. Another way of teaching people to identify their feelings with greater specificity is to teach them to identify the object or target of their feelings. Knowing that one is hostile toward one's sister, for example, adds definition to one's feeling and enhances one's ability to deal with it.

Once the specifics of a problem are identified, a solution can be sought. However, if individuals are suffering from mental stress denoting a psychological problem, it is essential to classify the problem as one of boredom or one of confusion. When such a diagnosis is made, the direction of the solution is indicated. Bored people find relief pursuing novelty and challenge. Confused people find relief by simplifying and regulating their lives as we explained in the last chapter.

Step 2: Setting Interest Priorities. After the sources of problems are identified, we then deliberate to decide which of our interests are more important to us. We answer the question, "To what extent does each of my problems bother me?" We attempt to rank order the problems by comparing them two at a time as we have explained and will elaborate at step 7.

Game theorists have developed a unique method for mathematically determining the utility of various options to an individual. The individual is given choices and asked for preferences. By systematically offering choices and noting the individual's preferences, the relative utility of the various options can be computed (see Rapoport 1960).

Matching for Prediction: To Determine What Is
Going to Happen without Intervention

Step 3: Predicting the Course of Events with No Interventions. We consider our high-priority interests to determine what may happen if we do nothing about them. We may decide that certain interests may be pursued later, while other interests must be attended to immediately. On the basis of these deliberations, we reassign priorities to our interests (see step 7).

Matching for Prediction: To Pursue a Preference

Once our interests are given priority, a master neuroprint is formed to predict the satisfaction of each interest. Of course, the high-priority interests would be dealt with first. This requires the following deliberations to be made in the following order.

Goals are considered next in the formation of a master neuroprint.

Step 4: Projecting Goals. We identify future states that can be expected to satisfy the interest. The projection of some goals is simple and automatic, like predicting that the eating of food (goal) will reduce one's hunger. The projection of other goals may be more complicated. A goal is projected by answering the question, "What future circumstances will satisfy my interest?"

Step 5: Assessing the Attainability of Goals. Next we review the projected remedies and decide which are attainable by making a series of two-alternative decisions. Reviewing each goal, we ask, "Is it or is it not attainable?" This decision is also made on a two-alternative basis by answering the question, "Is there or isn't there a program I can follow that will lead to achievement of the goal?" If the answer is yes, then the goal is attainable. Then all goals that are not attainable are eliminated from further consideration.

We should be taught that in considering which goals may be attainable in the future we are not concerned with the sacrifices that must be made to achieve them. This just confuses the immediate issue and is premature. We are simply concerned with what is possible. We become confused and discouraged by considering too many things at once and may eliminate an attainable alternative in the midst of such confusion.

Step 6: Assessing the Desirability of Achieving Goals. The remaining goals are assessed in terms of their desirability. Here we compare the appeal of pursuing each goal with the problems we would face in that pursuit. Some of the remedies may then be eliminated if they are deemed undesirable. The two-alternative question we ask here is, "Is it or is it not worthwhile for me to pursue this goal?"

Step 7: Setting Tentative Goals. The remaining goals are ranked in order of their desirability. The resulting ranking represents one's priorities for preferred goals. This ranking is also achieved by making a series of two-alternative comparisons. Suppose three goals remain. Let two alternatives be compared at a time, not all three, as that can strain anyone's powers of deliberation and can lead to an inaccurate decision. The highest-ranking alternative would be identified by first looking at any two goals and retaining the more desirable. The other is temporarily discarded.

Next we compare the goal that is retained (not discarded) to the third alternative and retain the more desirable of the two. That would be the highest ranking of the three.

To determine the second highest preferred goal, we compare the two alternatives previously discarded and decide which is more desirable. Of course, the less desirable of the two is the third-ranking goal.

This procedure can be followed to decide accurately the ranking of any number of alternatives.

Final goal decisions are not made until after programs are considered. When tentative goals are established it becomes necessary to design programs to achieve the goals.

Step 8: Designing Programs. We begin with the highest-ranking (most preferred) goal and design programs to achieve it. We should be taught that professional people are available to help us design programs, remembering that we are the ones who must tell the helper the goal we wish to achieve. Otherwise, the helper has no way of assisting us.

As programs are conceived, they are evaluated to determine whether or not they are preferred. A preferred program is chosen after considering two things: the efficiency of the program; and the desirability of implementing the program.

Step 9: Assessing the Efficiency of a Program. Here we consider the cost of implementing a program in terms of time, money, and effort. Inefficient plans are eliminated at this point by asking the question, "Is it efficient or not to adopt the program?"

Step 10: Assessing the Desirability of Implementing a Program. We review the remaining programs to decide whether or not we will enjoy implementing each program. If alternate programs are being considered, one may rank them in order of desirability as before, on the same two-alternative comparison basis (see step 7).

If a preferred program can be conceived to pursue the highest-ranking goal, it is adopted. If not, the pursuit of the goal may be abandoned. The question one asks to make this decision is, "Is it or is it not worth pursuing the goal if I must use this program?" If it is not, we can proceed to design programs to pursue the second highest-ranking goal. Even if we pursue the first goal, we can still start planning for the second, provided that all of our available resources are not committed to pursuing the highest-ranking goal. The decisions are the same for designing all programs. We can continue to design programs to achieve the highest-ranking goals until all allotted resources have been committed.

Step 11: Prescribing for Feedback. The design of the program must provide for feedback to determine whether the implementation of the program is leading to the goal as expected. This involves the identification of checkpoints and cues on the way to the goal. Typically, progressive checkpoints are identified after a certain number of planned activities have been performed.

Cues must be identified for each checkpoint to indicate whether or not (two alternatives) we are progressing toward the goal as predicted.

It is important to realize that when we are being helped by a professional we can monitor our own progress toward our goal, even though we may not understand how or why the professional's program works. We simply ask the professional to identify checkpoints and cues that indicate progress toward our goal. For instance, if we were ill, we might seek the help of our physician who would prescribe for our illness and would probably indicate when we should begin feeling better. If not, we should ask how soon we should start feeling better so that we could monitor progress toward our own recovery. To be master of our own future, we must set our own goals and learn how to monitor progress toward them when we avail ourselves of professional assistance.

Step 12: Prescribing for Error. In designing a program we must anticipate that people will stray and not make the desired progress toward their goal. Therefore, we must provide them with the means to correct their mistakes—either to understand how to correct their own mistakes or to get help from others or both.

Step 13: Learning the Program. Before beginning to implement any program it is important to know the rules to follow, the checkpoints at which progress is assessed, and the cues that indicate whether or not we are on the right track and when we have reached the goal. In addition, if assistance is not available should we go astray, we must learn how to take corrective measures ourselves. In following an extended program that is complicated, it may be necessary at each checkpoint to learn how to reach the next checkpoint.

For instance, assume that a salesman wants to find a potential customer's store and asks directions. If the route to the store is short and uncomplicated, he could understand the directions for the entire trip. However, if the directions were extended and complicated, the person helping him might direct the salesman to an interim point, say a gas station, and tell him to get further instructions there.

The design of programs is the final task in the formation of a master neuroprint to predict the satisfaction of an interest.

Activity

Step 14: Pursuing the Goal. Once the master neuroprint has been completed, we begin to pursue the goal by means of the program and assess our achievement.

Matching for Identification: To Test the Prediction

Step 15: Assessing Progress. We follow the directions of the program and at progressive checkpoints monitor the cues to determine whether we are on track. The question we ask is, "Am I or am I not progressing as predicted?" If there is a discrepancy between expectancy and actuality at any of these checkpoints, we proceed as follows. We reexamine our performances to that checkpoint to make certain that we have followed the directions correctly. If we have not, we correct our mistakes. If we find we have followed the directions and are not progressing toward the goal, we abort the program at that point and search for a new program so that we can proceed toward the goal. Presumably, provisions for errors would have been made, and we would know how to make corrections.

Step 16: Assessing the Outcome. Once arriving at the goal, we examine the situation to determine whether there is a discrepancy between the expected outcome and the attained outcome. This amounts to determining whether or not the problem is solved when the goal is reached. If the attainment of the goal does not satisfy the interest as predicted, then another goal must be substituted for the old one and plans must be made to pursue that goal.

Life goes on and we are always pursuing one goal or another with more or less success. The individual should be taught that it is normal to change our plans or goals. Unfortunately, in our society, too often mistakes are regarded as failures. It is necessary to plan for error and expect errors to occur. It is important to correct your errors and continue on your way without self-recrimination or discouragement. It is persistence as much as ability that contributes to the achievement of goals.

Afterword

We have attempted to explain and integrate individual and group behavior. In part I, we explained individual behavior; in part II, we explained group behavior; and in part III, we showed relationships between the two.

Although these explanations are based on some degree of empirical evidence, they should be regarded as hypotheses to be tested. A great deal more research must be done to confirm these explanations. On the other hand, prediction theory tends to be more integrating than refuting of existing data. A value of any theory is that it accommodates and integrates research findings. The research that has been conducted so far shows that the ability to predict contributes to adaptation and successful living in a number of areas. Friedman has developed tests to measure predictive ability and other constructs of the theory. Propositions in the theory continue to be tested, and further testing is encouraged.

The following are hypotheses that are germane to the validation of the theory. Naturally there is some overlap among them and some are more germane than others. The more germane hypotheses are marked with an asterisk.

Hypotheses Pertaining to the Individual

*1. If in a state of extreme unpredictability or confusion, the individual will seek relief from the confusion over any other alternative. When confused, the individual will seek familiarity and redundancy.

*2. If in a state of extreme predictability or boredom, the individual will seek relief from boredom over any other alternative, except the alternative of confusion. When bored, the individual will seek novelty and variability.

*3. To avoid confusion or boredom, optimum predictability is sought. Individuals seek situations that are sufficiently familiar to allow them to predict and sufficiently novel to present them with a challenge.

*4. Disorganized, erratic stimulation will cause confusion and increase arousal in the alert individual.

*5. Monotonous stimulation will generate boredom. If the individual is alert and energetic, the monotonous stimulation will increase the state of arousal. If the individual is fatigued, the monotonous stimulation will induce sleep.

6. If individuals feel the need to confirm a particular prediction (such as the successful completion of a duty) and their state of arousal is too low (for example, they are sleepy), they will attempt to increase their level of

arousal (for example, take a stimulant such as coffee) in order to confirm the prediction.

*7. The ability to predict contributes to successful performance of any kind.

*8. The ability to predict generates self-confidence.

9. The self-confident individual can tolerate delay in the confirmation of predictions more than an individual that lacks confidence. Similarly, the self-confident individual will persist in attempting to confirm predictions longer than the individual that lacks self-confidence.

*10. Individuals will tend to mentally organize activities into programmatic sequences (in order to improve their ability to predict).

*11. When an outcome satisfies a personal interest, the individual will mentally organize events into the form of the master neuroprint (in order to predict the satisfaction of the interest).

12. Individuals tend to organize their experiences into concept categories.

13. Images and concepts can be distinguished as types of ideas.

14. Individuals abstract salient features of an experience and store these features in memory.

15. Concepts tend to be organized into representational class-inclusion hierarchies.

16. Early learning in childhood proceeds from the concrete to the abstract.

*17. Isolated events are learned less readily than programs or master neuroprints.

*18. Individuals are impelled to confirm the predictions they make.

*19. When predictions are confirmed, the ideas that led to the confirmation are retained. When predictions are not confirmed, the ideas associated with the failure tend to be modified.

20. When the same type of problem is solved repeatedly, the solution will be relegated to habit.

21. When a habit fails to solve a problem, the problem will be deliberated.

22. When individuals become conscious of the autonomic functions of their bodies, they can control to some extent these functions.

23. Feedback enhances the confirmation of prediction and learning.

24. There is a tendency initially to attempt to base predictions on images. If no prediction is forthcoming, concepts are deliberated in search of a prediction.

25. Learning in early childhood proceeds inductively through association. Later learning, once concept hierarchies have formed, involves deliberating alternatives, deducing hypotheses, and then testing hypotheses.

26. Unfamiliar events are predicted by matching features of the unfamiliar event with a concept.

27. Learning through deductive hypotheses selection and testing is a discovery or insightful learning, whereas learning through inductive association in small graded increments is trial and error learning.

28. In matching for identification and prediction, a match is made on the basis of correspondence. The closer the correspondence between events and neuroprints or between two neuroprints, the more probable it is that a match will occur between them.

29. Attempts to alleviate boredom lead to discovery and invention.

30. The formation of more complex concept hierarchies increases with experience and intelligence.

*31. When individuals are excessively bored, they tend to defend against the boredom by shutting out redundant, familiar stimulation.

*32. When individuals are excessively confused, they tend to defend against the confusion by shutting out variable and novel stimulation.

33. When bored individuals fantasize, they will fantasize about novel situations.

34. When confused persons fantasize, they will fantasize about familiar, predictable situations.

35. Defensiveness temporarily reduces arousal.

36. When children are playing they are predicting.

37. Play and games improve the individual's ability to predict.

Hypotheses Pertaining to Social Groups

1. Humans create rules and live by the rules they create.

2. The impartial and consistent enforcement of rules contributes to group solidarity.

3. When rules are internalized and endorsed, there is increased likelihood that members will conform to them voluntarily.

*4. When conforming to rules enhances the members' ability to predict, they will conform. Conversely, when rules generate unpredictability and confusion, members will act to change the rules.

*5. The ability to confirm or prevent the confirmation of predictions of group members is positively correlated with the ability to control the enactment and enforcement of group rules.

*6. Greater conformity to group rules will occur when members are confronted with ambiguous unpredictable stimulation.

7. Group members will pursue group status because it gives them the authority to control the confirmation of predictions.

*8. The group gains support from its members when it provides for the reduction of confusion.

9. Writing rules in the master-neuroprint format aids the confirmation of predictions.

*10. Consensual predictions are supported because members believe that their personal predictions are more likely to be confirmed if they agree with the group.

*11. Predictability is facilitated when the group focuses on their common interests rather than on the different interests of group members.

*12. When the group (or the individual) believes its goal cannot be achieved, it will predict failure and act to confirm its prediction of failure.

13. It is an assigned responsibility of persons in high-status positions to reduce group confusion.

*14. Qualities of leadership are the ability to maintain predictability within the group, including the support of group rules; confirm the specific consensual predictions of the group; and change the rules for the benefit of the group.

*15. Because group members are interested in maintaining predictability, they solicit other members to confirm their views.

*16. Competition among group members (and groups) is primarily to gain control of the confirmation of predictions.

*17. Cooperation among group members is primarily to control the confirmation of consensual predictions.

18. Knowing what another person predicts will happen makes that person more predictable because that person can be expected to act to confirm his or her prediction.

19. One can increase the likelihood that one's predictions will be confirmed by convincing an opponent that they will be.

20. To confirm one's predictions, it is useful to make one's self unpredictable to an opponent.

21. A subordinate group is more predictable to a dominant group than a dominant group is to the subordinate group because the dominant group controls the confirmation of predictions in their interactions. The same would be true of dominant and subordinate individuals.

22. When people embark on a continuing relationship, they will create, adopt, and enforce rules to govern their behavior.

23. In competition, individuals and groups will attempt to make their actions unpredictable to the opponent.

24. In cooperative efforts, individuals and groups will attempt to make their actions predictable to their allies.

25. Group members can oppose pursuing existing group values without receiving negative sanctions, provided their actions are predictable to the group.

26. Group members can pursue their personal preferences without receiving negative sanctions, provided that the group does not perceive this as preventing the confirmation of consensual predictions.

*27. Rules that lead to the confirmation of predictions will be maintained by the group. Rules that do not lead to the confirmation of predictions will be modified or discarded.

Appendix:
The Predictive Ability
Test and Related
Research Reports

The following are sample items from Friedman's Predictive Ability Test (PAT) along with instructions to the respondent.

PART I

DIRECTIONS:

Print your name and today's date in the space provided below.

_____   _____
            NAME   DATE

On each of the pages in Part I you will see four pictures. You are to look at the first picture on each page. It is labelled A. The event shown in Picture A always happens first. Based on what you.see in Picture A, you are to decide whether or not the events shown in Pictures B, C, and D could happen.

SAMPLE ITEM:

There is a sample item on page 2. Turn to page 2 and look at the first picture labelled A. Picture A shows a boy and three blocks. Based on what you see in Picture A, you are to decide whether or not the events shown in Pictures B, C, and D could happen and mark your decisions on the sample item.

Look at Picture B and decide whether or not the event could happen. If you decide it could happen, then circle the letter Y (meaning YES) that appears on top of Picture B. If you decide it could not happen, then circle the letter N (meaning NO) that appears on top of Picture B. If you circled the letter Y you would be correct because the boy could stack the three blocks on top of each other as shown in Picture B.

Now indicate whether or not the event shown in Picture C could happen by circling the Y or the N for Picture C that appears on top of it. If you circled Y, you would be correct because the event shown in Picture C could happen also.

Finally, indicate whether or not the event shown in Picture D could happen by circling the Y or the N that appears on top of Picture D. If you circled Y you would be correct.

If all of your answers were correct for the sample item, it would be marked like the sample item on page 3. Turn to page 3 to see how the correct answers would appear.

SAMPLE

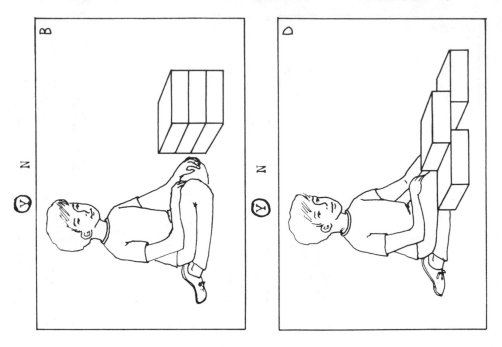

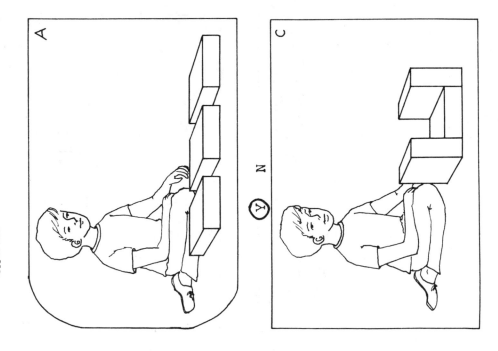

PART II

DIRECTIONS:

The items in Part II are different from those in Part I of the test. In Part II of the test, you will see four pictures on each page. You are to look at the first picture on each page and decide which of the other three pictures is MOST LIKELY to happen, which is NEXT MOST LIKELY to happen, and which is LEAST LIKELY to happen based on what you see in the first picture.

SAMPLE ITEM:

Look at the picture on the top left side of page 5. It shows a boy starting to slide down a sliding board. Now look at each of the other three pictures on page 5. These pictures show the way the boy landing at the end of the slide. Which picture shows the way he MOST LIKELY would land? Picture C shows the way he MOST LIKELY would land. So put the letters ML (meaning MOST LIKELY) on the line that is next to Picture C.

Now, which of the two remaining pictures is the NEXT MOST LIKELY to happen? The answer is Picture B. He could land that way. So put NML (meaning NEXT MOST LIKELY) on the line that is next to Picture B.

Which picture is LEAST LIKELY to happen? Picture A probably would not happen, so put the letters LL (meaning LEAST LIKELY) on the line next to Picture A. If you put ML next to Picture C, and NML next to Picture B, and LL next to Picture A, you are right.

If all of your answers were correct for the sample item, it would be marked like the sample item on page 6. Turn to page 6 to see how the correct answer would appear.

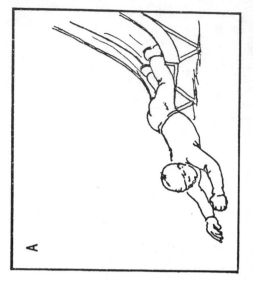

A

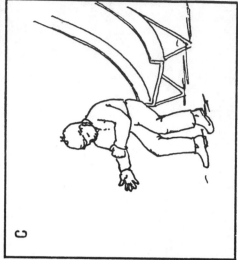

C

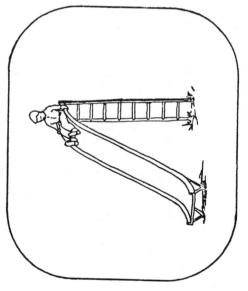

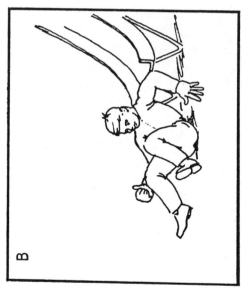

B

SAMPLE

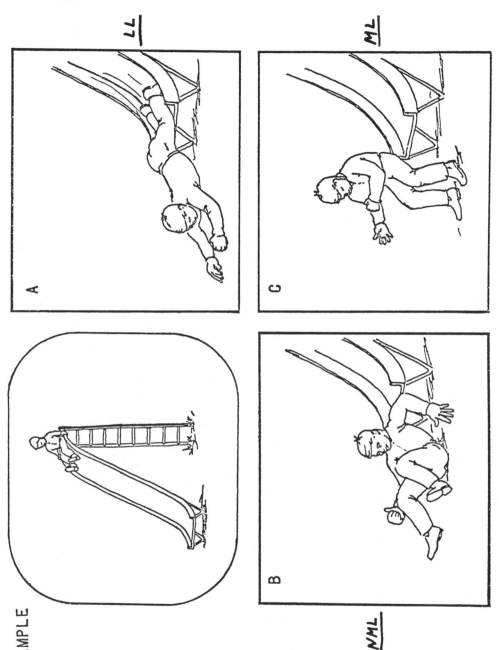

A LL

B NML

C ML

PART III

DIRECTIONS:

The items for Part III are different from the ones in Part I and Part II of the test. On each of the pages in Part III, you will see groups of pictures that can be arranged to show a correct order of events. On the top of each page you will see a picture of a beginning event on the far left and a picture of an outcome event on the far right. There are also a number of blank spaces in between. Some of the items have three blank spaces, and some have four blank spaces.

From the pictures shown on the lower portion of the page you are to fill in the blank spaces by selecting and ordering those pictures that lead from the beginning event to the outcome event. Each item has either two or three extra pictures that do not belong in the correct order.

SAMPLE ITEM:

Turn to page 8. At the top and far left of page 8 is Picture A which shows a boy about to make a high jump. Picture A represents the beginning event. On the far right is Picture F which shows the boy after he has made the jump. Picture F is the outcome event. Between the beginning and outcome events you see four spaces labelled B, C, D, and E.

Now examine the six numbered pictures on the lower portion of the page, and select and order the four pictures that will show the way the boy could complete the high jump. In the spaces labelled B, C, D, and E, place the numbers of the four pictures in the correct order. The correct order would be Picture 1, then Picture 3, then Picture 6, and then Picture 2.

If all of your answers were correct for the sample item, it would be marked like the sample item on page 9. Turn to page 9 to see how the correct answers would appear.

Now turn to page 10.

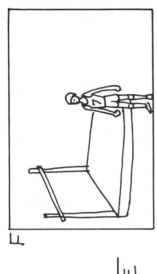

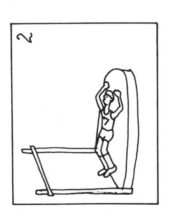

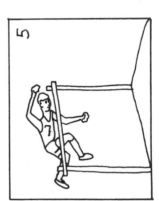

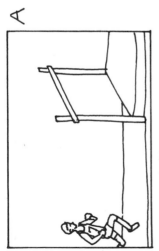

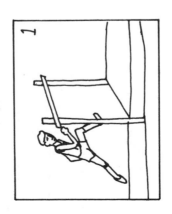

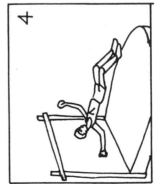

A B C D E F

1 2 3 4 5 6

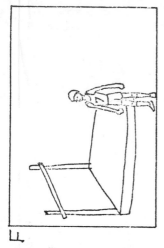

A

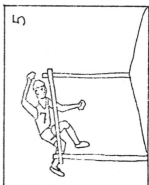

1 3 6 2
B C D E

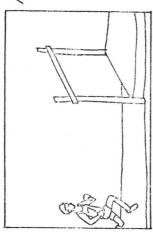

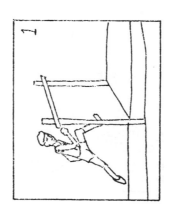

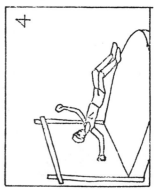

F

The drawings in the test are simple in order to eliminate visual discrimination as a contaminating variable. In developing and pilot testing the PAT, it was found that visually complicated and intricate drawings interfered with the preception of the content in the drawings. It was reasoned that if the subjects could not understand the content, they had no basis for making a prediction. So only simple line drawings were selected for test items.[1]

To validate the hypothesis that predictive ability is an index of successful living, the scores of the PAT were compared to various measures of successful living. It was reasoned that if predictive ability correlates positively with different indexes of successful living, it contributes to adaptation. The following evidence was obtained.

Social Adjustment as a Criterion of Successful Living

In one study the social adjustment of mental retardates at a state institution was correlated with PAT scores. The measure of social adjustment was the Vineland Social Maturity scale. PAT scores correlated with social adjustment scores substantially higher than scores on Binet IQ tests. The PAT scores correlated .43 with the Vineland Social Quotient scores, while the Binet IQ scores correlated .34 with the Vineland scores. There were forty-four subjects in the study with ages ranging from eighteen to forty-seven years. Their IQ scores ranged from 51 to 81, and their Vineland scores ranged from 31 to 98.

Success in Education as a Criterion of Successful Living

Successful and unsuccessful enlisted men were identified and tested at a large military establishment in May and June of 1974. The unsuccessful group consisted of privates who had been unable to meet the requirements of advanced training and who had either been recycled (reassigned) to a less demanding training or required to repeat certain parts of the same training. The group was comprised of a random sample of such persons available during the week when data were being collected. The successful group consisted of noncommissioned officers (NCOs) in grades E-6 through E-9 who had successfully completed advanced training and who had been promoted every time they had been eligible since entering the service.

Discriminant analysis was used to determine whether significant differences between the successful and unsuccessful groups could be found using the scores on the PAT as the discriminator. The PAT discriminated correctly 65 percent of the unsuccessful group and 78 percent of the successful group (significant at the .01 level). The PAT proved to be a significantly better discriminator between the two groups than the General Technical portion of the army classification battery, which is a verbal and nonverbal measure of learning presently used by the army. The PAT was also a better discriminator than the level of formal education, that is, the highest school grade completed. The results indicate that the PAT may serve as a basis for selecting and placing people in training programs.

In another study to determine whether the PAT is related to success in education, the PAT was correlated with student grade average and with scores on the Comprehensive Test of Basic Skills (CTBS). Data were gathered on 206 public high school seniors in a small urban southern city. The correlation between PAT scores and grade point averages was .49 (significant at the .001 level). The correlation between PAT scores and CTBS scores was .64 (significant at the .001 level). Thus there seems to be a substantial relationship between predictive ability and academic success in public high school.

Job Status as a Criterion of Successful Living

A large industrial organization administered the PAT to employees in different job classifications that were rank ordered to indicate status levels within the company. The results of discriminant function analyses follow.

Technicians: rank ordered by level of job status

Position: PAT means:
   craft apprentices $\overline{X}$ = 25.1
   chemical operators $\overline{X}$ = 22.3
   draw-twist operators $\overline{X}$ = 15.0
   general labor $\overline{X}$ = 4.6

Discriminant analysis between progressive pairs on the tests:

   craft apprentices versus chemical operators
      correct classification
         42/53 or 80 percent

   chemical operators versus draw-twist operators
      correct classification
         25/34 or 74 percent

   draw-twist operators versus general labor
      correct classification
         32/32 or 100 percent

When craft apprentices were compared to draw-twist operators, the PAT tests classified them correctly 91 percent of the time.

Managers
Position   PAT means:
    foremen and supervisors $\overline{X} = 20.4$
    executives $\overline{X} = 26.0$

Discriminant analysis between foremen and executives:
    correct classification
        32/36 or 90 percent

The PAT tests discriminated, on the average, 15 percent more accurately than the Otis Quick Score Intelligence Test for the above comparisons.

A description of the sample follows.

General Labor Group
Salary level: $6,000-$8,000
Job type: general maintenance and delivery services
Eligibility for promotion: usually can be promoted to production-
    level jobs
Sex: all male
Education: high school graduates or below

Craft-apprentice Program
Salary level: $6,000-$9,000 (low)
Job type: production (a four-year training program with a 10 per-
    cent dropout rate)
Eligibility for promotion: can be promoted within a production
    level up to rank of supervisor or foreman but not beyond because
    of educational limitations
Sex: all male
Education: high school graduates; a few with a year or two of
    technical school

Draw-twist Operators
Salary level: $6,000-$9,000 (low)
Job type: production
Eligibility for promotion: same as those in craft-apprentice program
Sex: 75 percent female
Education: high school graduates

Chemical Operators
Salary level: $6,000-$9,000
Job type: a one-time training program (2 to 3 months) for production workers for a new plant facility under construction.
Members were selected from operator-level jobs.
Eligibility for promotion: same as those in craft-apprentice program
Sex: all male
Education: same as those in craft-apprentice program

Foremen and Supervisors
Salary level: $9,000-$13,000
Job type: supervision of production workers
Eligibility for promotion: essentially none because of lack of education
Sex: mostly male
Education: high school graduates with a year or two of technical school

Executives
Salary level: $15,000-$25,000 (high)
Job type: administrative, planning, training, hiring, finance
Eligibility for promotion: all eligible for promotion and likely to be promoted under expanding plant conditions
Sex: all male
Education: college graduates

In addition, when noncommissioned officers (E6-E9) were compared to commissioned officers at an army installation, the PAT classified them correctly 75 percent of the time. The PAT plus level of education (highest grade achieved in school) classified them correctly 90 percent of the time. There were forty-eight noncommissioned officers and commissioned officers in the study.

In conclusion, the composite evidence indicates that predictive ability as measured by the PAT is substantially correlated with important indexes of successful living. There was a substantial relationship between predictive ability and social adjustment, success in education, and success on the job as indicated by job status. Therefore, predictive ability can be regarded as a significant index of adaptation in the populations tested.

Note

1. The test contains thirty items. The reliability of the test is .90 (using the KR 20 formula). The average discrimination index is .53. The average

difficulty index is .60. The chances of guessing the correct answers range from 1 in 6 for part II items to 1 in 360 for some part III items. A scoring key is provided making the test objective. A single factor emerged from a factor analysis of the test items indicating the construct validity of the test. A test manual is available. It describes the development of the test and provides other pertinent data such as norms. The test will be reviewed in O.K. Buros' *Eight Mental Measurements Yearbook* (Gryphon Press).

Bibliography

Abdurasulov, D.A. "The dependence of transfer on pattern analysis in mentally retarded children (translated title of Russian original)." *Defektologiya* 3 (1974):25-31.

Adams, J.A., and Xhigriesse, L.V. "Some determinants of two-dimensional tracking behavior." *Journal of Experimental Psychology,* 60 (1960):391-403.

Adams, J.S. "Inequity in social change." 2 vols. Edited by L. Berkowitz. *Advances in experimental psychology.* New York: Academic Press, 1965.

Aitken, P.O., and Hutt, C. "Do children find complex patterns interesting or pleasing?" *Child Development,* 45 (1974):425-431.

Allen, V.L., and Levine, J.M. "Social support and conformity: The role of independent assessment of reality." *Journal of Experimental Social Psychology* 7 (1971):48-50.

Allport, F.H. *Theories of Perception and the Concept of Structures.* New York: Wiley, 1955.

Anderson, L.W. "Student involvement and school achievement." *California Journal of Educational Research* 26 (1975):53-62.

Anderson, N.H. "Application of a model for numerical response to a probability learning situation." *Journal of Experimental Psychology* 80 (1969):19-27.

————— . "Information integration theory: A brief survey." *Contemporary Developments in Mathematical Psychology.* vol. 2. Edited by D.H. Krantz, R.C. Atkinson, R.D. Luce, and P. Suppes. San Francisco: W.H. Freeman, 1974.

Anderson, R.C.; Kulhaven, R.W.; and Andre, T. "Feedback procedures in programmed instruction." *Review of Educational Research* 40 (1970):349-370.

Aneshensel, C.S., and Rosen, B.C. "Domestic roles and sex differences in occupational expectations." *Journal of Marriage and the Family* 42 (1980):121-131.

Antes, J.R. "The time course of picture viewing." *Journal of Experimental Psychology* 103 (1974):62-70.

Aronson, E. "Dissonance theory: Progress and problems." In *Theories of cognitive consistency: A sourcebook.* Edited by R.R. Abelson et al. Chicago: Rand McNally, 1968.

Aronson, E., and Carlsmith, J.M. "Performance expectancy as a determinant of actual performance." *Journal of Abnormal and Social Psychology* 65 (1962):178-182.

Arvey, R.D. "Motivational models and professional updating." In *Maintaining Professional and Technical Competence of the Older Engineer.* Edited by S.S. Dubin, H. Shelton, and J. McConnell. Washington, D.C.: American Society for Engineering Education, 1973.

Asch, S.E. "Effects of group pressure upon the modification and distortion of judgment." *Group Leadership and Men.* Edited by H. Guetzkow. Pittsburgh: Carnegie Press, 1951.

_____ . "Studies of independence and conformity: I. A minority of one against a unanimous majority." *Psychological Monographs.* vol. 70 (9, Wh. N. 416, 1956). *Social Psychology, Understanding Human Interaction.* R. Baron, D. Byrne, and W. Griffith, eds. Boston: Allyn and Bacon, 1974.

Ashcraft, M.M., and Kellas, G. "Organization in normal and retarded children: Temporal aspects of storage and retrieval." *Journal of Experimental Psychology* vol. 103, no. 3 (1974):502-508.

Asher, S.R., and Markell, R.A. "Sex differences in high- and low-interest reading materials." *Journal of Educational Psychology* 66 (1974): 680-687.

Athey, I.J., and Holmes, J. *Reading Success and Personality Characteristics in Junior High School Students.* Berkeley: University of California Press, 1969.

Atkinson, J.W., and Feather, N.T. *A Theory of Achievement Motivation.* New York: Wiley, 1966.

Atkinson, R.C., and Shiffrin, R.M. *Mathematical Models for Memory and Learning.* Technical Report no. 79, Psychology Series, Institute for Mathematical Studies in the Social Sciences. Stanford: Stanford University Press, 1965.

_____ . "Human memory: A proposed system and its control processes." *The Psychology of Learning and Motivation* vol. 2. Edited by D.W. Spence and J.T. Spence. New York: Academic Press, 1968.

Atwood, N.K., and Shavelson, R.J. "An empirical test of predictions based on a semantic processing and a generative processing model of encoding." *The Journal of Educational Research* (1976):106-111.

Ault, R.L. "Problem-solving strategies of reflective, impulsive, fast-accurate, and slow-inaccurate children." *Child Development* 44 (1973): 259-266.

Ausubel, D.P. *The Psychology of Meaningful Verbal Learning.* New York: Grune and Stratton, 1963.

Bacon, S.J. "Arousal and the range of cue utilization." *Journal of Experimental Psychology* 102 (1973)81-87.

Bahrick, H.P.; Bahrick, P.O.; and Whittlinger, R.P. "Fifty years of memory for names and faces: A cross-sectional approach." *Journal of Experimental Psychology* 104 (1974)54-75.

Bales, R.F. *Interaction Process Analysis: A Method for the Study of Small Groups*. Reading, Mass.: Addison-Wesley, 1950.

————. *Personality and Interperson Behavior*. New York: Holt, Rinehart and Winston, 1970.

Bandura, A., and Adams, N.E. "Analysis of self-efficacy theory of behavioral change." *Cognitive Therapy and Research* 1 (1977):287-310.

Baron, R.; Byrne, D.; Griffitt, W. *Social Psychology, Understanding Human Interaction*. Boston: Allyn and Bacon, 1974.

Bass, B.M. *Leadership, Psychology and Organizational Behavior*. New York: Harper and Row, 1966.

Bass, B.M.; Wurster, G.R.; Doll, P.A.; and Clair, D.S. "Situational and personality factors in leadership among sorority women." *Psychological Monographs* 67 no. 16 (1953): (whole no. 366).

Beck, C.M.; Crittenden, B.S.; and Sullivan, E.V. "The theory of developmental stages in moral judgment." In *Moral Education: Interdisciplinary Approaches*. Edited by C.M. Beck, B.S. Crittenden, and E.V. Sullivan. New York: Newman Press, 1971.

Bell, G.B., and Hall, H.E., Jr. "The relationship between leadership and empathy." *Journal of Abnormal and Social Psychology* 49 (1954):156-157.

Bell, S.M. "The development of the concept of object as related to infant-mother attachment." *Child Development* 41 (1970):291-311.

Benz, D.A., and Rosemier, R.A. "Concurrent validity of the Gates Level of Comprehension Test and the Bond, Clymer, Hoyt Reading Diagnostic Tests." *Educational and Psychological Measurement* 26(1966): 1057-1062.

Berkowitz, L. "Group standards, cohesiveness and productivity." *Human Relations* 7 (1954):509-519.

Berlyne, D. *Conflict, Arousal and Curiosity*. New York: McGraw-Hill, 1960.

Berlyne, D.E. *Structure and Direction in Thinking*. New York: Wiley, 1966.

Berlyne, D.E., and Carey, S.T. "Incidental learning and the timing of arousal." *Psychonomic Science* 13 (1968):103-104.

Berlyne, D.E., and Ditkofsky, J. "Effects of novelty and oddity on visual selective attention." *British Journal of Psychology* 67 (1976):176-180.

Berlyne, D.E., and Lewis, J.L. "Effects on heightened arousal on human exploratory behavior." *Canadian Journal of Psychology* 17 (1963): 398-410.

Bernstein, H.E. "Boredom and the ready-made life." *Social Research* 42 (1975):512-537.

Bettleheim, B. *The Informed Heart*. New York: Avon Books, 1960.

————. "Play and education." *School Review* 81 (1972):1-13.

Bettelheim, B., and Janowitz, J. "Ethnic intolerance: A function of social and personal control." *American Journal of Sociology* 55 (1949):137-145.

Bickman, L., and Henchy, T., eds. *Beyond the Laboratory: Field Research in Social Psychology*. New York: McGraw-Hill, 1972.

Biderman, A.D., and Zimmer, H. *The Manipulation of Human Behavior*. New York: Wiley, 1961.

Bindra, D.A. *Motivation*. New York: Ronald Press, 1959.

Black, M., ed. *The Social Theories of Talcott*. Parsons, N.J.: Prentice-Hall, 1961.

Blake, R., and Mouton, J. "The intergroup dynamics of win-loss conflict and problem-solving collaboration in union-management relations." In *Intergroup Relations and Leadership*. Edited by M. Sherif. New York: Wiley and Sons, 1972.

Blake, R.; Shepard, H.; and Mouton, J. *Managing Intergroup Conflict in Industry*. Houston: Gulf Publishing Company, 1964.

Blau, P.M. "Cooperation and competition in a bureaucracy." *American Journal of Sociology* 59 (1954):530-535.

_____ . *Exchange of Power in Social Life*. New York: Wiley and Sons, 1964.

Bolles, R.C. "Reinforcement, expectancy and learning." *Psychological Review* 79 (1972):394-409.

Boocock, S.S. "The school as a social environment for learning: Social organization and micro-social process in education." *Sociology of Education* vol. 46, no. 1 (1973):15-50.

Borg, W.R. "Prediction of small group role behavior from personality variables." *Journal of Abnormal and Social Psychology* 60 (1960): 112-116.

Boucher, J., and Warrington, E.K. "Memory deficits in early infantile autism: Some similarities to the amnesic syndrome." *British Journal of Psychology* 67 (1976):73-87.

Bourne, L.E. *Human Conceptual Behavior*. Boston: Allyn and Bacon, 1966.

Bourne, L.E., and Dominowski, R.L. "Thinking." *Annual Review of Psychology* 23 (1972):105-130.

Bower, G.H. "Chunks as interference units in free recall." *Journal of Verbal Learning and Verbal Behavior* 8 (1969):610-613.

Bower, G.H.; Clark, M.C.; Lesgold, A.M.; and Winzez, D. "Hierarchical retrieval schemes in recall of categorized word lists." *Journal of Verbal Learning and Verbal Behavior* 8 (1969):323-343.

Bower, G.H., and Trabasso, T.R. "Reversals prior to solution in concept identification." *Journal of Experimental Psychology* 66 (1963): 409-418.

_____ . Concept identification. In *Studies in Mathematical Psychology*. Edited by R.C. Atkinson. Stanford: Stanford University Press, 1964.

Bower, T.G.R. *Development in Infancy*. San Francisco: Freeman, 1974.

Boyd, D.R. "The moralberry pie: Some basic concepts." *Theory Into Practice: Moral Development* vol. 16, no. 2 (1977):67-72.

Brayfield, A.H., and Crockett, W.H. "Employee attitudes and employee performance." *Psychological Bulletin* 52 (1955):396-424.

Brehm, J.W. *A Theory of Psychological Reactance.* New York: Academic Press, 1966.

Brickman, P., and D'Amato, B. "Exposure effects in a free-choice situation." *Journal of Personality and Social Psychology* 32 (1975):415-420.

Broadbent, D.E. *Perception and Communication.* Oxford: Pergammon Press, 1958.

———. *Decision and Stress.* New York: Academic Press, 1971.

Broen, W.E., Jr. "Limiting the flood of stimulation: A protective deficit in chronic schizophrenia." In *Contemporary Issues in Cognitive Psychology: The Loyola Symposium,* edited by R.L. Solso. Washington, D.C.: V.H. Winston and Sons, 1973.

Brown, A.S. "Examination of hypothesis sampling theory." *Psychological Bulletin,* 81 (1974):773-790.

Brown, D.G. "Masculinity-femininity development in children." *Journal of Consulting Psychology* 21 (1957):197-202.

Brown, R., and Lennenberg, E. "Studies in linguistic relativity." In *Readings in Social Psychology.* 3rd ed. Edited by T. Maccoby, E. Newcomb, and E. Hartley. New York: Holt, Rinehart and Winston, 1958.

Brown, R., and McNeill, D. "The 'tip of the tongue' phenomenon." *Journal of Verbal Learning and Verbal Behavior* 5 (1966):325-337.

Bruner, J.S.; Goodnow, J.J.; and Austin, G.A. *A Study of Thinking.* New York: Wiley, 1956.

Buelow, G.D. "Social and semantic rules." *Humboldt Journal of Social Relations* vol. 1, no. 2 (1974):89-92.

Burke, P. "The development of task and social-emotional role differentiation." *Sociometry* 30 (1967):379-392.

Burns, T., and Stalker, G.M. *The Management of Innovation.* London: Tavistock Publications, 1961.

Bursill, A.E. "The restriction of peripheral vision during exposure to heat and humid conditions." *Quarterly Journal of Experimental Psychology* 10 (1958):113-129.

Byers, J.L. "Verbal and concept learning." *Review of Educational Research* 37 (1967):494-513.

Byrne, D.; Rasche, L.; and Kelley, L. "When 'I like you' indicates disagreement: An experimental differentiation of information and affect." *Journal of Research and Personality* 8 (1974):207-217.

Camus, A. *The Fall and Exile and the Kingdom.* Translated by J. O'Brien. New York: Random House, 1957.

Carlsmith, J., and Aronson, E. "Some hedonic consequences of the confirmation and disconfirmation of expectancies." *Journal of Abnormal and Social Psychology* 66 (1963)151-156.

Carver, C.S.; Coleman, A.E.; and Glass, D.C. "The coronary-prone behavior pattern and the suppression of fatigue on a treadmill test." *Journal of Personality and Social Psychology* 33 (1976)460-466.

Cathcart, G., and Liedtke, W. "Reflectiveness/impulsiveness and mathematics achievement." *Arithmetic Teacher* 16 (1969):563-567.

Cattell, R.B., and Stuce, G.F. *The Dimensions of Groups and Their Relations to the Behavior of Members.* Champaign, Ill.: Institute for Ability and Personality Testing, 1960.

Chandler, M.J. "Relativism and the problem of epistemological loneliness." *Human Development* 18 (1975):171-180.

Clammer, J. "Rule-following and the social sciences." *Sociological Analysis* (Sheffield) vol. 3, no. 3 (1973):93-95.

Clark, D.C. "Teaching concepts in the classroom: A set of teaching prescriptions derived from experimental research." *Journal of Educational Psychology.* Manuscript submitted for publication, 1977.

Clark, R.D., III. "Group induced shift toward risk: A critical appraisal." *Psychological Bulletin* 76 (1971):251-270.

Clark, R.D., III; Crockett, W.H.; and Archer, R.L. "Risk-as-value hypothesis: The relationship between perception of self, others, and the risky shift." *Journal of Personality and Social Psychology* 20 (1971): 425-429.

Coch, L., and French, J. "Overcoming resistance to change." *Human Relations* 1 (1948): 512-532.

Cohen, A.R. "Upward communication in experimentally created hierarchies." *Human Relations* 11 (1958):41-53.

Cohen, A.R. "Situational structure, self-esteem and threat-oriented reactions to power." In *Studies in Social Power.* Edited by D. Cartwright. Ann Arbor, Mich.: Institute for Social Research, 1959.

Cohen, S.; Glass, D.C.; and Singer, J.E. "Apartment noise, auditory discrimination, and reading ability in children." *Journal of Experimental Social Psychology* 9 (1973):407-422.

Collins, A.M., and Quillan, R. "Retrieval time from semantic memory." *Journal of Verbal Learning and Verbal Behavior* 8 (1969):240-247.

————. "Does category size affect categorization time?" *Journal of Verbal Learning and Verbal Behavior* 9 (1970):432-437.

Condry, J., and Simon, M.L. "Characteristics of peer- and adult-oriented children." *Journal of Marriage and the Family* 36 (1974):543-554.

Conner, J.W. "Value continuities and change in three generations of Japanese-Americans." *Ethos* vol. 2, no. 3 (1974):232-264.

Conrad, C. "Cognitive economy in semantic memory." *Journal of Experimental Psychology* 92 (1972):149-154.

Coopersmith, S. "Studies in self-esteem." *Scientific American* 218 (1968): 96-102.

Cowell, C.C. "Mental hygiene functions and possibilities of play and physical education." *Elementary School Journal* 50 (1949):196-203.

Cuber, J.F. *Sociology: A Synopsis of Principles.* 6th ed. Englewood Cliffs, N.J.: Prentice-Hall, 1968.

Davenport, W.G. "Arousal theory and vigilance: Schedules for background stimulation." *The Journal of General Psychology* 91 (1974): 51-59.

Davis, O.L., Jr., and Tinsley, D.C. "Cognitive objectives revealed by classroom questions asked by social studies classroom student teachers." *Peabody Journal of Education* 45 (1967):21-26.

Deci, E.L. "The effects of contingent and noncontingent rewards and controls on intrinsic motivation." *Organizational Behavior and Human Performance* 8 (1972):217-229.

Depolito, F., and Struhar, W.J. "Effects of semantic organization on encoding and retrieval in recognition." *Perceptual and Motor Skills* 39 (1974):195-201.

Deutsch, M. "An experimental study of the effects of cooperation and competition upon group processes." *Human Relations* 2 (1949): 199-232.

Deutsch, M., and Krauss, R. "The effect of threat upon interpersonal bargaining." *Journal of Abnormal and Social Psychology* 61 (1960):181-189.

DeVore, I. *Primate Behavior: Field Studies of Monkeys and Apes.* New York: Holt, Rinehart and Winston, 1965.

Donahue, W.A. "An empirical framework for examining negotiation processes and outcomes." *Communication Monographs* 45 (1978):249-257.

Doran, R., and Ngoi, M.K. "Validation of a model for concept attainment levels with selected elementary school science concepts." *Child Study Journal* 6 (1976):21-32.

Dornbush, R.L., and Winnick, N.A. "The relative effectiveness of a stereometric and pattern stimuli in discrimination learning in children." *Psychonomic Science* 5 (1966):301-302.

Dostoevsky, F.M. *Letters from the Underworld.* New York: Dutton, 1944.

Draguns, J.G. "Values reflected in psychopathology: The case of the Protestant ethic." *Ethos* vol. 2, no. 2 (1974):115-136.

Durkheim, W. *The Rules of Sociological Method.* 8th ed. Glenco, Ill.: The Free Press, 1938.

Durkheim, E. *Suicide.* Translated by G. Simpson. New York: Free Press, 1951.

Educational Policies Commission. *The Central Purpose of American Education.* Washington, D.C.: National Education Association of the United States, 1961.

Eichorn, D.H. "The Berkeley longitudinal studies: Continuities and correlates of behavior." *Canadian Journal of the Behavioral Sciences* 5 (1973):297-320.

Eister, A.W. "An outline of a structural theory of cults." *Journal for the Scientific Study of Religion* vol. 11, no. 4 (1972):319-333.

Elliot, R. "Heart rate in anticipation of shocks which have different probabilities of occurrences." *Psychological Reports* 36 (1975):923-931.

Ellis, A. *Rational Living.* A journal review of the book *Rational Behavior.* New York: Institute of Advanced Study in Rational Psychotherapy, 1976.

Ellis, H.C., and Daniel, T.C. "Verbal processes in long-term stimulus-recognition memory." *Journal of Experimental Psychology* 90 (1971): 18-26.

Emerson, R. "Power-dependence relations." In *Interpersonal Behavior in Small Groups.* Edited by R. Ofshe. Englewood Cliffs, N.J.: Prentice-Hall, 1973.

Entwistle, D.R., and Huggins, W.H. "Iconic memory in children." *Child Development* 44 (1973):392-394.

Erickson, R.C.; Post, R.D.; and Paige, A.B. "Hope as a psychiatric variable." *Journal of Clinical Psychology* 31 (1975):324-330.

Erikson, E.H. *Childhood and Society.* 2nd ed. New York: W.W. Norton, 1950.

Estes, W.K. "Reinforcement in human behavior." *American Scientist* 1963 60 (1972):723-729.

Estes, W.K., and Vaughan, M. "Reading interests and comprehension: Implications." *The Reading Teacher* 27 (1973):149-153.

Etaugh, C.F., and van Sickle, D. "Discrimination of stereometric objects and photographs of objects by children." *Child Development* 42 (1971):1580-1582.

Etzioni, A. *Modern Organizations.* Englewood Cliffs, N.J.: Prentice-Hall, 1964.

Eysenck, M.W. "Extraversion, arousal and retrieval from semantic memory." *Journal of Personality* 42 (1974):319-331.

_____ . "Arousal and speed of recall." *British Journal of Social and Clinical Psychology* 14 (1975):269-277.

_____ . "Arousal, learning and memory." *Psychological Bulletin* 83 (1976):389-404.

Falk, C.T. "Object and pattern discrimination learning in young children as a function of availability of cues." *Child Development* 39 (1968): 923-931.

Feeney, S. "Breath of cue utilization and ability to attend selectively in schizophrenics and normals." Ph.D. dissertation, University of California at Los Angeles, 1971.

Festinger, L.; Schacter, S.; and Beck, K. *Social Pressures in Informal*

Groups: A Study of a Housing Community. New York: Harper and Row, 1950.

──────. *A Theory of Cognitive Dissonance.* Stanford: Stanford University Press, 1957.

Fitzgerald, F.S. *The Great Gatsby.* New York: Scribner, 1925.

Fleishman, E.A. "The development of a behavior taxonomy for describing human tasks: A correlational-experimental approach." *Journal of Applied Psychology* 51 (1967):1-10.

Fleishman, E.A., and Harris, E.F. "Patterns of leadership behavior related to employee grievances and turnover." *Personnel Psychology* 15 (1962):43-46.

Fleishman, E.A.; Harris, E.F.; and Burlt, H.E. *Leadership and Supervision in Industry.* Columbus: Ohio State University Bureau of Educational Research, 1955.

Fowler, H. "Satiation and curiosity." In *The Psychology of Learning and Motivation.* Edited by K. Spence and J.T. Spence. New York: Academic Press, 1967.

Fox, J.G. "Background music and industrial efficiency: A review." *Applied Ergonomics* vol. 2, no. 2 (1971):70-73.

Franck, J.D. *Persuasion and Healing.* Baltimore: Johns Hopkins, 1961.

Frerichs, A.H. "Relationship of self-esteem of the disadvantaged to school success." *Journal of Negro Education* 40 (1971):117-120.

Friedlander, F., and Greenberg, S. "Effect of job attitudes, training and organization climate on performance of the hard-core unemployed." *Journal of Applied Psychology* 55 (1971):287-295.

Friedman, M.I. Unpublished research. Columbia, University of South Carolina, 1967.

──────. *Predictive Abilities Test.* Published by author. Columbia, University of South Carolina, 1974.

──────. *Rational Behavior.* Columbia, S.C.: University of South Carolina Press, 1975.

Friedman, M.I., and Rowls, M.D. *Teaching Reading and Thinking skills.* New York: Longman, 1980.

Friedman, M.P.; Carterette, E.C.: and Anderson, N.H. "Long-term probability learning with a random schedule of reinforcement." *Journal of Experimental Psychology* 78 (1968):442-455.

Fromm, E. *Escape from Freedom.* New York: Avon Books, 1971.

Fu, V.R. "Preschool leadership-followership behaviors." *Child Study Journal* 9 (1979):133-140.

Gage, N.L. "The psychology of teaching methods." In *The Seventy-Fifth Yearbook of the National Society for the Study of Education.* Edited by N.L. Gage. Chicago: The National Society for the Study of Education, 1976.

Gale, A. "The psychophysiology of individual differences: Studies of extraversion and the EEG." In *New Approaches to Psychological Measurement*. Edited by P. Kline. London: Wiley, 1973.

Gallagher, J.J. "Expressive thought by gifted children." *Elementary English* 42 (1965):559-568.

Gamson, W.A. "An experimental test of a theory of coalition formation." *American Sociological Review* 26 (1961):565-573.

Garner, W.R. *The Processing of Information and Structure*. New York: Wiley, 1974.

Geller, E.S. "Preceding prediction outcome and prediction outcome probability: Interacting determinants of reaction time." *Journal of Experimental Psychology* 103 (1974):426-430.

Georgopolous, B.S.; Mahoney, G.M.: and Jones, N.W. "A path-goal approach to productivity." *Journal of Applied Psychology* 41 (1957): 345-353.

Gerard, H.B.; Willhelmy, R.A.; and Connelly, E.S. "Conformity and group size." *Journal of Personality and Social Psychology* 8 (1968):79-82.

Gersuny, C. "Punishment and redress in a modern factory." *The Sociological Quarterly* 8 (1967):63-70.

Gibbes, J.C. "Kohlberg's stages of moral judgment: A constructive critique." *Harvard Educational Review* vol. 47, no. 1 (1977):43-61.

Ginsburg, H., and Opper, S. *Piaget's Theory of Intellectual Development: An Introduction*. Englewood Cliffs, N.J.: Prentice-Hall, 1969.

Glaser, W. and Skills, D. *The Government of Associations, Selections from the Behavioral Sciences*. Totowa, N.J.: Bedminster Press, 1966.

Glass, D.C., and Singer, J.E. "Behavioral aftereffects of unpredictable and uncontrollable aversive events." In *Current Trends in Psychology*. Edited by I.L. Janis. Los Altos, Calif.: William Kaufmann, 1977.

Glass, D.C.; Singer, J.E.; and Friedman, L.N. "Psychic cost of adaptation to an environmental stressor." *Journal of Personality and Social Psychology* 12 (1969):200-210.

Glassman, W.E., and Levine, M. "Unsolved and unsoluble problem behavior." *Journal of Experimental Psychology* 92 (1972):146-148.

Goffman, E. "On face work: Analysis of ritual elements in social interaction." *Psychiatry Journal for the Study of Interpersonal Processes* 18 (1955):213-231.

_____ . "The nature of deference and dimension." *American Anthropologist* 58 (1956):473-502.

_____ . *The Presentation of Self in Everyday Life*. Garden City, N.J.: Doubleday, 1959.

_____ . *Behavior in Public Places*. New York: Free Press, 1963.

_____ . *Interaction Ritual: Essay on Face-to-face Behavior*. New York: Doubleday, 1967.

———— . *Relations in Public: Microstudies of Public Order.* New York: Harper Colopuan Books, 1971.

Good, K.J. "Social facilitation: Effects of performance anticipation, evaluation and response competition on free associations." *Journal of Personality and Social Psychology* 28 (1973):270-275.

Goodman, K.S. "A linguistic study of cues and miscues in reading." *Elementary English* 42 (1965):639-643.

———— . "Reading: A psycholinguistic guessing game." In *Theoretical Models and Processes of Reading.* Edited by H. Singer and R. Ruddell. International Reading Association, 1970.

Goodwin, W.L., and Klausmeier, H.J. *Facilitating Student Learning.* New York: Harper and Row, 1975.

Gove, W.R., and Herb, T.R. "Stress and mental illness among the young: A comparison of the sexes." *Social Forces* vol. 53, no. 2 (1974):256-265.

Gramza, A.F. "Responses to manipulability of a play object." *Psychological Reports* 38 (1976):1109-1110.

Grant, D.L. "A factor analysis of managers' ratings." *Journal of Applied Psychology* 39 (1955):283-286.

Greeno, J.G., and Noreen, D.L. "Time to read semantically related sentences." *Memory and Cognition* 2 (1974):117-120.

Grubb, E.A. "Assembly line boredom and individual differences in recreation participation." *Journal of Leisure Research* 7 (1975):256-269.

Hamblin, R.; Miller, K.; and Wiggins, J. "Group morale and competence of the leader." *Sociometry* 24 (1961):295-311.

Hammond, P.B. "The functions of indirection in communication." In *Comparative Studies in Administration.* Edited by J.D. Thompson. Pittsburgh: University of Pittsburgh Press, 1959.

Hartocollis, P. "Time as a dimension of affects." *Journal of the American Psychoanalytic Association* 20 (1972):90-107.

Hartup, W.W., and Zook, E.A. "Sex role preferences in three- and four-year old children." *Journal of Consulting Psychology* 24 (1960):420-426.

Havens, E.M. "Women, work and wedlock: A note of female marital patterns in the United States." *American Journal of Sociology* vol. 78, no. 4 (1973):975-981.

Hayden, B.; Nasby, W.; and Davids, A. "Interpersonal conceptual structures, predictive accuracy and social adjustment of emotionally disturbed boys." *Journal of Abnormal Psychology* 86 (1977):315-320.

Haythorn, W. "The influence of individual members on the characteristics of small groups." *Journal of Abnormal and Social Psychology* 48 (1953):276-284.

Haywood, H.C. "Novelty-seeking behavior as a function of manifest anxiety and physiologic arousal." *Journal of Personality* 30 (1962):63-74.

Hebb, D.O. "Drives and the C.N.S. (conceptual nervous system)." *Psychological Review* 62 (1955):243-254.

Heizer, J.H. "Manager action." *Personnel Psychology* 25 (1972):511-522.

Heller, J. *Catch-22.* New York: Simon and Schuster, 1961.

Helson, H. "Design of equipment and optimal human operation." *American Journal of Psychology* 62 (1949):473-497.

———. *Adaptation-level Theory.* New York: Harper and Row, 1964.

Henderson, E.H., and Long, B.H. "Correlations of reading readiness among children of varying backgrounds." *The Reading Teacher* 22 (1968):40-44.

———. "Decision processes of superior, average and inferior readers." *Psychological Reports* 23 (1968):703-706.

Heneman, H.G., and Schwab, D.P. "An evaluation of research on expectancy theory predictions of employees' performance." *Psychological Bulletin,* 1972.

Hernandez-Peon, R.; Scherrer, H.; and Jouret, M. "Modification of electrical activity in cochlear nucleas during 'attention' in unanesthetized cats." *Science* 1231 (1956):331-332.

Heron, W. "The pathology of boredom." *Scientific American* 196 (1957):52-56

Heron, W.; Bexton, W.H.; and Hebb, D.O. "Cognitive effects of a decreased variation in the sensory environment." *American Psychologist* 8 (1953):366.

Herzberg, F.; Mausner, B.; Peterson, R.O.; and Capwell, D.F. *Job Attitudes: Review of Research and Opinion.* Pittsburgh: Pittsburgh Psychological Services, 1957.

Hilgard, E., and Bower, G. *Theories of Learning.* Englewood Cliffs, N.J.: Prentice-Hall, 1975.

Hill, A.B. "Extroversion and variety-seeking in a monotous task." *British Journal of Psychology* 66 (1975):9-13.

Hippler, A.E., and Conn, S. "The changing legal culture of the North Alaska Eskimo." *Ethos* vol. 2, no. 2 (1974):171-188.

Hockey, G.R.J. "Effects of loud noises on attentional activity." *Quarterly Journal of Experimental Psychology* 22 (1970a):28-36.

———. "Signal probability and spatial locations as possible bases for increased selectivity in noise." *Quarterly Journal of Experimental Psychology* 22 (1970b):37-42.

Hoffman, L.W. "Early childhood experiences and women's achievement motives." *Journal of Social Issues* vol. 28, no. 2 (1972):129-155.

Hogan, R. "Moral conduct and moral character." *Psychological Bulletin,* 79 (1973):217-232.

Hogg, J.H. "Development of verbal behavior through cognitive awareness training." *Journal of Educational Research* 67 (1973):9-12.

Holding, D.H. *Principles of Training*. New York: Pergamon Press, 1965.

Hollander, E.P. "Competence and conformity in the acceptance of influence." *Journal of Abnormal and Social Psychology* 61 (1960):365-370.

Homans, G.C. *Social Behavior — Its Elementary Forms*. New York: Harcourt, Brace, Janovich, 1974.

Hunkins, F.P. "What to ask and when." *Yearbook of the National Council on Social Studies* 44 (1974):146-148.

Ibsen, H. *Eleven Plays by Henrik Ibsen*. New York: Modern Library, 1935.

Ingling, N.W. "Categorization: A mechanism for rapid information processing." *Journal of Experimental Psychology* 94 (1972):239-243.

Inhelder, B., and Piaget, J. *The Growth of Logical Thinking from Childhood to Adolescence*. New York: Basic Books, 1958.

Janis, I.L. Group identification under conditions of external threat. In *Group Dynamics*. Edited by D. Cartwritht and A. Zander. New York: Harper and Row, 1968.

Johnson, N.F. The role of chunking and organization in the process of recall. In *Psychology of Learning and Motivation: Advances in Research and Theory*. vol. 4. Edited by G.H. Bower. New York: Academic Press, 1970.

Jones, E.E.; Rock, L.; Shaver, K.G.; Goethals, G.R.; and Ward, L.M. "Pattern of performance and ability attribution." *Journal of Personality and Social Psychology* 10 (1968):317-340.

Kagan, J. "Reflection-impulsivity and reading ability in primary grade children." *Child Development* 36 (1965):609-628.

———. Developmental studies in reflection and analysis. In *Perceptual Development in Children*. Edited by A.H. Kidel and J.L. Rivoire. New York: International Universities Press, 1966.

Kagan, J., and Kogan, N. Individual variation in cognitive process. In *Carmichael's Manual of Child Psychology*. vol. 1. Edited by P.H. Mussen. New York: Wiley, 1970.

Katone, G. *Organizaing and Memorizing*. New York: Columbia University Press, 1940.

Keen, S. "Chasing the blahs away: Boredom and how to beat it." *Psychology Today* 10 (1977):78-84.

Kellas, G.; Ashcraft, M.H.; and Johnson, N.S. "Rehearsal processes in the short-term memory performance of mildly retarded adolescents." *American Journal of Mental Deficiency* vo. 77, no. 5 (1973):670-679.

Kellas, G.; Ashcraft, M.H.; Johnson, N.S.; and Needham, S. "Temporal aspects of storage and retrieval in free recall of categorized lists." *Journal of Verbal Learning and Verbal Behavior* vol. 12, no. 5 (1973):499-511.

Kelly, G.A. *The Psychology of Personal Constructs*. vol. 1. New York: W.W. Norton, 1955.

Kendler, N.H., and D'Amato, M.F. "A comparison of reversal and non-reversal shifts in human concept formation." *Journal of Experimental Psychology* 49 (1955):165-174.

Kendler, H.H., and Kendler, T.S. "Inferential behavior in preschool children." *Journal of Experimental Psychology* 51 (1956):311-313.

_____ . "Reversal and non-reversal shifts in kindergarten children." *Journal of Experimental Psychology* 58 (1959):56-60.

_____ . "Vertical and horizontal processes in problem solving." *Psychological Review* 69 (1962):1-16(a).

_____ . "From discrimination learning to cognitive development: A neobehavioristic odyssey." In *Handbook of Learning and Cognitive Processes.* Edited by W.K. Estes. Hillsdale, N.J.: Erlbaum, 1975.

Kendler, T.S. "Verbalization and optional reversal shifts among kindergarten children." *Journal of Verbal Learning and Verbal Behavior* 3 (1964):248-436.

Kendler, T.S., and Kendler, H.H. "Inferential behavior as a function of subgoal constancy and age." *Journal of Experimental Psychology* 64 (1962):460-466.

Kiesler, C.A., and Munson, P.A. "Attitudes and opinions." In *Annual Review of Psychology.* vol. 26. Edited by M.R. Rosenzweig and L.W. Porter. Palo Alto, Calif.: Annual Reviews, 1975.

Kifer, E. "Relationships between academic achievement and personality characteristics: A quasi-longitudinal study." *American Educational Research Journal* 12 (1975):191-210.

Kintsch, W. "Memory for Prose." Paper presented at the American Association for the Advancement of Science meeting. New York, 1975a.

_____ . "Memory Representation of Text." Paper presented at the Loyola Symposium. Chicago, 1975b.

Kintsch, W., and Keenan, J. "Reading rate and retention as a function of the number of prepositions in the base structure of the sentence." *Cognitive Psychology* 5 (1973):257-274.

Kipnis, D.M. "Changes in self-concepts in relation to perceptions of others." *Journal of Personality* 29 (1961):445-465.

Kitahare, M. "A function of marriage ceremony." *Anthropologica* vol. 16, no. 2 (1974):163-175.

Kitamura, S. "Studies on sensory overload: II." *Tohoku Psychologicia Folia* 29 (1970):45-69.

Klein, H.A.; Klein, G.A.; and Bertino, M. "Studying the use of context for word identification decisions." In *Diversity in Mature Reading: Theory and Research. Twenty-Second Yearbook of the National Reading Conference.* vol. 1 (1973), pp. 86-91.

Kleinsmith, L.J., and Kaplan, S. "Paired-associate learning as a function of arousal and interpolated interval." *Journal of Experimental Psychology* 65 (1963):190-193.

Klenmack, D.L., and Edwards, J.N. "Women's acquisition of stereotyped occupational aspirations." *Sociology and Social Research* vol. 57, no. 4 (1973):510-525.

Kohlberg, L. "The development of moral character and ideology." In *Review of Child Development Research*. Edited by M. Hoffman and L. Hoffman. New York: Russell Sage Foundation, 1964; In P.F. Peck and R.J. Havighurst, *The Psychology of Character Development*. New York: Wiley and Sons, 1960.

_____ . "Stages of moral development as a basis for moral education." In *Moral Education: Interdisciplinary Approaches*. Edited by C.M. Beck, B.S. Crittenden, and E.V. Sullivan. New York: Newman Press, 1971.

Kohlberg, L., and Turiel, E. "Moral development and moral education." In *Psychology and Educational Practice*. Edited by G.S. Lesser. Glenview, Ill.: Scott, Foresman and Co., 1971.

Kohler, W. *The Mentality of Apes*. New York: Harcourt, 1925.

_____ . *Gestalt Psychology*. New York: Leveright, 1929.

_____ . *The Task of Gestalt Psychology*. Princeton: Princeton University Press, 1969.

Komarovsky, M. *American Journal of Sociology* vol. 78, no. 4 (1973): 873-884.

Korman, A. "Organizational achievement, aggression and creativity: Some suggestions toward an integrated theory." *Organizational Behavior and Human Performance* 6 (1971):593-613.

Kotona, G. *Organizaing and Memorizing*. New York: Columbia University Press, 1940.

Kristofferson, M.W. "Shifting attention between modalities: A comparison of schizophrenics and normals." *Journal of Abnormal Psychology* 72 (1967):388-394.

Krupat, E. *Psychology Is Social*. Glenview, Ill.: Scott, Foresman and Co., 1975.

Kryter, K.D. *The Effects of Noise on Man*. New York: Academic Press, 1970.

Kuhn, D., and Phelps, H. "The development of children's comprehension of causal direction." *Child Development* 47 (1976):248-251.

Kulhavy, R.W.; Yekovich, F.R.; and Dyer, J.W. "Feedback and response confidence." *Journal of Educational Psychology* 68 (1976):522-528.

Kunce, J.T. "Vocational interests and accident proneness." *Journal of Applied Psychology* 51 (1967):223-225.

Kunkel, J.M., and Nagasawa, R.H. "A behavioral model of man: Propositions and implications." *American Sociological Review* vol. 38, no. 530 (1973):530-543.

Lackner, J.R. "Proprioceptive facilitation of open-loop visual pointing." *Perceptual and Motor Skills* 39 (1974):263-265.

Larson, L.E. "An examination of the salience hierarchy during adolescence: The influence of the family." *Adolescence* vol. 9, no. 35 (1974):317-332.

Lasswell, M., and Lobenz, N.M. *No Fault Marriage.* New York: Ballentine, 1976.

Lawrence, P.R. and Lorsch, J.W. *Organization Behavior and Administration.* Homewood, Ill.: Dorsey and Irwin, 1961.

Lazarus, R.S., and Averill, J.R. "Emotion and cognition: With special reference to anxiety." In *Anxiety: Current Trends in Theory and Research.* Edited by C.D. Spielberger. New York: Academic Press, 1972.

Leap, W.L. "Ethnics, emics and the new ideology." *Southern Anthropological Society Proceedings* 8 (1974):51-62.

Lee, A.M., and Lee, E.B. *The Fine Art of Propaganda.* New York: Octagon Books, 1972.

Lee, D. "Lineal and non-lineal codifications of reality." *Psychosometric Medicine* 12 (1950):89-97.

Leonard, J.A. "Advanced information in sensorimotor skills." *Quarterly Journal of Experimental Psychology* 5 (1953):141-149.

Lermontov, M. *A Hero of Our Time.* Translated by V. Nabokov. Garden City, N.Y.: Doubleday, 1958.

Levine, J.R., and Allen, V.L., eds. *Cognitive Learning in Children.* New York: Academic Press, 1976.

Levine, M. "A model of hypothesis behavior in discrimination learning set." *Psychological Review* 66 (1959):253-276.

_____ . "Mediating processes in humans at the outset of human learning." *Psychological Review* 70 (1963):254-276.

_____ . "Hypothesis behavior by humans during discrimination learning." *Journal of Experimental Psychology* 71 (1966):331-338.

_____ "A transfer hypothesis whereby learning-to-learn, einstelling, the PREE, reversal/non-reversal shifts, and other curiosities are elucidated." In *Theories in Cognitive Psychology.* Edited by R.L. Lolo. Potomac, Md.: Erlbaum Associates, 1974.

Lewin, K.; Dembo, T.; Festinger, T.; and Spears, P.G. "Level of aspiration." In *Personality and the Behavior Disorders.* Edited by J.M. Hunt. New York: Ronald Press, 1944.

Little, C.B., and Gelles, R.J. "Hey you: A study of the social-psychological implications of forms of address." *Sociological Abstracts* 20 (1972):1851.

Liu, J. Boredom and confusion cognitive inventory (BACCI). An unpublished test. Columbia, University of South Carolina, 1980.

London, H.; Schubert, D.S.; and Washburn, D. "Increase of automatic arousal by boredom." *Journal of Abnormal Psychology* 80 (1972):29-36.

Longstreth, L.E. "Tests of the law of effect on open and closed tasks." *Journal of Experimental Psychology* 84 (1970):53-57.

Lopes, L.L. "Individual strategies in a goal setting." *Organizational Behavior and Human Performance* 15 (1976):268-277.

Lorenz, K. *On Aggression.* New York: Bantam Books, 1966.

Lott, B., and Lott, A. "The formation of positive attitudes toward group members." *Journal of Abnormal and Social Psychology* 61 (1960): 297-300.

Lueptow, L.B. "Social structure, social change, and parental influence in adolescent sex-role socialization." *Journal of Marriage and the Family* 42 (1980):93-103.

MacCorquodale, K., and Mechl, P.E. "Edward C. Tolman." In *Modern Learning Theory.* Edited by W.K. Estes, S. Koch, K. MacCorquodale, P.E. Meehl, C.G. Mueller, W.N. Schoenfeld, and W.S. Verplanck. New York: Appleton-Century-Crofts, 1954.

McDavid, J.W., and Sistrunk, F. "Personality correlates of two kinds of conforming behavior." *Journal of Personality* 32 (1964):420-435.

McGhie, A., and Chapman, J. "Disorders of attention and perception in early schizophrenia." *British Journal of Medical Psychology* 34 (1961): 103-116.

McKinney, J.D. "Classroom behavior patterns of reflective and impulsive children." Paper presented at the meeting of the Southeastern Psychological Association. Hollywood, Fla., 1974.

McReynolds, P. "A restricted conceptualization of human anxiety and motivation." *Psychological Reports* 2 (1956):293-312.

McReynolds, P., and Bryan, J. "Tendency to obtain new percepts as a function of the level of unassimilated percepts. *Perceptual and Motor Skills* 6 (1956):183-186.

Maier, N.R.F. "Reasoning in humans. I: On direction." *Journal of Comparative Psychology* 10 (1930):115-143.

_____ . "Reasoning in humans. II: The solution of a problem and its appearance in consciousness." *Journal of Comparative Psychology* 12 (1931):181-194.

_____ . "An aspect of human reasoning." *British Journal of Psychology* 14 (1933):144-155.

_____ . "Reasoning in humans. III: The mechanisms of equivalent stimuli and reasoning." *Journal of Experimental Psychology* 35 (1945): 349-360.

_____ . "The quality of group decisions as influenced by the discussion leader." *Human Relations* 3 (1950):155-174.

Malmo, R.B. "Activation: A neuropsychological dimension." *Psychological Review* 66 (1959):367-386.

March, J.G. and Simon, H.A. *Organizations.* New York: Wiley and Sons, 1958.

Markle, S.M. and Tiemann, P.W. *Really Understanding Concepts.* Champaign, Ill.: Stipes, 1969.

Martin, E. "Transfer of verbal paired associates'." *Psychological Review* 72 (1965):327-343.

Maschette, D. "Moral reasoning in the 'real world'." *Theory into Practice: Moral Development* vol. 16, no. 2 (1977):124-128.

May, R., and Hutt, C. "Response to stimulus uncertainty in four-, six-, and eight-year-old children." *Journal of Psychology* 88 (1974):127-133.

Medow, H., and Zander, A. "Aspirations for groups chosen by central and peripheral members." *Journal of Personality and Social Psychology* 1 (1965):224-228.

Megarger, E.; Bogart, P.; and Anderson, B. "Prediction of leadership in a simulated industrial task." *Journal of Applied Psychology* 50 (1966): 292-295.

Merwin, W.C.; Schneider, D.O.; and Stephens, L.D. *Developing Competency in Teaching Secondary Social Studies.* Columbus, Ohio: Charles E. Merrill Publishing Co., 1974.

Messer, S. "Reflection-impulsivity: Stability and school failure." *Journal of Educational Psychology* vol. 61, no. 6 (1970):487-490.

Meyer, H.H. "Factors related to success in the human relations aspect of work-group leadership." *Psychological Monographs* vol. 65, no. 3 (1961) (whole no. 320).

Meyer, S.R. "Report on the initial test of a junior high school vocabulary program." In *Teaching Machines and Programmed Learning.* Edited by A.A. Lumsdaine and R. Glaser. Washington, D.C.: National Education Association, 1960.

Michener, J.A. *Sports in America.* New York: Random House, 1976.

Miller, G.A. "The magical number seven plus or minus two: Some limits on our capacity for processing information." *Psychological Review* 3 (1956):81-97.

Miller, G.A.; Galanter, E.; and Pribram, K.H. *Plans and the Structure of Behavior.* New York: Holt, Rinehart and Winston, 1960.

Mingle, C., and Roll, S. "Bugs in the flowers: A review of the nonviolent ethic of the hippie subculture." *Adolescence* vol. 9, no. 35 (1974):311-316.

Mitchell, T.R., and Biglan, A. "Instrumentality theories: Current uses in psychology." *Psychological Bulletin* 76 (1971):432-454.

Moran, J.J. "Problem-solving potential in elementary school children."
    Child Study Journal 6 (1976):39-47.
Morgenthau, H. *Politics among Nations.* New York: Alfred A. Knopf,
    1967.
Morten, E. "Transfer of verbal-paired associates." *Psychological Review*
    72 (1965):327-343.
Mueller, B.J. "Rural family life styles and sons' school achievement."
    Rural Sociology vol. 39, no. 3 (1974):362-372.
Murdock, B.B., Jr. "Short-term memory." In *The Psychology of Learning
    and Motivation: Advances in Research and Theory.* vol. 5. Edited by G.
    Bower, New York: Academic Press, 1974.
Nastovic, I. "Ego-psychological aspect of autism" (title translated from
    original Yugoslavic). *Neuropsihijatrija* 20 (1972):255-271.
Neissen, U. *Cognitive Psychology.* New York: Appleton-Century-Crofts,
    1967.
Nelson, D.L.; Brooks, D.H.; and Fosselman, J.R. "Words as sets of
    features: Processing phonological cues." *Journal of Experimental
    Psychology* 92 (1972):312.
Notz, W.W. "Work motivation and the negative effects of extrinsic rewards:
    A review with implications for theory and practice." *American
    Psychologist* vol. 30, no. 9 (1975):884-891.
Novack, T.A., and Richman, C.L. "The effects of stimulus variability on
    overgeneralization and overdiscrimination errors in children and
    adults." *Child Development* 51 (1980):55-60.
Nunnally, S.C., and Lemond, L.C. "Exploratory behavior and human
    development." In *Advances in Child Development and Behavior.*
    Edited by H.W. Reese. New York: Academic Press, 1973.
Nutten, J., and Greenwald, A.G. *Reward and Punishment in Human
    Learning.* New York: Academic Press, 1968.
Ornitz, E.M., and Rituo, E.R. "The syndrome of autism: A critical
    review." *American Journal of Psychiatry* 133 (1976):609-621.
Orphen, C. "Sociocultural and personality factors in prejudice: The case of
    white South Africa." *South African Journal of Psychology* 3 (1973):
    91-96.
Osgood, C.E. "The similarity paradox in human learning: A resolution."
    Psychological Review 56 (1949):132-143.
Osler, J., and Fivel, M.W. "Concept attainment: I. The role of age and
    intelligence in concept attainment by induction." *Journal of Experimental
    Psychology* 62 (1961):1-8.
Pallak, M.S., and Pittman, T.S. "General motivation effects of dissonance
    arousal." *Journal of Personality and Social Psychology* 21 (1972):
    349-358.

Palmer, G.J., Jr. "Task ability and successful and effective leadership." Technical Reports nos. 4 and 6. Louisiana State University, 1962.

Park, D., and Yonderian, P. "Light and number: Ordering principles in the world of an autistic child." *Journal of Autism and Childhood Schizophrenia* 4 (1974):313-323.

Parsons, T., and Shils, E. *Toward a General Theory of Action.* Cambridge, Mass. Harvard University Press, 1951.

Payne, B.P.; Platt, L.A.; and Branch, R.G. "Effects of rural recreation on attitudes of urban children." *Growth and Change* vol. 5, no. 1 (1974): 32-35.

Penfield, W. "Memory mechanisms." *Transactions of the American Neurological Association* 76 (1951):15-31.

Peteroy, E.T. "Effects of member and leader expectations on group outcome." *Journal of Counseling Psychology* 26 (1979):534-537.

Peterson, C.R., and Beach, L.R. "Man as an intuitive statistician." *Psychological Bulletin* 68 (1967):29-46.

Pfeiffer, I., and Davis, O.L., Jr. " Teacher-made examinations: What kind of thinking do they demand? *NASSP Bulletin* 49 (1965):1-10.

Piaget, J., and Inhelder, B. *Memory and Intelligence.* Translated by A.J. Pomeraus. New York: Basic Books, 1973.

Piaget, J., and Szeminska, A. *The Child's Conception of Numbers.* Translated by C. Gattegno and F.M. Hodgson, 1941. New York: Humanities Press, 1952.

Pickering, W.S.F. "The persistence of rites of passage." *British Journal of Sociology* vol. 25, no. 1 (1974):63-78.

Picton, T.W., and Hillyard, S.A. "Human auditory evoked potentials: II. Effects of attention." *Electroencephalography and Clinical Neurophysiology* vol. 36, no. 2 (1974):191-200.

Pines, M. "Cracking the mystery of memory: The race is on." *APA Monitor* 5 (1974):8.

Pood, E.A. "Functions of communication: An experimental study in group conflict situations." *Small Group Behavior* 11 (1980):76-87.

Porter, L.W., and Fowler, E.E. *Managerial Attitudes and Performance.* Homewood, Ill.: Irwin-Dorsey, 1968.

Poulton, E.C. "On prediction in skilled movements." *Psychological Bulletin* 54 (1957):467-478.

Powers, P.S.; Stavens, C.; and Andreasen, N.J. "The ontogenesis of intelligence: Evaluating the Piaget theory." *Comprehension Psychology* 16 (1975):149-154.

Premack, D. "Toward empirical behavior laws: I. Positive Reinforcement." *Psychological Review* 55 (1959):219-233.

———. "Rate differential reinforcement in monkey manipulation." *Journal of the Experimental Analysis of Behavior* 6 (1963):81-89.

_____ . "Reinforcement theory." In *Nebraska Symposium on Motivation: 1966.* Edited by M.R. Jones. Lincoln: University of Nebraska Press, 1966.

Preusser, D., and Handel, S. "The free classification of hierarchially and categorically related stimuli." *Journal of Verbal Learning and Verbal Behavior* 9 (1970):222-223.

Pribram, K.H. "Emotion: Steps toward a neuropsychological theory." In *Neurophysiology and Emotion.* Edited by D.C. Glass. New York: Rockefeller University Press and Russell Sage Foundation, 1967.

_____ . "The biology of mind: Neuro-behavioral foundations." In *Contemporary Scientific Psychology.* Edited by A. Gilgen. New York: Academic Press, 1970.

_____ . *Languages of the Brain.* Englewood Cliffs, N.J.: Prentice-Hall, 1971.

_____ . "Arousal, activation, and effort in the control of attentions." *Psychological Review* vol. 82, no. 2 (1975):116-149.

Pritchard, R.D. "Equity theory: A review and critique." *Organizational Behavior and Human Performance* 4 (1969):176-211.

Quay, H.C. "Psychopathic personality as pathological stimulation seeking," *American Journal of Psychiatry* 122 (1965):180-183.

Rafky, D.M. "Phenomenology and socialization: Some comments on the assumptions underlying socialization theory." *Sociological Analysis* vol. 32, no. 1 (1971):7-20.

Rapoport, A. *Fights, Games and Debates.* Ann Arbor: University of Michigan Press, 1960.

_____ . "The use and misuse of game theory." *Scientific American* 27 (1962):108-118.

_____ . *Strategy and Conscience.* New York: Harper and Row, 1964.

Raven, B.H., and Rietsema, J. "The effects of varied clarity of group goal and group path upon the individual and his relations to the group." *Human Relations* 10 (1957):29-44.

Raymond, J.G. "Beyond masculinity and femininity." *Andover Newton Quarterly* vol. 13, no. 3 (1973):214-221.

Reason, P. "Human interaction as exchange and encounter: A dialectical exploration." *Small Group Behavior* 11 (1980):3-12.

Reimer, J. "A structural theory of moral development." *Theory into Practice: Moral Development* vol. 16, no. 2 (1977):60-66.

Rest, J.R. "Recent research on an objective test of moral judgment: How the important issues of a moral dilemma are defined." In *Moral Development: Current Theory and Research.* Edited by D.J. DePalma and J.M. Foley. Hillsdale, N.J.: Erlbaum Associates, 1975.

Restle, F. "The selection of strategies in cue learning." *Psychological Review* 69 (1962):329-343.

Restle, F., and Greeno, S.G. *Introduction to Mathematical Psychology.* Reading, Mass.: Addison-Wesley, 1970.

Roach, D.E. "Factor analysis of rated supervisory behavior." *Personal Psychology* 9 (1956):487-498.

Robinson, S.; Winnick, H.Z.; and Weiss, A.A. "Obsessive psychosis: Justification for a separate entity." *Israel Annal of Psychiatry and Related Disciplines* 14 (1976):39-48.

Rogers, R.W. "Protection motivation theory of fear appeals and attitude change." *Journal of Psychology* 91 (1975):93-114.

Rogers, R.W., and Mewborn, C.R. "Fear appeal and attitude change: Effects of a threat's noxiousness, probability of occurrence, and the efficacy of coping responses." *Journal of Personality and Social Psychology* 34 (1976):54-61.

Roper, G., and Rachman, S. "Obsessional-compulsive checking: Experimental replication and development." *Behavior Research and Therapy* 14 (1976):25-32.

Rosenberg, B.G., and Sutton-Smith, B. "A revised conception of masculine-feminine differences in play activities." *Journal of Genetic Psychology* 96 (1960):165-170.

Roy, D. "Efficiency and 'The Fix': Informal intergroup relations in a piece-work machine shop." *American Journal of Sociology* 60 (1954): 255-266.

Saario, T.N.; Jacklin, C.N.; and Tittle, C.K. "Sex role stereotyping in the public schools." *Harvard Educational Review* vol. 43, no. 3 (1973): 386-416.

Saaty, T.L., and Vargas, L.G. "Hierarchical analysis of behavior in competition: Prediction in chess." *Behavioral Science* 25 (1980):180-191.

Salley, C.M., and Murphy, G. *Development of the Perceptual World.* New York: Basic Books, 1960.

Sartre, J.P. *No Exit.* New York: Knopf, 1947.

Savitz, J.C. "Diagnosis and Treatment of Emotionally Distrubed Clients Using Rational Behavior Theory." Ph.D. dissertation. Columbia: University of South Carolina, 1979.

Savitz, J.C., and Friedman, M.I. "Diagnosing boredom and confusion." *Nursing Research.* In press.

Schacter, S. "Deviation, rejection and communication." *Journal of Abnormal and Social Psychology* 46 (1951a):190-207.

———. *Human Relations.* 4 (1951b):229-238.

Schein, E.H. "Reaction patterns to severe chronic stress in American prisoners of war of the Chinese." *Journal of Social Issues* 13 (1957):21-30. Reprinted in E. Krupat, ed. *Psychology Is Social.* Glenview: Scott, Foresman and Co., 1975.

Schneider, K., and Posse, N. "Subjective uncertainty, attribution of cases, and choice of tasks: I." *Zeitschrift fur Experimentelle und Angewandte Psychologie* 25 (1978):302-320.

Scioli, F.P.; Dyson, S.W.; and Fleitas, D.W. "The relationship of personality and decisional structure to leadership." *Small Group Behavior* 5 (1974):3-22.

Seagoe, M.V. "A comparison of children's play in six modern cultures." *Journal of School Psychology* 9 (1971):61-72.

Seligmann, M.E.P. "Chronic fear produced by unpredictable electric shock." *Journal of Physiologic Psychology* 66 (1968):402-411.

Shakespeare, W. "The comedy of errors." In *The Complete Works of William Shakespeare*. Edited by W.A. Wright. Garden City, N.Y.: Garden City Books, 1936.

Shanas, E. "Older people and their families: The new pioneers." *Journal of Marriage and the Family* 42 (1980):9-15.

Shanas, E., and Hauser P.M. "Zero population growth and the family life of old people." *Journal of Social Issues* vol. 30, no. 4 (1974):79-92.

Shapiro, D., and Schwartz, G.E. "Biofeedback and visceral learning: Clinical application." In *Biofeedback and Self-control*. Chicago: Aldine, 1972.

Shaw, M.E. "Some motivational factors in cooperation and competition." *Journal of Personality* 26 (1958):155-169.

_____ "Acceptance of authority, group structure and the effectiveness of small groups." *Journal of Personality* 27 (1959a):196-210.

_____ . "Some effects of individually prominent behavior upon group effectiveness and member satisfaction." *Journal of Abnormal and Social Psychology* 59 (1959b):382-386.

Shaw, M.E., and Penrod, W.T., Jr. "Validity of information, attempted influence and quality of group decisions." *Psychological Reports* 10 (1962):19-23.

Shea, M. "Formulation of a generalization surface for the simultaneous variation of stimulus and response similarity." *Journal of Experimental Psychology* 80 (1969):353-358.

Shephard, R.N. "Recognition memory for words, sentences and pictures." *Journal of Verbal Learning and Verbal Behavior* 6 (1967):156-163.

Sherif, M. "An experimental approach to the study of attitudes." *Sociometry* 1 (1937):90-98.

_____ . *In Common Predicament*. New York: Houghton Mifflin, 1966.

_____ . "Superordinate goals in the reduction of intergroup conflict." In *Beyond the Laboratory: Field Research in Social Psychology*. Edited by L. Bickman and T. Henchy. New York: McGraw-Hill, 1972.

Sherif, M., and Sherif, C.W. *Groups in Harmony and Tension*. New York: Harper Brothers, 1953.

_____ . *An Outline of Social Psychology*. Rev. ed. New York: Harper and Row, 1956.

Sherif, M.; White, B.; and Harvey, O. "Status in experimentally produced groups." *American Journal of Sociology* 60 (1955):370-379.

Sheritz, R.N. *Leadership Acts: An Investigation of the Relation Between Exclusive Possession of Information and Attempts to Lead*. Columbus: Ohio State University Research Foundation, 1955.

Shotick, A.L.; Ray, A.; Bartow, A.; and Lewis, C. "Recall of familiar objects and projected color photographs of objects by mentally retarded individuals of comparable mental age." *Perceptual and Motor Skills* 42 (1976):139-145.

Shuell, T.J. "Clustering and organization in free recall." *Psychological Bulletin* 72 (1969):353-374.

Siegel, A., and Siegel, S. "Reference groups, membership groups, and attitude change." *Journal of Abnormal and Social Psychology* 55 (1957): 360-364.

Singer, D.G., and Lenahen, M.L. "Imagination content in dreams of deaf children." *American Annals of the Deaf* vol. 121, no. 1 (1976):44-48.

Sites, P. *Control and Constraints: An Introduction to Sociology*. New York: Macmillan, 1975.

Smith, R.J. and Cook, P.E. "Leadership in diadic groups as a function of dominance and incentives." *Sociometry* 36 (1973):561-563.

Smith, S.; Myers, T.; and Johnson, E. "Stimulation seeking as a function of duration and extent of sensory deprivation." *Proceedings of the 76th Annual Convention of the APA* (1968):625-626.

Snyder, E.E., and Spreitzer, E. "Orientations toward work and leisure as predictors of sports involvement." *Research Quarterly* 45 (1974):398-406.

Sokolov, E.N. "Neuronal models and the orienting reflex." In *The Central Nervous System and Behavior*. Edited by M.A.B. Brazier. New York: Josiah Macy, Jr. Foundation, 1960.

Solley, C.M., and Murphy, G. *Development of the Perceptual World*. New York: Basic Books, 1960.

Starr, M.K. "Some new fundamental considerations of variety-seeking behavior." *Behavioral Science* 25 (1980):171-179.

Steiner, I.D. "Group dynamics." In *Annual Review of Psychology: XV*. Edited by P.R. Farnsworth, O. McNemar, and Q. McNemar. Palo Alto, Calif.: Annual Reviews, 1964.

_____ . "Models for inferring relationships between group size and potential group productivity. *Behavioral Science* 11 (1966):273-283.

Stengel, E. "A study on some clinical aspects of the relationship between obsessional neurosis and psychotic reaction types." *Journal of Mental Sciences* 91 (1945):166-187.

Stevens, C. *Strategy and Collective Bargaining*. New York: McGraw-Hill, 1963.

Stogdill, R.M. "Personal factors associated with leadership: A survey of the literature." *Journal of Psychology* 25 (1948):35-71.

Stone, L.J.; Smith, H.T.; and Murphy, L. "The capability of the newborn." In *The Competent Infant*. New York: Basic Books, 1973.

Stotland, E. *The Psychology of Hope*. San Francisco: Jossey, 1969.

Student, K. "Supervisory influence and work group performance." *Journal of Applied Psychology* 52 (1968):188-194.

Suedfeld, P. "The benefits of boredom: Sensory deprivation reconsidered." In *Current Trends in Psychology*. Edited by I.L. Janis. Los Altos, Calif.: William Kaufmann, 1977.

Sugimura, A., and Terao, Yoko. "Children's concepts assessed by the abstraction and the identification tests." *Japanese Journal of Educational Psychology* 23 (1975):97-103.

Sumner, W.G. *Folkways*. New York: The New American Library, 1940.

_____ . *The Science of Sociology*. vol. 1. New Haven: Yale University Press, 1946.

Sussman, M., and Neil, W. "An experimental study on the effects of group interaction upon the behavior of diabetic children." *International Journal of Social Psychiatry* 6 (1960):120-125.

Sutton, S.; Tueting, P.; and John , E.R. "Information delivery." *Science* 155 (1967):1426-1439.

Szemanska, A. "Toward a radical sociology." *Sociological Inquiry* vol. 40, no. 3 (1954):3-12, 21-25.

Szurek, S.A., and Berlin, I.N., *The Antisocial Child, His Family and His Community*. vol. 4. The Langley Porter Child Psychiatry Series. Palo Alto, Calif.: Science and Behavior Books, 1969.

Thackray, R.I.; Jones, K.N.; and Touchstone, R.M. "Personality and physiological correlates of performance decrement on a monotonous task requiring sustained attention." *British Journal of Psychology*, 65 (1974):351-358.

Thibaut, J.W. "An experimental study of the cohesiveness of underprivileged groups." *Human Relations* 3 (1950):251-278.

Thomas, H. "Visual fixation responses of infants to stimuli of varying complexity." *Child Development* 36 (1965):629-638.

Thompson, J.D., *Comparative Studies in Administration*. Pittsburgh: University of Pittsburgh Press, 1959.

Thompson, R. *No Exit from Viet Nam*. New York: McKay, 1969.

Thorngate, W. "Must we always think before we act?" *Personality and Social Psychology Bulletin* 2 (1976):31-35.

Thurber, J. *My World and Welcome to It*. New York: Harcourt, Brace and World, 1942.

Tiger, L., and Fox, R. *The Imperial Animal*. New York: Holt, Rinehart and Winston, 1971.

Tolman, E.C. *Purposive Behavior in Animals and Men*. New York: Appleton-Century-Crofts, 1932. Reprinted, University of California Press, 1949.

_____ . *Collected Papers in Psychology.* Berkeley: University of California Press, 1951.

Totman, R. "An approach to cognitive dissonance theory in terms of ordinary language." *Journal for the Theory of Social Behavior* vol. 3, no. 2 (1973):215-238.

Trabasso, T.R., and Bower, G.H. "Presolution reversals and dimensional shifts in concept identification." *Journal of Experimental Psychology* 67 (1964):398-399.

_____ . *Attention in Learning: Theory and Research.* New York: Wiley, 1968.

Travers, R.M.W. *Man's Information System.* San Francisco: Chandler, 1970.

_____ . *Essentials of Learning.* New York: Macmillan, 1973.

Tulving, E. "The effects of presentation and recall of material in free-recall learning." *Journal of Verbal Learning and Verbal Behavior* 6 (1967):175-184.

_____ . "Episodic and semantic memory." In *Organization of memory.* Edited by E. Tulving and W. Donaldson. New York: Academic Press, 1972.

Tulving, E., and Patterson, R.D. "Functional units and retrieval processes in free recall." *Journal of Experimental Psychology* 77 (1968): 239-248.

Tulving, E., and Watkins, M.J. "Structure of memory traces." *Psychological Review* 82 (1975):261-275.

Uehling, B.S., and Sprinkle, R. "Recall of a serial list as a function of arousal and retention interval." *Journal of Experimental Psychology* 78 (1968):103-106.

Underwood, B.J. "Attributes of memory." *Psychological Review* 76 (1969): 559-573.

Vanek, J. "Time spent in housework." *Scientific American* vol. 231, no. 5 (1974):116-120.

Vaughan, M. "The relationships between obsessional personality obsessions in depression and symptoms of depression." *British Journal of Psychiatry* 129 (1976):36-39.

Veevers, J.E. "Voluntary childlessness and social policy: An alternative view." *Family Coordinator* 23 (1974):397-406.

Vos, K.; Doerbecker, C.; and Brinkman, W. "Success and cohesion in small groups." *Sociology Abstracts* 21 (1973):255.

Vroom, V.H. *Work and Motivation.* New York: Wiley, 1964.

Wagner, R.C.; Fitts, P.M.; and Noble, M.E. "Preliminary investigations of speed and load as dimensions of psychomotor tasks." *USAF Personnel Training and Research Center Report* no. 54-55 (1954).

Wallace, R.A. "The secular ethic and the spirit of patriotism." *Sociological Abstracts* vol. 34, no. 1 (1973):3-11.

Wallach, M.A., and Kegan, N. *Risk Taking.* New York: Holt, Rinehart and Winston, 1964.

Walster, E.; Aronson, E.; and Abrahams, D. "On increasing the persuasiveness of a low prestige communication." *Journal of Experimental and Social Psychology* 2 (1966):325-342.

Wangh, M. "Boredom in psychoanalytic perspective." *Social Research* 42 (1975):538-550.

Ward, W.C. "Reflection-impulsivity in kindergarten children." *Child Development* vol. 39, no. 3 (1968b):867-874.

Watkins, M.J. "Concept and measurement of primary memory." *Psychological Bulletin* 81 (1974):695-711.

Watson, D. "Reinforcement theory of personality and social system: Dominance and position in a group power structure." *Journal of Personality and Social Psychology* 20 (1971):180-185.

Weber, M. *The Theory of Social and Economic Organiation.* New York: Free Press, 1964.

————— . *Economy and Society.* New York: Bedminster Press, 1968.

Weidner, E. *Intergovernmental Relations as Seen by Public Officials.* Minneapolis: The University of Minnesota Press, 1960.

Weiner, N. *Cybernetics.* New York: Wiley, 1948.

Welch, M.J. "Infant's visual attention to varying degrees of novelty." *Child Development* 45 (1974):344-350.

Wertheimer, M. *Productive Thinking.* New York: Harper and Row, 1959.

West, L.J. "Vision and kinesthesis in the acquisition of typewriting skill." *Journal of Applied Psychology* 51 (1967):161-166.

Whitehill, S.; DeMeyer-Grapin, S.; and Scott, T.J. "Stimulation seeking in antisocial pre-adolescent children." *Journal of Abnormal Psychology* 85 (1976):101-104.

Whorf, B.L. "Science and linguistics." *Technology Review* 44 (1940): 229-231; 247-248.

Wicken, T.D., and Millward, R.B. "Attribute elimination strategies for concept identification with practiced subjects." *Journal of Mathematical Psychology* 8 (1971):453-480.

Wilensky, H. "Work, careers, and social integration." *International Social Science Journal* 12 (1960):543-560.

Wiley, M.G. "Sex roles in games." *Sociometry* 36 (1973):536-541.

Willis, M.R. An application of the predictive theory: A teaching plan for enhancing self-confidence in students. Unpublished manuscript. Columbia, University of South Carolina, 1974.

Willis, R.H., and Joseph, M.L. "Bargaining behavior. I. 'Prominence' as a predictor of the outcome of games of agreement." *Conflict Resolution* 3 (1959):102-113.

Wilson, E.K. *Sociology: Rules, Roles, and Relationships.* Homewood, Ill.: The Dorsey Press, 1966.

Wise, J.A. "Estimates and scaled judgements of subjective probabilities." *Organizational Behavior and Human Performance* 5 (1970):85-92.

Woodward, J. *Industrial Organization: Behavior and Control.* London: Oxford University Press, 1966.

Woolf, M.D. "Ego strengths and reading disability." *The Philosophical and Sociological Basis of Reading.* Edited by E.G. Thurston and L.E. Hafner. Yearbook of the National Reading Conference, 1965.

Yarbu, A.L. *Eye Movements and Vision.* New York: Plenum Press, 1967.

Zander, A. "Group aspirations." In *Group Dynamics: Research and Theory.* 3rd ed. Edited by D. Cartwright and A. Zander. New York: Harper and Row, 1968.

Zander, A., and Newcomb, T., Jr. "Group levels of aspirations in United Fund campaigns." *Journal of Personality and Social Psychology* 6 (1967):157-162.

Zentall, S. "Optimal stimulation as a theoretical basis of hyperactivity." *American Journal of Orthopsychiatry* 45 (1975):550-563.

Zuckerman, M.; Persky, H.; Miller, L; and Levin, B. *Proceedings of the 77th Annual Convention of the APA,* pp. 319-320. 1969.

Index of Names

Index of Subjects

About the Authors

Myles I. Friedman, Gambrell Professor of Education at the University of South Carolina, received the Ph.D. from the University of Chicago Graduate School of Education, where he specialized in educational psychology and research. Dr. Friedman has worked extensively in the public schools as a consultant and in the development of innovative approaches to education. His book *Rational Behavior* presented a new theory of human behavior, and he has coauthored such works as *Teaching Reading and Thinking Skills* and *Improving Teacher Education.*

Martha R. Willis, director of teacher education and associate director of the Graduate Program in Education at Converse College, received the Ph.D. degree from the University of South Carolina, where she specialized in educational psychology. Dr. Willis has extensive teaching experience and has worked in several clinical settings with a variety of populations. One of her major professional interests is adolescence, and she has served as a consultant to both professional and public groups who work with adolescents. Some of her work appears in the journal *Adolescence.*